The Sociomaterial Construction of Users

This book explores the intricate connections that link the current digitalization of manufacturing to our daily lives and identities as members of highly technologized societies.

Based on extensive research on the prosthetics industry in Germany, the US, Canada, and Haiti, the author analyzes the sociomaterial construction of users, by demonstrating the ways in which the introduction of 3D printing changes how artificial limbs are designed, manufactured, distributed, and used. Critically examining the capacity of digital technologies to afford greater diversity of user roles, enable the inclusion of marginalized groups, and increase user participation in the innovation process, the author presents a theory of user construction that sheds light on the dynamic relationship between industrial digitalization and the future of use.

An empirically grounded and conceptually informed study, *The Sociomaterial Construction of Users* will appeal to researchers in the fields of sociology, science and technology studies, and organization studies, as well as readers interested in 3D printing and the digitalization of society.

David Seibt is a post-doctoral research associate at the Institute of Sociology, Technical University of Berlin, Germany.

Routledge Studies in Science, Technology and Society

Books in this series consider social science aspects of science studies. Authors discuss how science is socially situated and mediated, how science and technology are shaped by society and society by science and technology. Books will consider the social impact of new technologies.

Titles in this series:

The Policies and Politics of Interdisciplinary Research
Nanomedicine in France and in the United States
Séverine Louvel

Public Communication of Research Universities
'Arms Race' for Visibility or Science Substance?
Marta Entradas, Martin W. Bauer

Emotion in the Digital Age
Technologies, Data and Psychosocial Life
Darren Ellis, Ian Tucker

Distributed Perception
Resonances and Axiologies
Natasha Lushetich, Iain Campbell

Rousseau and the Future of Freedom
Science, Technology and the Nature of Authority
Eric Deibel

The Sociomaterial Construction of Users
3D Printing and the Digitalization of the Prosthetics Industry
David Seibt

The Sociomaterial Construction of Users

3D Printing and the Digitalization of the Prosthetics Industry

David Seibt

Routledge
Taylor & Francis Group
LONDON AND NEW YORK

First published 2023
by Routledge
4 Park Square, Milton Park, Abingdon, Oxon OX14 4RN

and by Routledge
605 Third Avenue, New York, NY 10158

Routledge is an imprint of the Taylor & Francis Group, an informa business

British Library Cataloguing-in-Publication Data
A catalogue record for this book is available from the British Library

Library of Congress Cataloging-in-Publication Data
Names: Seibt, David, author.
Title: The sociomaterial construction of users : 3d printing and the digitalization of the prosthetics industry / David Seibt.
Description: Abingdon, Oxon ; New York, NY : Routledge, 2023. | Series: Routledge studies in science, technology and society | Includes bibliographical references and index.
Identifiers: LCCN 2022058315 (print) | LCCN 2022058316 (ebook) | ISBN 9781032180427 (hardback) | ISBN 9781032217215 (paperback) | ISBN 9781003269731 (ebook)
Subjects: LCSH: Prosthesis industry. | Artificial limbs—Economic aspects. | Three-dimensional printing.
Classification: LCC HD9995.P752 S45 2023 (print) | LCC HD9995. P752 (ebook) | DDC 338.4/76179—dc23/eng/20221207
LC record available at https://lccn.loc.gov/2022058315
LC ebook record available at https://lccn.loc.gov/2022058316

ISBN: 9781032180427 (hbk)
ISBN: 9781032217215 (pbk)
ISBN: 9781003269731 (ebk)

DOI: 10.4324/9781003269731

Typeset in Times New Roman
by codeMantra

Contents

Figures

Tables

Acknowledgments

Writing a dissertation thesis is a paradoxical thing. Sitting at your desk, reading many old books and some new, painstakingly navigating through field notes and interviews, writing, deleting, and writing anew—as years go by, it may feel like a very lonely enterprise. Yet, I know of nobody who has truly done these things all on their own, and neither have I. Even though academic conventions dictate that the final book be ascribed to a single author, the research and writing that give rise to it are inevitably enabled and shaped by a host of other actions. Therefore, before we jump into the book, I wish to acknowledge the people whose doings made this work possible and without whom it would not be the same.

First of all, I thank Uli Meyer and Sabine Maasen for giving me the opportunity to develop and write most of this book at the Munich Center for Technology in Society. Their guidance has allowed me to develop my way of thinking at the intersection of Science and Technology Studies, Sociology, and Organization Studies. Some of the most important cornerstones of this book, including the use of action net analysis, were inspired by their feedback. I also thank Attila Bruni for volunteering to contribute to our discussion, and for his honest review of an earlier version of this book. Attila, I hope you will find the ending of this one less shocking. Talking about guidance, I would also like to acknowledge my debt to Jochen Gläser, whose workshops about research questions and methodology have influenced my outlook on the social sciences more than he realizes and to whose high standards I fear I will never be able to do justice.

In terms of support and companionship, I am deeply grateful to the members of the Post/Doc Lab Reorganizing Industries and MCTS as a whole. These fine people, including Alex Wentland, Georgia Samaras, Klara Wenten, Verena Zink, Simon Schaupp, Cansu Birdal, Sarah Widmer, and others, provided not only a vibrant intellectual context but also the feeling of community, mutual support, and occasional silliness needed to survive in the forever foreign capital of Bavaria. Even as I acknowledge the support of the whole band, I would like to highlight the particular debt I owe to Tobias Drewlani and Johan Buchholz, who tirelessly commented on every aspect of the present book, and who have seen many versions of it that will never make it into print. I hope that someday I will be able to return the favor.

Much of the research for this book was done beyond the walls of German universities and I have particularly benefited from my stays in Canada, the US, and Haiti. Indeed, many of the people I met during my travels have inspired and contributed to this book far beyond the conventions of ethnographic research. I extend my heartfelt gratitude to Silvia Raschke and Lisa Boulton for their incredible work in co-organizing the Makeathons we held in Munich and Vancouver. These events, which you will read more about in Chapter 3, remain a milestone in my thinking about experimental STS, even though I still cannot fully wrap my head around all that happened during those days. I am equally grateful to Michael Peirone and Nick Dechev for being the most accommodating hosts and to Jade Myers for being the best company any ethnographer ever had. All of you have made this an unforgettable journey. The passion with which you approach your work has truly renewed my dedication to my own.

If fieldwork can be fun, and scholarly discussions enriching, getting a book ready for production is its own beast. At this point I would like to acknowledge the tremendous help of Jennifer Branlat, who copyedited almost all parts of this book, and some parts more than once. Jennifer, your work has taught me much about the finer points of academic writing and where I dared to ignore your advice, I have surely done so at my own peril. This book also benefited from the support I received from the whole Routledge team, and the detailed feedback of one anonymous reviewer. I am particularly thankful to Neil Jordan and Alice Salt for their professional editorial work and patience in steering me from book proposal to production.

And then there is life beyond this book. Or is there, really? Many of the people I am closest to would perhaps question that, citing the many occasions in which I let work interfere with friendship, family, and romance. This is not the place to work through these entanglements. Rather, it is the place to acknowledge your contributions to this book over the years. My gratitude belongs to Isa Schaller and Susanne Klimroth for always questioning my choices, for making plain the consequences of traveling the easy roads, and for reminding me of more rewarding alternatives. Finally, I thank my parents Simone Seibt and Frank Seibt, my aunt Elke Schröter, my beloved brother Jonas Seibt, and Antonia Glugla for trusting my judgment, encouraging me to pursue my dreams, and for staying with me in my happiest and most desperate hours. I promise you, there will be a life beyond this book and it would be my privilege to share it with you.

1 Introduction

How Do User Roles Change in Digitalizing Industries?

This book is about the construction of users in digitalizing industries. It is concerned with the ways in which the introduction of a new generation of digital fabrication technologies, subsumed under the term 3D printing, changes who industrial products are designed for and made available to, and how these products are engaged with in practice to carve out novel user roles and identities. This concern is mirrored by the two propositions which stand at the center of my work as well as its beginning.

The first of these propositions is that industries construct their users. In contemporary Western societies, the act of using any kind of physical product, from wheelchair to computer, presupposes the industrial practices of designing, manufacturing, and distributing. Who has access to what kind of technology and how industrially fabricated objects can be used is shaped by these activities. It is in this sense that industries construct and configure their users. Yet, as managers, designers, and sales personnel will eagerly point out, the continued operation of industrial organizations in turn depends on people using, and therefore buying, renting, or leasing, their products. Present day industrial organizing is therefore to some degree user-oriented and often reflexively integrates users into its operations. Thus, as things stand, industries and users are co-constitutive phenomena. They exist by virtue of their interlocking actions. From this perspective, users cannot be understood as pre-existing individuals with fixed attitudes waiting to buy, appropriate, or consume the things industry provides for them. Rather, the term *user* signifies a social role resulting from a complex net of actions, critically involving those associated with industrial production and those associated with the use of industrially made goods.

The second proposition is that industries are currently undergoing manifold reorganizations which are often summarized under the label of digitalization[1]. One central element of this development is the spread of digital fabrication, perhaps most prominently represented by a group of technologies commonly referred to as 3D printing. These machines come in many forms and include both industrial-grade and consumer-grade variants that use a large range of different mechanisms. Their common feature is that they enable the computer-controlled fabrication of almost any shape

DOI: 10.4324/9781003269731-1

out of some raw material and a digital representation of the final product. In contrast to their predecessors, particularly the computerized numerically controlled machine tools which have been part of production plants since the 1970s, 3D printers are a form of additive manufacturing. In essence, they create objects by successively adding layers of material rather than subtracting it from a pre-existing block, as is the case with conventional techniques such as cutting, grinding, or boring. These new technical capacities open up novel opportunities for industrial design, production, and logistics, as exemplified by discussions around the flexibilization and decentralization of manufacturing, as well as the changing role of users in the innovation process. In short, the digitalization of production is not merely a matter of exchanging one technical system for another, or of boosting corporate efficiency. What is at stake are the very ways in which contemporary industries are organized.

Taken together, these grounding assumptions lead to the expectation that the increasing digitalization of industries will be accompanied by significant shifts in user roles. After all, such roles are partly constructed in the very same industrial action patterns that digital fabrication promises to reorganize. From this perspective, the central question of this book becomes *how* user roles will change in digitalizing industries. Who will have the opportunity to use industrial products, as industries reorganize around digital production technologies and how will the users in such a digitalized future differ from the ones we have been used to?

1.1 Digital Fabrication and Users: The Literature and Its Gaps

The social science literature offers at best partial answers to these questions. Indeed, my interest in the connection between industrial digitalization and shifting forms of user construction falls into a blind spot between contemporary theorizing about industrial transformation on the one hand and the role of users in innovation on the other. While I will show that this blind spot stems from a longstanding division of scholarly labor between science and technology studies (STS) and organization studies (see Chapter 2), for now, my point can be illustrated by tracing the two major debates in which these fields of study have addressed the issue of 3D printing itself.

The first debate, rooted in organization studies, is concerned with the transformation of contemporary industries and positions 3D printing, or additive manufacturing, at the heart of the newest wave of automation (Brynjolfsson & McAfee, 2014; Srnicek & Williams, 2015). The ability to produce physical products directly from a given raw material and a digital representation of the final product is thought to continue a line of automation technologies that began with the development of numerical control (NC) and computerized numerical control (CNC) machines. Reviving some of the debates around automation from the 1970s and 1980s (e.g., Braverman,

1974; Noble, 1984; Shaiken, 1985), 3D printers are taken to be the ultimate machine tools and as such to further substitute human labor. The new twist on the automation debate stems from the argument that 3D printers are closely connected to an increasingly powerful, if not entirely new, range of other digital technologies. With the advancement of digital sensors, mass customization platforms, and machine learning, it is no longer only manual, but also cognitive labor that is being replaced by machines.[2] Some authors argue that we are entering what they call a "second machine age" (Brynjolfsson & McAfee, 2014) in which machines are becoming increasingly independent of their human operators and will eventually replace them entirely. Judy Wajcman succinctly summarized the spirit of that debate in her review of a selection of popular books on the topic:

> Where previous waves of automation ultimately created wealth and new sectors of employment, we are now witnessing a fundamental shift in the relationship between workers and machines. Machines are no longer tools; they are turning into the workers themselves.
>
> (Wajcman, 2017, p. 120)

This development is typically hailed as either a frightening source of mass unemployment (Frey & Osborne, 2013) or as a form of emancipation from the drudgery of work (Mason, 2015). Other commentators frame the debate in a historical perspective (Meyer et al., 2019; Wajcman, 2017) and identify it as a contingent struggle over possible futures (Dickel & Schrape, 2017; Urry, 2016; Urry & Birtchnell, 2016). They insist that both the effects and the causes of technology are political and therefore subject to negotiation. Accordingly, we should not try to predict the impact of technological change as much as engage in collectively shaping a desirable future—including the design of appropriate technologies.

In many regards, the current debate around 3D printing and the digitalization of manufacturing continues a long line of research into industrial automation (Braverman, 1974; Marx, 1976; Noble, 1984; Zuboff, 1985; Zuboff, 1988) and the relationship between technologies and organizing more generally (Barley, 1986; Leonardi et al., 2012; Orlikowski, 1992; Orlikowski, 2000). Keeping with that tradition, recent contributions are interested in the future of workers (or employees) and ask what consequences the introduction of digital technology might have for their work processes. With regard to my own project, there is something to be learned here about industrial reorganization in general, and digitalization in particular. However, within the scope of this debate, the treatment of technology *use* is limited to the interest in workers using production technology. The relationship between industrial automation and so-called end-users, who are faced with the technologies produced by increasingly digitalized industries, is not considered.

The situation appears to be reversed in a parallel debate, which is rooted in innovation studies and STS and addresses the potential of 3D printing to "democratize" production and innovation (Hippel, 2005). In this discussion, the increasing availability of affordable consumer-grade 3D printers outside of traditional industries is seen as a key development that will allow non-professional makers to produce physical goods adapted to their own needs. Building on discussions around open-source software (Raymond, 2001), commons-based peer production (Benkler, 2006; Söderberg & Maxigas, 2014) and the maker movement (Anderson, 2012; Gershenfeld, 2005), cheap 3D printers are considered to make the means of production available to everyone, be it in the form of privately owned machines, or as pieces of equipment in shared machine shops (Braybrooke & Smith, 2018). The grand vision negotiated in this debate is that the advancement of 3D printers and the adjunct peer production infrastructure, will eventually make the means of production available to everyone. In some of the more daring contributions, this is viewed as an opportunity to upend capitalist social relations (Rifkin, 2014); in others it is seen as further enabling users to produce (or repair) for themselves, decreasing their dependence on industrial manufacturers and, in some cases, allowing them to compete with the latter (Hippel, 2017; Söderberg, 2013a; Söderberg, 2016). Recently, however, evidence has mounted to support the hypothesis that many elements of seemingly emancipatory formations such as open-source communities and the maker movement tend to spawn, turn into, or be co-opted by the very capitalist organizations they were thought to oppose (Dahlander & Magnusson, 2008; Drewlani & Seibt, 2018; Ferdinand, 2018; Ferdinand & Meyer, 2017; Wenten, 2019). Even beyond such communities and movements, individual users are turned into working customers (Rieder & Voß, 2010), operators of firm owned configurator tools (Hippel & Katz, 2002) or even part of the infrastructure of digital platforms (Bruni & Esposito, 2019). The potential of users to produce for themselves is therefore complemented by a tendency to turn users into unpaid sources of labor, knowledge, or creative ideas (Hyysalo et al., 2016).

The debate around the potential of 3D printers to democratize production and innovation in many ways extends long-standing discussions in STS and innovation studies around users as active agents in technological change (Hippel, 1988; Hippel, 2005; Oudshoorn & Pinch, 2003; Pinch & Bijker, 1987). Contributions to this strand of scholarship have long been interested in the potential of users to innovate independently of corporate designers and manufacturers. From this point of view, the availability of 3D printers and other digital fabrication technologies makes the design and production of hardware much more scalable and accessible. Hence, these contributions provide important insights into the relationship between production technology and users. The difficulty with applying these findings to my own analytical project lies in the fact that they are interested in users only insofar as they engage in design and manufacturing outside of traditional industries. The relationship between users and industries is only considered to the extent that the latter increasingly perform the tasks of conventional manufacturers. Therefore, even though this debate repeatedly refers to roles such as "user innovator," it does not actually discuss how people use the technologies they help to develop. Consequently, these contributions do not address the relationship between digital fabrication and changes in the way user roles are constructed in and through the act of using itself.

I am hence left with a situation in which none of the current debates around 3D printing addresses the transformation of user construction in the way I am interested in. Current discussions are concerned with the reorganization of the system of production, and speak of users only insofar as they act as innovators or manufacturers. Whether it be in the form of a "Second Machine Age" (Brynjolfsson & McAfee, 2014), a "Third Industrial Revolution" (Rifkin, 2011), or an "Industrie 4.0" (Pfeiffer, 2017), whether production is carried out by skilled workers, machines, crowds (McAfee & Brynjolfsson, 2017), or prosumers (Ritzer & Jurgenson, 2010), all these contributions focus on the ways in which things are made rather than on how they are used and by whom. By contrast, I am interested in the question of how current changes in the system of production are related to the appearance of new users and use practices. I am not, in other words, concerned with the future of work, but the *future of use*.

1.2 The Case of 3D Printing in the Prosthetics Industry

To close this gap in the literature, I present a study of the introduction of 3D printing to the prosthetics industry. Prosthetics may seem like a rather unorthodox choice given my interest in industrial transformation. A sociological approach to artificial limbs may address issues connected to the social construction of (dis-)ability, the role of the body in social interaction, or the invisible labor involved in health care—but addressing prosthetics as an industry? In fact, I argue that the field of prosthetics has several properties that make it an ideal case to study the industrial construction of users and its relationship to changes in the technological means of production.

First of all, the fabrication of artificial limbs is remarkable because it features not one but two distinct modes of production—a division closely related to the organization of the field as a whole. The first of these modes, which involves the production of so-called fit components such as mechanical hands, feet, joints, and adapters can be characterized as properly industrial in the sense that production is highly centralized, standardized, machine-based, and products are fabricated in relatively large numbers (though on a significantly smaller scale than in sectors such as the automotive industry). In stark contrast, the prosthetic socket, the interface between the prosthesis and the human body, is mainly manufactured in a process of craftwork. Typically, production takes place in local workshops and depends largely on the hand skills of trained prosthetists and technicians. Moreover, every socket is custom made to fit the unique anatomy of its wearer, which means that production is notoriously difficult to standardize and is typically iterative, involving extensive testing and adaptation. Hence, studying prosthetics makes it possible to compare the effects of digitalization on both classical industrial and craft-based modes of manufacturing, helping me to put my findings into perspective without comparing prosthetics to an otherwise unrelated industry.

Second, prosthetics is an interesting case because the spread of new production technologies, such as 3D scanners and printers, is currently in full motion, and various trajectories of reorganization are becoming visible. Indeed, the introduction of 3D printing is in many ways challenging an industry structure that has been in place since World War I (Brown, 2002a; Harrasser, 2013b; Harrasser, 2016; Kienitz, 2008). This is a useful state of affairs for an analysis of user construction because, by contrast with other technologies and digitalization projects, it is clear that 3D printing is actually being implemented in prosthetics, rather than just being talked about (compare Meyer, 2019), and that the implementation of that technology is in fact related to shifts in the existing patterns of organizing (compare Pentland & Feldman, 2008). Moreover, the fact that the implementation of these technologies has only just begun to unfold means that established modes of production still exist in parallel and that several attempts at making 3D printing work are happening simultaneously—with varying effects on the construction of user roles. In the current situation, it is not at all unusual to find well-established prosthetists attempting to incorporate 3D scanning and printing into their traditional workflow, while start-ups set up digital mass customization platforms, open-source communities are pushing the private fabrication of low-cost prostheses, and NGOs are expanding the production of prosthetics to underserved regions of the world. All of these examples involve the reorganization of the prosthetics industry as well as changes in the user roles constructed in it. Being able to compare these different trajectories within the same industry allows me to arrive at a nuanced picture of the role of production technology in industrial user constructions.

My third, and final, reason for choosing prosthetics to address questions of user construction is that the design, production, circulation, and use of artificial limbs make the formation of user identities and roles particularly salient. As Lucy Suchman pointed out for the cases of AI and robotics, which are comparable in that regard, technology development projects in prosthetics "*involve a kind of doubling or mimicry in the machine that works as a powerful disclosing agent for assumptions about the human*" (Suchman, 2007, p. 226). The point is that the ways in which prostheses are designed, distributed, and used, make the formation of user roles much more explicit than would be the case in other industries, even though analogue processes may be at work. When a group of US 3D printing enthusiasts designs colorful superhero hands for children, their underlying ideas of who the users of their products are and how they are expected to engage with them become clearly visible in the material shape of the object. By the same token, when the same robotic-looking mechanical hands are most emphatically rejected by Haitian adults for fear of social stigma, this shines a light on the agency of users in carving out their own identities, while bringing into relief the importance of social, economic, and cultural position. It is because of their marked cultural significance(s) as well as their intimate connection to the human body that prostheses lend themselves so well to a study of user construction.

1.3 An Action Net Perspective on Industrial User Construction

Even though the transformation of user roles is currently observable in the prosthetics industry, the question remains of how to grasp them analytically. Which analytical stance makes it possible to explore the hypothesis advanced at the very beginning of this chapter, namely that the digitalization of production triggers changes in who has access to industrial products and how they are used? In other words, how do we arrive at a convincing theory of the digital future of industrial user construction? I suggest that the concept of "action nets" as developed by Barbara Czarniawska and colleagues (Czarniawska, 2004b; Lindberg & Czarniawska, 2006) offers a uniquely suitable basis from which to approach this task. On the one hand, an action net perspective offers insight into what it means to speak of the *construction* of users, while, on the other, it helps to make salient the relationship between user construction and *industry*.

The first key feature of an action net perspective concerns the notion of *construction*. As the name suggests, an action-net view grants analytical primacy to actions rather than actors. Actorial identities are not unimportant, but they are treated as the result of interrelated activities rather than their origin. This analytical principle helps me to clarify that who the users of a given product are and what exactly "using" means is *constructed* in action rather than being somehow given in advance. A person with limb loss is not automatically a prosthesis user, nor does amputation predict if, and how, an amputee will engage with an assistive device—a fact that is well documented by the high number of people who own a prosthesis but choose not to use it or use it only for very select purposes. Instead, what I call a *user role* emerges in the concrete practices of using a product, as well as in the relationship of these practices to other activities such as buying, repairing, customizing, and so on. Analytically speaking, *using precedes users*.

With this said, an action net perspective recognizes that some patterns of actions are repeated and do, over time, become institutionalized. That is to say, there will be taken-for-granted ways of doing and relating that will tend to be defended in normative terms when challenged (Czarniawska, 2014, pp. 21–22). Moreover, such institutionalized action patterns will often be inscribed into the artifactual world, including contracts, guidelines, buildings, industrial machines, and products (Joerges & Czarniawska, 1998; Latour, 1991). Concrete performances of user roles do therefore occur against the backdrop of an *institutional order* prevalent at a given time and place. For instance, the use of prostheses occurs in relation to the widely accepted belief that artificial limbs should approximate as closely as possible the form and function of their "natural" counterparts, thus rehabilitating a perceived disability. When this norm is challenged, as it often is with many of the more unconventionally designed 3D-printed prostheses, such performances will elicit strong reactions including rejection and belittlement, but also a positive sense of surprise marking the wearer of the device as particularly brave or otherwise extra-ordinary. As this example shows, the ongoing construction of user roles is to some degree influenced by historically grown institutions. However, insofar as these institutions are themselves the result of taken-for-granted ways of doing and relating, they can be challenged in action and vanish without it. The aesthetic norms connected to prostheses have changed throughout history and differ from place to place. Buildings are being refurbished to accommodate the mobility of individuals with non-standard bodies. Insurance policies are renegotiated, forgotten, or rediscovered. In other words, the term "user" signifies a temporarily stabilized social role that is constructed and de-constructed in action, rather than an embodied individual with given characteristics.[3]

This idea of *construction* sets an action net perspective apart from economically inspired views of a market populated by consumers, as well as from more recent ideas of user integration or user-centered design. All of these approaches posit that users are "people out there" with certain characteristics, needs, and wants, which firms should consider in their design and marketing activities. The same notion of users as pre-existing entities is also shared by studies of user innovation (Hippel, 2005; Shah & Tripsas, 2007) as well as accounts of users as "active agents in technology design" (Kline & Pinch, 1996; Pinch & Bijker, 1987). These diverge from traditional economic theory in that they focus on the agency of users rather than industrial actors in designing, producing, and marketing products. However, their focus remains on *the construction of technology*. By contrast, an action net perspective brings into view *the construction of users*, by homing in on the formation of their actorial roles and identities in interlinking sets of action. It shares this focus with other constructivist approaches, most prominently Actor-Network Theory (ANT). However, particularly in its "entrepreneurial" incarnations (Gherardi & Nicolini, 2005), ANT's analytical project is to show how powerful figures, such as scientists, engineers, or managers, construct unified macro actors by ordering heterogeneous actants, including humans, objects, animals, money, and so forth in relation to one another (Callon, 1984; compare the critiques by Haraway, 1988; Latour, 1987; Law, 1987; Lee & Brown, 1994; Star, 1991). An action net account, on the other hand, describes the complex interlinking of *processes*, which may be more or less stable and may give rise to a whole range of roles and identities depending on the circumstances. I am, thus, not interested in users as punctualized actor-networks.[4] Rather, I am interested in the patterned set of user and non-user roles that is constructed in the complex interlinking of industrial routines and situated use practices. My unit of analysis is thus neither *one* user (Latour, 1999, pp. 176–177), nor *the* user (Woolgar, 1991), nor a user *multiple* (Mol, 2002), but a *patterned multitude* of users and non-users, which may be termed a "user landscape."

The second major advantage of an action net perspective is that it makes intelligible how user construction relates to changes in industrial organization. As the name suggests, action net analysis focuses not on single sets or types of actions, but on the complex *interlinking* of action patterns. Indeed, it was originally developed to study contemporary organizing which quickly moves across places and routinely crosses organizational boundaries (Czarniawska, 2004). Hence, the notion of action net emphasizes that shifts in one kind of activity may have unexpected effects on very differently situated actions and the actorial roles and identities constructed therein. From this point of view, user roles are a result of using, but using is bound up with other actions that enable and concretize it in manifold ways. For instance, who can use a prosthetic aid and in which way is partly "configured" (Hyysalo, 2021; Woolgar, 1991) during the surgery that takes place at a hospital, the designing and testing of componentry at industrial R&D departments, the choosing and fitting at prosthetics workshops, the endless negotiating with insurance companies, as well as mental and physical training, continuous maintenance, and repair. By stressing the complex interrelation of these activities, an action net perspective brings into relief how the digitalization of prosthetics design and production, activities that are usually associated with the realm of industry, may be linked to changes in the way prostheses are used. An action net perspective thus attends closely to the organization and reorganization of actions in relation to one another, regardless of the fact that some may be considered "industrial" and others not.

To explain how diverse actions are connected across time, space, and communities of practice, the action net approach draws on the notion of *translation*[5] (Lindberg & Czarniawska, 2006). The central idea is that, for two actions to become linked, an intermediary needs to be passed along between them and convey meaning from one site to another. In theory, meaning can be conveyed by the movement of all kinds of intermediaries, including words, images, artifacts, bodies, and money (Callon, 1991; Latour, 1986, pp. 266–269). However, in addition to translation in the geometrical sense of "moving from one place to another" (Latour, 1987, p. 117), the term also captures the often subtle transformations in form and content that occur as intermediaries are transferred between differently situated actions. For example, while the actions transpiring at prosthetic clinics, manufacturers, insurance companies, and sites of use are clearly linked by the circulation of various intermediaries, what exactly these are and what exactly they *mean* shifts between sites. A person's limb may be translated into a plaster cast, which may be scanned and sent off to a technician who might never have seen or talked to the person represented in the scan. In this process, what precisely the amputee wished for, or what a specific marking means may easily be lost or re-interpreted. The notion of translation thus gives me a way of speaking about the connectedness of activities across technology design, distribution, and use without assuming that this connection is frictionless or works naturally. Rather, following the movement of intermediaries between differently situated actions focuses attention on the continuous work that is necessary to guarantee sameness across contexts, without ever forgetting the risk of subtle "betrayal" (Law, 2003) and obvious error.

The emphasis on studying the *interlinking* of action across time, space, and organizational boundaries helps me to close the gap left between research on the digital transformation of industries on the one hand, and the role of users in innovation on the other. These accounts may usefully sensitize analysis to specific subsets of action. They may speak to the prosthetists' fear of losing their jobs to increasingly sophisticated algorithms, or the engineers' drive toward developing such new tools. They may point me toward the increasing importance of open-source communities and the agency of users in developing their own prostheses. However, by focusing on one or the other kind of action, they are bound to miss how industrial and end-user activities are knotted together, defining who can use prosthetic devices and how. By contrast, an action net perspective emphasizes that user roles emerge as designing, producing, marketing, and using become interwoven in necessarily specific ways. It therefore also extends classical STS accounts which have repeatedly been criticized for overemphasizing the agency of designers (Akrich, 1992; Woolgar, 1991) or users (Pinch & Bijker, 1987; Silverstone et al., 1992) in shaping technology and associated use practices (Hyysalo, 2010; Hyysalo et al., 2019; Suchman, 2007; Williams et al., 2005). The approach suggested here does not make any such a priori decisions about which action in an action net is particularly important. The relevant units of analysis are the patterns of action that span the activities of both industry and the people who use industrially manufactured goods. It is in these patterns that user roles are constructed and transformed.

1.4 Digital Fabrication and Changes in Industrial User Construction: Three Findings

Taken together, the two aspects of the action net perspective (the construction of actorial identities in action and the interlinking of actions through translation) form the analytical basis for my theory of user construction in digitalizing industries. While unfolding their potential is the main purpose of this book, the usefulness of action net analysis can be demonstrated here by pointing to three instances in which it helped me to challenge commonly held beliefs about the relationship between the digitalization of production and changes in societal user roles. Based on my analysis of 3D printing in prosthetics, each of these examples concerns one specific aspect of the digitalization of production and links it to a newly emerging pattern in the *diversity*, *inclusion*, and *participation* of the people who use industrial products.

Finding 1: Flexible Production and the Diversity of User Roles

My first finding concerns the connection between the increasing flexibility of digitalized industrial production, as currently epitomized by the proliferation of mass customization platforms, and the promise of a massive increase in the diversity of user roles. In this instance, an action net perspective led me to a rebuttal of such overly optimistic predictions. Based on a comparison of the strings of translation involved in both conventional and digitalized production processes I suggest that *where mass customization replaces processes of mass production, the gain in the diversity of user roles will be limited, as the technology continues to rely on preset parameters or rules.* Moreover, *where mass customization replaces traditional processes of custom production, it runs the risk of reducing the diversity of possible user roles by subtly introducing new levels of standardization.* Hence, as I will spell out in Chapter 4, current forms of mass customization do not equally support the construction of all possible user roles. Instead of simply dissolving the biases produced by previous production systems, digital mass customization materializes novel patterns of industrial user construction that combine limited gains in diversity with new potentials for standardization.

This prediction goes against the grain of the mass customization gospel, prevalent in the management literature, which views the technology as potentially "[d]elivering affordable goods and services with enough variety and customization that everyone finds nearly exactly what they want" (Tseng et al., 2017, p. 2). Such expectations are rooted in the characterization of mass customization as a virtuous combination of the speed and scale of industrial automation with the individuality of craft-based production (Davis, 1987; Fogliatto et al., 2012; Hippel & Katz, 2002; Pine, II., 1993). Indeed, from the point of view of action nets, it is true that current mass customization processes involve both standardization and individualization. In a first translation, the diversity of potential users "out there" is molded into a generic digital template. Then, in a second translation, this template is re-inscribed with a particular user's individual characteristics in a semi-automated fashion, either by adjusting it along pre-given parameters (parametric mass customization) or by performing more complex transformations using rule-based algorithms (algorithmic mass customization). The digitally adjusted product can then be manufactured using multi-purpose fabrication technologies, such as 3D printing.

The decisive point is, however, that in that process the rigidity of standardized mass production is only slightly reduced, whereas the flexibility of craft production is exchanged for the potential of automation. While the first translation (the generation of digital templates) largely reproduces design practices typical of a regime of mass production, the second translation (the re-inscription of individual features) replaces a translation based on professional skill with one that is based on the adjustment of parameters or the application of preset rules. Mass customization systems may therefore bring about either modest gains or potentially dramatic losses of user diversity. In industries formerly based on mass production, parametric mass customization will allow for a slightly broader "distribution of the conventional" (Star, 1991, p. 43) likely to facilitate the performance of more varied user roles. However, no matter how many parameters are added and how fine grained they are, it is currently inconceivable that they would be able to capture the full range of human diversity. Parametric mass customization, like mass production, thus always constructs an outside of its "solution space" in the form of excluded user roles. Moreover, in industries formerly based on craft production, algorithmic mass customization may potentially introduce new levels of standardization and automation. This may speed up the inscription process and lead to more efficient services for people conforming to the standards and rules encoded into the mass customization software. However, by the same token, it will structurally exclude people not represented in these categories. Unlike a skilled craftsperson, today's mass customization systems are unable to adapt to a given situation by adding parameters or adjusting algorithms. They are also unable to react to user feedback in a way that would allow for continued tinkering and iteration. It is precisely because of such discrepancies that the idea of mass customization as a solution that fits *everyone* should be discarded (coons, 2022). When taken at face value, such a position may legitimize mass customization as *the only* mode of production suitable for contemporary industries. When put into practice, such a development would, however, risk new forms of exclusion and a reduction in the diversity of user roles.

Finding 2: Decentral Production and the Inclusion of New Users

My second finding is that the local fabrication of goods, enabled by the networked character of digital fabrication infrastructures may, under certain conditions, lead to an increased risk of misrepresenting potential users and contexts of use. With a view to the challenges involved in knotting together actions across socio-cultural contexts, I emphasize that, *where digitalization eases the distribution of things from industrial centers to diverse locations all over the globe, the action nets of user construction will grow ever more fragile and the potential for incongruities between the actions of users and industrial actors is likely to increase.* Where local fabrication is paired with centralized design, it may lead to the emergence of powerful actors, such as platform companies, that deploy novel strategies of control, including what one of my interviewees termed "techno-imperialism." Conversely, where local production is linked to the grass-roots design activities of open-source communities, it is precisely the lack of standardization and control over technology development that may prove problematic. *With the increasing availability of the means of design and production to hobbyists, the misrepresentation of users may result from the lack of professional routines and coordination on the side of amateur designers and manufacturers.* While the technologies for designing and producing all kinds of things have become widely available with the rise of private digital fabrication, the knowledge and skills necessary to design and produce *well* have not enjoyed the same level of diffusion.

This way of putting it is of course a challenge to the commonly held notion that digitally enabled decentralized fabrication is likely to engender locally meaningful products. This idea is based on two premises which my own study calls into question. The first of these is that *local fabrication* is typically linked to *local design* and hence brings about a reduction in the social and cultural distance between designers and the people they are designing for. This association was popularized through a large stream of literature which treats digital fabrication in the context of a growing polycentric peer-production infrastructure made up of FabLabs and shared machine shops (Gershenfeld, 2005; Schneider, 2018; Söderberg & Maxigas, 2014; Troxler, 2013) as well as a surge in private fabrication and "prosumption" (Rifkin, 2014; compare Schrape, 2019; Toffler, 1980). These authors posit that local fabricating will be linked to local designing and experimenting, either by allowing for increased interaction between a network of co-designers and users (as in the case of fabrication laboratories) or by allowing the prospective users to design and produce for themselves.

From an action net perspective, this preoccupation with the local is quite counterintuitive, particularly when articulated in conjunction with digital technologies. After all, one key characteristic of the new fabrication technologies is precisely that they are linked to globally distributed information and communication infrastructures. Hence, the ability to translate back and forth between material products and digital data is more likely a precondition for linking local production with various acts of decentralized designing that could happen almost anywhere. From this point of view, the availability of digital data as a new kind of intermediary in action nets is likely to increase the ability of newly emerging focal actors to centralize control over dispersed activities and disseminate their products and services around the world. While the idea of linking local design and production activities may be a valid political intervention, digital fabrication technologies make the opposite movement, the flow of products from one center to a vast number of heterogeneous localities, at least equally likely.

Unfortunately, this does not mean that, where digital fabrication *does* link local designing and producing, the representation of prospective users will necessarily be more sensible. Indeed, this vision is based on a second faulty premise, namely that digital fabrication is *easy*. Largely owing to utopian depictions of 3D printers as frictionless universal production machines, very much like the Replicator from Star Trek, the idea has emerged that 3D printing allows *everyone* to make *everything* literally by pushing a button (e.g., Rifkin, 2014, p. 92). Such depictions do, however, underestimate the potential "betrayals" associated with translating intermediaries from one form to another and the often invisible work necessary to maintain their sameness across contexts (Law, 2003). Sensibly representing potential users, even oneself, is *hard* and not always made easier by an abundance of digital tools. If such operations are to have any chance of success, they require time, skill, and sometimes costly equipment, let alone access to larger sociotechnical infrastructures. Where designing and producing are done by people with little prior know-how and experience, operating unbound—and unsupported—by professional norms and organizational routines, and equipped with sub-standard soft- and hardware, "translation errors" are bound to occur. Misrepresentation, frustration, and non-use are likely to become the flipside of the tinkering, learning, and playfulness commonly associated with private manufacturing. Moreover, the very fact that hobbyists are often designing and producing outside of the established institutional order may severely restrict the flow of their products through conventional distribution channels. This is likely to limit the range of prospective users and may even put user innovators "on the wrong side of the law" (Söderberg, 2013b, p. 78). In short, local fabrication may extend action nets of user construction to new groups by tapping into digital information infrastructures for distribution or by bypassing existing norms and regulations. However, within this process the likelihood of at least initial misrepresentation of these groups is high, making the construction of non-users an important issue.

Finding 3: Digitalization and the Role of Users in Innovation

The third finding I would like to put forward is that shortly after the introduction of digital fabrication, unconventional use practices are more likely to occur and to challenge institutionalized ideas of who the users of a given product are and how they ought to engage with it. More specifically, I argue that *insofar as the digitalization of design and distribution makes industrial products available to hitherto excluded or marginalized social groups, the likelihood of unexpected use practices is going to increase, due to these group's specific social, cultural, and economic situatedness.* Moreover, not only are these novel use practices prone to diverge from ingrained norms, but they are also likely to become part of the industry's common sense more rapidly. *Owing to the shortened redesign cycles characteristic of digital design, rapid prototyping, and rapid production, unconventional use practices are going to feed back into new design iterations more quickly, aiding the fast institutionalization of new roles and identities.*

In a way, this formulation is similar to the common assumption that the influence of users on the design of industrial products increases with digital fabrication (e.g., Hippel, 2005). However, an action net perspective focuses the view on the differential ways in which various forms of using are translated back into processes of designing. This stresses that some people's actions become consequential for the construction of new user roles, while others do not. Also, by contrast to widespread notions of the "prosumer" (Ritzer & Jurgenson, 2010; Toffler, 1980), the "user innovator" (Hippel, 2005), or the "free innovator" (Hippel, 2017), an action net perspective does not make any assumptions about *who* incorporates feedback from situated use practices into new design iterations. From that vantage point, the question is not whether there is a new regime of innovation in which the same people who use also innovate. The decisive question is, whose ways of using are taken into account in new design iterations—regardless of whether design is done by industrial firms, open-source communities, or other actors—and what we can say about the mechanisms through which these feedback loops contribute to the formation of new roles and identities.

Against this backdrop, I assert that the digitalization of industrial design, production, and distribution changes whose actions become consequential and which groups may become newly marginalized. Some people may suddenly find themselves in the focus of a digitalizing industry, while others may become newly "orphaned" (Callon, 2007) and in need of collectively rearticulating their interests through means including "user innovation," "peer production," or "research in the wild" (Callon & Rabeharisoa, 2003). In the first scenario, which is the one I will concentrate on, these newly relevant social groups are likely to engage with industrial products in unconventional, and often unforeseen ways for the very same reasons that had previously led to their exclusion: their bodies as well as social, cultural, and economic positions differ from the norms institutionalized within established industrial configurations. As the new roles and identities they perform become commonplace and are inscribed into new generations of products, we may speak of the co-evolution of users and technology (Oudshoorn & Pinch, 2003).

It would be prudent to expect similar processes wherever the introduction of a new production technology triggers changes in industrial organization. What is specific about *digital* design and production technologies is that this feedback process is drastically sped up. Given a well-maintained digital fabrication infrastructure, the feedback time between using and re-designing is reduced, because it is relatively easy to make design changes and translate them into a material product or prototype. In effect, surprising use practices can be reacted to more quickly, aiding the rapid materialization and institutionalization of new user roles. Overall, then, I am with Michel Callon in asserting that the reorganization of techno-economic networks contributes to a "proliferation of the social," in my case in the specific form of new user roles and identities. Callon writes that…

> …These new forms of innovation and economic agencies increase the possibility of overflowings and have the effect of inducing the exceptionally rapid emergence of new groups with new problems and

> expectations, fighting for recognition of their identity and a place in a common world. What is new is not the fact that markets overflow and therefore produce matters of concern; it is the amplitude and frequency of those overflowings.
>
> (Callon, 2007, p. 151)

What a focus on feedback and institutionalization adds to this is the idea that out of this rather chaotic proliferation of user roles, some will be taken into account, while others remain or newly become excluded. In short, it alerts us to the fact that which identities can be successfully articulated, what kind of feedback can be translated into new design trajectories, and which kinds of user roles become dominant in a digitalizing industry is necessarily a question of power. From this perspective, digital fabrication may advance the influence of some social groups, but it is unlikely to lead to a truly democratic innovation process in the sense of an equality of chances across social groups to participate in the industrial construction of users.

1.5 Sketching out the Structure of the Book

The chapters following this introduction are dedicated to further developing a theory of industrial user construction and to explicating its theoretical and methodological foundations as well as its practical consequences.

In Chapter 2, I put the two propositions with which I began this introduction on a more solid theoretical basis. I develop the idea that *industries construct their users*, by engaging with three decades of STS literature on the topic. I argue that the limited focus of most approaches on the agency of either technology developers or the people who use technology makes it difficult to examine just how the digitalization of design, production, and distribution are linked to changes in situated use practices (Section 2.1). To facilitate such analyses, I develop an *action net perspective on industrial user construction* by combining insights from organization studies and biographical studies of artifacts and their (use) practices (Section 2.2). Finally, I weave in the proposition that the *digitalization of production is linked to industrial reorganization* (Section 2.3). I show that STS focused on the role of technology as a product, while neglecting its role as a means of production. To extend existing concepts, I again turn to the field of organization studies, where the relationship between production technologies and organizing has long been a central concern. The upshot of this section is a notion of *production devices* that highlights two key aspects of production technologies in user construction: Their capacity for translating intermediaries from one form (input) into another (output) and their recursive relationship with institutionalized patterns of organizing.

In Chapter 3, I discuss the *methodological challenges* raised by an action net perspective on industrial user construction. I consider how to use qualitative methods to collect data on large-scale phenomena such as a globally distributed net of industrial (and non-industrial) activities. I also detail my own compound strategy, including mapping the field by means of explorative interviews, following the action through a series of focused ethnographic case studies, and bringing the action to me by means of experimental, user-centered design workshops (makeathons), reflecting on my own implication in the processes under study. Finally, I turn to the challenge of analyzing data by beginning from action rather than actors. In the absence of a thorough treatment of this problem by Czarniawska herself, I explain how I operationalized her action net approach and how to interpret the drawings that populate my analytical chapters.

Chapters 4–6 present my analysis of user construction in the prosthetics industry and its transformation following the introduction of 3D printing. Each chapter zooms in on one of the major sets of action involved in industrial user construction and develops one of the three findings advanced above by way of comparing the established action nets with the ones now forming around digital fabrication. Chapter 4 investigates the different modes of technology design related to craft-based custom production, industrial mass production, and two forms of digital mass customization. Positioning the introduction of 3D printing within a century-old struggle for professional dominance between craftspeople and engineers, the main theme is how the introduction of digital technologies offers an opportunity to renegotiate strongly institutionalized patterns of user construction. Chapter 5 is concerned with how users and non-users are constructed during the distribution of prosthetic components from the sites of production to the sites of use. Investigating the issue of the uneven global distribution of prosthetic components, I zoom in on the power asymmetries built into the infrastructural and institutional foundation of the field and discuss the potential of using digital technologies to bypass them. Chapter 6, the final empirical contribution to this book, analyzes how situated practices of *using* industrial products relate to the emergence and institutionalization of new user roles. Paying close attention to the feedback loops between re-interpretation in use and re-inscription in design, I elaborate how digital technology may change the relationship between industrial organizations and their users by allowing for new forms of including user feedback.

In Chapter 7, I attempt an answer to the question of how the digitalization of industrial production shapes the future of use. To this end, I examine the large-scale patterns that become visible when combining the insights about user construction during technology design, production, distribution, and use. To capture these patterns, I introduce the concept of *modes of user construction* and differentiate between an industrial and a craft mode. I then go on to argue that genuinely new, *digital modes of user construction*, such as those linked to digital platforms or open-source communities, do tend to emerge as flexible re-combinations of deeply ingrained nets of action. While the opportunities for re-combination depend on the translational capacities of new technologies, the direction of change remains inextricably tied to the practical lives of the people constituted as users.

Notes

1 I will use the term *digitalization* instead of digitization throughout this book in an attempt to go beyond purely technical connotations and capture the manifold processes through which technology and organizing continuously shape each other (Seibt et al., 2019).

2 Such arguments should be taken with a grain of salt. While today's digital technologies can certainly perform tasks that their 40 years older counterparts could not, claims about the increasing automation of cognitive work are by no means new. For instance, Blau and colleagues wrote in 1976: "Technological innovation in factories used to be confined largely to production, substituting machines for manual labor, but the recent development and spread of computer systems now also substitutes automated operations for white-collar work" (Blau et al., 1976).

3 Of course, prostheses are used by concrete people, whose bodies do have identifiable properties, sizes, shapes, weights, colors, etc. The point is that they only become users, of one kind or another, in action and cannot be identified as such beforehand.

4 The fact that prosthesis users depend on the assemblage of human and non-human elements is plain enough and not particularly remarkable in a world where most of us are cyborgs in one way or another (Haraway, 1991). I do not consider users to be leviathans in need of unscrewing (Callon & Latour, 1981). Nor am I interested in claiming that the introduction of digital fabrication will bring about a new anthropological ideal, such as a "body 2.0" (Harrasser, 2013a), which would suggest a society-wide shift in orientation. In my view, 3D printing may enable the construction of several novel user roles, including that of prosthetic superheroes. But these are likely to coexist with all sorts of other roles, including quite ordinary ones.

5 Czarniawska borrows this term from early actor-network thinkers (Callon, 1984; Latour, 1987), who in turn borrowed it from the philosophy of Michel Serres (see Brown, 2002b, pp. 5–8), who bases it in information theory.

2 Theoretical Foundations of Industrial User Construction

In order to lay the theoretical foundation for analyzing the link between the reorganization of contemporary industries and the future of use, I return to the two propositions put forward in the introduction. The first is that industries construct their users and the second is that the ongoing digitalization of manufacturing is transforming the ways in which they do so. Building on these ideas, I argue that the *construction* of user roles and identities needs to be understood as a net of interlinked activities spanning technology design, distribution, and use, and occurring throughout a technology's biography (Hyysalo et al., 2019). To facilitate this kind of analysis, I draw on the notion of *action net* (Czarniawska, 2004b) and adapt it from the study of organizations to the study of users. To also capture the influence of the *digitalization of manufacturing*, I then introduce the idea that *production devices* act as pivotal mediators in the action nets linking technology supply and use. Taken together, these concepts form the theoretical backbone for analyzing the construction of user roles throughout the biographies of artifacts, as well as on the industrial scale.

2.1 The Construction of User Roles and Identities

Industries and users are co-constructed phenomena, one depending on and elaborating the other. From this perspective, differences between individual users and user groups, or changes in prevalent use practices, cannot simply be explained in terms of pre-existing characteristics of the "people out there." Instead, research needs to begin by examining *user construction*, by which I mean the recurring sociotechnical processes through which certain groups of people come to use a given technology in specific ways, while others might use the same kind of product differently or not at all. This is not a new idea. In fact, a focus on the co-construction of users and technology (Oudshoorn & Pinch, 2003) has been of pivotal importance in defining the identity of science and technology studies (STS) as a field of research. Several major STS traditions have contributed to our understanding of this dynamic relationship and this work has already been aptly summarized (Hyysalo et al., 2016a; Oudshoorn, 2019; Oudshoorn & Pinch, 2008; van den Scott et al., 2017; Wilkie, 2010).

DOI: 10.4324/9781003269731-2

A theory of industrial user construction builds on this rich field of scholarship, while extending it in several directions. Most importantly, an action net perspective offers a basis for the critical theory bridging suggested in recent biographical analyses of the co-construction of users and technology (Hyysalo et al., 2019; Hyysalo, 2021). As will become clear, this is a particularly salient challenge in the field of user studies, where a wealth of concepts from different analytical traditions exists side by side, often incorporating different notions of what users are and what user construction entails. An action net perspective is not the only feasible theoretical orientation for such an endeavor, but it does offer several advantages. Foremost, it allows for the conceptualization of the emergence of user roles and identities in action rather than assuming these to be inherent properties of preexisting individuals and groups. Further, an action net perspective addresses how spatially and socially distributed activities (e.g., design, production, distribution, and use) are linked into larger constellations, in which user roles, and indeed entire user landscapes, are constructed. Finally, it makes visible processes of institutionalization and the importance of prevalent institutions in these processes. Before I explore these themes in greater detail, I will first review the existing STS literature on user construction to more closely determine the point of departure of an action net analysis.

2.1.1 Users as Constructed in Technology Design

A first strand of STS user research concerns the construction of user roles during technology design and development. Starting in the 1980s, several constructivist approaches including the Social Shaping of Technology (SST) (MacKenzie & Wajcman, 1985; Williams & Edge, 1996), the Social Construction of Technology (SCOT) (Bijker, 1995; Pinch & Bijker, 1987), and Actor-Network Theory (ANT) (Latour, 1987; Law, 1987) criticized linear models of technological innovation and the tenets of technological determinism that underpinned them. These authors emphasized that technology should not be conceptualized as an external force with unambiguous impacts on society but was rather to be understood as socially constructed to begin with.

Marxist and feminist authors working under the label of the SST conducted important historical studies that demonstrated the pervasiveness of *social choice* in technology design and the effects of those choices on the possible usages of new technologies (MacKenzie & Wajcman, 1985). The idea that technological change resembled a "garden of forking paths" (Williams & Edge, 1996, p. 866) emphasized that technology could, in principle, take various forms and be put to varied uses. The co-construction of users and technology was thus cast as a political question open to negotiation between various social groups. However, early empirical studies highlighted that the result of such controversies was usually constrained by ingrained social relations and power constellations. In the field of industrial technology, David Noble (1978, 1984) found that the development of automated machine tools involved the choice between "numerical control" and "record-playback" technologies. Yet, he also concluded that the decision for the former was made in the interest of greater managerial control, reproducing the asymmetrical relationship between management and workers. In the realm of household technology, Ruth Schwartz Cowan (1983) demonstrated that viable alternatives to domestic appliances, such as the humming compressor refrigerator, existed and promised to reduce the workload of women. Yet, they ironically resulted in *More Work for Mother* as new machines were designed, marketed, and used in ways that not only served the financial interest of powerful manufacturers, but also reproduced the social institutions of family autonomy and the allocation of household work to women. Overall, despite drawing attention to the prevalence of social choice, early social shaping studies emphasized that ingrained user roles tended to be reproduced in the design of new technologies.

Another line of scholarship, often associated with ANT, treated the construction of users in the tradition of material semiotics (Latour & Akrich, 1992; Latour & Woolgar, 1986). Working against the metaphor of "machine as text," Steve Woolgar proposed that developers, or writers, oriented their development activities toward anticipated users, or readers, of the technology. Design thus involved a process of *configuring the user*, which included "defining the identity of putative users, and setting constraints upon their likely future actions" (Woolgar, 1991, p. 59). What made Woolgar's approach so appealing was that it allowed scholars to talk about "users in the semiotic sense: users as imagined by the designers of a technology" (Oudshoorn et al., 2004, p. 31). What is materialized in the physical shape of the machine and its accompanying contracts and instructions is not the user as an embodied individual, but the user as a social category constructed through the designers' activities. However, even though Woolgar offered a provocative view of technology development, he remained mostly silent with respect to the relationship between the user configured in technology development and the user "in-the-flesh" (Latour, 1992, p. 237).

Other material-semiotic approaches, such as Pfaffenberger's "technological dramas" (1992) or the script approach by Akrich and Latour (Akrich, 1992; Latour, 1992; Latour & Akrich, 1992) took a broader perspective. In a seminal article, Akrich noted that a big part of any innovator's work is that of defining and inscribing into the artifact a certain vision of the world in which it was to be inserted (Akrich, 1992, p. 208). The object, itself understood as a network, is therefore thought to contain a *script*—a somewhat richer, theatrical metaphor compared to Woolgar's generic *text*.[1] Scripts define actors with certain properties, their relationships to others, and the activities they are expected to engage in and refrain from. In this view, using the artifact amounts to the situated enactment of the role inscribed into the object. Akrich tellingly refers to these performances as "de-scriptions," which necessarily involve "mechanisms of adjustment (or failure to adjust) between the user, as imagined by the designer, and the real user" (1992, p. 209).[2] *Description*, then, takes on the double meaning of challenging the script defined by an object and making intelligible the structure of the sociotechnical network in which the object is embedded. Unlike Woolgar's notion of configuring the user, the script approach thus acknowledges that inscribed user roles can be redistributed, recombined, or ignored, including the possibility of physically altering the artifact itself.

Despite its underlying network imagery, early work in ANT was criticized for according too powerful a position to designers and entrepreneurs (Gherardi & Nicolini, 2005; Haraway, 1988; Star, 1991; Suchman, 2007). Similarly, related work in SST was viewed as giving an over-politicized account of technology design (Williams et al., 2005), while disregarding the negotiation of user roles during marketing or in the appropriation of technology (Mackay & Gillespie, 1992). These attempts at deconstructing technological determinism ran the danger of replacing it with a social determinism whereby technology reflected the interests of powerful social groups and clever network builders. If technology had negative effects, it was due to its existence as an instrument of power (Noble, 1984) or because the biased worldviews of engineers had led them to misrepresent the users of the objects they helped to bring about (Oudshoorn et al., 2004). Even common strategies to alleviate these problems, such as user-centered design, were viewed as reproducing the "design fallacy" (Stewart & Williams, 2005; Williams et al., 2005, pp. 100–104) of overestimating the degree to which situated use practices could be anticipated in or controlled through technology design.

Subsequent scholarship served to decenter the position of the designer in various ways. Several authors paid close, often ethnographic attention to the daily practices of technology development. Their studies provided insight into the various factors constraining the choices of engineers and other technologists. Contemporary technology development was described as highly regulated, both through formal rules set by state actors or standard-setting organizations (Sørensen, 1996), and in the form of professional norms, organizational procedures, and user requirements (Mackay et al., 2000). Development work was oriented by shared *frames* (Bijker, 1995) or *paradigms* (van den Belt & Rip, 1987), as well as ideology and culture more generally (Mackay & Gillespie, 1992; Oudshoorn et al., 2004). The construction of technology and its possible usages was further found to be influenced by visions of future industrial development (Brown et al., 2000; Pollock & Williams, 2009) and *practice-bound imaginaries* of how these visions might be practically realized (Hyysalo, 2006; Hyysalo, 2010). Finally, contemporary design projects, particularly in the field of ICT, were found to reuse and build on established techniques and pre-existing components (Pollock & Williams, 2009), along with the user representations they contained. Ironically, within these tightly structured settings of technology development, designers may come to feel as if they had little latitude in their work.

The early focus on the agency of technology designers was further undermined by another set of studies, which point out that the work of constructing user roles is not restricted to product development by industry and does not end once the artifact is first marketed. Rather, user roles are negotiated between a wide range of relevant groups well beyond the R&D department (Williams et al., 2005). Empirical studies, particularly from the fields of health and medicine, found that multiple groups and organizations such as public-sector agencies, health advocacy groups, user communities, and social movements advanced their own representations of users and their practices, which designers were forced to contend with (Callon & Rabeharisoa, 2003; Epstein, 2003; Oudshoorn, 2003; van Kammen, 2003). Perhaps unsurprisingly, the most important among these groups were users themselves.

2.1.2 Users as Active Agents in Technological Change

From the inception of STS user research, several important contributions complemented the concern with technology development by focusing on users as active agents in technological change. These studies emphasized the agency of users in choosing between or ignoring the products offered to them by suppliers. They also stressed the work of interpretation, adaptation, and re-invention that goes into making technologies useful in local contexts. The co-construction of technology and user roles, they contend, does not end at the doorstep of the laboratory or factory, but extends well into the organizational and domestic settings in which technology is used.

The SCOT approach was among the first to pay attention to the active role of users in technological change. In their famous study of the social construction of the bicycle, Pinch and Bijker (1987) emphasized the *interpretative flexibility* of technology, and included users and non-users as relevant social groups attributing particular meanings to it. In their account, interpretations by user groups, such as "women cyclists" and "young men of nerve," would point to certain problems with a given technology that were, in turn, addressed by developers in subsequent product variations. Following an iterative and potentially multidirectional process of variation and selection, several mechanisms ultimately lead to a closure of the controversy and the stabilization of a dominant design, such as the "safety bicycle." In the SCOT model, users therefore played an important role in the evolution of technology, chiefly through their interpretation and selection of designers' offerings. In similar fashion, Cowan also draws attention to the importance of consumer choice in explaining why some versions of a technology succeed, while equally promising variants do not. She reversed the focus on network builders present in ANT and related work on Large Technical Systems (LTS) (Hughes, 1983) to focus on the *consumption junction*, "the place and the time at which the consumer makes choices between competing technologies" (Cowan, 1987, p. 255). Rather than studying technology development and depicting sociotechnical networks from the point of view of designers, she focused on technology's diffusion and aimed to reconstruct which sets of relations played a role in the users' selection of one or the other product variation.

As these examples show, even though much social constructivist scholarship focused on the early phases of technology design, these approaches were in general agreement that the fate of a technology is ultimately decided through the interpretation of its users. Technology suppliers may try to influence potential users by changing the design of a technology, by restricting choice in a product range, or by altering the context of use. They may promote specific meanings through advertising (Cowan, 1983, pp. 136–138; Pinch & Bijker, 1987, pp. 37–38) or discursively surrounding the artifact with myths and rituals (Pfaffenberger, 1992). They may even engage in the tedious work of altering culturally ingrained perceptions and norms (Oudshoorn, 2003). However, the success of these strategies always depends on the people who decide to take up the artifact or not. As Latour put it in articulating the problem of the network builder: "The fate of facts and machines is in later users' hands" (1987, p. 259).

While the various social constructivist brands of technology studies stressed the role of users in choosing between available offerings and providing cues for further technology development, scholars from the areas of cultural and media studies treated consumption as a central component of identity construction in its own right. Drawing on anthropological work on material culture (Appadurai, 1986; Douglas & Isherwood, 1979), they emphasized that consumption is not merely an economic, but a cultural activity. Consumers actively construct meaning even, and especially, for the mass-produced commodities of large-scale industries (Miller, 1987). Simultaneously, they construct and signal their own identity through acts of consumption (Baudrillard, 1998), even as these identities are socially, culturally, and economically patterned (Bourdieu, 1984). Of particular importance to STS was the notion of *domestication* (Berker et al., 2006; Lie & Sørensen, 1996; Silverstone et al., 1992). It refers to the process in which artifacts and media are imbued with specific meanings as they move from being commodities in the "formal economy" of the market to being objects in the "moral economy" of a local context such as the household (Silverstone & Hirsch, 1992). In the model developed by Silverstone et al. (1992, pp. 18–23), domestication is understood as a four-stage process including the appropriation of the artifact by users, its objectification through placement and display, its incorporation into routines and practices, and its conversion through the enactment of a certain status and identity vis-à-vis others. Overall, the domestication approach allowed for a more detailed appreciation of consumption as identity-making. It emphasized that the meanings ascribed to an object by its users may be radically different from those imagined by its designers, and it underlined that the symbolic dimension of objects may matter as much as their functionality.

While undoubtedly important, early conceptualizations of users as active agents in technological change have been both criticized and extended. The concept of "relevant social group" was criticized by feminist scholars for excluding groups that do not influence technological change but might nonetheless be affected by it. They argued that many users fall into this category of "implicated actors" (Clarke, 1998, p. 16) and therefore remain invisible in the SCOT framework. In a similar vein, Sally Wyatt argued that "non-users also matter" (Wyatt, 2003). While the importance of anti-cyclists was recognized in Pinch and Bijker's original study, Wyatt distinguished between different kinds of *non-users*. "Resisters" have never used a technology because they do not want to; "rejecters" have stopped using it voluntarily; "the excluded" cannot use it for a lack of access, and finally, "the expelled" are forced to stop using it against their will. Nelly Oudshoorn (2011) further refined this view by drawing attention to the phenomenon of *selective use* rather than complete rejection. These feminist critiques underscore the fact that users are not a homogenous group. Differences in gender, age, ethnicity, or technological expertise matter, as do social, cultural, and economic contexts. Similarly, authors writing in an actor-network register argued that the configuration of users' (dis-)abilities occurs within larger networks that include material as well as discursive elements (Latour, 1999, p. 176; Moser, 2006).

A second strand of critique has been directed at the narrow depictions of technology use in both social constructivist and consumption studies. With a view to social constructivist approaches, the idea that the interpretative flexibility of an artifact decreases after the closure of a controversy, seemed to make users "relevant" only during the early phases of an artifact's biography, such as development or market introduction. Users, then, were important only insofar as they influenced designers. Conversely, the domestication framework was criticized for limiting the view to technology use in the household, while neglecting other sites of use as well as its relationship to the realm of development and production. Within the SCOT tradition, subsequent empirical studies reacted to this critique by demonstrating that users do reinterpret and in fact materially redesign even seemingly stabilized technologies like the Ford Model T (Kline & Pinch, 1996).[3] With regard to the domestication framework, the research focus was extended to technology use in other settings, such as the workplace (Lie & Sørensen, 1996). Moreover, more interactive models of social learning were developed (Lie & Sørensen, 1996; Sørensen, 1996), which essentially merged insights from cultural studies and social constructivist technology studies. Together, these developments signaled a move toward more encompassing models that spanned iterative cycles of technology design and use over extended periods of time.

2.1.3 User Construction Across Multiple Innovation Cycles

Early STS accounts produced a wealth of knowledge and concepts on the mutual shaping of technology and user roles. It also became clear, however, that their accounts differed widely between theoretical traditions and methodological vantage points. Work in both SST and material semiotics treated user roles as constructed and inscribed during technology *design*, with SST emphasizing the importance of social structure and power relations and material semiotics the situated practices of scientists and engineers. Conversely, work in SCOT and cultural anthropology treated roles and identities as constructed in technology *use*. Yet, SCOT emphasized the importance of users' shared social, cultural, and economic positions, whereas anthropologists studied the concrete use practices of individuals and small collectives. Given these incongruities, calls for more integrative research became louder. In the early 2000s, several edited collections took stock of the range of processes involved in the co-construction of users and technology. They stressed the complementarity of earlier approaches and contributed to the inception of user studies as a recognizable sub-field in STS (Oudshoorn & Pinch, 2003; Rohracher, 2005; Sørensen & Williams, 2002). At about the same time, several more encompassing frameworks were proposed (Callon et al., 2002; Flichy, 2007b; Hyysalo, 2010; Williams et al., 2005). Theoretically, these incorporated multiple concepts from STS and neighboring fields. Methodologically, they suggested study designs that extended investigations longitudinally, covered diverse settings, and combined multiple scales of analysis.

One of the most elaborate approaches was the social learning in technological innovation (SLTI) framework (Williams et al., 2005), which resulted from a large-scale research project spanning twenty-seven case studies in European ICT innovation. The SLTI approach was explicitly based on earlier work in SST (MacKenzie & Wajcman, 1985), but extended its focus to include technology implementation and use. To this end, researchers took on board concepts from the anthropology of consumption (Lie & Sørensen, 1996; Silverstone & Hirsch, 1992), as well as work on "innofusion" (Fleck, 1988) and the learning economy (Lundvall, 1988). Methodologically, rather than focusing exclusively on technology design or use, they investigated how the two were related throughout the innovation process and compared insights across several development projects and technological systems. Whereas research on the learning economy had mostly studied the aggregate level of national innovation systems, these studies showed in greater detail, how technology designers gradually came to learn about potential users, and how users, individually and collectively, learned to use and adapt the products offered by technology suppliers (Sørensen, 1996). Moreover, proponents of the SLTI framework found that the evolving relationship between designers and users was frequently enabled and regulated by entire ecologies of intermediary actors (Stewart & Hyysalo, 2008).

A key contribution of these studies was to conceptualize the nexus of technology design and use in innovation contexts that diverged from the idealized view of economics (Williams et al., 2005). The baseline of economic innovation research had long been a linear model, in which technology supply and demand are linked by an impersonal market. By contrast, the SLTI studies developed models that drew attention to contexts characterized by direct interaction, mediated feedback cycles, and the cumulative effects of social learning. For instance, the "pick and mix" model, typical of complex ICT systems, involves conventional market transactions, but allows for the gradual combination and configuration of generic components at the site of use. The user-centered design model captures the direct interaction between designers and (proxy) users during early stages of the design process. In the innofusion and domestication model, social learning instead takes place in the interaction of adopters and suppliers during technology implementation and early use. Finally, the evolutionary experimental model describes more extended interactions, as users and developers collaborate over several iterations of design, use, and re-design, progressively bringing in larger groups of actors. In sum, the social learning perspective offers a cyclical understanding of the relation between technology design, implementation, and use, and demonstrates the variety of ways in which the user-designer nexus can be organized.

Methodologically, the SLTI framework was further refined by the biography of artifacts and practices (BOAP) approach (Hyysalo, 2010; Hyysalo et al., 2019; Hyysalo, 2021; Pollock et al., 2003; Pollock & Williams, 2009). This strand of scholarship pointed out that the conceptual shortcomings and incongruencies of earlier user studies were partly rooted in their preferred research templates and data types. Ethnographic studies, conducted by scholars affiliated with ANT and cultural studies, had a propensity to miss larger contexts and jump to questionable conclusions based on findings from local sites (Hyysalo, 2021, p. 16; Pollock & Williams, 2009). Conversely, the historical accounts preferred by SST and SCOT, tended to address the co-construction of technologies and user roles on a scale and level of granularity that made it impractical to attend to the detailed meanings and materialities of the practices involved (Hyysalo, 2021, p. 17). To arrive at more balanced accounts, the biographical approach sought to combine insights from multiple vantage points by knitting together a string of close-up studies conducted at different biographical moments, with investigations using other sources of empirical material, such as historical or quantitative studies (Pollock & Williams, 2009, p. 110). Such flexible research geometries were thought more appropriate to capture the "social life" (Appadurai, 1986) or "biography" (Kopytoff, 1986) of complex artifacts (Pollock & Williams, 2009) and their accompanying (use) practices (Hyysalo, 2010).

Biographical studies, in combination with conceptual frameworks like SLTI, brought into view the changing constituencies and practices implicated in co-construction processes over the long term. For example, Pollock and Williams (2009) showed that, despite common diagnoses of initial misfit in single-sited "snapshot," or implementation studies, large ICT platforms could become extraordinarily successful over time. The success of such configurational technologies did not depend solely on their initial *localization* to a specific site and usage. In the long run, it also required the *generification* work of stripping away idiosyncrasies as well as re-using, packaging, and commodifying functionalities developed for local settings. In the same vein, Hyysalo's study of healthcare technology noted that contemporary (digital) technologies are heterogenous assemblages whose biographies feature long sequences of *pre-, de-, re-,* and *co-configuration* (Hyysalo, 2009; Hyysalo, 2010). Configuring the user of such technologies is therefore not a one-off effort as implied by Woolgar (1991). Rather, as an emerging technology changes, it may, over time, relate to different users and usages. With a view to long-term innovation processes, the co-construction of technology and user roles was thus depicted as a *series of configurational movements* (Hyysalo et al., 2019; Hyysalo, 2021). In this process, not only did the shape and meaning of the technology change during its "diffusion" (compare Rogers, 1983), but so did the composition and identities of the "relevant social groups" (compare Pinch & Bijker, 1987) that helped to shape it.

The new focus on long-term co-construction also refined the understanding of several mechanisms already found in previous ethnographic and historical studies. Regarding user role construction during technology design, a social learning perspective invariably led to the question of how designers produce knowledge on future users (Williams et al., 2005). Subsequent studies thus elaborated on the theme of *user representation* (Hyysalo, 2010, p. 234; Hyysalo & Johnson, 2016) that had first been highlighted in the tradition of material semiotics (Akrich, 1995; Oudshoorn et al., 2004). Extending Akrich's original typology (Akrich, 1995, p. 169), designers were shown to deploy explicit representational techniques ranging from arm's length requirements gathering to direct user involvement. Indeed, organizations were found to use digital technologies to set up extensive "knowledge infrastructures" (Johnson, 2007; Johnson et al., 2014) through which they monitored user activities. These representations could be reflexively used as resources in the design process (Wilkie, 2010), or they could be accumulated, commodified, and traded (Pollock & Williams, 2009). Moreover, a biographical perspective highlighted that user representations become reified and accumulate over several design iterations (Hyysalo, 2010). They may become inscribed in extant infrastructures and hardware systems (Bowker & Star, 1999), but particularly in algorithms (Glaser et al., 2021) and re-purposed layers of software (Ametowobla, 2022). At the same time, particular ideas about users may form part of familiar genres or common narrative structures used in technology design (Hyysalo, 2010, p. 234). More implicitly, designers draw user representations from professional lore and societal conventions (Hyysalo, 2010; Oudshoorn et al., 2004). Johnson and Hyysalo (2016, p. 83) further added that particular imaginations of the user underpin both business concepts and regulatory demands, thereby taking deep roots in organizational and institutional contexts.

Following technologies through several cycles of innovation also stressed the previously neglected mechanisms of *mediation* between industrial technology supply and use, and revealed the spectrum of actors involved. While this theme was touched upon by earlier social constructivist studies, it was fully articulated in more encompassing models (Callon et al., 2002; Williams et al., 2005) and longitudinal studies (Hyysalo, 2010; Hyysalo, 2021; Johnson, 2007; Oudshoorn, 2003; Pollock & Williams, 2009). Entire ecologies of actors, like resellers, consultants, trainers and technical support, local experts, advocacy groups, and user communities, were found to be involved in *intermediation* between technology supply and use (Stewart & Hyysalo, 2008). Together, they support and regulate the physical distribution of products while enabling users to learn about new technologies, and reciprocally, designers to learn about users. Stewart and Hyysalo (2008) stressed that these tasks are particularly important in the case of new products, for which no relationship between demand and supply has yet been established. Similarly, Kivimaa and colleagues (2019) were concerned with intermediaries in periods of sociotechnical transition. Conversely, Callon et al. (2002) emphasized the role of intermediaries in stable markets by drawing attention to the "economy of qualities" in which products and consumer tastes are constantly re-shaped and fitted to one another through processes of *qualification* and *singularization*. The latter contributions also point out that, while the problem of intermediation may have initially emerged under conditions of centralized mass production (Hyysalo et al., 2016a, compare Chapter 5), it takes on new forms in the wake of digitalization. Chains of intermediation become longer and more diversified as supply chains are globalized, processes of outsourcing abound, and new mediators such as platform providers rise to prominence. Industrial organizations evolve more flexible production and distribution systems to address, track, manage, or enroll users, while the latter gain greater access to information about available offerings and routinely share their knowledge, or pool resources in translocal networks and communities (Hyysalo et al., 2016b).

A final set of findings generated through social learning and biographical studies concerns the active contributions of users in shaping and asserting their own roles and identities. They underlined that, far from simply choosing between existing products or imbuing them with new meaning, users actively participate in almost all aspects and phases of the innovation process (Hyysalo, 2021; Schot et al., 2016). They actively contribute to the design process with varying intensity ranging from use as-is to outright user innovation (Kohtala et al., 2020). Yet, they also generate new meanings, use practices and settings (ibid.) and contribute to the diffusion of innovations by championing, lending legitimacy to, or creating markets for new products (Hyysalo, 2021, pp. 106–112). It is also important to point out that many relevant contributions are made by user collectives (Kohtala et al., 2020; Mozaffar, 2016). Users provide assistance to their peers, be it as "local experts" (Stewart, 2007), in shared machine shops (Kohtala et al., 2020) or via emerging online communities (Hyysalo, 2021) (Flichy, 2007a; Hippel, 2005; Hippel, 2017). They share, organize and collectively create knowledge about existing technologies (Grabher & Ibert, 2014), or collectively innovate new ones (Hippel, 2005; Hyysalo & Usenyuk, 2015). For all these reasons, there is a long history of attempts by industrial organizations to harness the creative potential of their customers. With a focus on individual users, Rogers (1983) stressed the importance of opinion leaders, while von Hippel proposed "lead users" as "a source of novel product concepts" (1986). With digital technology, outsourcing parts of the innovation process to individuals (Hippel & Katz, 2002) or crowds (Bauer & Gegenhuber, 2015) has become viable. In the same vein, newer management tactics advocate the management of innovation communities (Dahlander & Magnusson, 2005; Dahlander & Magnusson, 2008) or ecosystems (Gawer & Cusumano, 2014). Social learning and biographical studies have contributed to moving these discussions from the economically-oriented registers of user innovation (Hippel, 2005) and open innovation (Chesbrough, 2003) to the core of STS. This move has led to more balanced accounts that capture users' innovative potential, as well as the tendencies of companies to foster active users and benefit from their activities (Bruni & Esposito, 2019; Drewlani & Seibt, 2018; Ferdinand & Meyer, 2017; Hyysalo et al., 2016a; Johnson et al., 2014; Neves da Rocha & Pollock, 2019; Pollock & Hyysalo, 2014).

2.1.4 From Critical Eclecticism to Theory Bridging

Over the last two decades, the social learning approach and related models have significantly advanced STS user research. Through this work, we have arrived at a very complex and empirically-grounded picture of the construction of user roles in processes that span industrial technology supply and technology use. Yet, the richness of this picture also creates new challenges, not least of which is the problem of theory bridging: How to integrate insights generated with concepts originating from different theoretical backgrounds, addressing different kinds of settings, and pitched at varying levels of granularity?

Until recently, SLTI and BOAP mainly addressed issues of theoretical incongruency by developing heuristic frameworks and elaborate study designs that help to analyze the same subject matter from multiple analytical vantage points. However, they largely neglected the tedious task of conceptual integration between these perspectives. SLTI demonstrated the need for studies to address the relationship between (industrial) technology supply and use, including a range of intermediary activities. To this end, scholars mapped extant concepts with regard to the processes and actors they addressed, and pragmatically combined them into an abstracted cyclical model of co-construction between user roles and technologies (Williams et al., 2005). BOAP further substantiated this work from a methodological perspective, highlighting that incongruencies between early conceptualizations of users and user construction stemmed from attention to various points in a technology's biography, different scales of analysis, and the reliance on data of different levels of granularity. In response, biographical studies advanced complex methodologies that helped to generate robust empirical coverage of co-construction processes over several cycles of innovation, primarily by stringing together series of sub-studies and integrating different kinds of materials.

Taking stock of these contributions, it is possible to map the relevant mechanisms of user construction along the innovation cycle (see Figure 2.1). This kind of simplified framework, which builds on similar work in SLTI and BOAP, is no doubt useful. Most importantly, it highlights the insight that, in the long term, the co-construction of user roles and technology is based on a complex relationship between industrial technology supply and use, which features constant feedback loops and a whole range of intermediary activities. Together, these constitute long and winding "biographies" of technologies and (use) practices that may span multiple design-use-redesign cycles and longer periods of transition (Hyysalo, 2021; Pollock & Williams, 2009).

Yet, for all the conceptual ordering and sophisticated empirical studies that have emerged from SLTI and BOAP, these approaches have not yet articulated something like an integrated theory of user construction. Indeed, the encompassing research journeys they prescribe often

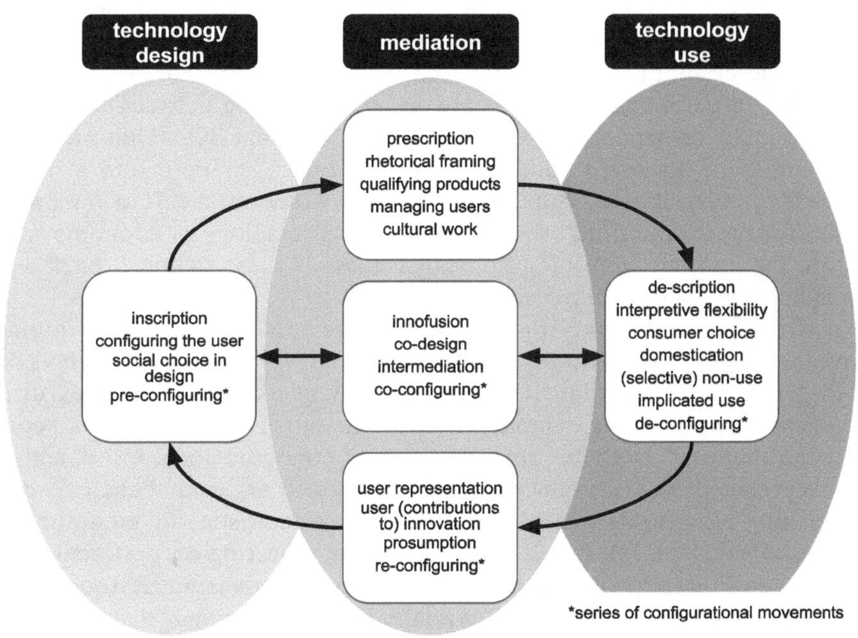

Figure 2.1 STS concepts describing the co-construction of user roles and technology. Own figure.

pragmatically combine concepts from various areas of the social sciences (Hyysalo et al., 2019; Pollock & Williams, 2009; Williams et al., 2005). Most social learning studies were based on the "broad church" of social constructivist approaches, including influences from SST, SCOT, ANT, and LTS (Russell & Williams, 2002; Williams & Edge, 1996), which were further extended by concepts from innovation studies and consumption studies (Sørensen, 1996; Williams et al., 2005). Tapping into such a wide range of frameworks, SLTI offered researchers a rich toolbox for studying different aspects of the user-designer relationship but it did little to unpack the underlying assumptions of the respective concepts. Similarly, when Pollock and Williams formulated their biographical approach, they argued for "a certain level of critical eclecticism in relation to broader worldview, and the theories and concepts that inform it" (Pollock & Williams, 2009, p. 110). While acknowledging that concepts should not be combined on "a pick-and-mix basis" (ibid.), they were more wary of the rigidities of theoretical purism, arguing that biographical studies should be compatible with multiple theoretical orientations.

This does not mean, however, that biographical and social learning studies do not attend to theory. It simply means that, rather than elaborating a unified theoretical foundation, researchers pragmatically combine concepts and middle-range theories relevant to the phenomena they encounter during a string of snapshot studies (Silvast & Virtanen, 2021). The drawback of this strategy is that authors may accumulate a rather large and potentially incoherent bunch of theories as they string together multiple sub-studies. To the degree that differences between theoretical frameworks, say SCOT and ANT, are not reducible to study design, mediating between these perspectives may present a sizable challenge. The fact that BOAP has provided little guidance on how to address this problem has made it into a rather unwieldy approach and arguably impeded its wider uptake. It also made it easier for more traditional disciplines, such as sociology or economics, to ignore the findings from biographical studies, as these switched back and forth between analytical registers.

It is only more recently that calls for more principled theory bridging have been articulated by proponents of the biographical approach. Hyysalo et al. (2019) suggested that BOAP studies may be used to advance existing theoretical concepts, as demonstrated by the move from Woolgar's "configuring the user" to the notion of "series of configurational movements." In his recent book, Hyysalo went even further to argue that the capacity for theory bridging is one of the distinct characteristics of biographical studies (Hyysalo, 2021, pp. 21–24). In essence, reflecting on pertinent phenomena from multiple methodological vantage points is understood as an opportunity for extending and potentially linking previously disparate theoretical concepts. Rather than in an ad-hoc manner, Hyysalo argues that this kind of theory bridging is best done on the ground of a wider, well-articulated theoretical orientation or what Silvast and Virtanen (2021) have called a "meta theory." In his view, it is this general theoretical perspective that should guide theory bridging in a biographical study.

Clearly, there are several theoretical orientations that lend themselves to grounding a BOAP study (Hyysalo et al., 2019). Each combination would yield a differently poised "theory-method package" (Silvast & Virtanen, 2021), conducive to answering particular kinds of research questions. For instance, theoretical bridging may be performed on the basis of activity theory (Hyysalo, 2010), symbolic interactionism (Hyysalo, 2021), or potentially a theory of social learning (Williams et al., 2005). The requirement is, however, that the underlying theory provides sufficient range to analyze *geographically and socially distributed processes of sociotechnical change that cut across multiple timeframes and scales of analysis.*

It is this aim that guides the action net analysis of industrial user construction that follows. I argue that a theoretical orientation that views the sociotechnical world as composed of more and less stabilized nets of action provides a basis for grasping the relationship between a range of narrower concepts (e.g., representation, inscription, intermediation, re-interpretation) that describe mechanisms occurring at different points in the biography of an artifact and its usages. In contrast to more elaborate frameworks such as the multi-level perspective (Hyysalo, 2021; Schot et al., 2016) or social theories such as structuration theory (DeSanctis & Poole, 1994; Orlikowski, 1992; Orlikowski, 2000), action net analysis is very lightweight and less likely to produce major rigidities vis-à-vis existing concepts. At the same time, it offers a few key features that make it particularly useful for the present study.

1 It explicitly conceptualizes the emergence of actorial identities and roles from action. It therefore offers a clear idea of what it means to speak of user construction.
2 It clarifies, through the notion of translation, what it means to speak of the connection between actions that span time, space, and social settings. It thus allows for the conceptualization of the relation between activities relating to, for example, technology design, production, distribution, and use.
3 It recognizes the role of non-human mediators within action nets, allowing me to account for the role of production technology and the effects of digitalization.
4 It offers ways of talking about the stabilization of action nets and user roles in terms of institutionalization in addition to the recognition that the institutional order co-evolves with material tools and infrastructures that reify and stabilize it. The analysis of user construction is thus linked to overarching patterns of industrial organization and transformation.

Action net analysis lends itself well to the kind of theory bridging that appears necessary to further advance STS user research. As I will continue to show, it is a particularly useful foundation for a study of industrial user construction in digitalizing industries.

2.2 An Action Net Approach to User Construction

The previous section has shown that it is possible to understand the different mechanisms of user construction described in the STS literature as complementary insofar as they occur at different points and levels in a technology's biography. The goal of the present section is to bridge existing concepts by treating the processes they describe as interlocking actions within *action nets* (Czarniawska, 2004b; Czarniawska, 2014). By building on this general theoretical orientation, it becomes possible to capture the construction of user roles and identities across technology design, production, distribution, and use. Moreover, an action net approach provides tools for addressing the influence of prevalent institutions and power relations, which are important for investigating user construction on larger scales of analysis.

Action net analysis was first developed for the field of organization studies by Barbara Czarniawska who was dissatisfied with the tendency of existing theories to focus on action in single localities. Just like theorists in the social learning and biographical traditions of STS, Czarniawska saw the problem as stemming from the inability of the field's prevalent methods to grasp the fact that contemporary organizing spans several locations and frequently moves across organizational boundaries.

> The aim is rarely to study a place, but the result is often just that. To study 'Volvo' is to study its headquarters in Gothenburg, its plant in Kalmar and perhaps its Polish branch in Wroclaw. This move is dictated by the common sense of fieldwork: practices are situated, and so are their students. One has to be somewhere in order to study something. [...] The point is not, however, that of methodological purity, but of missing what is important in practice: contemporary organizing moves quickly from one place to another and happens in several places at once.
>
> (Czarniawska, 2004b, p. 779)

To address these issues, Czarniawska broadly conceived of action nets as "collective actions related to one another within a given institutional order" (Joerges & Czarniawska, 1998, p. 364), where

> [T]he collective actions concerned need not necessarily be performed within the bounds of a specific 'organization.' On the contrary, an action net may involve a great variety of organizations or organized groups of people of a loose or temporary nature.
>
> (Lindberg & Czarniawska, 2006, p. 293)[4]

Defined in this way, I suggest that the concept holds promise for the study of user construction, which similarly involves the interlinking of actions across different times and places and across organizational boundaries. In particular, I would like to stress two advantages gained by transferring the notion of action net from the study of organizations to the study of users. One of them concerns the notion of the *construction* of user roles and identities in action, the other that of *translation* as a way of describing the interlinking of relevant processes across technology design, distribution, and use. Taken together, these two concepts offer a toolkit with which to capture the mechanisms of user construction both on the scale of a single technology's biography (Hyysalo et al., 2019) and on the scale of industries that give rise to a patterned multitude of user roles.

2.2.1 Constructing User Identities and User Roles

The first advantage of action net analysis is that it allows me to view "users" as the result of interlocking actions rather than as something given in advance. This perspective helps to make plausible how the reorganization of industrial activities may correspond to the appearance of new user roles and identities. The key insight of action net analysis is that actorial identities emerge from action rather than the other way around. In contrast to other approaches (e.g., SCOT), analysts do not start by identifying the relevant actors (e.g., users) followed by an observation of how they act. Instead, researchers identify the kinds of action they are interested in (e.g., using) and then study which human and non-human actants[5] are involved in accomplishing it. Importantly, in this type of analysis, whoever or whatever the "author" of an action is, is treated as an open question. It is assumed that actorship can, in principal, be attributed to any type of actant (e.g., a human, an organization, an algorithm), but only in a process of sensemaking after the act has occurred (Weick, 1995). It is with a view to the latter aspect that actorial *identities* should be considered as posteriori narrative constructions (Czarniawska, 1998; Weick, 1995, pp. 18–30) since they are attributions that make sense of a given sequence of events. Within such processes of sensemaking, attributing an identity to an actant means to endow it with a certain degree of sameness across the manifold transformations it undergoes and interactions it participates in over a relevant period of time. Following the same logic, I use the term *user identity* in reference to those aspects of the narrative construction that make sense of the use of a specific technology and flag them as particularly important parts of the identities of human actors in highly technologized societies.

The assertion that analytically speaking, action precedes the attribution of actorial identities should not be taken to mean that all attributions will be equally likely or legitimate. In fact, the narrative construction of identity occurs against the backdrop of a prevalent "institutional order" (Czarniawska, 2004b) that regulates who or what can legitimately be considered an actor and which actions should conventionally be linked together.[6] For now, it will suffice to point out that insofar as patterns of action are *repeated*, they may give rise to specific sets of expectations regarding the properties of actants and the kinds of activities they should and should not be involved in. Where actions interlink in a regularized fashion, they therefore give rise to actorial *roles* that, while still subject to a degree of interpretation, can be said to persist independently of individual actors and their identities.[7] For instance, in Lindberg and Czarniawska's example, the knotting together of several acts of patient care into a trans-organizational "chain-of-care" created the role of the "chain-of-care coordinator" (Lindberg & Czarniawska, 2006, p. 302). This role was clearly created by concrete individuals engaging in a novel pattern of action. Yet, as the new pattern was repeated, it created a generalized sense of the requirements, competences, and obligations for the healthcare workers performing it. In result, the pattern of action persisted while individual actors could be exchanged. More generally speaking, while roles are constructed in action ("role-making"), stable roles constitute sets of requirements and expectations confronting actors that aspire to take part in the action ("role-taking").

With regard to user construction this means that, while it is an actor's individual history of using a technology that provides the material for the narrative construction of *user identities*, it is the repeated performance of specific action patterns involving technology use, and occurring independently of individual actors, that lead to the emergence of socially recognizable *user roles*. Given that both processes do not occur independently of one another, it is reasonable to assume that the history of each user will give rise to a more or less pronounced individual user identity, while likely involving the performance of roles that are the stabilized-for-now result of repeated patterns of actions.

Overall, the concepts of *actorial identity* and *role* allow me to treat "users" as the result of nets of interlocking actions. From an action net perspective, who will use a specific technology and how it will be used is neither viewed as determined by readily available properties of "people out there," nor by powerful technology designers and their representation practices. In contrast to most approaches that focus on users as active agents in technology design (e.g., SCOT), the temporal order of action and the attribution of identities and roles is reversed. It is not that people start out as users with a particular attitude toward a technology. Rather, user roles are slowly constructed through a series of activities involving technology. Even in relatively stabilized action nets, individuals (or other currently legitimate actors such as organizations) must actively take on and interpret prevalent user roles, and "being a user" may only gradually become part of their identity. Particular ways of using a technology are also viewed as being linked to rich nets of other actions involving both the practical lives of the people who engage with a piece of technology and the realm of technology design, production, and distribution that made that object available in the first place.

It follows from this that the practices of technology development are seen as important. Yet, unlike approaches that focus on the agency of technology designers to configure or inscribe users (e.g., in material semiotics), action net analysis does not grant these activities analytical priority. It emphasizes that the user roles constructed in design can be reinterpreted, contested, or ignored in subsequent action. From an action net perspective, user identities should thus be viewed as narrative constructions that (potentially) take into account all kinds of actions that transpire throughout the biography of a given technology, often including the conditions of a technology's design and production. Similarly, user roles are viewed as the result of larger patterns of action that span technology design and use, are repeated, and become stabilized. In both cases, what counts is the way in which heterogeneous sets of activities become interlinked.

2.2.2 Translating Between Technology Development and Use

The second advantage of an action net approach to user construction is that it specifies the mechanism for connecting actions performed over time, as well as across spatial and organizational boundaries. In this way, it provides a suitable foundation for theorizing how the various processes described in the user studies literature interlink. To clarify her position on that point, Czarniawska draws on the notion of *translation*, which she borrows from early actor-network thinking (Callon, 1984; Latour, 1987). Translation, in her view, does not only refer to the linguistic operation of equating the meaning of words from different languages. Instead, in keeping with ANT's principle of symmetry, translation is understood as the general mechanism of creating equivalence between all kinds of actants (Callon, 1991). It is this equivalence between whatever is acted upon that creates compatibility between actions. According to this position, it is not only words that can be translated into other words. Instead, translations may occur between all kinds of actants including words, numbers, images, objects, people, and so forth. Actions become connected by creating chains of equivalence between the intermediaries that are passed on between them. It is when no translation can be achieved that action nets fall apart.

Considered from this perspective, the processes involved in user construction are a series of actions linked by various kinds of translations. During *technology design*, the activities of people represented as potential users may be transformed into words or numbers, which are translated into drawings, which form the basis of the inscriptions made into prototypes and final products. The *mediation* between technology supply and demand involves translations that ensure the circulation of these objects from the sites of design and production to the site of use. This may involve the rhetorical framing or qualification of products, as well as their physical configuration and re-configuration (e.g., some products are assembled, or refined, others may require freezing or careful handling to remain the same between actions). Finally, depending on the practices of *technology use,* the product may again be reinterpreted or physically altered to facilitate its function within its new context. Frequently, reinterpretations and reinscriptions made by users then feed back into new iterations of technology design. It is ultimately through the translation (connection) of all these actions into relatively stable action nets that rich sets of user roles are formed and specific ways of using emerge as dominant.

There are two caveats that should be attached to the notion of translation as the mechanism of knotting together the action nets of user construction. The first is that translation is never a smooth or frictionless process. Establishing a connection between two different actions is likely to require either the adaptation of the activities involved or the transformation of whatever is passed between them. Consequently, both the forms and meanings of actants may be "displaced" as actions are connected with one another, potentially altering the actorial identities attributed to them. To describe these shifts, Latour points to the geometrical meaning of translation as "moving from one place to another" (Latour, 1987, p. 117). Law goes one step further in writing that "to translate is to also betray (traductore, tradittore)" (Law, 1999, p. 1; compare Law, 2003). The general idea is similar: Whether intentionally or not, the act of translating always modifies that which is translated. To be translated is necessarily to be changed. From this perspective, the common finding of critical design research that designers "misinterpret" their users is quite unsurprising, as is the engineers' disappointment when their products are used differently than they had intended. It is only by following these displacements (or conversely the work that goes into establishing the conditions under which two different things can be considered equivalent) that we can understand how heterogeneous sets of action are connected and how their interlinking gives rise to specific kinds of user roles and identities.

The second caveat that should be attached to the notion of translation is that, in the action net perspective, actions are seen as connected in relation to the *institutional order* prevalent at a specific place and time. Czarniawska takes the idea of "institutional orders" from the new institutionalism in organization studies (Powell & DiMaggio, 1991), where it is meant to signify the sets of rules and norms governing the legitimacy of action. Similarly, Czarniawska writes:

> ...In each time and place it is possible to speak of an 'institutional order,' a set (not a system) of institutions (not necessarily coherent) prevalent right then and there. Such institutions shape organizing inasmuch as they dictate which actions, conventionally, should be tied together.
>
> (Czarniawska, 2004b, p. 780)

Consequently, certain links between actions have become institutionalized to such a degree that it is hard to challenge their connection. For instance, in contemporary capitalist societies, producing tends to be linked to selling, and consuming and it would seem strange to us if this order was changed or if the large-scale production of goods was linked to other actions such as gifting, sacrificing, or destroying.[8] This does not mean that institutions are ontologically distinct from other action nets. At no point are they turned into a structure that somehow exists outside of concrete actions.[9] The difference is merely that institutions are *repeated* patterns of actions that become *taken for granted* over time and that, when questioned, will be *justified* in normative terms (Czarniawska, 2014, p. 22). Institutionalization can thus be thought of as a case of what Michel Callon has termed "irreversibilization," that is, a state in which it has become difficult for the actors involved to conceive of legitimate alternatives to a given translation. In this case, an existing pattern of action becomes a norm and is likely to shape future translations within the same network.

> In a word, irreversibilisation, taken as the predetermination of translation and as the impossibility of a return to competing translations, is synonymous with normalisation [...]. A network which irreversibilises itself is a network that has become heavy with norms.
>
> (Callon, 1991, p. 151)

The concept of institutional order can thus be understood as a set of taken-for-granted, or at least widely accepted, ways of doing that are tied together by successful past translations and have taken on a normative character. Past translations, although in principle reversible, will continue to have a strong influence on the way in which subsequent actions can be related to one another in practice. On the one hand, this makes it possible to account for highly stabilized user roles, which may appear natural and hard to change from the perspective of the actors involved. On the other hand, it makes intelligible the complications involved in the knotting of action nets that span radically different institutional settings, as the same kinds of translations that so seamlessly work in one context, might not be recognized as legitimate in another.

Overall, treating user construction as a set of actions connected into action nets through the mechanism of translation offers a theoretical foundation for analyzing the ways in which the different processes described in the user studies literature interlink. Individual user identities and institutionalized user roles are treated as the result of sensemaking within various interlocking actions, spanning industrial technology development and use. Translation is the mechanism that creates equivalence between the actants passed on between these actions. Even though it is likely to involve some displacement or "betrayal," it is these translations that create compatibility between heterogeneous processes carried out in different times and places. Finally, as patterns of action are repeated, they may, over time, be sanctioned by corresponding rules and norms, and eventually become taken for granted.

In this case, they become part of the institutional order influencing which patterns of action are viewed as legitimate and, therefore, which user roles are likely to become reproduced over time.

2.2.3 Patterns of User Construction on an Industrial Scale

Up until now, I have discussed the connection of actions into *chains*, mostly as an effort to describe user construction throughout a single technology's biography (Hyysalo et al., 2019). Yet, when considered on an industrial scale, it is not sufficient to follow the construction of "the user" in the singular, as is often done by close-up ethnographic studies. Nor is it enough to focus on the formation of multiple user groups around a single dominant technology, as is common in high-level historical accounts. Instead, we must consider that industries produce a wide range of similar but different products and thereby construct what can be described as a patterned multitude of user roles or, in my terms, a *user landscape*. The same interlinked processes that so self-evidently constitute some people as "users of course" will almost as naturally exclude others from that category and will further differentiate between all those that fall in between these extremes. To capture this "distribution of the conventional" (Star, 1991), it is useful to elaborate on the idea that *industrial* user construction occurs in *nets* rather than simply in *chains* of action. This final analytical move builds on all that has been said so far and makes possible the study of *user construction on an industrial scale*. In doing so, it is intended to make visible the constructed differences between users and include the effects of power in the analysis.

The term *industry*, as defined in the Cambridge Dictionary, signifies "the companies and activities involved in the process of producing goods for sale."[10] Industries are typically categorized according to the kinds of products they produce, which means that the automotive industry comprises all companies that participate in designing, producing, or selling cars, the aerospace industry encompasses all companies that do the same for planes and space crafts, and the prosthetic industry is the set of companies that design, produce, and sell prostheses. However, in practice, it is difficult to clearly delineate industries in this way. Should the automotive industry include motorcycles? Is the production of helicopters part of the activities comprising the aerospace industry? And how to deal with the fact that most organizations involved in the production of prostheses *also* make orthoses, and consider themselves as part of "P&O," a shorthand for "prosthetics and orthotics"? For reasons such as these, scholars associated with the new institutionalism in organizational analysis have moved away from the term "industry" and toward the notion of "organizational field." In its original formulation by DiMaggio and Powell, the concept referred to the production of similar services and products common to many definitions of "industry," but also encompassed the idea that actors are involved in a mutually recognized "area of institutional life":

> By organizational field, we mean those organizations that, in the aggregate, constitute a recognized area of institutional life: key suppliers, resource and product consumers, regulatory agencies, and other organizations that produce similar services or products.
>
> (DiMaggio & Powell, 1983, p. 148)

What the concept of organizational field clarifies is that action in industries is not only sequentially linked into *chains* constituting a set of similar production processes. Instead, there is also heightened interaction and mutual awareness between the actors involved in those parallel processes (ibid.). Industries are therefore tightly knit action *nets*. Action chains become interlinked both in the form of direct interaction and in the sense of actors being aware of what others are doing and adapting their own actions accordingly. In the latter case, chains of action may be linked through the circulation of words, figures, myths, and other intermediaries of seemingly ephemeral character (Czarniawska & Sevón, 2005). These may nonetheless become consequential as they are transformed into white papers, contracts, machinery, and so forth (Joerges & Czarniawska, 1998). The analytically relevant point here is that, for action chains to be linked, "[t]he different actors need not know one another or meet, but they may serve one another as role models, competitors, dream figures" (Czarniawska, 2004b, p. 781).[11]

Viewing industries as relatively dense action nets with a mutually recognized institutional order has consequences for the present characterization of industrial-scale user construction. Most importantly, it signals a departure from the notion of "the user" in the singular, as advanced in the tradition of Woolgar's "configuring the user."[12] The problem is not merely that any given product can be used in a variety of ways, thus configuring different (groups of) users and non-users. The true challenge is that, when considered on an industrial scale, this effect is multiplied as there is a whole range of similar but different products which are often *designed for, delivered to*, and *used by* slightly different groups of people in slightly different ways (Callon et al., 2002). It is not enough to follow the way users are constructed in the biography of a single product, such as Woolgar's computer, or even to study the emergence of one "dominant design" among several competing options (Pinch & Bijker, 1987). At an industrial scale, we need to examine the construction of an entire landscape of user roles, unevenly dispersed across an entire class of products. To understand this change in emphasis, just consider that, even after the closure of the controversy described by Pinch and Bijker (1987), there were still a lot of different types of bicycles in use, despite the fact that all but one type did *not* represent the dominant design inscribed with the dominant user role.

This turn to the industrial scale, and to patterned multitudes of users, opens up my analysis to the effects of *power*. By this I do not simply mean the typically obvious power asymmetries marking the relationship of users and producers, but the subtle ones that construct slight differences *between users*. Inequalities may accrue because the existing institutional and infrastructural conditions favor the performance of some chains of action (and thus the construction of some user roles) rather than others. For instance, some social groups may not be represented in *research and development* because they escape the representational techniques taught to engineers as part of their professional education. Conversely, the prevalent management jargon may legitimize some potential users as "trendsetters," "influencers," or "lead users." Certain design ideas will be harder to *manufacture* with the available means of production because of material constraints or the inability to deviate from routinized production practices. At other times, products may face barriers to *distribution* because of existing regulations or non-existing infrastructure. Finally, some *use practices* will be taken for granted in a specific socio-cultural context, while others may be shunned or ruled illegal. As a result, while in any given industry a multitude of different users may exist, the construction of some user roles will be relatively likely, while that of others will become a practical impossibility.

The pattern of an industry's user landscape will also be shaped by the horizontal linkages between different chains of action that result from heightened interaction and mutual awareness between the actors involved (DiMaggio & Powell, 1983). Industrial companies do not only interact with their suppliers and customers in vertical strings of action. They also regularly monitor what their competitors are up to. They may try to create products with features that set them apart from the competition, thus trying to create niche markets. Similarly, they may copy successful products originally developed by others, or try to improve on their less successful designs. Another set of processes may lead to the interlinking of situated use practices. Users may imitate the consumption practices of others, or consciously distinguish themselves from them (Bourdieu, 1984). They may share the use of a product or convince others to stop using it. In effect, the construction of different user roles within the same industry or field cannot easily be evaluated independently. Capturing how patterns of interaction and mutual awareness shape the topology of user landscapes is one of the main contributions of action net analysis and explains why the performance of some user roles is favored, while the performance of others is foreclosed.

2.3 The Role of Production Technology in Action Nets

In this section, I theorize the role that production technology plays in processes of industrial user construction. The starting point of the discussion is the second proposition advanced at the beginning of this book, namely that the ongoing digitalization of manufacturing, as exemplified by the introduction of 3D printing, is connected to a far-reaching reorganization of contemporary industries. Several of these developments directly impinge on the processes of user construction. Digital fabrication technologies promise to open new opportunities for industrial *design* under headings such as mass customization or AI-driven product optimization. They are connected to new practices of *distribution*, as they enable the circulation of products as digital files and their polycentric fabrication by service providers or private makers. Finally, digital fabrication is linked to innovation processes that are more closely informed by situated *practices of use*, as product designs are updated more rapidly, and the means of production become more widely available.

Interestingly, STS research on user roles has had little to say about industrial production technology and the introduction of digital fabrication. This may be partly attributed to the origin of user studies, where attention to the agency of users was intended to counterbalance a focus on powerful figures such as scientists, engineers, entrepreneurs, and other actors commonly associated with industry (Cowan, 1987; Oudshoorn & Pinch, 2003). Another explanation may be that industrial production in general has fallen out of favor both as an empirical phenomenon in Western societies and as a topic for the social sciences (Seibt et al., 2019). Whatever the reason, STS researchers have mainly been concerned with *technology as a product*, while they have largely ignored *technology as a means of production*.

To capture the role of industrial machinery in the construction of users, I begin by revisiting the concepts of *technological frame* and *inscription device* as put forward in the social constructivist and material-semiotic literature on the topic. To extend these concepts to industrial production technology, I draw on insights from the field of organization studies, where manufacturing technology has been a central issue for decades. As the upshot of that discussion, I introduce the concept of *production devices* and explain how it relates to an action-net analysis of industrial user construction.

2.3.1 Social Constructivism: Interpretative Flexibility and Interpretative Frame

As the name implies, social constructivist approaches to technology deal first and foremost with *technology as a product of human action*. The central idea is that technological change does not follow a linear progression determined by a force outside of society but is better described as a socially patterned evolutionary process (SCOT) or garden of forking paths (SST). In this model, technology is *interpretatively flexible*. Designers (including user innovators) generate multiple variations of a technology as they find and pursue different solutions to pertinent problems. Users and other social groups in turn interpret new variations in accordance with their socially-, culturally-, and economically-patterned perspective, often articulating new challenges for technology design. A particular version of a technology will stabilize once it is viewed as solving the perceived problems and is adopted into routine use. From an action net perspective, social constructivist approaches thus treat technological artifacts as intermediaries that are passed back and forth between the activities of designing and using, and are gradually shaped in the translations that occur in each cycle. Technologies are, hence, the malleable objects or stable results of social action.

By contrast, the social constructivist model has less to say about the *technologies of production* that influence the co-construction of products and user roles. The direction of technological change is understood as the result of controversies between different social groups, without much analytical regard for the means of production at their disposal. The closest the social constructivist tradition comes to dealing with manufacturing technology is the notion of *technological frame* (Bijker, 1987; Bijker, 1992). Similar to Kuhn's idea of "paradigm," frames include all "concepts and techniques employed by a community in its problem solving" (Bijker, 1987, p. 164). In essence, they shape the interpretations a relevant social group is likely to construct of a given technology, including the definition of problems and the strategies for solving them. What sets technological frames apart from similar concepts, such as *technological paradigm* (van den Belt & Rip, 1987) or *technological regime* (Nelson & Winter, 1982), is that it is meant to be applicable to all relevant social groups, rather than just those actors traditionally involved in technology design. In Bijker's words, "a technological frame should be understood as a frame with respect to technology, rather than as the technologist's frame" (Bijker, 1987, p. 167), which makes it a promising concept for capturing the relationship between industrial technology supply and use.

Unfortunately, the definition of technological frames offered by Bijker is extremely broad and includes "current theories, tacit knowledge, engineering practice (such as design methods and criteria), specialized testing procedures, goals, and handling and using practice" (ibid.: 164), in addition to "devices, material networks, and systems used in a community" (Law & Bijker, 1992, p. 301). Recast through the lens of action net analysis, this definition suggests that, insofar as they become part of relevant frames, production technologies, and infrastructures constitute part of an industry's institutional order. As such, they would take on a normative character that orients the action patterns in which they become involved. They may orient the problem-solving strategies of engineers and designers,[13] require certain kinds of state regulation, or feature in the consumption decisions of reflexive consumers. Despite the plausibility of this idea, Bijker's original concept is too broad to provide guidance on how to analyze the specific qualities of production technologies as part of technological frames.

A relevant extension of Bijker's model is provided by Paul Rosen in his book *Framing Production* (2002). Rosen criticizes the sociology of technology's focus on processes of technology design and consumption, noting the lack of attention to production as an intermediary process. In particular, he criticizes the concept of technological frame for missing both the important role of manufacturing equipment and the relevant social groups that participate in production (Rosen, 2002, p. 20). Rosen then goes on to include these elements in his extended concept of *sociotechnical frame*, which he uses to analyze the evolving relationship of production and use in the British bicycle industry, covering the three successive periods of small-batch production, centralized Fordist mass production, and flexible globalized production. However, while this work is analytically inspiring and empirically relevant, the notion of *sociotechnical frame* does little to specify the framing qualities of manufacturing equipment, as it adds even more elements to the analysis.

2.3.2 Material-Semiotics: Script and Inscription Device

The material-semiotic tradition, like the social constructivist one, is primarily concerned with technologies as products mediating between designers and users. The basic idea is that technologies can be understood as *texts* (Woolgar, 1991) or as containing *scripts* (Akrich, 1992). In this line of thought, designers are the writers of the text or script, while users are its readers or the ones enacting it. In both versions, writers try to compose the technology in such a way that it will influence readers' interpretations. Hence, in contrast to social constructivist approaches, the emphasis is not so much on the technology's initial interpretative flexibility and subsequent evolution, but on the ways in which it enables and constrains the actions of its users. Material-semiotic accounts do, therefore, attribute to technological objects the potential of contributing to the ordering and re-ordering of the settings in which they become involved. Nonetheless, from an action net perspective, the role of technology in those accounts is chiefly that of an intermediary meant to translate between the actions of designing and using.

As things stand, the metaphors of *text* and *script* offer an interesting perspective on technologies as products. Yet, despite the recognition that design is enabled and constrained by institutionalized patterns of organizing (Mackay et al., 2000), the production technologies involved in these activities have hardly received any analytical attention in material-semiotic studies of *user* construction.[14] A close approximation can, however, be found in the field of science studies, where technology was not conceptualized as a text or script but as the *means of writing* or *inscribing.* Indeed, the literature on the construction *of scientific knowledge*, from which much of the material-semiotic tradition draws, has long paid minute attention to the material settings and devices involved in the production of "inscriptions" (Latour, 1983; Latour, 1990; Latour & Woolgar, 1986) or "scriptures" (Knorr-Cetina, 1981). Given the common analytical starting point of both strands of work and the often explicit depictions within science studies of laboratories as "unusual factories"[15] (Latour & Woolgar, 1986, p. 47) or "assembly lines" (Latour & Woolgar, 1986, p. 224, 236) in which knowledge is "manufactured" (Knorr-Cetina, 1981), some of the latter's ideas can be used to inform a material-semiotic perspective on production technology.

The notion of *inscription device*, as developed in Latour and Woolgar's seminal book *Laboratory Life* (1986), is the most promising concept in this regard, not least because its terminology was later taken up in user studies (Latour & Akrich, 1992). One of the central observations of the original study was that, in their attempt to establish facts, scientists are constantly making what Latour calls "inscriptions." The term "designates an operation more basic than writing" and is used "to summarize all traces, spots, points, histograms, recorded numbers, spectra, peaks, and so on" (Latour & Woolgar, 1986, p. 88) which were produced during the construction of scientific facts. The graphs, tables, and diagrams resulting from this constant writing activity could be considered the very *products* of science, as they were directly used in the publication of scholarly articles. Importantly, Latour argued that the successful manufacturing of inscriptions, and thus scientific facts, was not the result of the brilliant minds of individual scientists. Rather, it was made possible through routinized acts of organizing equipped with a whole range of *machines*, which he aptly named "inscription devices."

> [A]n inscription device is any item of apparatus or particular configuration of such items which can transform a material substance into a figure or diagram which is directly usable by one of the members of the office space.
>
> (Latour & Woolgar, 1986, p. 51)

In other words, inscription devices are key to the making of scientific facts, because they transform given raw materials into an inscription. Understood as a means of production, they are to science what manufacturing technology is to industry.

Starting from this recognition, several analogies to the realm of industry can be drawn to form a basis for an action net approach to manufacturing technology. Indeed, Latour himself famously suggested that there is "no distinction [...] between what is called a 'scientific' fact and what is called a 'technical' object or artefact" (1987, p. 131). As far as he is concerned...

> ...[T]he problem of the builder of 'fact' is the same as that of the builder of 'objects': how to convince others, how to control their behaviour, how to gather sufficient resources in one place, how to have the claim or the object spread out in time and space.
>
> (ibid.)

Although a more careful distinction will be necessary in the context of user construction (Section 2.3.5), several similarities between inscription devices and manufacturing technology bear mentioning.

First and most importantly, inscription devices produce inscriptions by transforming one kind of intermediary into the next. In the field of science, a whole array of laboratory equipment may be involved in a series of translations transforming "[b]leeding and screaming rats," into "a tiny set of figures" (Latour, 1990, p. 39). By analogy, in industrial manufacturing machines and workers are arrayed along a production line to gradually transform raw materials into consumer products—a process that similarly involves the materialization of specific scripts of users and their activities (Akrich, 1992).[16]

Second, inscriptions are useful to scientists only insofar as they help them to support claims about complex objects (e.g., bleeding and screaming rats) beyond the laboratory in which they were produced. It is only as these statements are *faithfully taken up by others*, that they are turned into accepted facts. Similarly, in industrial user construction, it is not enough to manufacture consumer products in a central factory. It is only as these objects are taken up in variously situated use practices, that we may speak of the industrial construction of users.

Finally, even though inscription devices are used in the production of scientific facts, they are themselves the reifications of prior fact construction that has typically occurred in other fields.[17] As Latour notes:

> The apparatus and craft skills present in one field thus embody the end results of debate or controversy in some other field and make these results available within the walls of the laboratory. [...] The inscription device provides inscriptions which can be used to write papers or to make points in the literature on the basis of a transformation of established arguments into items of apparatus. This transformation, in turn, allows the generation of new inscriptions, new arguments and potentially new items of apparatus.
>
> (Latour & Woolgar, 1986, p. 66).

Accordingly, inscription devices embody the results of years of scientific activity that has been transformed into a single piece of equipment. Similarly, economists concerned with industrial production like to stress that industrial machines are the "produced means of production." Understood in this way, both inscription devices and industrial production technology may be viewed as stabilizing established patterns of action by lending them a mechanized form.

2.3.3 Including Production Technology in User Studies

The action nets that link contemporary industries and their users involve technology as both *product* and *means of production*. In processes of user construction, industrial products are featured as the evolving objects of design, as the intermediaries[18] that move between development, production, and use, and most importantly, as the technologies that are used, changed, or abandoned. Product technologies both enable and constrain the actions of their users, but they do so as actants that are *acted on*. By contrast, industrial production technology includes the tools of design and the machines of industry. In one sense, industrial machines are themselves the products of prior action, although they are typically operated by other groups of users (e.g., technicians, workers). Yet, in another sense, production technology may itself take on an actorial character to the degree that it "takes the last generation of intermediaries and transforms (combines, mixes, concatenates, degrades, computes, anticipates) these to create the next generation" (Callon, 1991, pp. 140–141). *Production technologies* may then be understood as *active mediators* that translate between actions (e.g., design, distribution, use) by transforming one kind of intermediary into another.

This far, the user studies literature has largely neglected industrial manufacturing technology, concentrating instead on technology as product. Available concepts do not therefore adequately capture the former's role in user construction. The social constructivist tradition stresses the interpretive flexibility of products, adding to this the idea that manufacturing equipment constitutes a part of the sociotechnical frames that shape the interpretation process of relevant social groups. While this suggests that manufacturing technologies form part of the institutional order of contemporary industries, we learn little about which of their dimensions or qualities account for these framing effects. Moreover, it remains unclear under what conditions production technology can count as part of a stable frame and when it becomes the object of contestation and change. The material-semiotic tradition offers the notion of industrial products as texts or as containing scripts, while the complementary idea of technology as the means of writing or inscribing is only elaborated in the context of scientific laboratories. While interesting analogies with the realm of manufacturing may be drawn, talking about laboratories is not the same as talking about factories, and science is not equivalent to industry. Conceptually equating the two means losing sight of both the differences between and intertwined nature of science and industry. This becomes apparent in the case of user construction, where the generation of facts about potential users matters as much as the inscription of user roles into technical objects in spite of these processes occurring at different points in time, involving different kinds of equipment, and depending on translations between different types of intermediaries.

To sharpen the view of manufacturing technologies as active mediators in action nets of user construction, I devote the remainder of this chapter to introducing the concept of "production devices" as the counterpart to Latour's inscription devices. In fact, I will argue that production devices are to industry what inscription devices are to science.[19] To account for the specific relationship between manufacturing technology and institutionalized patterns of industrial organizing, I now turn to three classical accounts of production technology as elaborated within the field of organization studies.

2.3.4 Production Technology and Patterns of Industrial Organizing

The field of organization studies has long been concerned with conceptualizing the link between industrial organizing and the technologies of production. By focusing on technology use in (and by) industrial organizations, the debate often complemented developments in the STS discussion on end-users. Early studies treated production technology as an independent variable to which organizations must adapt to function efficiently (Blauner, 1964; Woodward, 1958; Woodward, 1965). Similarly, the introduction of new production technology was characterized as an external force punctuating phases of incremental change in the organization of established industries (Dosi, 1982; Nelson & Winter, 1982). Other authors contested that production technology was itself designed and applied according to the interests of powerful groups of human actors and could, in theory, be designed differently (Child, 1972; Trist et al., 1963). Indeed, the design and introduction of new machines was a focal point in the conflict between capital and labor (Braverman, 1974; Burawoy, 1979; Burawoy, 1985). Following that debate, more symmetrical approaches depicted technology, specifically digital technology, as enabling and constraining the patterns of organized action through which it is itself re-produced (D'Adderio, 2010; DeSanctis & Poole, 1994; Orlikowski, 1992; Orlikowski, 2000; Pentland & Feldman, 2008). Today technology is increasingly seen as part of the sociotechnical practice of organizing itself (Leonardi, 2013; Orlikowski & Scott, 2008).

For the purpose of this chapter, it is not necessary to reconstruct the debate in its entirety, but rather to focus on what it adds to the characterization of production devices in user construction. With this goal in mind, I examine three particularly influential approaches, with a focus on their depiction of production technologies *as active mediators* in industrial organizing, and their ideas about the relationship between production technology and the *institutionalization* of specific action patterns. Representing the three major streams of research mentioned above, the models examined here are the *technological imperative model*, pioneered by Joan Woodward (1965), the *deskilling thesis* advanced by Harry Braverman (1974), and Wanda Orlikowski's *practice lens* (2000).

2.3.4.1 The Technological Imperative Model

The relationship between production technology and the organization of industrial firms has been at the heart of organization studies from the beginning. A first important approach to this topic was the technological imperative model developed by Joan Woodward and her team (Woodward, 1958; Woodward, 1965). Of particular relevance are Woodward's idea of distinguishing production systems by the quality and quantity of intermediaries they set into motion, and her treatment of production technologies as taken-for-granted factors in organizational life.

The starting point of Woodward's work was the question of how to best run industrial firms. In this regard, her ideas were in line with the *Principles of Scientific Management* pioneered by Frederick Winslow Taylor (1919), an approach still dominant in management thinking during her time. However, Woodward took issue with Taylor's notion that there was *one best way* of managing *all* types of organizations. Based on a study of 100 English manufacturing firms, she argued that the best—meaning the most commercially successful—way of organizing a firm was not determined by an adherence to a set of universal principles. Instead, it was contingent on several variables, the most prominent of which was the firm's production system. In particular, her study showed that there was a correlation between types of production technology, patterns of organizing, and commercial success. Woodward went on to deduce that...

> ...[T]he fact that organizational characteristics, technology, and success were linked together [...] suggested that not only was the system of production an important variable in the determination of organizational structure, but also that one particular form of organization was most appropriate to each system of production.
>
> (Woodward, 1965, pp. 69–71)

Production technology was thus not seen to determine organizational structure in a strong sense, as the label "technological imperative model" may suggest. Technology was just one of many variables and *empirically* there was always a range of different ways of organizing, even among firms with similar production systems. Technology was seen as imperative in the *normative* sense that firms should try to fit their patterns of organizing to their production technology, because doing so correlated to a firm's success.

It should be noted that in Woodward's analysis, technology did not directly refer to the tools and machines used in manufacturing. Rather, it referred to a combination of the organization's *production task*—specified as "the type, quantity and quality of the goods to be produced, and their rates of production" (Reeves et al., 1970, p. 4)—and the *machines, tools, and technical procedures* used to fulfill it. In fact, Woodward argued that, in the long term, the goals set for production strongly influenced the machines used:

> It soon became obvious that firms with similar goals and associated manufacturing policies had similar manufacturing processes—*the range of tools, instruments, machines, and technical formulas was limited and controlled by manufacturing policy.*
>
> (Woodward, 1965, p. 38, my emphasis)

Thus, in her famous typology of 11 types of production systems (ibid.: 39), Woodward gave analytical primacy to the *production task* they were designed for rather than the hardware they were equipped with. She defined three types of unit & small batch production, producing goods to customers' orders, four types of large batch and mass production producing standardized integral products such as cars, and two types of process production, putting out standardized dimensional products such as liquids, and gases. The final two categories are combined systems which play a minor role in her further analysis. Essentially, production systems were defined in terms of the type and quantity of their output, as well as the rate at which this output was produced.[20] Concrete tools and machines were not seen as unimportant, but were considered to be relatively unproblematic means to fulfill the organization's production task.

Despite this decentering of technological artifacts, two aspects of Woodward's work are relevant for understanding the role of production technology in action nets of user construction, one concerning its quality as active mediator, the other its relationship to institutionalized patterns of organizing. Beginning with the former, Woodward offers a typology of production systems defined by the quantity and quality of products they set into circulation. Hence, if we consider production technologies as active mediators between technology supply and use, their translational capacities are differentiated in terms of their *outputs*. Some production technologies are geared toward the translation of raw materials into one-off products that meet a user's individual requirements, while others produce large quantities of integral or dimensional products for entire populations of users on a mass market. In short, Woodward's typology provides a way for thinking about the interrelation between an industry's user landscape and the products industrial organizations are able to manufacture with available technology.

The second relevant aspect of Woodward's work concerns the relationship between technology and institutionalized patterns of organizing. Thus, Woodward's study showed that different types of production systems tend to be associated with different patterns of organizing within the firm (Woodward, 1965, 125 ff.). For example, while in unit production the activities of developing, producing, and marketing were found to be so closely linked that it was difficult to discern between them, in systems of mass production they were more strictly separated. They were carried out by people with different professional backgrounds in different organizational units, often located in different places or even working for different companies. Accordingly, design, production, and marketing often followed different rationalities to the point of open conflict between the respective departments. In Woodward's analysis, such correlations demonstrate that firms may be organized around a system of production that is viewed as practically unchangeable due to the enormous cost and effort required to replace it. In my own terms, this view suggests that production technologies frequently take on such a strong normative character that the rest of the action net becomes molded around them. While in the long run, the system of production may be changed, from the perspective of the actors operating it, it has become a materialized part of the institutional order, to which the ongoing action must be adapted.

Despite its contributions to theorizing the relationship between production technology and organizing, the technological imperative model has been subjected to heavy critique from the beginning. Authors trying to replicate Woodward's findings criticized the definition of her variables, particularly the idea of an increasing technological complexity within the scale of production systems (Hickson et al., 1969; Starbuck, 1965). Moreover, other variables, such as firm size, were found to be more important than technology (Blau et al., 1976; Hickson et al., 1969; Pugh et al., 1963). Most importantly, critique centered on Woodward's modeling of production technology as a factor immutable by human action.[21] In the eyes of her critics, her model essentially ignored human choice in the design, appropriation, and use of technology. In sharp contrast, researchers studying the labor process found that work may be organized in different ways, even within the same production system. Similar to later findings in STS, they deduced that the configuration of organization and technology involves organizational choice (Trist et al., 1963). As a result, (production) technology was no longer seen as an external factor impinging upon organizations, but as one of many factors in the organization's environment that was subject to the influence of powerful social actors (Child, 1972). This line of critique was most forcefully developed by Marxist scholars.

2.3.4.2 The Deskilling Thesis

The 1970s saw another debate about the relationship between production technology and organization. Kindled by Harry Braverman's (1974) reading of Karl Marx's *Capital*, it focused on the interplay between manufacturing technology and the labor process.[22] Braverman's work provides a useful contrast to the model proposed by Woodward, as he depicts production technology as the product rather than the determinant of the prevalent institutional order. At the same time, his typology of production technologies is oriented toward the inputs with which such machines can be controlled rather than the products they set into motion.

In his analysis of the labor process, Braverman understood technology not as the cause of social relations, but as their manifestation. Since, according to Braverman, the central social relationship in capitalism, regardless of the means of production, is the control of capitalists over the productive labor of others, the development of industrial machinery in capitalist societies tends to fortify and increase that control. This approach explicitly rejects the technical classifications of production processes advanced by contingency theorists such as Woodward (1965) and Blauner (1964). For Braverman "the key element in the evolution of machinery is not its size, complexity, or speed of operation, but the manner in which its operations are controlled" (1974, p. 129). It was this focus that drew his attention to the process of automation and specifically to the development of numerical control (NC) technology.[23]

The central point of his analysis is that, under conditions of capitalism, the development of automated technology increasingly wrests control over the labor process from the workers themselves. With hand tools, workers control both the mental and physical aspects of the labor process, but with the development of machines and their integration into large-scale machinery, this control is gradually lost (Braverman, 1974, 127 ff.; Marx, 1976, 492 ff.). The more the movement of the tool is predetermined by a larger mechanism, the less control is exercised by the worker. The lathe, for instance, guides the movement of the tool, but can still be adjusted to different operations. By contrast, the large production lines typical of mass production perform a single pre-fixed series of operations, resulting in only one kind of product, and reducing worker control to a minimum. According to Braverman, the third level in the automation of production technology comes about, when control over the machine's operation is no longer fixed within the mechanism itself but exercised through information encoded on some external medium. What is significant about this change is that…

> ...The ability to guide the machine from an external source of control in many cases restores the universality of the machine. It can now regain its adaptability to many purposes without loss of control, since that control is no longer dependent upon its specialized internal construction. A lathe can be controlled even more efficiently by a punched-paper or magnetic tape, and be immediately adaptable to work of every kind suitable to its size and power.
>
> (Braverman, 1974, p. 132)

Braverman sees in these features of multi-purpose production technology, and especially in NC technology, the mechanized manifestation of the Tayloristic management principle of separating planning from execution.[24] Braverman famously concluded that with the introduction of such technology workers would be progressively transformed into unskilled attendants of the machine, while the control over the labor process increasingly rested with management and engineers.

An important aspect of this argument is that, unlike Woodward, Braverman does not distinguish production technologies by their output, but by the way in which they are controlled. From the point of view of action net analysis, he explicitly disregards the intermediaries set into circulation by production devices[25] and instead focuses on the intermediaries that inform the movement of the machine itself. Recast through this lens, Braverman tells us that with *tools* operated by hand, the tool's movement depends on the input of skilled workers, who, from the point of view of management, may turn out to be rather recalcitrant mediators. With the development of *single-purpose machines*—typical of modern mass production—the tool's movement is increasingly fixed within the mechanism, and it is the human operator who must adapt his or her actions accordingly. Finally, with the introduction of *programmable multi-purpose machines*, production technology is controlled using intermediaries such as punched tape cards or digital files, which can be handled by relatively unskilled workers. Braverman's model thus highlights that production devices can be distinguished by the intermediaries that inform their operations and that, in this way, they are deeply entangled with issues of control and domination.

The second aspect of Braverman's work I would like to make salient is that he viewed production technology as the materialization of social relations which preceded its development. Rather than simply determining patterns of action, to him, the means of production reflected the same institutional order that had made their development possible in the first place. From this point of view, the ability to control machine movement through non-human intermediaries is a reification of management strategies that extend control over the labor process. Production technology therefore clearly affects organizational processes but "behind the technology that affects social relations lie the very same social relations" (Noble, 1979, p. 19). In this sense, Braverman saw machinery as a mechanization of managerial control previously implemented through disciplinary measures (1974, p. 134).[26] In my own terms, this makes production devices into a material expression of the prevalent institutional order in which they emerge. They are "society made durable" (Latour, 1991).

Braverman's account of automation triggered a massive debate in organization studies and beyond, in which many aspects of his work, including the two emphasized here, were heavily criticized. The deskilling thesis was criticized for overestimating the capability of management to fully grasp the situation and act accordingly. Similarly, Marxist scholars contended that it understated the skill required by maintaining and operating modern machines. Hence, Braverman's model did not adequately explain the relative control that workers retained over operations on the shop floor, nor did it describe their ability to resist managerial intent and enter into effective negotiations (Aronowitz, 1978; Burawoy, 1979; Noble, 1984). Despite these criticisms, the deskilling thesis has inspired much subsequent work on industrial automation. Most importantly, it was taken up in debates about the automation of white-collar work (Cooley, 1980) and is still relevant in contemporary discussions around the replacement of workers by artificial intelligence and other automated technologies (Brynjolfsson & McAfee, 2014; Frey & Osborne, 2013).

Braverman's notion that the design of technology reproduces the logic underlying the organization of labor has equally elicited a split reaction. On the one hand, it inspired much empirical work on the effects of automation technology. Burawoy (1985) took on the important task of comparing factory regimes under capitalism and socialism. Andersen (1988) compared the different trajectories of NC technologies in Norway and the US. More recently, Söderberg (2013) pointed to the different social relations underlying the introduction of CNC machinery in capitalist firms of the 1970s and the use of desktop 3D printers in contemporary hobbyist communities. On the other hand, Braverman's work was criticized as a form of social determinism as opposed to material determinism (Leonardi & Barley, 2008, p. 160). For instance, the history of numerical control written by Noble (1984, 1985) showed that there was social choice involved in machine design and that there were viable alternatives to numerical control, including those retaining greater worker control over the labor process. In combination with the increasing emphasis on the study of software artifacts, the upshot of these discussions was that, even though technology does affect the social organization of work, it is itself constantly designed, redesigned, and reinterpreted through human action.

2.3.4.3 Technology-in-Practice

In the late 1980s and early 1990s, scholars studying industrial organizing turned to various strands of practice theory to move beyond views of technology as either an objective force impinging on human action or a passive object of human construction. With a view to the translational capacities of production technology, this work explains how different action patterns may emerge around the same technology (Barley, 1986; Orlikowski, 2000). Regarding the relationship between production devices and prevalent institutions, it depicts technology as a continuously malleable part of ongoing social practices, particularly where it includes reprogrammable software components (Orlikowski, 1992; Pentland & Feldman, 2007). It is this focus on technology-in-action that makes this body of work especially relevant for the conception of user construction in action nets featured in the present work.

The development of a practice lens moved from an understanding of technology as a medium and result of human organizing, based on sociological practice theory, to a view of organizing as a fundamentally sociomaterial practice, influenced by STS analytics. This shift can be retraced in the highly influential work of Wanda Orlikowski (Feldman & Orlikowski, 2011; Orlikowski, 1992; Orlikowski, 2000; Orlikowski, 2007; Orlikowski & Scott, 2008). Her first major study focused on the development, introduction, and use of a range of computer-aided software design tools in a multi-national software consulting firm. The new tools were meant to transform the development of custom software applications for end-users from a labor-intensive idiosyncratic process into a more thoroughly standardized one, thereby promising management tighter control over the quality of the products. In her study, Orlikowski observed that the software tools in question featured as both the outcome and the means of human action. They were the outcome of action in the sense that they were developed, manufactured, appropriated, and modified by people working for the firm she studied. Yet, they also took on the role of a means of action in the sense that they facilitated and constrained the development of end-user products. Given this finding, Orlikowski rejected both Woodward's technological imperative model and various social choice models (including that of Braverman) as "partially correct, but also one-sided" (1992, p. 423).[27] Instead, she opted for a conception of technological objects based on the theory of structuration proposed by Anthony Giddens (1984). This allowed her to treat the software tools as both *product* and *medium* of human action. As technical artifacts, production technologies embodied possible "structures" of technology use that could be "appropriated" by their human operators. Technology and social action were thus implicated in an ongoing process of structuration that re-produced and sometimes changed the overall organizational order.

Orlikowski later proposed an extension of her model, which reacted to the critique of her earlier conceptualization (e.g., DeSanctis & Poole, 1994) and integrated new insights gained from a study of so-called "groupware."[28] Making use of "a practice lens for studying technology in organizations" (Orlikowski, 2000), she no longer theorized technology beginning with the artifact, but from the activities in which it became implicated. In contrast to her earlier work, she described the structures of technology use, or what she now called "technologies-in-practice," as *emerging* in action rather than as *inscribed* into technological objects. It followed that technology was no longer thought to be consequential in and of itself, but only insofar as it was taken up *in practice*. The focus of analysis then shifted from a preoccupation with the more or less faithful enactments of pre-existing scripts, to the question of which improvised and routine patterns of action could be "crafted" with the material properties of the artifact at hand. This new perspective highlighted that technology, and particularly software, could be used to generate and support multiple patterns of action with different relationships to prevalent institutions. It could be used to reproduce well-established ways of working, to enact the new organizing patterns intended by management, or to creatively generate new practices. In either case, Orlikowski's "practice lens" focused on the action patterns of *using* technology, rather than on the technological artifact as such.

For the current conception of production devices, I draw on two aspects of Orlikowski's work. First, I stress that the translational capacities of a given production technology may support the generation of multiple different action nets. A production device will have certain discernible characteristics including those that allow it to transform one generation of intermediaries (input) into another (output). Yet, depending on which of its material and symbolic properties are drawn on in practice, it may knit together different actions by translating between various qualities and quantities of intermediaries. A 3D printer, for instance, may be part of digital craft production, industrial mass production, or mass customization, which are likely to correspond to the construction of very different user roles. While this is true of any technology, the re-programmability and modularity of digital technologies, and particularly software, tend to allow for a particularly large range of possible usages (Yoo et al., 2010).

The second relevant aspect of Orlikowski's practice lens is her insistence that, as the possible roles of "technologies-in-practice" are multiple, their relationship to the prevalent institutional order is not given in advance. The introduction of a new production technology may lead to the further entrenchment of existing institutions (similar to Braverman's account), it may intentionally or unintentionally change ingrained patterns of organizing (as in Woodward's examples), or it may not be taken up in ongoing organizational processes at all (e.g., Pentland & Feldman, 2008). As some ways of engaging with technology are repeated, perhaps because they are considered successful, or because there is no viable alternative, they may be fortified by formal rules or informal norms, and eventually become a taken-for-granted part of the institutional order. However, the study presented in this book shows that even strongly institutionalized ways of manufacturing may eventually be challenged, and the production devices involved in them may be materially and symbolically altered to facilitate novel ways of organizing.

2.3.5 An Action Net Perspective on Production Technology: Inscription and Production Devices

In industrial user construction, technology is important both as product and as means of production. However, the STS literature on the topic focuses almost exclusively on products, sidelining the technological means by which they are designed and manufactured. To advance our understanding of user construction, it is therefore helpful to draw on research conducted under the broad umbrella of organization studies, where the relationship between production technology and organizing has been theorized over the course of the last half century. In this spirit, the three theoretical models presented above can be used to inform my own conception of *production devices* (and their relationship to inscription devices) in the industrial construction of users. To do so, they need to be systematically recast along two important dimensions of action net analysis: the role of production technology as an active mediator in a series of translations and the relationship of the resulting action patterns to the prevalent institutional order.

From an action net perspective, the first decisive characteristic of production technology is that it acts as a *mediator* between heterogeneous actions. Rather than being passed around and transformed through the actions of others, it is a configuration of equipment that itself transforms one generation of intermediaries into another, where the first is a range of inputs (e.g., raw material, a medium carrying information) and the second is a product intended for use. By translating between technology supply and use in this way, production technology will influence the structure of the action nets in which it becomes involved. It is because of this quality that the introduction of a novel production technology has the potential to transform established patterns of action and the user roles constructed in them. The three perspectives outlined above shine a light on a different aspect of this translation. Woodward's Technological Imperative Model concentrates on the *output* of the production process, classifying production systems by the kinds and quantities of intermediaries they set into motion (e.g., single units or large batches, integral or dimensional products). Here we learn that industrial action nets tend to take on different forms depending on their main production task. By stark contrast, Braverman's deskilling thesis emphasizes the importance of the kinds of *input* with which production technology is controlled. Here we are taught that the patterns of industrial organizing depend on whether manufacturing technologies are operated by the manual input of skilled workers, or by readymade intermediaries, such as a punched tape cards, which are supplied from beyond the shop floor. Finally, Orlikowski's practice lens highlights that the translational mechanisms of production technologies are not fixed, especially where they are modular or reprogrammable. They may participate in transforming multiple kinds of input into multiple kinds of output and may therefore be involved in knotting together many different kinds of action nets. Hence, in processes of user construction, the concrete role of technology is not fixed within the machine itself regardless of its material properties and the character conventionally ascribed to it. Its material properties may support a large, though always patterned, multitude of possible user roles.

The second relevant aspect of production technology in action nets is that it plays a key role in the *stabilization and institutionalization* of specific action patterns and the user roles they support. Again, the literature reviewed above provides a number of interesting insights. Woodward's model stresses that in industrial contexts, production systems will appear to most actors involved as an unchangeable reality. At least in the short run, there may be virtually no legitimate alternatives to the way products are manufactured, which is why production technologies tend to take on a normative, or even imperative character. In this case, we can say that they form part of the institutional order pertinent to a specific organization or industry. Braverman adds to this that, while production technologies do shape social relations, in the long run, they are themselves the product of those very same social relations. Hence, production technology will often reflect existing patterns of action, particularly where they are backed up by social norms and power relations. Finally, Orlikowski emphasizes that, while specific ways of using production technology may become institutionalized the relationship of new technology and the existing institutional order is neither predetermined, nor fixed once and for all. Insofar as the character of technology emerges in action, there are always multiple alternatives for how it may relate to established institutions.

Combining these insights from the field of organization studies with the concepts developed in the STS literature, specifically Latour's notion of inscription devices, it is now possible to define the role of production

Table 2.1 Contributions of selected work in the field of organization studies to the concept of production device

	Production Technology as Mediator in Action Nets	*Relationship between Production Technology and Institutional Order*
Technological Imperative Model (Woodward, 1958, 1965, 1970)	Production technologies can be distinguished by the quantity and quality of intermediaries they set into circulation (e.g., unit-, batch-, mass- or process production, or combinations of these).	In the short run, production technologies may take on a normative character. If they cannot easily be changed by their operators, they appear as part of the institutional order.
Deskilling Thesis (Braverman, 1974)	Production technologies can be distinguished by the intermediaries used to control their operation (e.g., manual tools, single-purpose machines, re-programmable multi-purpose machines)	Production technologies are shaped by the same social relations that they tend to write forth. They are not immutable in principle but reflect the institutional order in which they were constructed.
Practice Lens (Orlikowski, 1992, 2000, 2007)	Production technologies can be used to generate and support various patterns of action, although their material properties constitute boundary conditions.	Production technologies may be used to support or undermine existing institutions. They are themselves materially and symbolically adapted in action.

technology in action nets of user construction. It also becomes possible to see how the means of industrial production interact with the machines used in the construction of scientific facts to contribute to the construction of user roles. To this end, I will use the term *production devices* to denote the tools and machines that participate in the translation of the objects of design into the products intended for use. Production devices may include everything from the tools used in a workshop to the sophisticated machines and assembly lines typical of modern industry. The decisive criterion is that they transform the intermediaries constructed in design (e.g., user representations, models, blueprints) into the objects meant for use. In principle, the same production device may be involved in various action patterns. Yet, successful devices tend to take on a normative character to the degree that the translations they help to perform come to be viewed as the only legitimate course of action. In that case, they form part of the overall institutional order of a given industry. Nevertheless, the symbolic and material properties of a production device are shaped by its position in an overall pattern of action, while its status as active mediator is the result of a collective attribution. Therefore, in times of controversy or crisis devices may, once more, take on the character of malleable objects that are updated, tinkered with, or exchanged for other pieces of equipment.

Despite the close analogy between production and inscription devices, their roles in action nets of user construction are different. *First,* inscription devices, in the Latourian sense, transform complex and unwieldy intermediaries into "[t]hin readable traces" (Latour & Woolgar, 1986, p. 246). They are the pens, surveys, or scanners implicated in converting potential users of any form[29] into the drawings, numbers, and models directly usable in design activities. By contrast, production devices take the result of the design process, such as a blueprint encoded in a punched tape card, or digital file, and transform it into a "thick material object," such as a car, or a prosthetic hand. *Second,* in the construction of scientific facts, the mobility of the inscription is increased with each transformation with the effect that the object it represents can be easily moved from its place of origin to a "center of calculation" (Latour, 1999, p. 304), such as an R&D department or a laboratory (Latour, 1990). Conversely, in industrial production, the emphasis is on the multiplication of products and their distribution to a large number of heterogeneous sites of use, despite the fact that they tend to be less mobile than the intermediaries that informed their production. *Finally,* in the construction of facts about users, inscriptions are taken up by designers insofar as they convincingly represent "the users out there." By sharp contrast, the products manufactured by industry are taken up by potential users insofar as they are convinced that the artifact will be a useful addition to their practical lives. In this context, the goal of scientists is to "extract" information from likely future users, while the goal of engineers is to "inform" the activities of those same users.

Because they perform different kinds of translations, inscription devices, and production devices work in tandem in processes of user construction. Most importantly, the output of inscription devices needs to be directly usable as an input for production devices. Afterall, NC machines need punched tape cards to operate (compare Braverman, 1974, 132 ff.; Noble, 1985, p. 110), injection molding needs molds, and 3D printers need 3D models encoded in a machine-readable format. Therefore, to guarantee their compatibility, a chain of translation needs to be established between the two kinds of devices. Measurements may be transformed into drawings, drawings into CAD models, and CAD models into the input processable by a CNC mill or 3D printer. Analyzing how these chains of translation are organized will provide insight into some of the most interesting phenomena in industrial user construction. Regarding *technology development,* such analyses may demonstrate how, despite a firm's commitment to user-centered design, any reference to potential users is lost, as the logic of the process moves from representing the needs of concrete people to generating inscriptions compatible with the available means of production (Chapter 4). In terms of the *mediation* between technology supply and use, studying the interplay between inscription and production devices may help to show that, far from simply increasing the accessibility of products, the decentralization of production may easily reproduce global patterns of domination where it is paired with centralized modes of inscription (Chapter 5). Last but not least, with reference to the processes of *technology use*, this model may explain why the focus on "making," prevalent in many contemporary grass-roots movements, runs the risk of delivering sub-standard products as long as these movements fail to pay equal attention to the careful inscription of prevalent use practices and subsequent user feedback (Chapter 6). As these examples demonstrate, the role of production devices in user construction should not be narrowly understood as the unproblematic fulfillment of design. Instead, the necessity of production reverberates through the larger action net like ripples on a pond. To grasp the effects of ongoing processes of digitalization on the future of use, we need to understand how science and industry work together to knot action nets that permeate our lives in highly technologized societies. The theory of industrial user construction presented here is intended as a modest step in that direction.

Notes

1 Donna Haraway uses yet another textual metaphor in her approach to material-semiotics, drawing on Katie King's treatment of the *poem* (Haraway, 1988, p. 595). Haraway's approach to material-semiotics, while notoriously difficult to pin down, did have some bearing on user studies, particularly through her notion of *figure* and *figuration* (Haraway, 1997, p. 11), and particularly the cyborg figure (for a general discussion see Suchman, 2012; for examples directly relevant to user studies see Hyysalo, 2009; Oudshoorn, 2016; Oudshoorn, 2020; Drewlani & Seibt, 2018).

2 The relationship between script and de-scription is similar to Suchman's ethnomethodological notions of "plan" and "situated action" (1987). For Suchman, a plan, no matter how elaborate, can never fully specify the actions to be taken in an actual situation. This is why plans get used as resources in situated action rather than fully determining it. The plan shapes the action and is elaborated in it. In this sense, "the inscription perspective entails something like an 'ethnomethodology of machines'" (Joerges & Czarniawska, 1998, p. 375).

3 This stronger focus on re-design as well as re-interpretation meant that social constructivist scholars also moved closer to positions taken in the user innovation literature (Hippel, 1988; Hippel, 2005; Shah & Tripsas, 2007).

4 In Czarniawska's conception, action (as opposed to behavior) is always related to the prevalent social order. She writes: "I understand action as a movement or an event, to which an intention can be attributed by relating the event to the social order in which it takes place (Harré, 1982)" (Czarniawska, 2004b, p. 782). For that reason, Czarniawska also tends to equate "collective" and "social" action. As actions always relate to the social order, either by confirming it or by consciously departing from it, they are "social or collective, even when they are performed by individuals" (Lindberg & Czarniawska, 2006, p. 293).

5 Czarniawska borrows the term from Greimas and Courtés and, quoting from their analytical dictionary of semiotics, defines it as "that which accomplishes or undergoes an act" (Greimas & Courtés, 1982, p. 5 quoted in Czarniawska, 2004b: 788; see Czarniawska, 2004a, p. 79 for a more in-depth treatment). Interestingly, the original entry, provides not only a far more elaborate characterization of the term actant (and its relationship to others such as role, identity, actor, or action) but also the interesting remark that it is borrowed from French linguist Lucien Tesnière. It is befitting of the way that Czarniawska uses the term that it should be passed around so much.

6 This means that some narrative attributions of actorhood become institutionalized and thus taken for granted. For example, Meyer and Jepperson (2000) trace the process through which individuals, organizations, and nation states became the quintessential actors of current day Western societies.

7 The difference to sociological role theory (see Turner, 2001 for a review) is that roles can be attributed to non-humans, including animals, machines, trees, etc. (for an elaboration and critique of that move see Schulz-Schaeffer, 2016). Perhaps the most relevant example of non-humans taking on the generalized role of "user" are organizations (Czarniawska, 1997).

8 Of course, anthropological studies have shown that, in other times and places, this can be quite different—see for instance Mauss (1990), or Appadurai (1986).

9 They do, however, become inscribed into the material world, most often by organizations (Joerges & Czarniawska, 1998). This echoes Latour's famous point that "technology is society made durable" (Latour, 1991).

10 Cambridge Dictionary, https://dictionary.cambridge.org/dictionary/english/industry, accessed 2020-06-17.

11 Czarniawska tends to associate direct interaction with the "old institutionalism" exemplified by Selznick's "interorganizational fields" (1949), whereas she attributes what she calls "virtual connections" to the new institutionalism (Powell & DiMaggio, 1991). While I agree that the new institutionalism stresses mutual awareness, loose coupling, and the role of myths, I do not find that its proponents have stopped looking at direct interactions altogether.

12 It should be noted that Woolgar himself treated the use of the singular as an empirical finding. He was intrigued by engineers referring to users in this way since "[c]learly, one criterion for a successful text is precisely its appeal to a wide range of users." (Woolgar, 1991, p. 71). He made sense of the singular "the user" by interpreting it "as a generalized formulation produced for purposes of establishing contrasts between insiders and outsiders. The generalized user provides a more successfully stark contrast with us/the company/members of the company than would a heterogeneous rag-bag of customers with varying attributes" (ibid.: 73).

13 The practical relevance of manufacturing in design (e.g., through manufacturability, price) is emphasized in Hyysalo's concept of practice-bound imaginaries, which he deploys in his analysis of the biography of Vivago-Wirstcare (Hyysalo, 2010, 82 ff.).

14 This is quite remarkable considering the close ethnographic attention these studies have given to technology design. One might speculate that since in contemporary industries design tends to be separated from production in time and space, production might have been beyond the scope of these studies.

15 Latour was always playing with the parallels between his discussion of science and Marx's discussion of industry. Beyond his discussion of the laboratory as a factory and his remarks concerning the proximity between fact and fetish (Latour & Woolgar, 1986, p. 259), his description of machines as automatons also bears a striking resemblance to Marx's discussion of the same topic (Latour, 1987, pp. 128–131; Marx, 1976, pp. 492–508).

16 Inscription devices are therefore not necessarily the analogue of single pieces of production technology, but of their combination into machines and even machinery in the Marxist sense (see Section 2.3.5). They may comprise "a particular combination of machines, pieces of apparatus, and technicians" (Latour & Woolgar, 1986, p. 58), which produces a useful inscription.

17 With regard to industries, the observation that the means of production are often the result of other fields suggests the that designers often use technology that was not originally designed for them. Their work may thus be configured by the norms and procedures of an entirely different industry or discipline.

18 This distinction keeps the terminology of ANT in which intermediaries are the actants passed around between actions. Note that in other relevant STS discourses the term intermediary denotes what I call an active mediator (Stewart & Hyysalo, 2008, p. 298).

19 Kathryn Henderson's (1991) notion of "conscription device" can be read as a step in this direction. It transfers Latour's idea of inscription devices from science to engineering in order to analyze how drawings configure the design process. However, the concept refers to visual representations of the product like drawings or sketches and is not extended to manufacturing machines.

20 Note that Woodward originally thought of her types of production systems "as being positioned on a continuum from low to high technical complexity," the latter allowing for increased control over the production process (Woodward, 1965, p. 40). Framing the list in terms of "the goals of production," is closer to Woodward's later work (Reeves et al., 1970).

21 In her later work, Woodward explained that her model was meant to address the short-term aspect of organizing only, but by that time the label of technological determinism had already stuck. Woodward herself noted:

> [W]e would expect to find a two-way relationship between social and technical aspects [...]. In the long term, the technology of an organization is for the most part a result of a series of managerial decisions to serve specific markets, to acquire or build plant, to accept certain types of raw materials, and to address the organization to certain production tasks. But in the short term, as our definition of technology suggests, most of these considerations can be taken as given, and we may expect to see certain salient features of the technology of the organization limiting the administrative structures.
>
> (Reeves, Turner, & Woodward, 1970, p. 5)

22 Most organization theorists before Braverman had read Marx as a proponent of technological determinism (see MacKenzie, 1984 for a review; Blauner, 1964 for an influential example). For them, the evolution of production technology went on in the direction of ever greater complexity and/or efficiency, while generating social relations compatible with its current state of development.

23 The numerical control (NC) and computerized numerical control (CNC) of machine tools are of particular interest, because they represent the technical foundation for the development of additive manufacturing, or 3D printing. The control mechanism behind a CNC mill and a desktop 3D printer are more or less the same in that a tool is moved through a three-dimensional space according to external specifications in the form of machine-readable code.

24 Subsequent studies of CNC machines did not always confirm this separation (Orlikowski & Barley, 2001, p. 150).

25 Braverman makes it very clear that for him the problem with capitalism does not stem from the unequal distribution of the products of social labor, but in the organization of the production process itself.

26 This symmetry between control by organizational and mechanical means is a key feature of Latour's own analysis of automation as a mechanization of forces (Latour, 1987, pp. 128–132).

27 In line with a biographical perspective, Orlikowski emphasizes that characterizations of technology depend on when and where it is studied. The dominance of one-sided accounts may thus be explained by the temporal and spatial divide between technology development and use typical of industrial societies (Orlikowski, 1992, p. 421).

28 Orlikowski describes groupware as a specific type of software "designed to facilitate the working together of individuals by providing support for distributed electronic interaction over time" (Orlikowski, 2000, p. 413). It is thus not per se a case of production technology. Yet, given the generality of her argument, it can be applied to all kinds of technologies involved in contemporary organizing.

29 In most sociological accounts users will turn out to be human individuals, groups, and organizations, but other potential users are possible. In my own research, I was confronted with 3D-printed prostheses for birds, dogs, and other animals. Similarly, in the beginning of the study it was unclear whether mechanical hands for robots should be considered.

3 Methods for Studying Industrial User Construction

In this chapter, I present a set of *methods* for studying user construction at the industrial scale. These methods are intended to translate between my action-net-based theoretical framework and the empirical reality of my field. This is in line with the finding that many pressing theoretical limitations in contemporary user studies are rooted in methodology (Hyysalo et al., 2019). Close-up ethnographic studies examine the construction of user roles during technology design or use but miss both the historical embeddedness of situated action and its connection to activities in other geographical settings. Historical case studies do better at capturing a larger scale, but only at the cost of brushing over the manifold practicalities that shape the construction and negotiation of user roles. From a point of view of theory, an action net perspective offers a solution to this dilemma as it moves the focus to the relationships (translations) of heterogeneous actions across settings, while situating the emerging patterns within the institutional order prevalent at a given time and place. Yet, the question remains of how to implement these theoretical ambitions in an actual study.

In the following pages, I address three aspects of my methodology in some detail. First, I briefly sketch out my general strategy for generating the data necessary to capture a connection between industrial transformation and changes in user construction. Here I concentrate on the issues of study design implied by the geographical scope of industry and the historical dimension of changing user roles. Second, I discuss the "fieldwork devices" (Law & Ruppert, 2013) I used to collect that data. Focusing on the three examples of interviews, ethnography, and makeathons, I pay particular attention to the ways in which my research activities became entangled with the action constituting my field of study. Third, I detail the ways in which I went about analyzing the data collected in accordance with the theoretical foundation laid out in the previous chapter. Here I explain how to re-construct an action net from interview transcripts and fieldnotes and how to render those findings intelligible.

DOI: 10.4324/9781003269731-3

3.1 Study Design

How does the introduction of a new kind of production device lead to changes in the ways in which user roles are constructed in an industry? From the point of view of a researcher trained in qualitative methods, collecting the data necessary to answer this question poses at least two methodological challenges. On the one hand, it raises the issue of how to capture the diverse actions contributing to user construction at an industrial scale, given the geographical scope and distribution of contemporary industries. On the other, it points to the problem of establishing a transformation in institutionalized user roles, given the historical dimension of such a change. Taking inspiration from anthropologists and other ethnographers, who have been faced with similar challenges, these issues can be interpreted as a problem of following action through space and time (Appadurai, 1986a; Czarniawska, 1998; Hine, 2007; Hyysalo, 2010; Latour, 1987; Marcus, 1995; Pollock & Williams, 2009; Star, 1999).

3.1.1 Following Action Through Space

As Barbara Czarniawska observed, "contemporary organizing moves quickly from one place to another and happens in several places at once" (Czarniawska, 2004b, p. 779). The actions that contribute to industrial user construction are no exception. Indeed, contemporary industries are both archetypical examples and key drivers of the dispersion of action nets, as evidenced by the networked coordination of research and development (Powell & Grodal, 2005), the uneven globalization of manufacturing (Castells, 2010, pp. 417–433) and the ever-growing scale of logistic distribution networks (Pfeiffer, 2022). Accordingly, to understand user construction at an industrial scale, a study of a single site, such as the headquarters of an industrial manufacturer or a local group of users, will not suffice. Research needs to focus on multiple loci of action and on the interlinking of actions across them (Hyysalo et al., 2019). However, given that it is both impossible and pointless to study how everything is connected to everything else, the question becomes how to choose a manageable number of strategic sites from which to begin the investigation (Marcus, 1986; Pollock & Williams, 2009, pp. 110–114).

In the previous chapter, I argued that it is necessary to investigate the interlinking of processes of user construction across technology *design, distribution,* and *use*. Methodically, the connections within and between these sets of action may be explored by following the "social life" (Appadurai, 1986b) or "biography" (Hyysalo et al., 2019; Kopytoff, 1986; Pollock & Williams, 2009, pp. 80–118) of industrial products. The fundamental idea is, thus, to follow the action by following that which is acted on.[1] Yet, in actual research practice what exactly the product of a given industry *is*, is not as obvious as it may appear. Both the *multitude* and the *heterogeneous character* of industrially made goods complicate the elaboration of a manageable research design. As both issues feature prominently in my own case, I will briefly address each in turn.

The first complication in following a particular "product" is that contemporary prostheses, like many industrially manufactured goods, are not monolithic entities but rather heterogeneous assemblages (Hyysalo, 2010, pp. 249–250; Latour, 1987). While a prosthetic leg or arm may, ideally, behave as one thing *in use*, during *design*, *production*, and *distribution* it is not a single object at all. In fact, any one prosthesis can consist of hundreds of different parts, that may be grouped into about half a dozen major components, all of which may be developed, produced, and sold by different organizations.[2] Depending on the height of the amputation, a contemporary leg prosthesis (Figure 3.1) will include a foot-ankle, a pylon, a knee unit, and a socket, which are held together by various joints, screws, and adapters and may or may not be clad into an anthropomorphic cover made of foam or silicone. Some types of prosthesis are worn with a special sock and liner, and the entire package may come with batteries, charging units, and smartphone apps. Hence, the closer one studies any actual prosthesis, the more one discovers a complex technical system consisting of a heterogeneous assemblage of objects, each with its own "biography," and each likely to be inscribed with a slightly different representation of its potential users.

As the task of studying the journey of all of these components seemed both impractical and uninteresting, I decided to simplify it by drawing a heuristic distinction between *sockets* and *fit components*. Not only did this represent the common view of people in the field that a prosthesis consists of "a socket and everything that attaches to the socket" (Fieldnote, 2016-05-06), it also worked to capture one of the most fundamental features of the industry's institutional order: The distinction between the worlds of *craft-based custom production* and *industrial badge- or mass production*. By studying the journey of prosthetic sockets, I entered local clinics, workshops, and rehabilitation facilities. I learned about the relationship between amputees, prosthetists, technicians, and doctors, about "magic hands" and the transformation of plaster, about pain, sweat, and the always specific histories of particular human bodies. In contrast, by studying the social life of fit components, such as prosthetic feet or knee joints, I was pointed to R&D departments, factories, testing labs, and distribution centers. I talked to engineers, scientists, and sales personnel and learned about industry norms, certification, anthropometry, and the specificity of populations and markets. In short, by strategically reducing the internal heterogeneity of prostheses to just two kinds of objects, namely sockets and fit components, I moved closer to a manageable research design, while retaining much of the complexity of the spatially distributed action net I was exploring.[3]

A second layer of complexity needs mentioning in a study of user construction at an industrial scale. It refers to the *multitude* of industrial products and stems from the fact that industries produce not one product but a wide range of different ones, for a variety of intended users. Here the question is not so much which parts of a prosthesis should be studied to represent the product as a whole, but which products should be studied to represent the mechanisms of user construction prevalent in a larger product class (Pollock & Williams, 2009, pp. 107–109). For instance, most of my interlocutors thought of themselves as part of the "orthotics and prosthetics industry," the major product classes of which include prostheses, but also orthoses, braces, cranial helmets, insoles, orthopedic shoes, and other assistive devices such as wheelchairs. Even narrowing the focus to prosthetic technology, and here only to artificial limbs, the variety is still large. There are upper limb devices which perfectly resemble human hands, complete with matched complexion, and details such as hair, spots, and freckles. Yet, many of these are for aesthetic purposes only and have little mechanical functionality. Then there are devices that look slightly more robotic but often have a remarkable range of motion and dexterity. These come with features such as motors, batteries, sensors, and mobile apps. Yet, next to these high-tech devices, body-powered prostheses, many of them shaped like metal hooks, also have their place. Artificial legs, too, are more diverse than one might initially imagine. There are, of course, lower limb prostheses for walking (Figure 3.1 right), but also for running (Figure 3.1 left) and other kinds of specialized activities such as skiing, or bathing (Figure 3.1 middle). Again, some of these are packed with electronics, while others are essentially bent plates of carbon fiber, and yet others are simply foot-shaped pieces of wood and rubber.[4]

Given the large differences in the way these products represent their potential users, the choice of which of them to study was inevitably going to shape the account of the action nets I was likely to encounter and record. In the study presented here, I began from the distinction between the two product classes of *upper* and *lower limb* prostheses, reasoning that these are intended for radically different use practices and user bodies[5] and may thus bring out the way in which the construction of user roles functions under different conditions. Both of these classes were in turn represented by focusing on a small number of products that were particularly common in the places I visited or were presented to me as defining examples of their respective class. While people in the industry were adamant about the fact that there is no such thing as a standard prosthesis, these *exemplary artifacts* nonetheless helped to orient their actions by working as templates for how things are commonly done and by serving as reference points in illustrating arguments or justifying courses of action. In this spirit, artifacts such as thermoformed sockets, the mechatronic knee C-Leg, the wooden SACH foot, and the infamous Running Blade, the multiarticulate hand prosthesis i-Limb, or the body-powered split hook will be recurring examples throughout my account of user construction in prosthetics. Serving as representatives of their respective product classes, these exemplars helped me to reduce the complexity of my field, while keeping in focus some of the key

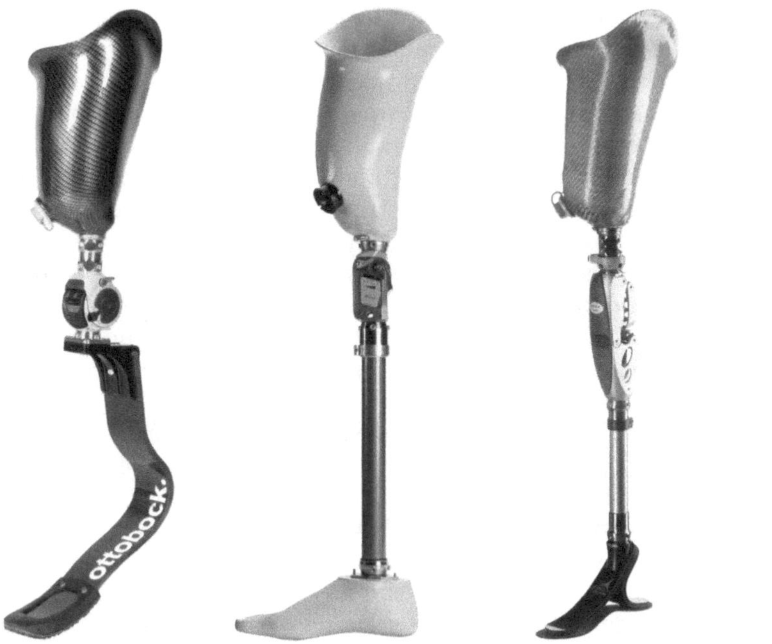

Figure 3.1 These examples of lower limb prosthetic systems by German manufacturer Ottobock showcase both the diversity and modular design of contemporary prosthetics. Photos credit: Ottobock SE & Co. KGaA.

distinctions it produced. Most importantly, studying how these objects were *designed, distributed,* and *used* allowed me to identify the mechanisms that contributed to the construction of a strongly patterned multitude of user roles that presented a wide range of possibilities for some, while limiting courses of action for others.

3.1.2 Following Action Through Time

In addition to the spatial dispersion implied by my focus on industrial scale, addressing the effects of industrial transformation entails the challenge of capturing a *change* in the processes underlying the construction of user roles. On a theoretical level, an action net perspective is ideally suited for this task, as it focuses on the ways in which the connections between situated actions give rise to actorial identities that may, over time, congeal into recognizable social roles. From such a starting point, serendipity and change appear always just around the corner, ready to be observed in situ. Yet, as Czarniawska points out, the process of role construction occurs against the backdrop of an institutional order which not only regulates and orients actions and their relationships but also offers widely accepted scripts for the attribution of specific roles to specific kinds of actants. Hence, while in theory user roles remain malleable and may change at any time, in practice, strongly institutionalized action nets are more likely to change incrementally. For this reason, the transformation of an industry such as prosthetics is hard to observe from just a single temporal vantage point. To demonstrate changing practices of user construction, one needs to find ways of *following action through time.* Czarniawska herself named three strategies of doing this. According to her, "[a]ction nets need [...] to be observed as they are being established and re-established, which can be done *progressively, deduced speculatively* or, in Foucault's terms, *studied genealogically*" (Czarniawska, 2004b, p. 782, my emphasis). These techniques offer a useful way of summarizing the approaches I used to capture a transformation in the action nets of user construction.

My first strategy, which may be described as a *progressive* research design, consisted in paying attention to the ways in which established manufacturers implemented 3D printing into their own development and production processes. By paying attention to the phase of introduction, I hoped to observe not only the shaping of new routines around a new set of production technologies, but the way in which prevalent ways of doing were called into question, revealing underlying principles which might otherwise remain invisible (compare Barley, 1986 for a successful example). Unfortunately, this was scarcely the case at the beginning of my study, although toward the end of it, 3D printers were being implemented at both prosthetic workshops and industrial manufacturers. Even though digital technologies such as 3D scanning and CNC milling had gradually been introduced since the 1980s, 3D printing was still viewed as an "experimental technology" that, from the perspective of the industry's incumbents, had yet to outperform existing processes. For this reason, it seemed difficult to select a site for prolonged observation without incurring the risk that nothing of interest would happen there. Accordingly, while this first strategy helped me to give an account of the norms and practices constituting the existing institutional order of prosthetic user construction, it hardly helped me to capture their transformation.

It proved more useful to engage with the industry's history in what could be dubbed a *genealogical* approach. While not originally a part of my study design, the field's history was a recurring theme throughout my research. On the one hand, it was an important element from an emic perspective, as I was studying the industry at a time when several of its most important organizations, such as the American Orthotics and Prosthetics Association (AOPA) (founded in 1917), or world market leader Ottobock (founded in 1919) were celebrating their centennials, often sponsoring special exhibitions, or printing small pamphlets summarizing their own history. On the other hand, the history of prosthetics was the most prevalent topic in the scholarly treatment of the field, with several impressive studies offering insight into the time of its early industrialization (Brown, 2002; Cohen, 2001; Harrasser,

2016; Herschbach, 1997; Kienitz, 2008). Relating my own findings to both the academic debate and the way in which the industry remembered its own history, I was able to reconstruct the gradual evolution of its institutional order which would otherwise have remained part of the implicit background of the action observed in situ. In theoretical terms, engaging with the industry's history allowed me to learn about its central institutions at a time when they had not yet become taken for granted.

Another useful technique for studying industrial transformation was to attend to new entrants to the industry that tried to change the status quo by building their businesses around digital technology. In what might be termed a *speculative* approach, I treated these as "hopeful monsters," as "things born perhaps slightly before their time; when it's not known if the environment is quite ready for them" (Mosley, 2000 [1990], p. 71, see also Law, 1991, p. 1). Naturally, the impact of these companies on the industry at large could not be predicted. However, they explicitly challenged established institutions and, in doing so, made visible how the existing system could potentially be organized differently. To be sure, these hopeful monsters were moving targets with both their technologies and practices changing quickly. Yet, by selecting a range of variously organized "challengers," including industrial reorganization projects, start-ups, university-based nonprofits, and a globally dispersed open-source community, I was able to reconstruct several models of how things *might* be done, and how they *might* work under different conditions.

Taken together, these strategies enabled me to construct an account of the processes of user construction as they were established and re-established throughout important turning points of the field's history. By *following the action through space* I was able to shed light on processes of user construction along the biography of industrial products and product classes.

Table 3.1 Methodological framework and methods used

		Biographical Dimension (Product)		
		Designing (Chapter 4)	*Distributing (Chapter 5)*	*Using (Chapter 6)*
Historical Dimension (Industry)	*Industrialization* (1861/1914–ca. 1950)	Document analysis (historical) Reference to academic literature		
	Normal operation of industry (ca. 1950–today)	Document analysis (historical and current) Qualitative interviews Multi-sited ethnography		
	Digitalization of industry (ca. 1980–today)	Document analysis (current) Qualitative interviews Multi-sited ethnography		
	Implementation of 3D printing (ca. 2012–today)	Qualitative interviews Multi-sited ethnography Participatory makeathons		

Following the action through time allowed me to trace the transformation of the involved mechanisms throughout the industry's history. These dimensions constitute the methodological framework of a study that addresses both the *industrial scale* and *historical transformation* of user construction in the field of prosthetics (Table 3.1).

3.2 Data Collection

To implement the ambitious research design just sketched out, I deployed several different methods, most importantly interviews, focused ethnographies, and participatory workshops including makeathons. The primary purpose of these *fieldwork devices* (Estalella & Sánchez Criado, 2019; Law & Ruppert, 2013) was, of course, to generate the data necessary to answer my research question. Yet, like all devices, they were prone to do much more than originally intended. Most importantly, the methods I used tended to become entangled, each in its own way, in the very action nets they were supposed to generate data on. In the process, my own techniques defined for myself specific actorial identities that squarely put me *within* my field of study and, in turn, shaped the ways in which I could act in my primary role as a researcher (compare Czarniawska, 1998, pp. 33–50). To give the reader an understanding of how I came to collect the material presented in this book, I will briefly sketch out my methods.

3.2.1 Interviews

The first technique I used consisted in identifying and interviewing the relevant stakeholders in the industry. Starting from some first explorative conversations with prosthetists, I successively built a representation of my field by asking to be referred to other relevant actors or sites of action at the end of each interview. In this way, I came to talk to prosthetists, and technicians, developers of software tools and 3D printers, engineers working for industrial manufacturers and engineers working for non-profits, research scientists and managers, business owners and 3D printing enthusiasts, and of course I talked to people who use prostheses. In all, I ended up doing 84 interviews, the outlines of which constantly evolved reflecting the differences between my interlocutors as well as my growing understanding of the industry.[6] Overall, these interviews roughly fell into two groups: 38 shorter semi-structured interviews and 42 longer expert interviews.[7] To make these available for subsequent analytical work using qualitative data analysis software, 55 of these interviews were fully transcribed, while memos were made summarizing the central aspects of the remaining 27.[8]

The first set, consisting of 38 semi-structured interviews, was conducted at international trade fairs and conferences, and intended to give me a broad overview of the field.[9] These interviews were often spontaneous and exploratory in character and usually lasted between 15 and 30 minutes. Interviewees were selected based on the scientific program or exhibitor directory of the event, as well as previous referrals. Roughly following a recurring guideline, these conversations would cover at least three topics: First, my interviewee's personal activities with regard to prosthetics; second, how these activities linked to those of other actors within the industry and, third, how these nets of activity had changed, or were expected to change, with the introduction of digital fabrication. Based on these data, I successively built a broad representation of the industry as described by the actors themselves, while slowly developing an understanding of how the processes described to me corresponded to my analytical categories. Moreover, I was able to establish a first notion of the way in which 3D printing was expected to transform the industry and the often less spectacular ways in which it was already being applied.

Building on that general overview, almost all of the remaining 42 interviews were more extensive conversations with selected experts (Gläser & Laudel, 2009, pp. 111–196), which were either conducted on site (e.g., in a lab, makerspace, or workshop) or, where necessary, through video conferences or telephone calls. These interviews went into more detail and usually lasted about an hour, with some taking up more than two hours. In these interviews I more freely diverted from the prepared guidelines, focusing on the expert knowledge of my interlocutors and adding new questions on the unexpected details that inevitably came up. Using these data, I was able to substantiate my general understanding of the field with several concrete narratives and detailed practical examples (compare Czarniawska, 2004a). This helped me to build up a "thicker" understanding of how things worked and to correct initial misunderstandings.

3.2.1.1 Promises of Future Collaborations

Interviews were one of the central ways to get in touch with my field. However, they did more than generate data. Interviews were also occasions at which I entered and was drawn into the field in ways that extended beyond the interview situation itself. The most relevant example of this was what I call *promises of future collaboration*. These promises bear mentioning here since they importantly altered my position within the field and, to some modest degree, contributed to shaping the latter. In short, they were a sort of mutual "interessement" (Callon, 1984) that was most pertinent when arranging and wrapping up interviews, but sometimes pervaded the interview situation itself. On the one hand, I viewed (and was trained to view) at least some of my interviews as possible entry points for subsequent ethnographic research. On the other, several of my interview partners wanted something out of the interview themselves. Some interviewees asked me about specific details of my research in the hope of learning something new about their field including, of course, information about competitors. Others saw my work, my perspective, or my affiliation as genuinely relevant to their own agenda. In some cases, they tried to enroll me into their own endeavors, for instance by suggesting joint research projects, or grant proposals, or by having me write an article in their journal.

As a researcher in need of both field contacts and funding, I was not usually disinclined to pursue those ideas and sometimes actively encouraged them. In several cases, some sort of action was taken. I wrote outlines of grant proposals, or protocols of interviews, I organized and sat on various brainstorming and coordination meetings, commented on patient interview guidelines, or tried to put together user-centered design toolkits. While some of these projects are still ongoing or were successfully completed, other initiatives were discontinued or put on hold until an unspecified future. Reflecting on my methods, the question remains: what to make of these failed promises? For one thing, they added to my perspective. They were pathways to questions I would not otherwise have asked. Collaborating with my interlocutors gave me a better understanding of their hopes, attitudes, and fears, as well as of the necessities and resistances of the field. Yet, they frequently left open ends behind, loose strands of action that were never woven back into the larger action net. Where such situations left behind a feeling of disappointment, failure, or even betrayal, they were prone to hamper my further access to the field.

3.2.2 Ethnography

Ethnographic research was an essential part of studying user construction in action nets. Attempting to "follow the action," I entered prosthetic clinics and workshops, engineering labs and research facilities, 3D printing factories and makerspaces, conferences, and trade fairs. In one case, I was invited into the home of a person living with limb differences. I attended patient fittings, business meetings, and product testing sessions, I watched prosthetists scanning limbs and working plaster, engineers adapting CAD models, and 3D printers extruding plastic. I saw people using their prostheses in all sorts of ways and, not least of all, I met those who chose to forego the use of their assistive devices. Entering the field in an ethnographic mode helped me to gain a more profound understanding of many of the processes talked about in the interviews, while simultaneously drawing my attention to relationships between actions that had not been touched upon. Most importantly, an ethnographic approach gave me a better sense of the material dimensions of prosthetics, its spaces, practices, bodies, machines, and products. Much of this ethnographic experience was recorded in field notes as well as a wealth of audiovisual material such as audio recordings, photographs, and videos.

Given the broad usage of the term ethnography, I should qualify my own approach as both *multi-sited* (Marcus, 1986) and *focused* (Knoblauch, 2005). It was multi-sited in that I tried to generate data on processes occurring at various geographical settings and spanning both national and organizational boundaries. In this way, I followed the action to four different countries (Germany, US, Canada, and Haiti) and a large number of different organizations, bit by bit constructing an ethnographic account of user construction in prosthetics. At the same time, my style of ethnography was focused (Knoblauch, 2005) or strategic (Pollock & Williams, 2009, p. 112), in that my research stays in these locations were relatively short and concentrated on specific aspects of the overall action net. Lasting between a few hours and seven weeks instead of the year-long research design suggested for traditional anthropological ethnographies, they were intended to explore particular processes or situations rather than aiming at a holistic description of the local culture (e.g., of a lab, an organization, a society). Such a focused approach required me to establish a general understanding of the field *prior* to the ethnographic moment and it presupposed that I shared much of the implicit cultural knowledge relevant to the places studied. Moreover, the brevity of my field stays was, to some degree, compensated by the intensity of data collection. In addition to taking field notes, I was usually equipped with a camera, video camera, or audio recorder, to document specific settings, artifacts, and activities for later analysis. Overall, while it was impossible to ethnographically explore all aspects of user construction talked about in the interviews, this particular style of *multi-sited* and *focused* research allowed me to arrive at a deeper understanding of a comparably large number of key processes.

3.2.2.1 Role Spillovers in Ethnographic Research

Studying prosthetics ethnographically meant constructing my role in the field quite differently than in the interviews discussed above. In interview situations, my role as a researcher was clear to all involved and needed little additional justification. By contrast, the more I was allowed to participate in the activities I studied, the more it seemed necessary to justify my presence in the terms of the field itself. Particularly when encountering people who had not taken part in negotiating my field access, it was often unsatisfactory to simply point to my mission of contributing to the disciplinary knowledge of sociology.[10] Being in the field for any extended period of time, some role had to be assigned to me that made sense to the people I worked with.

Since I was not an expert in the field and couldn't easily conjure up any directly valuable contributions, my role was usually that of a helpful companion carrying out small tasks for the people I studied. I pointed potential customers to the booth of a start-up I was working with, I ran errands, kept company, carried prosthetic arms not currently in use, I shared food. At other times, I was already part of the game before I knew it. Sometimes, people used my academic role to reflect positively on their own activities, depicting themselves as particularly innovative (*We even attract the interest of researchers!*) or particularly responsible (*We even thought of bringing in a sociologist!*). Finally, my very presence in the field could itself have some effects on it and, at times, make or unmake it in more than a metaphorical way. German funding lines, for instance, often *require* the inclusion of social scientists to assess the societal consequences of a given project, which means that without someone to study them, many of these projects would not exist. Similarly, when the group of researchers I was part of delayed their trip to Port-au-Prince due to political upheaval in the Haitian capital, we jeopardized the very activities we wanted to study, since the local clinic's 3D printing center in part depended on the money, materials, and reputation we were expected to bring in. As an ethnographer, then, one does not only constitute one's own object by doing research on it (Clifford & Marcus, 1986). One may also contribute to its demise by ceasing to do so.

It was in these ways that my activities in the field systematically "spilled over" (Michael, 2012) the frame set by my role as a researcher. This confronted me with situations that were challenging from the point of view of traditional research ethics. However, it was through these very spillovers that I developed a sense for the many layers of action that would not have counted as integral parts of the field of prosthetics from an armchair perspective, despite being critical to its continued practical operation. In this sense coming to terms with such unforeseen entanglements should be considered an important part of the ethnographic method.

3.2.3 Makeathons

My third major fieldwork device consisted of a number of participatory workshops, foremost including two so-called *makeathons* held in Munich and Vancouver.[11] This technique differed from the ones mentioned previously in two respects. First, it did not tackle the large historical and geographical extension of my field by retracing its activities, but by bringing the action to me. Second, it did so by drawing on a format familiar to people in the field of 3D printing and adapting it to facilitate social scientific data collection.[12] In the four-day makeathons, we brought together prosthesis users with engineers, prosthetists, 3D printing experts, industrial designers, and STS scholars in a user-centered design exercise that ran them through a digitalized process chain from ideation to sketching, to CAD modeling, 3D printing, and public discussion. Through these makeathons, which were moderated by STS scholars and professional designers, interdisciplinary teams developed speculative prototypes of 3D-printed prosthetic devices for and with their envisioned users, presenting their results at a final exhibition (Figure 3.2). Arranging my field in this way, enabled me to study the beliefs and orientations of individuals and groups of actors (e.g., prosthetists) as they were asked to collaborate and discuss their approaches with members of other groups (e.g., engineers, users). These encounters clearly brought out the idiosyncrasies of institutionalized practices and underlying patterns of legitimation that I, as a non-expert, would not have been able to unearth by other means. As a method

Figure 3.2 A makeathon participant holding a 3D-printed prototype he helped design. Own photograph.

of data collection, makeathons were therefore an important way of putting my hard-won beliefs about the field to the test and adding new perspectives on what I had learned from working with individual experts and groups. The rich material generated at the events was subsequently scanned (e.g., drawings, sticky notes) or otherwise stored (3D files, material prototypes) for future reference. Selected recordings of group sessions or presentations were transcribed and most of the remaining material summarized in memos for further analysis.

In contrast to the two fieldwork devices discussed so far, makeathons can be described as *experimental* in that they brought together pre-selected participants in a controlled setting to produce an unknown and open-ended outcome. Rather than studying action within its globally dispersed settings and over long periods of time, I brought the action to me based on existing field contacts and my evolving model of prosthetic user construction. Instead of studying action "naturalistically," it was compressed in space and time, and arranged with regard to the composition of groups, the rules, including the goals and temporal structure, of the process, and the infrastructural setting of the event. Roughly, the process followed a possible digitalized workflow—from ideation to sketching, digital modeling, 3D printing, and feedback. It also ran in the direction of greater social complexity—from individual exercises to in-group discussions, to interdisciplinary work, to an engagement with an interested public.

Despite this high degree of control within the setting, the outcome of the events was unknown. Makeathons were designed to answer a set of specific questions around the effect of digitalization on user construction in prosthetics. How do the various groups (e.g., users, prosthetists, engineers) envision a digitalized future? What are their concerns, hopes, and challenges? How do users construct their own identities and how are these translated by the professionals of the industry using, among other things, the digital technologies at their disposal? Yet, it was unclear how possible answers to these questions would be articulated and whether the events would work as intended. In hindsight, I dare say that they were successful in terms of generating large amounts of useful data. In addition, an equally interesting set of insights was generated in the process of organizing these events and in the various relationships and collaborations they fostered beyond their use as instruments of sociological research.

3.2.3.1 Assembling My Field

A defining feature of makeathons was that, in contrast to interviews and ethnography, they can be described as *deliberately interventionist.* Rather than representing what would have happened without my being there, makeathons reflexively assembled my field in a way that was informed by and conducive to my own research process. The decisive difference to traditional qualitative methods was that makeathons purposely generated relationships within the field that would not have existed without them. Indeed, some of the most interesting findings of these events resulted from reflecting on the various resistances we faced in organizing them and observing which of the generated relationships continued after the event was over. It was instructive to observe the ways in which the field's actors facilitated and resisted my efforts to enroll them into specific positions within the makeathons. Several large companies, for instance, were keen on participating in the events but only on the conditions that none of their competitors attended and that they would be allowed to bring not only the engineers I had requested, but also their own prosthetists and users. In doing so, they taught me a lot about the intricate structures of competition and cooperation between the actors involved in the making of prosthetic devices. In another example, people with limb differences were the group that was most difficult to recruit except through manufacturers or prosthetists. As they did not constitute a professional group in their own right, they were more difficult to contact and, usually, could not participate in the event as part of their regular jobs. Surprisingly, even though industrial activity centered around them, in some ways they were rather marginal participants in the field. As these examples show, by trying to make people play specific roles in my experimental setup, I was confronted with the difference between my own perception of these roles and the perspective of the role-takers themselves. Given these resistances, it was all the more interesting to see how participants reflected on the makeathons afterward and how some of the newly created relationships outlasted the events themselves. This included new contacts between firms, but also meant that one participant became a test user for an attending company, while a participating user innovator utilized the event to kick-start his professional network. Most remarkably, makeathons enabled people with limb differences to participate in designing their own devices—an experience that, several participants assured me, most amputees never get to make.[13] Seeing which of the newly created relationships were viewed as novel and valuable by the people attending further added to my understanding of the existing institutional order, while reaffirming my intention of reflexively contributing to its ongoing transformation.

3.3 Data Analysis

In this concluding section, I describe the process through which I generated answers to my research question based on both my analytical framework and the empirical data collected. That is, I outline my methods of data analysis. This will cover the extraction of relevant information from the large corpus of data collected and the re-construction of the underlying processes of user construction from this material, including the graphical representation of action nets. I will indicate the kinds of questions that oriented my own interpretations for each step.

3.3.1 Structuring the Empirical Material Using Deductive/Inductive Coding

The first challenge in analyzing the expansive collection of empirical material was to locate in it the information relevant to my question about the relationship between digitalizing industries and user roles. For this task I chose a deductive/inductive form of *coding* (Schreier, 2012, p. 89), which I carried out using a qualitative data analysis software called Dedoose. This approach was favored over a more strictly inductive one (e.g., as in the early stages of grounded theory per Glaser & Strauss, 1967) for two reasons. First, because I had already constructed an analytical framework based on my research question and my review of the user studies literature, I started coding with a fair idea of the *kinds of things* I was looking for. Second, although it might have been rewarding to analyze the material in an entirely open fashion, given the sheer size of the text corpus, it appeared necessary to approach it in a more clearly delimited way.

My theoretically informed starting point was expressed most clearly in the fact that I used basic mechanisms of user construction, such as *inscribing, circulating, and re-interpreting,* as the initial set of categories structuring my coding scheme. Moreover, my analytical perspective also shaped the way in which I went about inductively adding new categories. As I worked from an action net perspective, I aimed to organize my data around specific *actions* rather than around actors, or social worlds. Hence, categories described recurring actions or processes which I deemed relevant to user construction, while information about actors was dispersed across categories. For instance, the code "scanning" (a subcategory of "inscribing") was applied regardless of who was doing the scanning (e.g., a prosthetist or an amateur), with what technology (e.g., an iPhone scanner or a high-end device), or who was scanned (e.g., a person missing an arm or a leg). Relevant information associated with actors was retained through subcategories describing important *conditions* of scanning, such as "scanning skill," "kind of scanner," and "bodily characteristics of patient." Nonetheless, the primary goal was to discover *recurring ways of doing* and not so much to elucidate the characteristics of the actors involved.

Coding involved a certain degree of interpretation that informed, for instance, which codes to apply to which portions of the text, and when to add or merge categories. For example, my material contained information on a number of different ways of "scanning." Sometimes the body of the prospective user was scanned directly, at other times, its position was corrected using a sock or fixture, while in yet other cases, a positive plaster mold was scanned rather than the body itself. Each performance involved a slightly different choreography and cast of actants. Hence, the question arose which of these actions to subsume under the label of "scanning," and whether there should be a further subdivision of that code. To inform my decisions, I used a set of orienting questions based on my analytical perspective. For example, to identify relevant actions, I would ask whether they performed a translation relevant to the construction of user roles and thus constituted an important link within the action net. Similarly, for separating distinct processes, I would ask, whether these translations differed in important dimensions, such as acting on a different quality or quantity of inputs, generating a different quality or quantity of outputs, or being triggered and sustained by a different set of adjacent actions. The result of coding was a text indexed with a set of categories that described the actions relevant to user construction, along with information on the conditions of their performance and the translations performed in them.

3.3.2 Reconstructing and Interpreting Processes

In order to re-construct an action net from an index of categories, the actions described by these categories had to be related to one another. Doing this involved going through the excerpts of each code (e.g., scanning) and identifying which other codes (e.g., modeling, sending) they were linked to. However, recording and analyzing the emerging patterns proved cumbersome with text-based QDA software. I therefore started experimenting with visual modes of representation. Beginning with a number of simple sketches, I eventually developed a more formalized procedure that provided the basis for the action-net-renderings shown in the empirical chapters of this book (see Figure 3.3).[14] Unfortunately, despite the wealth of network concepts in STS and organization studies, *analytical* renderings of the relationships between *actions* are not very common and I initially found little guidance conducive to my analysis.[15]

One of the few successful approaches is outlined by Pentland and Feldman (2007) in their description of "narrative networks." Narrative networks are representations of actual and hypothetical patterns of technology in use (Orlikowski, 2000). They contain nodes of "narrative fragments" connected by ties indicating sequence and coherence, the latter usually provided by the unity of purpose from the point of view of the narrator. Narrative networks are close to renderings of action nets (Czarniawska, 2004b; Czarniawska, 2014, pp. 17–22) in that their central elements, narrative fragments, "consist of at least two actants and some kind of action that occurs with them or between them" (Pentland & Feldman, 2007, p. 788). Hence, following the directed network graph (ibid. 789), one will end up reciting possible stories describing a purposeful sequence of activities involving human and non-human actants.

Even though my own method for reconstructing the processes of user construction is inspired by the approach of Pentland and Feldman, it deviated from it in at least three ways, reflecting my own theoretical understanding of

Concept	Depiction
Nodes describe actions and the actant that is acted on.	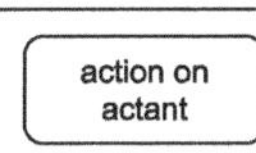
Ties signify translations of actants. Translation can be established by an actant being passed on between actions or by equivalence being established between two different actants. *Tie direction* indicates sequence.	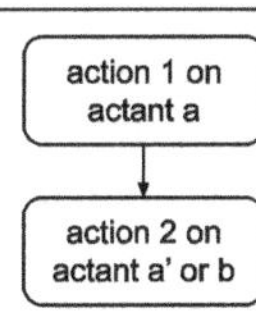
Action nets depict a pattern of action that can be observed repeatedly in the field. They form the basis for the formation of actorial roles (e.g., user, prosthetist, engineer). The action nets in this book depict basic processes of user construction (e.g., inscription). The example to the right shows the relationship between a conventional inscription process using the plaster cast method (white) and a digitalized inscription processes using 3D scanning and 3D printing (grey).	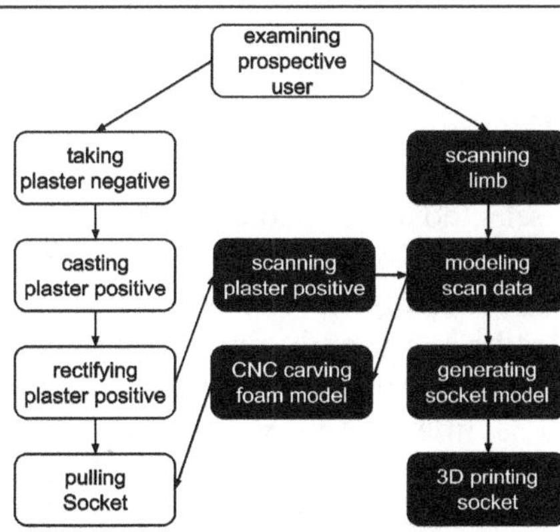

Figure 3.3 Basic concepts in the graphical representation of action nets. Own figure.

action net analysis (Figure 3.3). First of all, the *nodes* in my action nets are not narrative fragments, but *actions* (see also Pentland, 1999). The major difference is that, whereas narrative fragments need a defined subject (the first of the two actants in Pentland and Feldman's account), I treat the subject carrying out the action as exchangeable within certain limits. Leaving the subject of an action undetermined limits one of the ways in which narrative fragments multiply in narrative networks, thereby simplifying the figures that result. For instance, instead of distinguishing between the narrative fragments "prosthetist scanning limb" and "technician scanning limb," I simply write "scanning limb"). In fact, insofar as actions precede the formation of actorial identities, including the latter may easily become tautological (e.g., "user using prosthesis").

The second difference between my approach and that of Feldman and Pentland concerns the *ties* of the network. Where in narrative networks ties indicate sequence and coherence established by unity of purpose, I emphasize that in action nets coherence between actions is established by *translation*. This is why, in my own drawings, ties indicate that some kind of intermediary (e.g., object, money, word, human) has been passed on between actions or has been equated with another actant. Hence, actions indicate *what is acted on* and in following their sequence the gradual transformation of intermediaries becomes apparent (e.g., scanning limb → modeling scan data → generating socket model). It would be tempting to say that this way of constructing ties retains the second actant in Pentland and Feldman's narrative fragments, but unfortunately, they seem to oscillate between intermediaries that pass between actions (e.g., e-mail) and the means by which they are made to move (e.g., browser).

The final and most important difference between action nets and narrative networks is that the former are not *networks of all possible stories*, actual and hypothetical. Rather, in my account, action nets depict *sequences of actions occurring repeatedly in reality*.[16] That is to say, I exclude not only hypothetical actions and relations, but also idiosyncratic ones that only occur once. Doing so is necessary because my goal is to model a change in the institutional order of user construction rather than to describe the variability of technology-in-practice.[17] Yet, making these simplifications is no trivial matter. Which of the processes emerging from the analysis should be selected as particularly typical or relevant is not inherent in the resulting drawings. Nor can such renderings *explain* why something happened and not something else. Hence, rather than taking the action nets constructed thus far as the endpoint of analysis, they should be viewed as both an outcome of interpretation and a scaffold for further analysis.

The interpretive work underpinning the account given in this book involved continuously moving back and forth between visual model, and empirical data. One advantage of the simplified visual models was that they lend themselves nicely to comparison. They helped me to evaluate whether a given performance of a process recorded in the material differed in important ways from the patterns I had established previously. They also facilitated comparison between processes occurring under different conditions. For instance, it was interesting to ask how processes of user construction differed between product classes (e.g., is scanning an arm the same as scanning a leg?), or between the major components of a single product (e.g., are there different distribution processes associated with sockets and fit components?). Most importantly, the simplified models allowed me to evaluate the mediating role of production devices in action nets of user construction. How does the use of a specific production device require, enable, or shape each of the translations in a given action net? Are there multiple processes associated with the same production device? Why are some of these processes used in some cases and not in others? Answering these questions, required a constant switching between the models I was building and the empirical material I had collected. The results of this work form the centerpiece of this book and are presented in the following three chapters.

Notes

1 Note the difference here between the dictum of "following the actors" (e.g., Latour, 1987) and "following that which is acted on" (Czarniawska, 2004b, p. 781).

2 While some large manufacturers aim to offer *all* types of components, most specialize in just a few. Any actual prosthesis may, therefore, contain parts manufactured by multiple firms.

3 Some issues became more difficult to grasp with this study design, as some components deviate from standard trajectories. Prosthetic feet used in competitive sports may be viewed as fit components but are neither standardized nor necessarily made in large factories. Similarly, several "adjustable sockets" are neither custom nor manufactured at prosthetic workshops. Some prostheses have no socket at all but are integrated directly into the bone using a technique called osseointegration. Despite these omissions, I am confident that the distinction between sockets and fit components helps to represent the basic institutional order of the industry in a way that is relevant to my research question and compatible to an emic understanding of the field.

4 Initially, it seemed to me that there must be some sort of hierarchy associated with these differences: Surely, a robotic hand was *better* than a hook, a powered ankle *superior* to a foot carved out of wood! Yet, the longer I participated in the field, the clearer it became that there was no one best device. The appropriateness of a prosthesis depended on who was using it, what it was used for, where, and when. It was only in this relational view that I was able to grasp the diversity of user roles constructed in the field.

5 The causes of amputation tend to differ dramatically between upper and lower limbs. According to Baumgartner and Botta (2008, p. 16), 85–90% of lower limb amputations in "industrialized countries" are due to arterial occlusive diseases (50–60% of those following diabetes mellitus), while 50–70% of amputations of the upper limb are due to trauma. Not only does the cause of amputation entail psychological and physical differences, it also corresponds to demographic factors such as age, with most young amputees (aged 0–20) suffering limb loss due to trauma, while most older amputees (aged 60 and older) lose limbs due to disease (ibid.).

6 See also the strategy of "theoretical sampling" per Glaser and Strauss (1967, pp. 45–78).

7 The other four included two early exploratory interviews and two interviews that were conducted alongside ethnographic research and had to be stopped as my interviewees had to attend to more urgent matters.

8 The transcribed material amounted to 55 hours and roughly 88% of the recorded material. Seven interviews were not recorded at the wish of my interviewees, in which case I took notes during and after the conversation. Twenty interviews were only partially transcribed, focusing on passages that contained new information.

9 Most of these interviews were conducted at conferences taking place in Germany in 2016 and 2018, and the US in 2017. This allowed me to get information from two of the places in which the modern prosthetics industry first emerged. It also enabled me to alternate between data collection and analysis and select new interview partners to address remaining gaps in my emerging model.

10 Identifying as an STS researcher was slightly more useful because a role could be defined with regard to a specific field of study rather than an abstract discipline. This made it possible to argue that I was producing knowledge about *the prosthetics industry*, which could be useful to my interlocutors in the future. Yet, such an argument, too, appeared somewhat fragile, because it was never certain that I would succeed in producing such practical knowledge and, even if I did, whether I would do so in an acceptable timeframe.

11 In developing and conducting these events I was aided by many people. My gratitude belongs, in particular, to Lisa Boulton for her untiring work on the user-centered design process and materials, and to Silvia Raschke for her invaluable help in developing the prosthetics dimension of the workshop and enrolling participants from the Canadian P&O community. Further, I am indebted to *Innovationsmanufaktur*, the *British Columbia Institute of Technology*, and *Wiivv* for hosting the events and their final exhibitions and to *Makerbot* and *Cimetrix* for contributing printers and other materials. Last but not least, I am grateful for the help of the people of *MCTS* and *BCIT*, from student assistant to professor, in running the events as smoothly as they did.

12 Makeathons, in the terms of the field, are events in which people come together in one place for a relatively short period of time and collaborate on the design and prototyping of new technology. In the realm of hardware development, the capacity of 3D printers to facilitate "rapid prototyping" (compare Chapter 6) is of great help in this activity.

13 Typically, people with limb differences participate only in the process of choosing between readymade components.

14 One of the main advantages of sketching was that it forced me to extract the relevant relational information from specific portions of text. Even though this lost a lot of contextual information, it also made the material more manageable by radically reducing its complexity. In this respect, the technique is similar to the *extraction* part of the "extractive qualitative data analysis" developed by Gläser and Laudel (2013; 2019).

15 In organization studies, theories are usually built around networks of *actors* rather than actions, while methods are frequently oriented toward the mathematical analysis of *quantitative* rather than qualitative data (e.g., Granovetter, 1973; Powell & Grodal, 2005). In STS, all sorts of network concepts exist (e.g., Deleuze & Guattari, 1987; Haraway, 1994; Laet & Annemarie Mol, 2000; Law, 1987). However, while these are often theoretically elaborate, they tend to be underdeveloped as methods of empirical analysis (but see Callon et al., 1986). More precisely, the few visualizations that do exist, tend to be either simplistic

illustrations of basic social processes (Latour, 1987, p. 120) or metaphorical depictions of analytical concepts (Czarniawska, 2014, pp. 17–22).

16 Insofar as Czarniawska (2004b, p. 782) defines action as an "event, to which an intention can be attributed," this is close to what Gläser and Laudel (2019) describe as a "candidate for a mechanism."

17 One way of keeping both the variability of individual performances *and* the focus on institutionalization would be to introduce weighted ties, as demonstrated by Pentland (1999). In the resulting drawings, possible ways of doing would be preserved, while typical ways of doing would stand out. However, this necessitates a level of standardization in the collection of data which is at odds with the openness of most qualitative research.

4 Designing Technology

User Representation and Inscription

In this chapter, I take up a familiar line of research in STS by studying the construction of user roles during technology design. I hope to further an understanding of the processes involved by considering their relation to the organization of manufacturing and attending in particular detail to the introduction of 3D printing. To capture the mediating role of production technology, I examine how specific sets of production devices (e.g., manual tools, large-scale assembly lines, 3D printers) become linked to distinctive modes of representing and inscribing users, while other alternatives are rejected as inferior or impractical. I then argue that the introduction of new production technologies may transform user roles by triggering the renegotiation and recombination of ingrained practices.

To demonstrate this argument, I compare the action nets that have formed around various production devices in the prosthetics industry. I show that since the very inception of prosthetics as a large-scale industry, the field has featured two vastly different modes of user representation and inscription, one associated with the *machine-based mass production* of prosthetic fit components, and the other with the *tool-based craft production* of prosthetic sockets. I trace the history of that divide and show that it emerged around a professional conflict between engineers and prosthetists, with each group engaged in different practices of user representation and inscription (Section 4.1). The current trajectories of digitalization, including the rise of different varieties of *digital mass customization*, must be understood against that background. When digital production technologies were first introduced in the 1980s, prosthetists and engineers alike tried to use them in accordance with their institutionalized routines, often adapting new technologies to ingrained practices. It was only as new groups of designers—research engineers, start-ups, and the maker movement—introduced new ways of organizing digital fabrication that institutionalized action nets became subject to renegotiation and novel user roles began to emerge (Section 4.2). Concluding my analysis, I spell out its major implications for a theory of industrial user construction. I contend that multiple modes of user inscription may simultaneously exist within the same industry and that these constitute stable links between professional routines, manufacturing

DOI: 10.4324/9781003269731-4

technologies, and products. As digital inscription and production devices introduce new translational capacities, they allow for a renegotiation of these connections, although new modes of user construction may emerge as re-combinations of well-rehearsed practices (Section 4.3).

4.1 Between Craft and Industry

The term "inscription" refers to a set of processes through which the features of potential users and their envisioned activities are translated into design criteria and eventually into physical artifacts. User representations, whether based on concrete embodied individuals or the designer's abstract imaginings, influence the way technology is made. By studying a technical object, it is possible to recover something of the designer's ideas concerning its potential users. From this vantage point, a striking feature of modern prostheses is that they are highly modular products with two very different kinds of components. The interface between the machine and the human body, the so-called socket, is *custom-made* to conform to the anatomy of each individual amputee. However, all the components that attach to that socket, such as prosthetic hands, feet, or joints are highly *standardized* and produced by a process of machine-based mass (or batch) production. While this may appear to be a natural way of building something that attaches so intimately to the human body, I argue that studying how that difference came into being is a useful starting point to unravel the principles underlying user construction in prosthetics. By attending to the history of the field, it can be demonstrated that the distinction between customized sockets and standardized fit components is merely the current state of affairs in a century-old professional struggle over how to represent users in the design of prosthetic devices.

Tracing the roots of the two dominant forms of inscription in contemporary prosthetics reveals that artificial limbs have existed for much of human history. Most engineers, prosthetists, and surgeons working in the industry know this, and frequently point to the field's ancient origins.[1] Examples include the metal hand of a Roman general from the period 218–201 BC (Wellerson, 1957) or the wooden leg of a Persian soldier dated back to 484 BC (Wilson, Jr., 1992), with the oldest prosthesis referenced during my fieldwork being the wooden toe found in the tomb of an Egyptian mummy from ca. 1065 to 740 BC (Nerlich et al., 2000). Early technical drawings and construction notes date to the time of German knight Götz von Berlichingen with his famous "Iron Hand" (ca. 1509; Contini, 1954) and the mechanical leg developed by French surgeon Ambroise Paré (ca. 1561; Hernigou, 2013). However, while there is some evidence that such designs were occasionally imitated, prostheses were usually designed and manufactured on an individual basis by locksmiths, armorers, or other craftspeople. The 18th century saw a growing disciplinary concern with the mechanical "correction" and "repair" of the human body, as exemplified by the publication of the famous *Orthopædia: or the art of correcting and preventing deformities in children* (Andry, 1742), which introduced the term "orthopaedics" to the English language.[2,3] Yet, partly due to the very small number of surviving amputees, there was still little interaction between the makers of artificial limbs, and there was no independent trade or profession to develop shared norms or representational practices.

The professionalization of prosthetic design and production gained momentum in the wake of war. The US Civil War (1861–1865), World War I (1914–1919), and to a lesser degree the German-French War (1870–1871) had left behind more amputees than ever before due to the industrialization of warfare and the simultaneous advances in medical technology allowing many wounded soldiers and civilians to survive amputation. During the US Civil War about 60,000 amputations were performed (Herschbach, 1997, p. 26), and the number of surviving amputees after WWI is reported as approximately 70,000 in Germany alone (Kienitz, 2008, p. 156). In both cases, the goal of reintegrating the maimed masses into the social fabric, and especially into industrial production,[4] was of paramount importance for the (re-)building of post-war nation-states in Germany and the US (Harrasser, 2009; 2013; compare Herschbach, 1997; Kienitz, 2008; also Chapter 6). Initially, this strengthened the position of craft-based limb makers whose work was now viewed as being of national importance. The wars gave rise to guilds and professional associations such as the Artificial Limb Manufacturers Association (ALMA)[5] in the US (est. 1917; Hanger, Jr., 1956) and the *Reichsinnungsverband der Orthopädiemechaniker und Bandagisten* in Germany (est. 1923; Dittmer, 2018, p. 3).[6] These associations greatly increased the exchange of knowledge among limb makers and led to the establishment or strengthening of professional standards and education programs, leading to the birth of a *craft-based mode of inscription*. At this time, virtually all elements of the prosthesis, whether foot, hand, joint, or socket, were produced manually in small-scale local workshops and, while specific templates and models existed, skilled craftspeople often introduced variations reflecting their own style or the requirements of individual amputees.

At the same time, the sheer number of amputees, combined with the symbolic and financial importance attributed to their rehabilitation, facilitated the rise of competing modes of representing and inscribing users.[7] The most important of these was the application of engineering principles to prosthetic design and manufacturing, which eventually led to the partial industrialization of the field.[8] Notably, many of the engineers that engaged in prosthetics production had previously worked in different areas and modeled their understanding of prostheses on experiences gained developing industrial machines or weapons of war (Harrasser, 2013b, p. 103).[9] Partly because of that, the engineering approach advanced by organizations such as the *Prüfstelle für Ersatzglieder* in Germany (compare Harrasser, 2009; Hartmann, 1919), or the Artificial Limb Program in the US (Committee on

Artificial Limbs, 1947; Strong, 1954) was based on principles of technology design and manufacturing that were directly opposed to those underpinning the emerging craft-based profession.

Both approaches involved a different set of *production devices*. Craftspeople aimed to provide prostheses to the large number of wartime amputees by expanding tool-based production in a decentralized system of small-scale workshops. By contrast, the engineering approach centered on machine-based mass production within an industrial-scale factory system. These differences in the organization of production were linked to two distinct forms of representing and inscribing users in technology design, each of which involved the use of specific *inscription devices*. The craft approach favored a skill- and experience-based inscription process that relied on the iterative adaptation of human body and technology and was therefore dependent on sustained interaction between designer and user, with physicians acting as important mediators, particularly in the early phases after an amputation. Engineers, on the other hand, aimed to standardize prosthetic design based on the scientific study of human anatomy and movement. They were aided in this endeavor by the availability of unparalleled quantities of human measurement data. These, in turn, were the result of advances in measurement technology (e.g., stroboscopy, photography) and their frantic application in the military[10] as well as Tayloristic industrial organizations[11] (see Chapter 6).

These discrepancies between the modes of inscription favored by craftspeople and engineers respectively had remarkable consequences for the kinds of user roles constructed. Engineers developing limbs for industrial mass production stressed standardization and mechanical functionality. In the name of reproducibility and efficiency of production, the limbs were abstracted from the bodies of individual amputees, while the emphasis on mechanical functionality often led them to abandon anthropomorphic shapes altogether. For instance, engineers in WWI Germany were torn over the question of whether upper limb prostheses should be designed as replacement-arms (*Ersatzarm*) or arm-replacements (*Armersatz*) (compare Kienitz, 2008, pp. 174–176; Schlesinger, 1919, p. 322). The former would be modeled after the shape and function of the human body; the latter were conceived of as mechanical tools that did not resemble human physiology but were designed for specific tasks, sometimes directly interfacing the human body with industrial machines (see Figure 4.1). The designs of artisans, by contrast, aimed to imitate the unique shapes and outer appearance of their wearer's body as closely as possible (see Figure 4.2). Primarily working with hand tools, they avoided mechanical features in favor of natural form and symmetry between limbs. However, as described by Kienitz (2008, pp. 163–164), their products were often rejected as impractical, or merely ornamental "Sunday hands" (ibid.) by engineers and physicians alike, contributing to the relative decline in influence of the craft-based mode of user inscription.

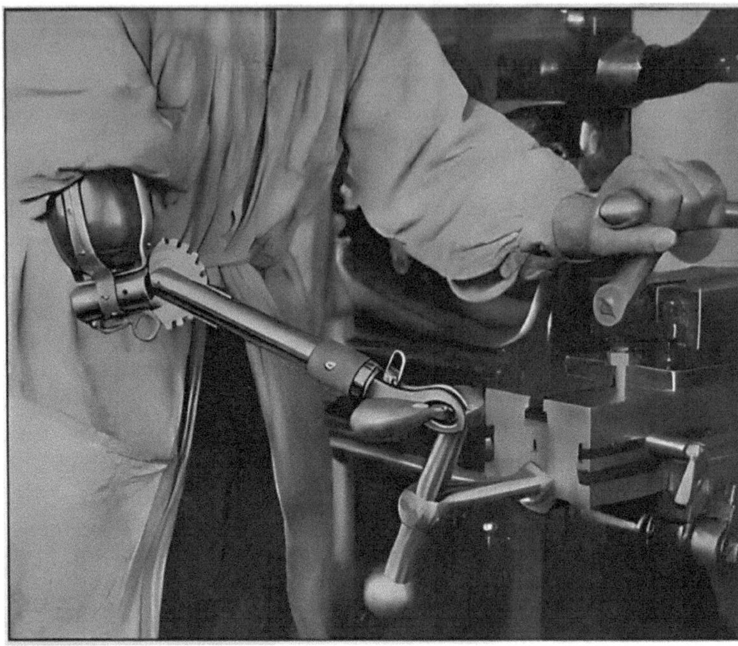

Figure 4.1 An upper limb prosthesis developed by engineers. Reprinted by permission from Springer Nature Customer Service Centre GmbH from: Schlesinger (1919, p. 488).

The prosthetics industry has therefore since its inception been marked by a peculiar professional struggle over how to represent users in the design and manufacturing of prostheses. While craftspeople, like orthopedic mechanics and truss-makers, favored a skill- and experience-centered process of custom production, engineers favored a process of standardization and mass production. The relative influence of these two modes of inscription varied over time, each extending over specific parts of the product. Yet, with the progressive industrialization of the field, the influence of the craft-based approach was increasingly circumscribed. Whereas until the early 20th century, craftspeople would be tasked with constructing the entire prosthesis, by the middle of the century they were procuring most components from large manufacturers, resulting in the division of labor characteristic of the field today. Regarding what is now known as *fit components*, the role of the craftsperson was, with very few exceptions, reduced to choosing and assembling. The *socket* presented one exception: as it forms the interface between fit components and the human body, it proved much more difficult to standardize and remained outside the scope of industrial production. As such, the design and production of this crucial component have remained a craft-based process to this day.

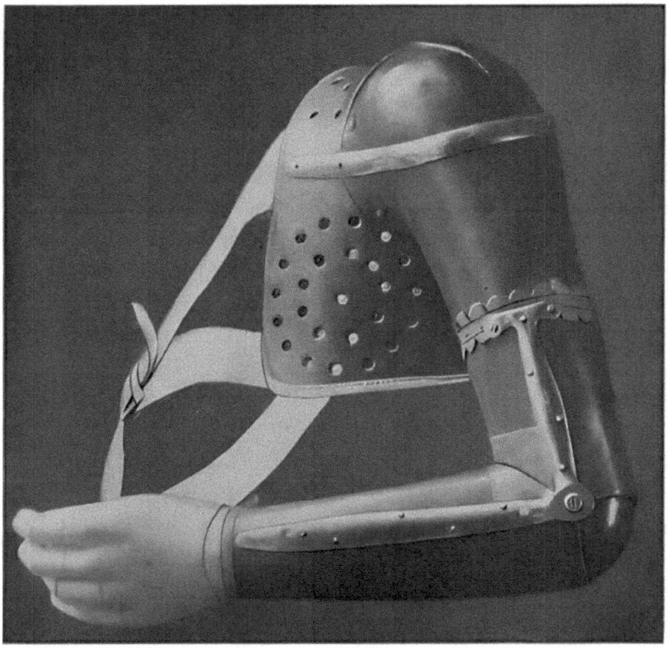

Figure 4.2 An upper limb prosthesis built by a craftsperson. Reprinted by permission from Springer Nature Customer Service Centre GmbH from: Nicolai (1919, p. 696).

Of course, there have been many changes in both socket and fit component design over the past hundred years. Sockets are no longer made from wood, but from thermoplastics and occasionally carbon fiber. Prosthetic hands, joints, and legs were similarly advanced, including the introduction of microprocessor technology to allow for better control and intricate articulation of artificial limbs. On the organizational side, the 1990s saw a degree of centralization, with industrial manufacturers buying prosthetic clinics and workshops and hiring craftspeople to work in central manufacturing facilities. However, the professional division of labor—associating mass-produced fit components with engineering and custom-made sockets with craftsmanship—remained intact and was further entrenched materially and institutionally. In the 1960s, standard adapters for connecting sockets and fit components were introduced. These further disentangled design interdependencies between professions, by materially defining the interfaces between component classes and establishing a truly modular product architecture. Moreover, engineers and prosthetists have established different education programs, work in different kinds of organizations (e.g., local shops and multinational corporations), and face different sets of regulations with regards to their products. In what follows I will reconstruct in finer grain the contemporary inscription processes typical of these two groups.

4.1.1 Sockets: In the Hands of the Prosthetist

It is a widely accepted view in the field that the single most important component of both upper and lower limb prostheses is the socket, which forms the interface between the device and the user's body.[12] It is the socket that is most critical for wearing comfort and an uncomfortable socket is among the most common reasons for people to abandon their prosthetic aid. It is therefore crucial to design sockets that are uniquely tailored to their user's anatomy. The manufacturing of sockets is one of the central tasks of professional prosthetists and technicians, who go about this challenge using a craft-based approach. There are different classes of sockets, and specific styles of designing and manufacturing have developed within each school and firm. Yet, despite a degree of routinization, prosthetists emphasize that "every stump is unique and requires unique care" (Fieldnote, 2018-05-17, own translation). The ability to deviate from standard processes is therefore considered the mark of a skilled artisan as designing a custom socket to fit an individual user's unique anatomy is often accomplished through a lengthy process of trial and error. The most illustrative example of the craft-based inscription process is the so-called plaster cast method. This technique, which is considered by many to be the "gold standard" (Fieldnote, 2016-05-06) of socket design, is taught to every prosthetist during vocational training.

4.1.1.1 Translating Limbs into Plaster

Following the sequence of translations involved in the plaster cast method clearly demonstrates how the body of an individual amputee is transformed into a unique inscription that forms the basis of craft-based manufacturing. Besides casting the socket itself, activities at the prosthetic workshop involve other kinds of inscription, too. Upon meeting a new client, prosthetists interview them regarding their experience with wearing prostheses and their goals for using a prosthesis. They take a range of measurements and note them down in several forms. Yet, when it comes to determining the form of the socket itself, prosthetists usually rely on their manual skills to inscribe the amputee's anatomical features into plaster.

When crafting a socket, the prosthetist begins by taking a plaster impression of the user's residual limb. To do that, a parting agent is applied to the limb (or it is wrapped in plastic foil) and a sock is pulled over it.[13] Importantly, the clinician touches the limb and moves it into a slightly flexed position to locate soft tissues, pain zones, bones, tendons, and so forth, while indicating these things on the sock using a transferrable marker. S/he then cuts a number of plaster bandages, soaks them in water, and applies them around the residuum. The prosthetist does not merely capture the limb's outer shape but models the plaster to capture important features of its inner structure such as bones and tendons. After the plaster has set, the cast, including the marked sock on the inside, is removed. The prosthetist may do some quick remodeling with additional plaster bandages and have the patient try on the impression. If this so-called *negative* conforms nicely around the leg, the prosthetist will take it to the workshop. There it is transformed into a *positive model* by filling it with liquid plaster. To be able to mount the model for later modifications, a metal rod is embedded in the center of the cast. Once the plaster has hardened (see Figure 4.3), the model is mounted on a vice and the negative model is removed. In this process, the original markings are transferred from the sock on the inside of the negative to the surface of the positive. This leaves the prosthetist with a marked block of solid plaster that corresponds roughly to the shape of the user's residual limb.

In the sequence of actions described here, the prospective user's anatomy has been inscribed into plaster. This is to say, the activities performed by the prosthetist have established a chain of equivalence leading from the residual limb of one specific person to its representation in the form of a plaster cast.[14] The subsequent production process is based on this peculiar inscription alone, so that the person it represents may leave and return to the clinic only to try on the final product.

Figure 4.3 Four positive casts are left to dry alongside a cast that will be used for an orthosis (left). Own photograph.

Figure 4.4 A rectified positive model of a socket. Own photograph.

4.1.1.2 From User Representation to Custom Production

Once the prospective user has left, the logic of the processes shifts from one of representation to one of manufacturing. In some places, this shift is marked by a change in setting and personnel, as the process moves from a clinical setting to the workshop, and may be performed by a technician rather than a certified prosthetist. In either case, from an action net perspective, the major translation involved in the manufacturing of the socket is the one between the representation of the amputee's body—the plaster cast—and the shape of the actual product.

Guided by experience and the marks on the plaster model, the prosthetist rectifies the shape of the positive cast by adding material in areas that are supposed to be tighter and removing material where the fit is to be slightly looser.[15] Once s/he is happy with the shape, the model is sanded down until it is perfectly smooth (Figure 4.4). When I asked how they determined the best shape for their users, prosthetists often referred to "the magic in their hands," hinting at the importance of experience and embodied knowledge in the process. Indeed, the rectification of the plaster cast is among the steps in the process that demands the greatest experience and skill. It is here that the prosthetist decides on the inner shape of the future socket and thus determines how it will relate to the wearer's body.

After the plaster model has been rectified, the final product is manufactured in a vacuum-forming process referred to as "pulling the socket" (Figure 4.5). For this step, the plaster impression is mounted on a special rack. The prosthetist (or the technician) will take a sheet of the desired material, often fiberglass or thermoformable plastic, and heat it in an oven until it softens. The flexible sheet is then placed over the rectified positive,

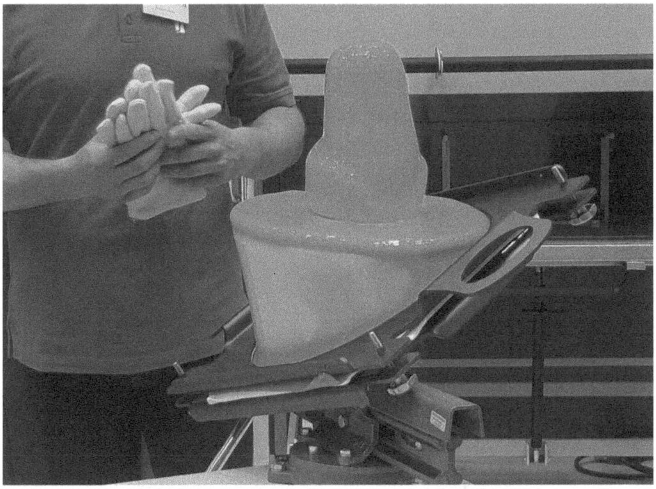

Figure 4.5 A socket being "pulled" to demonstrate a new material at a trade fair in Leipzig, Germany. Own photograph.

patted down, and sealed at the bottom. The pump included in the rack then sucks out the air between the plaster and the softened sheet, creating a vacuum that "pulls" the material around the cast in a process that was described to me as the equivalent of "producing yoghurt cups in a lot size of one" (Fieldnote, 2016-05-06). After the material has hardened, the plaster cast is removed and, if possible, retained for possible reuse. The socket is then sanded and may be carefully adjusted using a heat gun. The prosthetist may also laminate the socket with carbon fiber to add strength or decorative fabrics to satisfy the requests of individual clients (Figure 4.6). Finally, the necessary adapters are added to allow for the connection of the socket to the rest of the device.

As a result of this process of craft-based custom production, the user representation inscribed into each socket corresponds to one specific person and may reflect parts of that person's identity. As the socket is further refined, it may be adapted to incorporate further user feedback. Overall, then, the action net underlying socket production represents users as individuals. Even though the process itself follows a relatively routinized order, it ascribes to each user a unique character.

4.1.1.3 User Inscription in Custom Production

The process of socket design and manufacturing exemplifies the inscription process associated with custom production. Most importantly, the action net underlying socket design can be described as a series of actions that translate the features of one unique person into a custom product. The process configures a one-to-one relationship between an embodied individual

Figure 4.6 Many sockets are laminated to their wearer's specifications. While this process often aims at the imitation of individual complexion, other expressions of user roles and identities are possible. Own photograph.

and the user representation inscribed into the product. These inscriptions do, however, rarely construct more widely shared user *roles*, as the same socket would not be useful to any other person. When new socket designs are reproduced elsewhere, considerations usually pertain to questions of style or ease of manufacturing (e.g., how to wrap the plaster bandages, or which materials to use) and almost never aim beyond the deeply ingrained idea that each socket is unique and made for a unique user.

The second point to note is that the inscription process is performed *manually*. The prosthetist's "magic hands" function as the primary inscription and production device along with a range of tools and simple contraptions. For this reason, the fit between socket and user-body, the single most important criterion of the artifact's usability, largely depends on the skill of the craftsperson. Professional skill is involved in every translation described above from imprinting the user's anatomy into plaster to manufacturing a product based on that representation. The inscriptions produced by the plaster cast method simply cannot be reproduced precisely; they differ between workshops, prosthetists, and individual performances—a fact that deeply irritated many of the engineers I talked to and frequently inspired hopes of future standardization or partial automation.

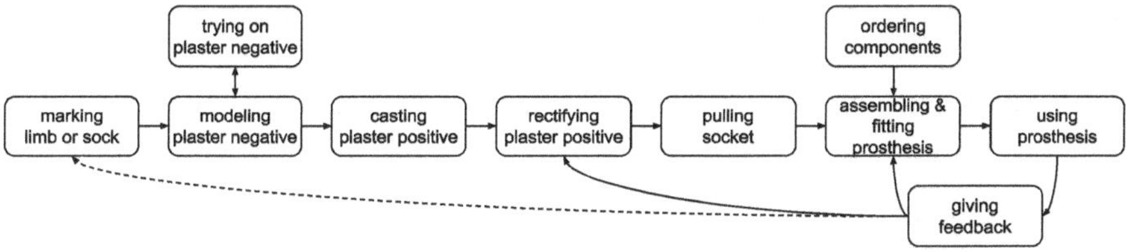

Figure 4.7 Craft-based custom production of prosthetic sockets. Own figure.

Despite the singularity of the inscription process, patterns of user construction do emerge in craft-based custom production. These are due to the institutional order of the industry as well as the patterns of people's lives that lead to specific kinds of limb loss in the first place. For instance, while the factors contributing to a prosthetist's skill are notoriously hard to determine, they are not entirely individual but shaped by professional training, patterned by levels of certification, as well as differences between university- and apprenticeship-based schemes. The accumulation of experience, too, depends on the overall pattern of action. For instance, prosthetists in the US or Germany, unless they are highly specialized, would see far more lower limb than upper limb amputees, simply because lower limb loss is far more common (Baumgartner & Botta, 2008, p. 16). According to upper limb specialists in the industry, this may occasionally lead to the erroneous application of principles of socket design in legs to the upper extremity, making for a less-than-ideal fit.[16]

The patterns in the private and collective lives of people with limb loss are also important factors for determining what appears to be a purely individual fit between socket and user. Specific shapes and lengths of the residuum require greater skill from the craftsperson, as do possible neuroma or sharp bony overgrowth. Yet, the likelihood of these things depends on the kind of amputation itself, the risk of which is socially patterned. In North America and Europe, most amputations of the lower limb are due to cardiovascular diseases. They can thus be planned and performed by a professional surgeon, leading to residual limbs that tend to be relatively easy to fit. By contrast, traumatic amputations through war, landmines, or accidents will result in stumps that professionals find more challenging. The user landscape of custom production is further shaped by the tendency of some human bodies to change more rapidly or frequently than others, as prosthesis users gain or lose weight, grow up, or become pregnant.

In summary, the inscription process associated with custom production generates a multitude of user identities in which no two users are alike. Each socket is custom-made for an identifiable individual, based on their anatomy and incorporating their feedback. Yet, recognizable differences between categories of users still emerge due to the professional and regulatory order against which inscription occurs and due to the patterns of people's individual and collective lives that underlie bodily development and limb loss. As a result, some sockets may fit their users well, while others might cause pain or skin abrasion or be too tight or too loose to wear at all.

4.1.2 Fit Components: Mobilizing the Average User

Most parts of contemporary prostheses are so-called fit components. This category includes components such as hands, feet, or knee joints that give the prosthetic limb its specific mechanical functionality; it also includes the dozens of screws, adapters, pylons, and so forth that integrate the device into a functioning whole. Fit components are the dominion of engineers, and the inscription process associated with them differs markedly from the process previously described for sockets. A first difference is that there is usually little interaction between technology designers and potential users, and engineers rely, often begrudgingly, on a range of mediators to speak for their prospective users. A second discrepancy arises from the difference in production devices. Due to the fact that fit components are manufactured in large quantities using industrial machinery, the inscription process emphasizes the reduction of differences between user roles and their aggregation into larger categories that represent entire "populations" instead of single individuals.

4.1.2.1 Inscribing Absent Users

During the development of new fit components, prospective users are rarely present as embodied individuals. Instead, I found that engineers typically work with a range of highly abstracted user representations that have been constructed and aggregated long before they ever reach the research and development (R&D) department.[17] While there are doubtlessly many different sources from which engineers draw their knowledge about users, I argue that the action nets underpinning them share a common structure. On the one hand, representational practices aim at the *aggregation of user roles* rather than at the detailed representation of individual users. On the other hand, the translation between the activities of users and engineers involves *additional mediators* that are trusted to speak for potential users. These points can be demonstrated by examining three chains of translation involving intermediation by prosthetists, governments, and competing manufacturers.

PROSTHETISTS AS TRANSLATORS: RELYING ON CRAFTSPEOPLE

One of the reasons for embodied users' absence during the design of fit components can be found in the structure of the prosthetics industry. Industrial manufacturers do not sell directly to people with limb differences, but to prosthetic clinics and workshops where the prosthesis is assembled and fitted to the amputee. Local prosthetists thus mediate between component development and situated use practices, meaning that engineers lack direct access to potential users. Instead, they must rely on craftspeople to speak for their users, despite the fact that they otherwise tend to be skeptical of the latter's representational practices.[18]

Large firms typically collect feedback and survey data from prosthetists on a regular basis. When I interviewed the director of research of one such company, he described the process as follows:

> We've got this mechanism that [the members of the sales department] go out and get this feedback. And, you know, the prosthetists are definitely not end-users, but I think they do have a good feel for, you know, [...] what do my own patients tell me? [...] I don't know that it's a perfect surrogate for talking directly to amputees, but it is the thing that we have access to. And getting access to the amputees is a little bit more difficult.
>
> (interview, director of research at industrial company, 2017-09-09)

As becomes clear in this excerpt, the process of representing users in the design of new fit components is predicated on the input of prosthetists who act as spokespersons for prospective users. And they are not the only mediators involved. The collected data is further transformed by the organization itself, as the sales department aggregates and analyzes it to inform decisions about product development. For example, the same interviewee talked about how the aggregated results of a large-scale survey informed a decision of their R&D group regarding the battery life of a new socket cooling device:

> So the surveys will say, [...] you know, what do we do for the battery? Is it okay to have it be removable? [...] If it is not removable, how many hours would it have to last? Does it have to go 16 hours? Or could we get away with eight? [H]ow long between swapping out batteries would you [the prosthetist, DS] think your patients are willing to go? So, this is great because for the most recent survey we got 402 responses. Now, that's all the US. But we get not just Massachusetts, we get guys in San Antonio and Oregon, so all over the States, which is a nice tool for us.
>
> (interview, director of research at industrial manufacture, 2017-09-09)

What becomes quite clear in this example is that before user representations enter the R&D department, they are inscribed and re-inscribed several times in a cascadic process that reduces differences between users (e.g., in Massachusetts and San Antonio) and consolidates them into homogeneous categories amenable to statistical analysis. Users tell prosthetists about their experience with using prostheses, prosthetists then fill out a questionnaire provided by the sales department, which then aggregates the data collected from hundreds of prosthetists all over the US. As described in the above excerpt, in the design of fit components, the quality of a useful inscription is not its correspondence to the characteristics of one potential user, but its ability to represent large aggregates of users that engineers often refer to as "markets" or "populations."

Governments as Translators: Development Grants and User Representation

Another source of user representation is development grants. These are offered by external funding bodies, usually governments, with vested interests in the provision of prosthetic care for highly specific groups of people. Hence, grant solicitations usually come with a general description of the device to be developed and the group of users for which it is intended. For instance, consider the following goal statement:

> Develop and demonstrate a prosthetic foot that provides normalized biomechanics and function, with no external power requirements, for patients with below the knee amputation performing military relevant tasks.
>
> (Small Business Innovation Research: https://www.sbir.gov/sbirsearch/detail/1188821, accessed 2018-09-19)

As in the previous example, users are not represented as individuals but are aggregated into categories such as "patients with below the knee amputation performing military relevant tasks." However, in the case of grants, the mediator translating between the activities of using and engineering is not the prosthetist, but an organization directly involved in funding R&D. The group of users translated here will not be determined by the accumulated experience of the prosthetist, but by the mechanisms of a granting agency, which may overrepresent particular groups of amputees. As in the case of the US Department of Defense soliciting devices for military personnel with lower limb loss, the imagined and actual activities of these people may differ drastically from those of most other groups. Development grants will then represent some users and not others. This is of major significance for an understanding of the co-construction of users and technology in prosthetics since grants make up a significant portion of overall R&D funding.

One example of such biases is the DEKA arm, named after the firm originally charged with developing the device. It is also dubbed the Luke Arm for its highly advanced functionality reminiscent of the hand prosthesis worn by Jedi Knight Luke Skywalker in George Lucas' Star Wars. The Defense Advanced Research Projects Agency (DARPA) invested more than 100 million dollars into the development of the DEKA system, which was intended for veterans returning from the Iraq war. This staggering investment, one of the largest in the history of prosthetics, yielded an extraordinarily sophisticated device, which was represented as one of the industry's major innovations during the centennial exhibition of the American Orthotic and Prosthetic Association (AOPA). The display read as follows:

> This prosthetic system utilizes a series of electrodes capable of reading muscle movement so that a wearer feels as though the appendage is being naturally operated by the brain. This system can handle fine motor operations like picking one grape from a bunch and bringing it to a person's mouth. Vibrations generated by the prosthetic device can tell a person if they are gripping fruit, keys or some other item too hard.
>
> (AOPA centennial exhibition, 2017, Las Vegas)

The DEKA arm thus promises to be highly functional, but that functionality does not reflect the use practices of all upper limb amputees. First of all, the various batteries and motors that allow for the arm's marvelous dexterity make it quite heavy. Second, mastery of the device depends on training the muscles that are tapped for electrical signals. While these constraints pose less of a challenge for young military veterans, they might be more challenging for other groups such as elderly or child users. Third, the continued function of this advanced prosthesis depends on the availability of electricity for charging the batteries as well as regular access to spare parts and a skilled prosthetist. These are just some of the reasons why it would be impractical to amputees who live in places where they cannot meet these conditions (see Chapter 5). Lastly, the device is so expensive that insurers don't tend to cover its cost for civilians. In the end, the category of users inscribed into the Luke Arm is so narrow that it becomes impractical for the vast majority of people with upper limb differences.

Competitors as Translators: Me-Too-Products

A third important source of user representations in fit component design is the pre-existing product landscape. Companies routinely scan the products developed by competitors as well as the insurers' decisions to pay for them. Once a manufacturing firm conducts the clinical studies necessary to convince large insurers to cover a given product, that device—along with the user roles it helps to construct—may become the benchmark for further product development efforts. A good example of that mechanism was provided by an engineer reporting on the development of a mechatronic foot-ankle.

> Power Comp (a pseudonym, DS) came up with the Power Foot (also a pseudonym, DS), which is a microprocessor foot-ankle. They invested

> all their own money, probably some [...] government money too, [...] in creating this foot-ankle. They fit it, they gave it to patients, they said it provides these values. The Medicare system, the government medical system here in the United States said: 'Yes we see the value and we will reimburse. We will pay for that device at a rate of about 15.000 $.' So, all of a sudden, as soon as that happens, everybody who hasn't spent any time thinking about that says: 'Wait a minute! If I make one of those things, people pay me 15.000 $ for that. [...].' So, the first microprocessor foot-ankle was released in 2008. CMS [Center for Medicare and Medicaid Services, DS] said they would code for it in 2010 and by 2012 there were four new devices on the market.
>
> (interview, mechanical engineer, 2017-12-01)

The so-called "me-too-products" described here would aim to provide a similar device at a lower price or to improve on the functionality of the existing product. In the first case, R&D efforts attempt to copy the user inscriptions made by another company (e.g., by means of "reverse engineering"), in the second one they take them as a starting point. As in the two previous examples, engineers do not draw the inspiration for their designs directly from embodied users. Instead, they build on the design work of other companies. This process of re-inscription may lead to the development of entrenched innovation trajectories. Where this happens, an ever-expanding range of similar and improved products will become available for specific groups of people, while others go underrepresented.

Overall, the three mechanisms of inscription described in this section demonstrate that there are various ways through which user representations enter the engineering process associated with fit components. In spite of this diversity, from the point of view of action net analysis, all these processes share two common features. First, in all of them, user representation involves *intermediation* by one or more other actors, including prosthetists, governments, and competing manufacturers, but also insurance organizations and a firm's own marketing department. Such intermediation is prone to steer the chain of translation into specific directions, even as the processes involved usually remain intransparent from the point of view of engineers. Second, all of the chains of translation described here involve forms of *aggregation* that lead from a diversity of people and practices toward simple numbers, statements, or papers (compare Latour, 1990). In the context of user construction, the specific effect of this process is *to construct representations not of users as individuals but of users as populations.*[19]

4.1.2.2 Scaling Production, Standardizing User Roles

I now shift my attention to the processes through which engineers translate the user representations that arrive in their laboratories and R&D

departments, into design specifications. Following the action nets leading from the decision to develop a product to the point at which that product is manufactured means tracing processes of translation that link a specific user group, say geriatric users with lower limb loss, to choices about sizes, materials, or functions of specific products, such as prosthetic hands or feet. How do engineers know how large to make a foot? How do they know which forces it will need to withstand? How do they represent the preferences of "geriatric patients"? In answering questions such as these, engineers tend to refer to both pre-existing standards and to considerations linked to technologies of mass production.[20]

Reliance on Standards

Engineers' reliance on standards is exemplified by their use of *anthropometric tables*. These tables are collections of all kinds of average measures of the human anatomy broken down by categories such as sex or age. When designing a prosthetic hand for a given population, engineers may refer to such tables to determine things like the distributions of hand width or finger length. Even though such measures have usually been collected for other purposes, in other times and places, they are taken as unproblematic representations of users and often no additional investigation is conducted. One engineer, when asked how she determined the sizes of new devices, replied:

> So, if I needed to know about the sizes of the body or typical distribution of finger lengths or hand sizes or leg lengths or weights, I can go to these government data sets of anthropometrics [...] Often in this country, it's from the military. We have all kinds of standardized charts for people's size distribution that we can use, statistics to determine [...] what the typical sizes are.
>
> (interview, design engineer in a small manufacturing company, 2018-07-11)

Recasting this practice in terms of user inscription, we can say that the user representations drawn from the various sources described in the previous section are merged with yet another source of highly aggregated representations. This operation adds additional information, couched in terms of standard distributions, to the population model of users that has already been established at this point.

Prescribed *testing procedures*, including both norms and physical test stands, are a further source of standardized user representations. Being classified as a medical product, each prosthetic fit component must undergo such testing prior to being approved for sale by regulatory agencies such as the Food and Drug Administration (FDA). For example, prosthetic feet are developed in accordance with the International Organization for Standardization's (ISO) standard number 22675, which describes a cycle testing procedure for simulating the forces such a device would be subjected to during walking. Such testing procedures thus include codifications of average users that present the basis for the design of physical test stands, which quite literally *automate* the expected use of a prosthesis in accordance with the standard. As in the previous example, the inscriptions relevant to the design of fit components correspond to entire populations of users, represented as readymade categories. They are the result of long chains of translation in which people are transformed into numbers, that are aggregated into averages, that are, in turn, objectified in the form of tables or test rigs. When engineers use such objects to inform their design decisions, they end up inscribing standardized user representations into their products.

Fitting Users to Machines

A final type of translation that occurs in determining the specifications for prosthetic fit components is directly linked to manufacturing. This is the further adaptation of aggregated user representations to the material requirements and institutionalized practices surrounding production devices tailored to mass production. Whereas prosthetic sockets are custom-made, fit components are designed to be produced in large quantities using production devices such as injection molding or metal casting.[21] In my interviews, it became clear that such technologies had taken on a normative character in several of the largest firms operating in the field. They had become so deeply ingrained in a net of taken-for-granted practices that it was difficult for the people working with them to conceive of viable alternatives. In particular, representational practices that aggregated potential users into populations were closely linked to, and justified by, the availability of technologies of mass production and the economic imperatives linked to them.

The concept of "economies of scale" marked the most common way in which user representations were transformed to allow for efficient manufacturing rather than the other way around. When asked about possible alternatives to standardization offered by the implementation of 3D printing, interviewees reminded me that mass production made sense economically, since it allowed for economies of scale, in which the price of a product is related to its lot size. In other words, the more units made, the cheaper each individual unit will be. To explain this concept, practitioners repeatedly linked it to the technology of injection molding. In this process, a molten material, typically some type of thermoplastic, is injected into a preformed mold and left to harden to yield the product. Since the process of making the initial mold is very time consuming and requires extensive development effort, large financial investment is needed. By contrast, the costs associated with using the mold repeatedly are only marginal. This is why, with production technologies like injection molding, the key to economic success is believed to be increasing lot sizes and reusing the same mold as often as possible. Further following this line of argument, the easiest way to guarantee sufficient lot sizes was to reduce the number of product variants in dimensions such as size or color. Accordingly, in a world molded around mass production, it is thought unviable to make prosthetic components to fit the preferences of *just one user*. Instead, designing for economies of scale means making the same product for a large number of people and covering the full population with as few variations as possible. The effect of this logic is to ascribe the same role to as many people as possible to allow for efficient production. As one engineer put it in an offhand remark: "There are always exceptions. But there are always averages, too" (Fieldnote, 2017-09-18).

4.1.2.3 User Inscription in Mass Production

From the point of view of industrial user construction, the foregoing examples make at least three aspects of user inscription in prosthetic fit components pertinent. The first characteristic of the action net is that it involves no direct link between the use of prosthetic devices and the activities of design and development (see Figure 4.8). Whereas in socket production, potential users enter the design process as embodied individuals, engineers rarely have direct access to the people for whom they design. Instead, they know their users through inscriptions generated in chains of translation that involve several *mediators*, each with their own agenda and procedures.

The second decisive point is that these mediators *aggregate* the users they represent. Prosthetists base their answers to a company's survey on years of experience with hundreds of amputees. Governments are clearly more concerned with large groups than individuals. Even the clinical studies conducted by industrial firms themselves require aggregation to convince anyone. Moreover, wherever the information originally came from, it will be further aggregated by marketing or other departments that translate between the activities constituting the organization and those that transpire in its constructed environment. Consequently, at the time they are taken up in development practice, user representations are already aggregated to the point where they refer to entire "populations" or "market segments."

A third notable point is that, while engineers are often intensely skeptical of the idea of the prosthetists' "magic hands," user inscription in engineering is similarly oriented by the prevalent production devices, although this connection is legitimated in economic rather than mythical terms. The *normative character* of industrial production technology becomes clear in the observation that, when challenged about prevalent practices of user representation, engineers often begin their argument for standardization with the material and economic necessities of a specific production technology. In this way, the connection between the aggregation of user representations and the reliance on technologies of mass production is deeply institutionalized in engineering practices relating to prosthetic fit components.

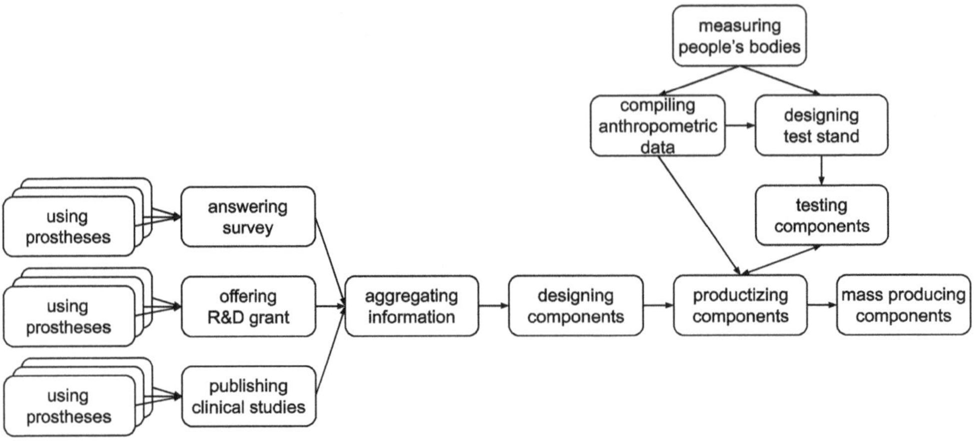

Figure 4.8 Inscription in processes of mass production relies on intermediation and aggregation.

The result of the inscription process described here (see Figure 4.8) is that thoroughly engineered and tested prosthetic components become available at a massive scale. Each component is inscribed with a relatively broad category of potential users, which means that individual differences are glossed over. Some people may be well represented by these categories, but others will invariably be situated at the margins. Even though the range of products is more diverse in some areas (e.g., because of the development of me-too-products), the force of this "distribution of the conventional" (Star, 1991) is generally felt most clearly by people who do, for whatever reason, not fit the constructed averages of fit component design. For instance, most bionic hands come in three or four different sizes. Since hand sizes and shapes of actual people differ beyond being "small," "medium," or "large," most recipients will end up with two differently sized hands (Figure 4.9). Similarly, foot shells for prosthetic feet usually come in only two or three different skin tones. Users with different complexion, will therefore end up with mismatched feet, unless they can afford an expensive custom-made foot shell.

The process of user construction in the design of fit components differs markedly from the one described for prosthetic sockets. Both cases can be understood as processes of translation in which potential users are transformed into inscriptions, which are then transformed into product specifications. However, as a result of the different action nets involved, the two processes construct very differently patterned user landscapes. As I have shown, both forms of inscription are deeply institutionalized, interlinking with professional routines and organizational contexts as much as with material settings at workshops and R&D departments. In both cases, the prevailing production devices, hands and tools on the one side, large-scale machines on the other, have taken on a normative character. They have

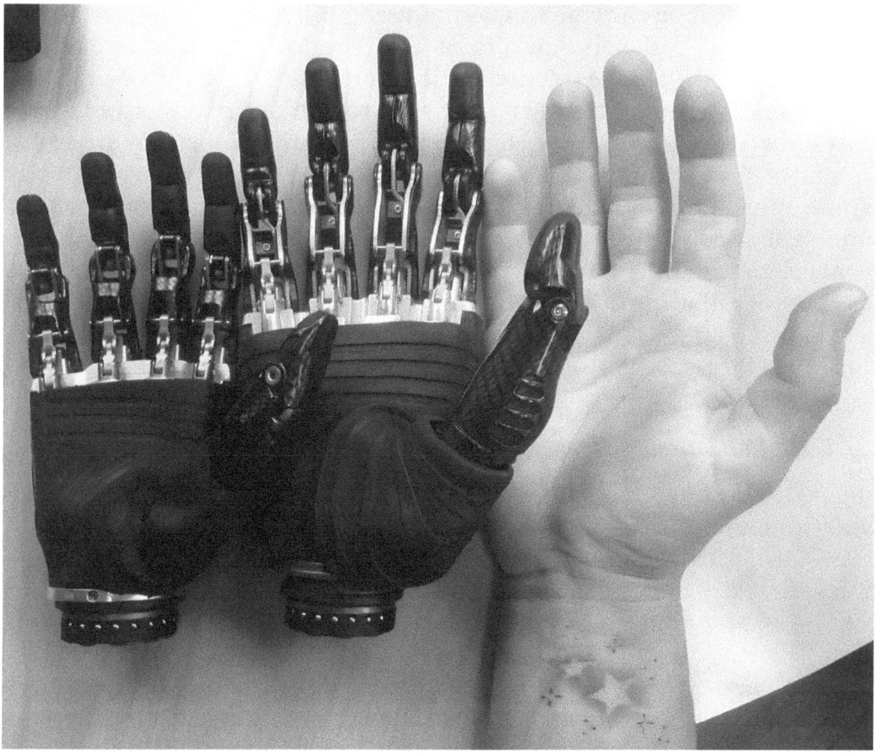

Figure 4.9 A small and medium version of a popular bionic hand prosthesis compared to the hand size of an actual user. Photograph courtesy of Philipp-Asmus Barluschke (Barluparts3D).

become linked to institutionalized ways of designing and manufacturing a specific kind of prosthetic component. In acting as mediators in action nets of user construction, production devices clearly shape the patterns in which user roles may emerge. They also have become integral parts of the identities of both engineers and prosthetists. For these reasons, the implementation of a new set of production devices may appear hopeless, undesirable, or outright dangerous. Yet, this is exactly what has been happening in the prosthetics industry.

4.2 3D Printing as an Opportunity for Renegotiating Inscription Practices

The introduction of 3D printing has led to changes in the ways users are inscribed into prosthetic sockets and fit components. Yet, the effects of 3D printing were not fully determined by the technology itself. When digital fabrication was first introduced to prosthetics in the 1980s, it did not have any major effect on the construction of users. Instead, the different groups of professional designers interpreted the new production technology in accordance with their respective institutionalized practices. When digital technologies were adopted at all, it was the technology that was adapted to existing action nets of user construction rather than the other way around. It was only as 3D printing was woven into new patterns of organizing that an opportunity arose for renegotiating the prevalent institutional order underpinning user construction. New groups like start-ups and the maker movement began to use digital fabrication in ways that resonated with the vested interests of either prosthetists or engineers. As alliances formed between new entrants and established groups of designers, the institutional order was called into question and parts of the user landscape started to change.

4.2.1 Digitalization Without Reorganization

Digital fabrication is not new, nor is it new to prosthetics. Early experiments with Computer Aided Design and Computer Aided Manufacturing (CAD/CAM), which can be viewed as precursors to the current wave of digitalization in the field, date back to the 1970s. By the late 80s and early 90s, CAD/CAM was becoming a commercially viable option and a growing number of prosthetists adopted 3D scanners, 3D modeling software, and computerized numerical control (CNC) mills into their workflow. The two additive manufacturing techniques most relevant to prosthetics today, *selective laser sintering* (SLS) and *fused deposition modeling* (FDM), were developed in 1986 and 1989 respectively, and both prosthetists and engineers have been experimenting with them for almost as long.[22] Both groups of professionals have been keeping an eye on these technologies, now known as 3D printing, and in more than a few cases tried them out themselves. However, almost all of them found 3D printing wanting in several respects including quality, durability, price, and production time. As a consequence, the technology was only slowly adopted and played a negligible role in the production of commercial products.

The slow adoption of 3D printing was at least partly due to the technology being interpreted in accordance with the field's established action nets of user construction. Both engineers and prosthetists evaluated the usefulness of 3D printing in reference to their ingrained practices. They would only adopt digital technologies, if they helped them to do what they were already doing faster, better, or more efficiently (compare Christensen, 1997). If this was not the case, it was the technology that had to be adapted and not the professionals' practices of representation, and manufacturing.

Early uses of 3D printing in industrial manufacturing nicely illustrate the point. It would be incorrect to say that the established firms were "surprised" by 3D printing. Most of them had been watching the technology for years and almost every large firm in the field had at least a couple of people on staff whose job it was to explore the opportunities it offered. Some firms conducted entire research projects on the viability of digital fabrication. Convinced that 3D printing was the technology of the future, organizations invested time and money into understanding it. However, in all of the tests that engineers recounted to me, they were evaluating the merits of 3D printing based on existing processes and products. In short, engineers, being used to produce standardized fit components, searched for ways to use 3D printing to make *better* standardized fit components. As one engineer who had worked for several of the industry's foremost manufacturing firms put it:

> What I need is a concrete example where [3D printing] creates benefits for the patient. And this is, I think, what is lacking a little bit at the moment. There are many visions, but the visions are not yet far enough developed to show: Here is a breakthrough regarding one of the many problems of prosthetics and orthotics.
>
> (interview, engineer, 2017-01-25, own translation)

Engineers were constantly searching for ways to use 3D printing to make their products lighter, cheaper, or stronger, or to add new functionality to them. However, few, if any, of these solutions were readily forthcoming. Judged against their existing practices and products, virtually all manufacturers decided that 3D printing was "not ready yet" (ibid.).

When 3D printing was adopted at all, it was used to enhance existing processes such as prototyping or tooling. For example, in *rapid* prototyping or *rapid* tooling, instead of adapting the final product, engineers would use digital technologies to produce prototypes faster or make cheaper molds for injection molding. While this use of 3D printing helped industrial manufacturers to speed up development times and reduce costs, they did not initially change much about the processes through which user representations were aggregated and inscribed into products.[23] For this reason, the early implementation of digital fabrication at large manufacturing firms did not lead to the emergence of new user roles.

For prosthetists, the situation was very similar. They too interpreted digital tools in accordance with their own established workflow. Their goal was to use the ability of 3D printing to enhance the custom production of prosthetic sockets. However, when they first started experimenting with technologies like 3D scanning or CAD software in the 1980s, they found that the new inscription and production devices were not compatible with the institutions of craft-based manufacturing. Indeed, most of these technologies had been developed for engineers, and often for design practices of entirely different industries. One software developer with a background in prosthetic craftsmanship recalled those early days saying:

> You had to be half engineer to make it work and your typical clinician has extremely little engineering background. [...] Technology-wise O&P

> [orthotics and prosthetics] is too small to go to [...] design firms and say: 'I want you to build me a scanner that does this and for a certain price point.' We're just too small. Most of our technology used to come [...] from aerospace. Scanning technology comes from the automotive industry. [...]. So, our CAD development has really been predicated on other industries.
>
> (interview, software developer, 2017-09-09)

The main problem with most early CAD/CAM systems was that they disregarded the prosthetists' institutionalized techniques of representing users and inscribing them into their products. Having been developed for engineering components in the automotive or aerospace industry, neither scanners nor CAD software was well suited to facilitate the touching, feeling, and sculpting through which prosthetists represent the bodies of their users. Clearly many craftspeople found it difficult to integrate the new technology into their work, as one of my German interviewees neatly articulated:

> The problem is, I see it in front of me in 2D and I cannot touch it. Someone once said: 'It is only with the heart that one can see rightly.' For prosthetists it is 'one can see rightly only with the hands.' I need to have felt it and only then do I have an idea that I can transfer to the model. [...] That is something I simply cannot do with the screen. The screen is simply something dead to me. I have nothing but the visual information.
>
> (interview, prosthetist, 2016-06-01, own translation)

Interestingly, instead of prosthetists adapting their workflow to facilitate the new technology, it was initially the software that was adapted to the prosthetists and specifically to their way of representing users. The above-quoted software developer explained to me how she went about translating the traditional workflow into the digital world.

> We designed [our software] with the intended user being an orthotist or prosthetist. We use their terminology, we use their thought processes, we don't make it engineering [...]. We want people to feel comfortable of trying to change from hand skills to CAD/CAM. You're taking them out of their comfort zone. And of course, they say: 'It's my hands! My hands!' And that's something we've been battling with for years: 'No, it's not! It's your brain! It's not your hands! You can use your hands on a computer and a keyboard as well, and with the scanner, too [...].' And I tell people, show me how you would do this right now. And then my job is to match it up to how to do it in the software.
>
> (interview, software developer, 2017-09-09)

The degree to which the new digital production technologies have been adapted to prosthetists' traditional methods is best captured by the metaphor of the "digital plaster cast" that is now commonly used to refer to the manipulation of scan data in CAD software. The interfaces, tools, and language of 3D modeling software have been adapted to the work of prosthetists and in some cases, firms even sell digital sculpting tools that give haptic feedback to the prosthetist when she "touches" the digital model. Thus, while some prosthetists did selectively adopt digital technology, this did not involve major changes in the basic premises of the underlying action net. Prosthetists still interacted directly with prospective users, they still represented them with a view to their unique bodily characteristics, and they still relied on manual skill for transforming those representations into custom products.

In summary, even though digital fabrication technologies, including scanning, 3D modeling, CNC milling, and 3D printing have been around for more than 30 years, they did not fundamentally change the institutional order underpinning the inscription practices of engineers and prosthetists. Overall, the adoption of these technologies is better characterized as a slow process of learning and mutual adaptation (Williams et al., 2005). When they were implemented, digital technologies were usually adapted to the established practices of user construction, with the basic structure of the action net remaining unchanged. Engineers still relied on intermediaries and standards to represent whole populations of users, even though they were now using rapid prototyping or tooling technologies. Prosthetists were still performing manual modifications of representations taken off individual users, even though they now applied the "digital plaster cast" technique. The new translational capacities of digital production technology were thus integrated into existing action nets of user construction. It was not until more recently that digital fabrication became involved in new patterns of organizing that grew into a serious challenge to the status quo.

4.2.2 New Patterns of Action, New Users

3D printing became an opportunity for renegotiating the ingrained institutional order when its novel translational capacities were used to weave together new patterns of action. It was around such new processes of user inscription that a host of start-ups, research labs, and open-source communities emerged, and that firms from other industries established a foothold in the prosthetics industry. The analysis that follows will focus on the ways in which these new groups of designers related to the longstanding division of labor in the way users were represented in the industry. The prevalent institutional order tied together engineering, mass production, and fit components on the one hand and craftsmanship, custom production, and sockets on the other. At the same time, new digital production technologies allowed for the creation of new connections between these elements while flexibly aligning with the ingrained practices of one or the other established group of designers. New organizations seized these opportunities to shape genuinely new patterns of inscription that gave rise to new user roles and identities. However, the specific translational mechanisms of digital technologies also introduced new biases into the resulting user landscape, linking new organizations to the lives of highly specific groups of people, such as fashion-conscious young adults or children with congenital limb differences, while steering them away from others.

4.2.2.1 Algorithmic Mass Customization: Turning Craft into Science

3D scanning and modeling has become more and more common in socket design within the last ten to twenty years and has begun to call into question the dominance of the plaster cast method. In the scanning process, the amputee's body is captured with a handheld 3D scanner, or even an iPad sensor, and the digital representation is further modified by using a range of software tools. Yet these technologies are still very much part of a craft-based process relying heavily on the prosthetist's skill at both scanning and modeling. Likewise, production itself is in most cases still done manually, as the digital model is not directly usable for manufacturing. Instead, it is sent to a CNC mill, often located in a central factory (see Chapter 5), which carves a foam model equivalent to the plaster positive (see Section 4.1.1). The prosthetist then uses the manual technique of pulling the socket over the foam model just like s/he would have done using a plaster cast.

While prosthetists interpreted digital tools as a means toward a digital craft, many engineers viewed them as an opportunity to turn socket design into a "science," thereby making it amenable to the representational techniques used in engineering. One of the most prominent efforts in that direction is what Hugh Herr, MIT professor and himself a double amputee, termed "the science of comfort" (conference presentation, 2017-09-07). Herr's idea is to substitute the prosthetist's skilled labor with semi-automated machine-based design and production. In view of the insufficiencies of 3D scanning, a technique that only captures the outer shape of a person's limb, Herr does not want to fall back to the plaster cast method, as doing so would leave user representation dependent on the prosthetist's hand skills. Instead, Herr's strategy is to add to optical scanning techniques a host of other digital inscription devices such as CT scanners and pressure sensors. Combining the data obtained from these machines into a model of what he calls the "digital human" is meant to allow the simulation and analysis of important use scenarios such as donning the socket, walking, or standing. His group aims to develop algorithms that would use these simulations to automatically design a prosthetic socket that would "fit perfectly" and could be readily produced using advanced, multi-material 3D printing.

The vision behind this project, and others like it, is to advance the fit between socket and user by wresting socket design from the hands of the prosthetist that are viewed as all too unreliable inscription devices. Prosthetists would still be involved in the process, yet their role would change from that of a skilled craftsperson mainly concerned with manufacturing to what an interviewee termed a "human measurement expert." Their task would be that of operating digital inscription devices, which link to a semi-automated production process designed by engineers and are amenable to the latters' renderings of the amputee's anatomy. In this particular vision, turning socket design into a science would mean making user representation in sockets the dominion of engineering.

User Inscription in Algorithmic Mass Customization

The visions of technological projects like Herr's "science of comfort" differ markedly from the established practices of inscribing embodied users into prosthetic sockets. While such projects still configure a one-to-one relationship between embodied and inscribed users, the quality of the translation would be independent of the prosthetist's skill, safe for providing measurements of the user's body. The decisive factor in the translation from user representations to the final product is now the *algorithm* programmed by software engineers.

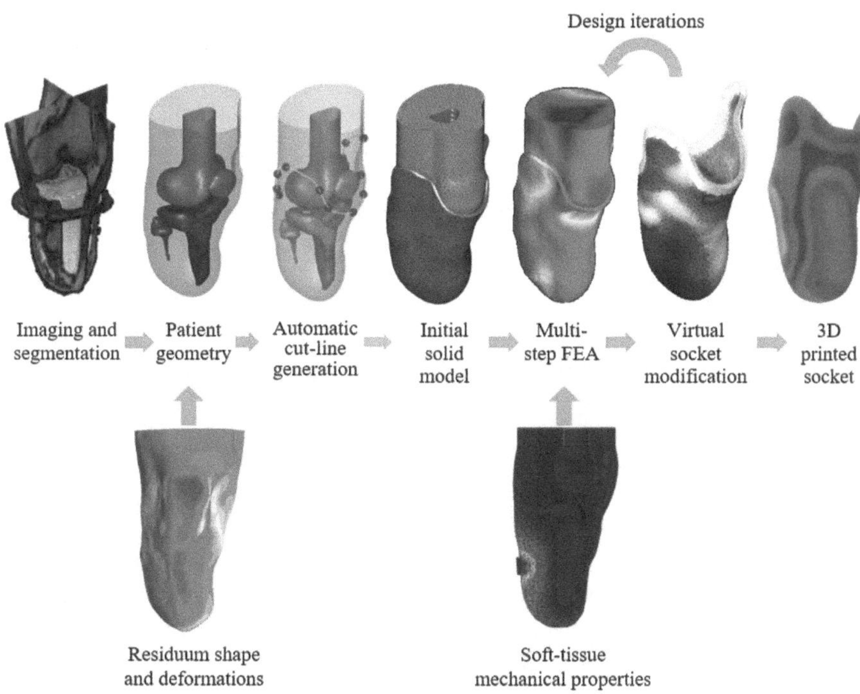

Figure 4.10 Visualization of a possible translation process involved in Herr's science of comfort. © 2022 IEEE. Reprinted, with permission, from Solav et al. (2019, p. 2).

It is still an open question as to what kind of user roles might emerge from this change, as only very few projects like this have been implemented. However, it is worth pointing out that there are a number of important differences between algorithmic mass customization and craft-based custom production. In algorithmic mass customization, even though the resulting product will be unique in each case, the procedure of designing and producing is more thoroughly standardized than in craft-based custom production. Whereas prosthetists may vary (voluntarily or not) the way in which they design sockets, the sequence of actions performed by the algorithm is fully repeatable. The program will be the same for every user and will be based on a standardized model of human anatomy that allows the algorithm to "interpret" the digital inscriptions of a prospective user's body that an operator provides to it. However, a standard process like that, whether performed by hand or by machine, will not work equally well for everyone. The more a person's body deviates from the standard inscribed into the algorithm, the more problems will arise. As a developer of such a program explained for the case of partial hand prostheses, the fit that could be achieved between prosthesis and user body depended on the shape of the limb. Depending on the user's anatomy, the process could fail entirely.

> Partial hands are really complex cases because there are different combinations. Persons can be missing one finger, two fingers, three fingers, three fingers in a row, three fingers sequentially at different heights, each finger at a different height [...]. That makes it really hard to say that it will be fully automatable [...]. Let's say the patient has an amputation for his [whole] hand. Then, most likely, it [the algorithm, DS] could do over 95 percent. But even then [...] the shapes of those [hands] are really different, so it still would have to be overseen [by a prosthetist]. But I would say that good code could definitely achieve somewhere around an efficiency of 80 percent if the template doesn't change. If there are different levels of amputation, different combinations of anatomy, then it's complex [...]. I had some thoughts about that, but at the current point, basically the result is that it requires too much effort for persons who are going to need that.
>
> (interview, software developer & prosthetist, 2017-10-10)

What this example illustrates is that algorithmic mass customization may introduce the idea of a standard user into socket design, by replacing the prosthetists' skill-based performance with an automated process and the custom inscription with an adjustable "digital template." As in custom production, there would still be a unique product for each user. Yet, the fit between the two would not be determined by the skill of the prosthetist but by the algorithm. While the former process allows for manual adjustments to facilitate individual divergence from the norm, the latter begins from a standard user representation that is automatically adapted based on a series of digital representations. Given that such automated processes only work within what is called a "fixed solution space," the possible diversity of inscriptions in sockets would be limited. The further a potential user deviates from the standard, the worse the resulting fit between product and user. In the absence of solutions that work for all potential users, many current approaches in the automation of socket design take a less extreme approach and aim to integrate the established representational practices of the crafts. They work with only partly automated design tools, or only automate design work in what are considered straightforward cases, thus retaining the craftsperson's control over a part of the inscription process. These approaches, in essence, are hybrids between the manual process currently performed by prosthetists and the automated processes envisioned by engineers.

4.2.2.2 Parametric Mass Customization: Bringing Customization Back in

While the idea of automated mass customization is still highly experimental in socket design, it has become much more of a practical reality in the area of fit components. As previously noted, engineers working for large manufacturers in the prosthetics industry tended to interpret 3D printing mainly as a prototyping technology to speed up product development. They neither questioned the institutionalized link between fit component design and mass production, nor did they perceive 3D printing as an already viable production technology. This situation was challenged by a number of start-ups that took the digital fabrication process as the starting point from which to construct their action nets. These companies evolved around a new form of inscription, parametric mass customization, which made use of the new translational capacities offered by digital technologies. In doing so, they gave rise to action nets that combine elements of user representation from both mass and custom production, thereby constructing novel kinds of user roles.

The basic model of user inscription around which these start-ups formed can be described as *parametric mass customization*. This process begins from constructing a standardized digital product model that is then adapted to a user-specific input. The difference to algorithmic mass customization lies in the form of that input, which must be rendered in the form of predefined parameters, such as sizes or colors.[24] As with algorithmic forms of mass customization, the construction of the initial digital template does not differ significantly from the inscription process associated with conventional fit components in that it draws on aggregated user representations.[25] However, in contrast to processes of mass production, digital inscription devices such as CAD software allow for the automated adaptation of that digital template to user-specific inputs, while 3D printers allow for the translation of the resulting digital model into a unique material product. As a result,

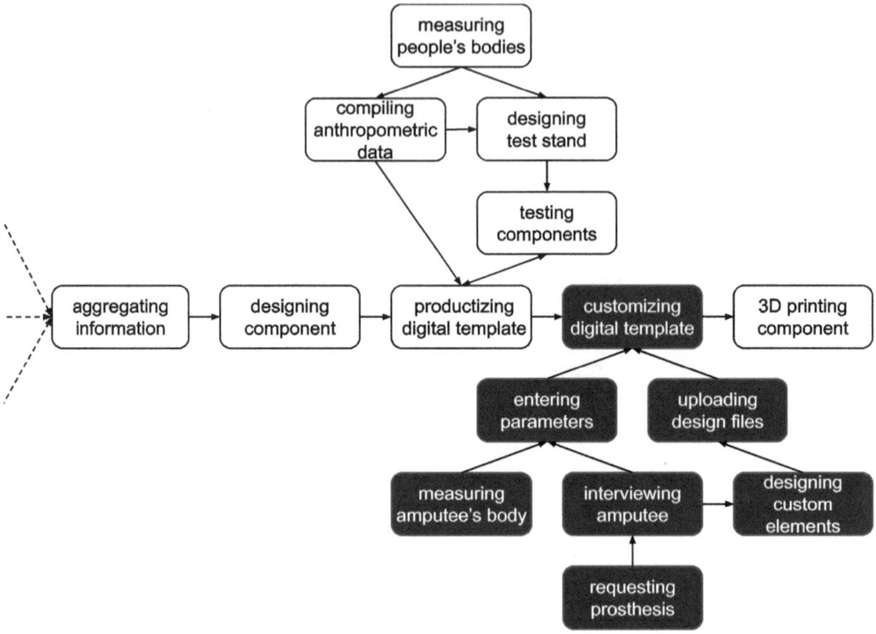

Figure 4.11 The inscription process underlying mass customization begins from constructing a standardized template (compare Figure 4.8), but subsequently adapts it to a user-specific input. The figure shows the parametric version of the process. Own figure.

standardized inscriptions can be altered to account for certain characteristics and preferences of individual users.

In this inscription process, start-ups perform the bulk of the design work, including the definition of a product's basic design and parameters. They do, however, leave the configuration of those parameters to amputees and their prosthetists. To this end, several firms developed web-based platforms or mobile apps on which prosthetists could configure products by choosing the device's size and colors or by adding individual patterns and branding to predefined areas. Once the preferred parameters were entered, the digital model would automatically be adjusted and could be ordered with the press of a button.

The implementation of parametric mass customization most commonly affected the construction of user roles in conjunction with the products' aesthetic qualities. Several start-ups applied such systems to the design of protective covers for prosthetic arms and legs, which featured startling aesthetics that could be configured by the intended users themselves.[26] Remarkably, they often framed these products as fashion items or wearables instead of prosthetic aids that would rehabilitate or hide disability. As illustrated in the following quote from a start-up's website, these companies envisioned scenarios in which users would wear prosthetic covers to proactively express their unique identity instead of trying to pass as "normal."[27]

> Our users have different stories to tell, share different interests, have different lifestyles and different goals and that is why they should all have the opportunity to personalize their own prosthetic in order for it to be much more than just a facilitation (sic!). Gamma [a pseudonym, DS] gives you a possibility to express your personality. It's a stylish addition to your look. It isn't just another prosthetic - it's an accessory that suits YOU. It is the first prosthetic crafted to suit your individual needs.
> (Website of the start-up Gamma, accessed 2018-10-01)

The idea of transforming prostheses into individual accessories resonated particularly well with young, fashion-conscious adults who, in turn, shaped the image of start-ups as particularly innovative compared to the manufacturers of mass-produced standard covers. In effect, the new inscription process afforded by digital fabrication linked start-ups to a highly specific group of users, while contributing to the construction of particular identities for both sides.

It is interesting to note how the new user roles constructed here were shaped by the specific translational capacities of 3D printing. Clearly, mass customization was key to the claim of individuality and would not have been possible without the automation afforded by CAD software and the

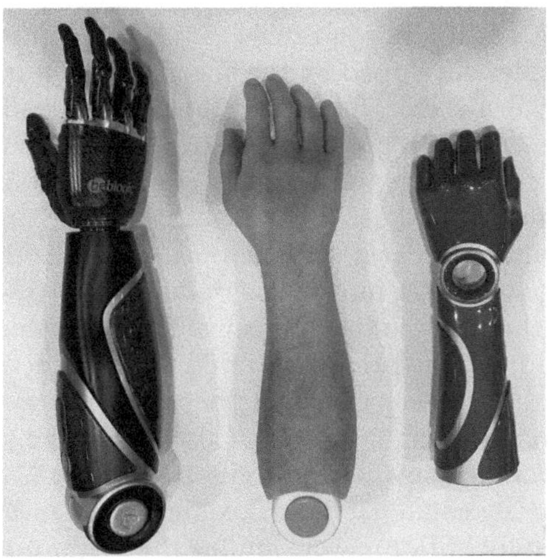

Figure 4.12 Three prostheses on display at a start-up's exhibition booth: Right: 3D-printed arm with glossy finish and passive hand; middle: 3D-printed arm covered with custom-made silicone glove produced by a specialized artisan; left: 3D-printed forearm combined with an advanced myoelectric hand by an industrial manufacturer. Own photograph.

flexibility of 3D printing. Yet the product's eye-catching aesthetics were linked to digital production in other ways, too. For instance, 3D printers eased the exact fabrication of intricate patterns and engravings, while printable materials (e.g., polyamide and other plastics) favored glossy finishes and stark, uniform colors (Figure 4.12, right). 3D printing thus afforded the inscription of user roles underlining fashionable distinction. By contrast, it would have been next to impossible to use the technology to produce a truly humanlike appearance comparable to the custom-made silicone covers manufactured by specialized craftspeople in a time- and labor-intensive process (Figure 4.12, middle). Similarly, the integration of electronic components, typical of advanced mechanical hands manufactured by industrial companies proved difficult to realize in a mass customization process with constantly changing sizes and geometries (Figure 4.12 left).

A notable example of parametric mass customization that went beyond exterior design to involve some aspects of mechanical functionality, was the web-based platform of the German start-up Omega. Logging into this platform, prosthetists could customize and order a range of products including several different prosthetic feet (Figure 4.13). These could be adapted in several dimensions including size, color, and branding, with the firm working on features that would allow adjusting the mechanical performance of their devices to make them feel either "sporty" or "safe" according to one of the company's developers. This strategy would have allowed Omega to design products adapted to individual recipients and their envisioned activities beyond the fixed standards typical of mass production.[28] Yet, once more, the specific user roles that emerged were shaped by the materiality of digital production devices beyond their capacity for mass customization. For instance, the feet developed by the start-up relied on purely mechanical principles rather than on the integration of electronic components as is typical of many advanced prosthetic feet in the field. This reflected both the ability of 3D printers to manufacture complicated mechanical structures, and the inability of those machines to print electronics. Moreover, the specific 3D printing process used here—called selective laser sintering (SLS)—linked the price of a foot to the build volume it would take up inside the printer rather than to the number of feet produced, as in mass production.[29] Accordingly, the price for a child's foot tended to be high when using conventional technologies, simply because there were only very few children with lower limb amputations. Conversely, the price of a similar product was particularly low when produced with SLS, simply because it was very small. Surely enough, colorful, waterproof, and mechanically robust prosthetic feet for children were among the first products marketed by Omega. Once more, production technology had acted as a mediator, linking specific kinds of industrial activity to the lives of very specific groups of potential users.

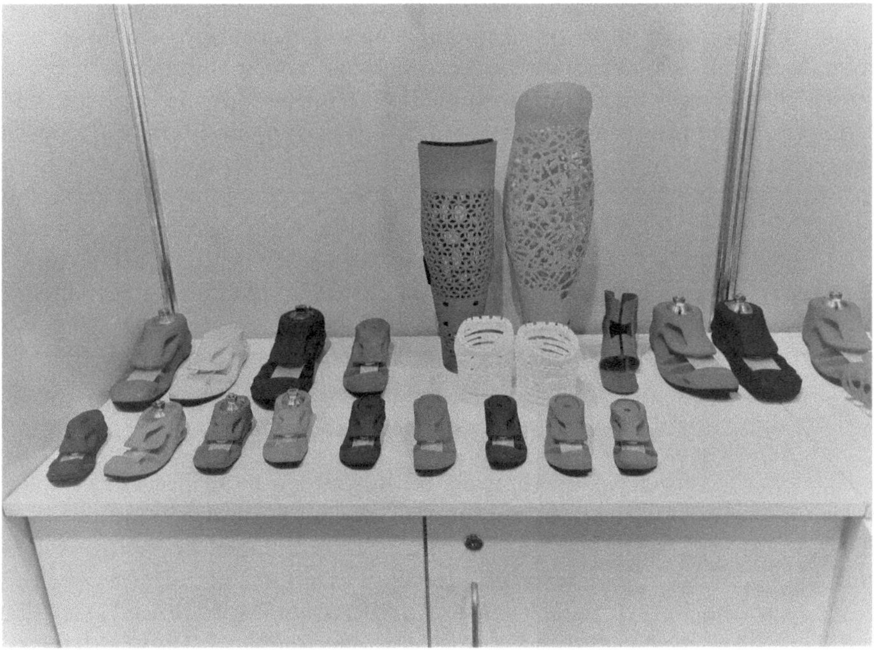

Figure 4.13 Mass customized products of a German start-up including prosthetic feet for adults and children, covers, and one orthosis.

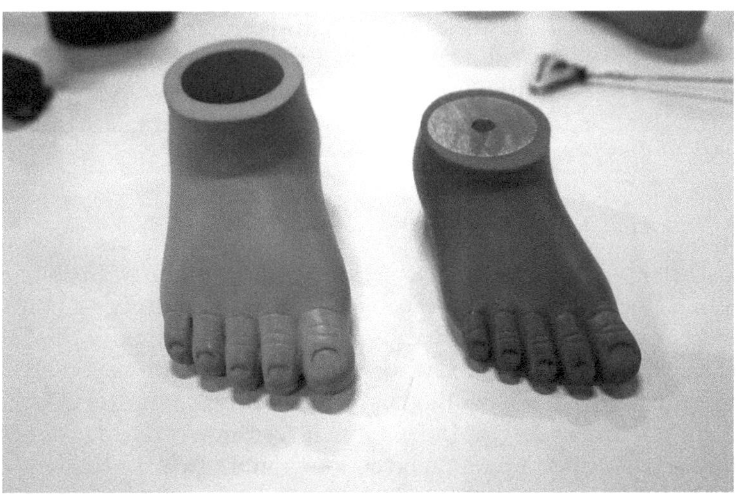

Figure 4.14 Prosthetic feet for children in the two available standard foot shells offered by a conventional manufacturer. Own photograph.

From the point of view of user construction, the above examples are remarkable for two reasons. On the one hand, they demonstrate ways in which the action net woven around digital production technologies led industrial start-ups to construct specific ideas of their users. Parametric mass customization connected the activities of prosthetic design and manufacturing to the lives of a highly specific cast of people who, in turn, stabilized the newly founded organizations by becoming their first customers. On the other hand, the examples illustrate how mass customization gained legitimacy in a highly institutionalized context by combining elements of already established practices. To engineers, it demonstrated how 3D printing could be applied to further enhance standardized mass production. To prosthetists, the same technique presented a way of re-introducing a long-lost degree of customization to the production of fit components.

Yet, mass customization was neither "mass" nor "custom" production. In contrast to true mass production, it allowed a greater diversity of user roles to be inscribed into the component. By enabling users and prosthetists to manipulate the parameters of digital templates, mass customization led to a multiplication of choices along product dimensions such as color, size, and style. In effect, mass customization tools allowed start-ups to break down the populations of users inscribed into standardized fit components into much smaller segments. However, despite these changes, parametric mass customization fell short of configuring a custom fit between amputees and fit components (coons, 2022). While products could be adjusted to reflect certain individual characteristics, this process invariably yielded variations of existing digital templates. These templates, however, narrowed the solution space in which user roles could be constructed. Even though mass customization offered more variability than conventional mass production, it still constructed users along predefined categories.

4.2.2.3 Scalable Custom Production: Sharing a Helping Hand

The most striking example of an emerging inscription process, in conjunction with 3D printing, is practiced by a global community of non-professional makers that I will refer to as Alpha. This community consists of a distributed group of volunteers, who has little in common beyond their passion for 3D printing, their willingness to help others, and their lack of experience in prosthetic design. Indeed, the inscription process around which the community formed was influenced much more by practices and norms of open source projects and the maker movement than it was by the prevailing institutions of the prosthetics industry. Even though the devices produced by volunteers were often custom-made for specific users, distributed 3D printing and the free sharing of design files allowed for their potentially rapid diffusion and large-scale uptake. Accordingly, I will refer to this form of inscription as *scalable custom production*.

Alpha's origin story is indicative of both the community's loose organization and the way in which its members go about the inscription of user roles. The original 3D-printed hand, around which the community later formed, was developed by a South African carpenter who had lost part of his hand in a work accident and an American prop maker whose model of a giant prop hand he had found online. In hope of developing a low-cost assistive device that would fit the specific needs of the carpenter, the two started collaborating through e-mail and video calls. Using technologies such as aluminum milling, they built various prototypes of what was later called the Robofinger, with the prop maker's wife documenting their progress online. Not long after, the mother of a young boy with a congenital limb difference called amniotic band syndrome discovered their blog and hoped that her child could also benefit from a homegrown device. Despite the challenges of long-distance collaboration, a prototype of a second device, the so-called Robohand, was developed and tailored to the boy's condition. To further pursue the Robohand's development, the prop maker enrolled the help of Makerbot, a company selling desktop 3D printers. Using the printers sponsored by the company helped speed up the distributed development process, as it allowed them to produce, test, and adapt new iterations more quickly than would have been possible with conventional production devices.

To the two inventors, this experience signaled the potential scalability of their approach, which they now saw as applicable not just to one individual user, but more generally to children born with congenital limb differences. They decided to upload the Robohand's printable files to the sponsoring company's online repository under an open-source license. At the same time, the company itself published a video that documented the Robohand's development on YouTube, in the hopes of advertising their printers. The video, in turn, caught the attention of a US-based professor interested in collective intelligence. On a whim, he set up an online map with the goal of connecting people in need of a Robohand with people who had access to a 3D printer. Within weeks, hundreds of volunteers rallied around the cause of providing open-source 3D-printed hands for children, quickly scaling up the production of Robohands in the US and beyond. In the eight years that followed, Alpha volunteers have developed a plethora of simple hands, arms, and other 3D printable assistive devices, many of which began as custom solutions for individual recipients. According to one of the community's main blogs, Alpha has grown into a global movement counting some 20,000 volunteers in over 100 countries and has delivered 3D-printed devices to approximately 8,000 recipients around the world. The inscription process that emerged around the community's use of CAD software, privately owned desktop 3D printers and a shared, if fragmented, digital communication infrastructure is unique and merits closer examination.

User Inscription in Scalable Custom Production

From the point of view of user construction Alpha is unusual, as it draws on a set of digital technologies to combine custom production with scalability. In this pattern, Alpha devices are first developed for specific individuals, such as the above-mentioned carpenter, or the recipient of the original Robohand. The development of new designs usually happens in a process of intense collaboration that is reflected in the fact that many of these hands are named after their first recipient (e.g., "Isabella edition" or "Ody Hand"). Yet, the fact that devices are designed digitally allows them to be shared with others who may reproduce them using desktop 3D printers or adapt them to new users using CAD software. In the spirit of an open-source project, these new adaptations would then be reported back to the larger community.[30] Hence, what begins as a process of custom production can subsequently be scaled up thanks to the mobility, reproducibility, and malleability of digital models and the capacity of 3D printers to translate them into usable products at low cost.

The inscription process described here differs from the two forms of mass customization discussed above in at least two ways. First, the digital product files that Alpha volunteers use are the result of *custom* production meaning they take an individual person, rather than a statistically aggregated population, as their starting point. Second, due to the community's open-source practices, the process by which these templates are adjusted to the characteristics of new users is, in principle, open-ended. Whereas in mass customization, the limits of adaptation are defined by rule-based algorithms or fixed parameters, in the Alpha community customization is done manually. The kind and degree of adaptation depend on the volunteer's skill and relationship to the intended user. As there originally were no institutionalized norms for how to customize devices, several patterns emerged simultaneously.

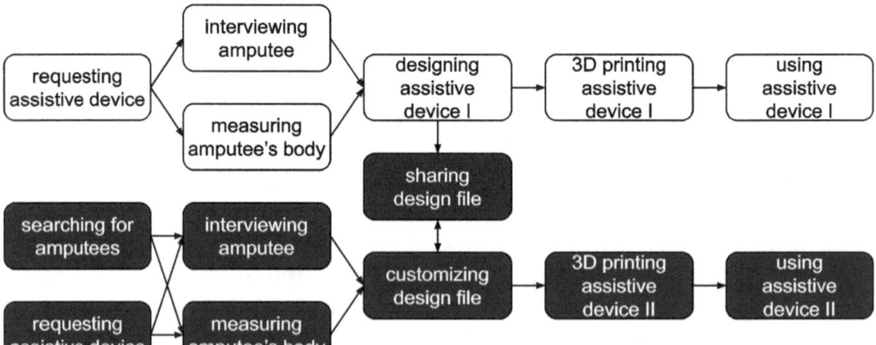

Figure 4.15 "Scalable custom production" begins from the design of a custom product but allows for its distributed reproduction and adaptation through subsequent sharing. Own figure.

Many of the early Alpha volunteers were fascinated by the story of the Robohand and viewed the community as a demonstration of the charitable potential of open-source hardware, desktop 3D printing, and grass-roots organization. Wanting to join a noble cause, they began actively searching for potential recipients of available Alpha hands.[31] In these cases, the level of customization tended to be relatively low. Most often customization was limited to categories such as colors and sizes and did not differ much from parametric mass customization. At other times, customization efforts were reminiscent of hobbyist versions of craft-based socket design, with volunteers thermoforming plastic gauntlets or adding padding to make the devices more comfortable to wear. Finally, volunteers that were more adept with digital design tools decorated the hands with custom embossings or superhero-themed decorations, such as Batman logos or Wolverine claws, which were viewed as corresponding to the preferences of American children, Alpha's main user group.

In another set of cases, the inscription process was closer to full-fledged custom development. Here entirely novel devices were made to facilitate the requests of people that could not be fitted with one of the available designs. These processes often involved intense collaboration between makers and recipients. They also tended to add new functionality to existing Alpha devices, thereby making them usable to people with different preferences and body types. Some volunteers designed devices for different amputation heights, extending Alpha's portfolio from arms to hands. Others made devices specific to the activities that children wanted to engage in, such as

Figure 4.16 Two Alpha devices demonstrating different kinds of customization. Left: A device with an adapter for exchangeable terminal devices, such as this baseball bat holder. Right: A common Alpha design with superhero-themed painting.

playing the violin, shooting glitter, or throwing Star Wars-themed snowballs. In extreme cases, volunteers designed entirely new kinds of prostheses that bore little resemblance to previously existing devices within Alpha or the conventional prosthetics industry (Figure 4.16). Where new devices were shared with the wider community, they could be taken up in further development and production activities, thus expanding the landscape of possible user roles.

As these examples demonstrate, the specific translational capacities of digital fabrication could support a wide variety of different inscription processes, giving rise to a multitude of different user roles. But desktop 3D printers are far from the universal replicators they have been claimed to be in public discourse. Rather, at least between 2015 and 2020, the time of this study, consumer-grade 3D printers could only be used for a narrow range of products. Most importantly, limitations in strengths and durability meant that the pattern of *scalable custom production* remained limited to non-weight-bearing upper limb prostheses.

The scope of the Alpha approach has also been limited by its incompatibility with ingrained professional practices in the industry. Engineers not only found the material properties and mechanical functionality of Alpha devices far below their standards, but also rejected them for a lack of laboratory-based testing and clinical studies. Prosthetists, while often fascinated by the potential of 3D printing to facilitate a digital craft, criticized Alpha volunteers for their inability to represent their users' bodies in anything approaching the craft's professional norms. Most importantly, Alpha devices did not include anything like a traditional socket, working instead with cut-outs and thermoformed gauntlets, or padding—an idea rather repulsive to prosthetists, whose own professional role was so centrally premised on socket design. Remarkably, prosthetists and engineers alike proved to be much less concerned about Alpha operating *outside* of their respective profession's zone of influence. For instance, several of the interviewees in this study combined their general dismissal of Alpha with the idea that a community approach could be useful for people in the Global South, who they pictured as having practically no access to professionally made prostheses. As a result of this rejection, and the volunteers' general distaste for for-profit organizations and proprietary design, Alpha mainly continued to exist at the margins of the conventional industry.

4.3 Industrial Reorganization and Patterns of Inscription

This chapter has addressed different forms of user inscription. I have analyzed, how people become represented as potential users with specific preferences, tastes, and bodily features, and how these representations, in turn, form the basis for the design of new technologies. My central argument has been that a number of different forms of inscription processes can be distinguished, each of which is linked to a specific mode of production, and each contributing to the construction of a differently patterned user landscape. By comparing the action nets constituting machine-based mass production, tool-based custom production, and several forms of digital fabrication, based on CNC milling and 3D printing, I have shown that production devices are important mediators in the inscription process. Therefore, the introduction of production devices with new translational capacities opens an opportunity for the emergence of new patterns of inscription. Several findings from this analysis of the prosthetics industry from the beginning of the 20th century onwards are of wider relevance for the study of user construction and industrial reorganization.

One set of findings concerns the institutionalization of the dominant patterns of user construction and their emergent relation to production devices in both mass and custom production. The first noteworthy finding is that multiple stable patterns of inscription may emerge within the same industry. Each of these links specific parts of the industry's product (e.g., prosthetic sockets and fit components), a group of designers (e.g., prosthetists and engineers), and a set of production technologies (e.g., hand tools and machines). In prosthetics, the representational processes favored by engineers and craftspeople involved different forms of translation, so that they ended up producing two distinct user landscapes, each with its own principles of inclusion and exclusion. In mass production, users were rendered as populations, with the conformance to fixed standards being the decisive criterion for inclusion. In custom production, users were rendered as individuals, with the main determinant of inclusion being the skill of the craftsperson. Essentially, the specific division of labor between the professions meant that multiple different user representations were inscribed into each prosthesis, facing the device's potential user with a complex set of bodily requirements and scripts for future use practices.

We have also seen that specific inscription processes may become deeply institutionalized as they are linked to the rules and norms of professional education systems, testing regimes, and industrial standards as well as material infrastructures and technical equipment in places like factories and workshops. Production devices often took on a deeply normative character, as evidenced by the intense reactions of prosthetists to challenges regarding their "magic hands" and the astounding tendency of engineers to justify their representational practices with the requirements of the available machines and infrastructures. Yet, even though certain patterns of user construction have become taken for granted in the prosthetics industry, there is nothing inevitable about the way their underlying action nets are organized. In fact, institutionalized practices of inscription that today seem so self-evident to people in the field have their historical origin in the catastrophe of war. It was in these massively dis-organized events that the institutions of modern prosthetics evolved and the contemporary links between professions, production devices, and product components were forged. On the one hand, war led to the professionalization of craft-based prosthetics. On the other, it allowed engineering, mass production, and the population logic to establish a foothold in the industry and to gain a firm hold over most components of modern prostheses.

Another set of findings makes intelligible the relationship between user construction and industrial digitalization. The first of these insights was that, when digital technologies were first introduced, they were interpreted in accordance with institutionalized patterns of user inscription. At that early stage, they neither lead to significant changes in the organization of the industry nor did they affect the ways in which technology designers and manufacturers represented their users. By contrast to the revolutionary scenarios sometimes associated with digital fabrication (e.g., Anderson, 2012; Rifkin, 2014), new technologies were mostly used in ways that were compatible with—and at times equivalent to—institutionalized patterns of user inscription. Engineers that were used to designing standardized fit components, applied 3D printing with aims to produce *better* standardized fit components. Most prosthetists, similarly, did not adopt the new production devices until they allowed them to perform a digital version of the traditional plaster cast method. The slow uptake of 3D printing may be interpreted as a case of innofusion (Fleck, 1988) or social learning (Williams et al., 2005), in which complex technical systems are gradually adapted to an already organized setting, such as a factory or R&D department. In terms of industrial user construction, the effect was that for more than two decades, the introduction of digital technologies to prosthetics changed the former much more than the latter. Digital technology did not act as an external force impinging upon the industry with invariable effectiveness. Rather, while new production devices were constantly adapted, the action patterns underpinning user inscription changed at a glacial pace at best.

An action net perspective emphasizes that digital production devices only give rise to new users when their novel translational capacities help to bring about novel patterns of action. Yet, even new forms of inscription need to be established against the backdrop of an existing institutional order. A second finding concerning digital modes of user construction was that novel forms of inscription often became the object of struggle between incumbent groups of professional designers and their entrenched modes of representing users. For example, *algorithmic mass customization* promised to turn socket design into a science and bring it under the control of engineers while *parametric mass customization* promised to restore a degree of customization to fit components, granting prosthetists more control over the design of the overall prosthesis. Interestingly, the most radically new form of inscription, namely *scalable custom production*, was rejected by both incumbent groups. Being incompatible to existing institutions, it was relegated to the margins of the industry and linked to marginalized groups, such as children or people in the Global South, whom incumbent professionals had not constituted as users of their own.

Despite the importance of existing institutions in shaping the use of 3D printing, it would be wrong to depict the introduction of the new production technologies as merely a trigger (Barley, 1986) that allowed for a new round of political maneuvering and reshuffling between pre-existing positions. Instead, a third relevant insight was that the specific materiality of digital production devices eased the construction of some action nets and foreclosed the realization of others. Hence, the user roles that emerged were shaped by the concrete translational capacities of digital production devices in dimensions such as build volume, compatible materials, and file formats.[32] In practice, even though 3D printers are often depicted as universal machine tools that can produce pretty much everything imaginable (Gershenfeld, 2012), they cannot make everything equally well. While each group of designers pitched their vision as benefitting "patients," "customers," or "users" this never meant *all* users, and sometimes only the tiniest fraction of all people who might have benefitted from prosthetic technology. As a result, digital technologies first became relevant in mediating a small number of highly specific connections between industrial activities on the one hand and the lives of people with limb differences on the other. That is, they only constituted a select few groups of people (e.g., young adults, children) as potential users. These, in turn, acted as "early adopters" (Rogers, 1983) or "lead users" (Hippel, 1986), stabilizing new product classes and design trajectories such as fashionable prosthetic covers, or robotic-looking superhero hands, as well as the organizations that developed and manufactured them. These early relationships importantly shaped the user roles subsequently constructed in the industry, for instance by emphasizing unorthodox outward design, and non-anthropomorphic functionality in upper limb prosthetics. Which new user roles become dominant in digitalizing industries is thus a complex question, involving industrial re-organization, situated use-practices, and the evolving translational capacities of inscription and production devices mediating between them.

Concluding this chapter, it is important to comment on some of the new possibilities for user construction opened up by the novel translational capacities of 3D printers, and on the ways in which an action net perspective makes them more intelligible. The two most relevant digital forms of inscription in the industry were associated with *parametric* and *algorithmic* varieties of *mass customization*, both of which have long been enthusiastically discussed in the management literature (Hippel & Katz, 2002; Pine, II., 1993; Tseng et al., 2017), but have rarely been the explicit focus of critical analysis by STS scholars (for a notable exception see coons, 2022). Both variations combined elements of inscription processes commonly associated with custom and mass production. This allowed these patterns of inscription to gain legitimacy with established groups of designers and to be taken up in the professional struggle between craftspeople and engineers. Yet, as an action net analysis makes clear, their specific effects differed from both custom and mass production. As a result, the recombination of existing patterns of action gave rise to genuinely new forms of inscription that helped to construct new user roles in the industry.

Parametric versions of mass customization re-introduced a degree of customization to standardized fit components such as prosthetic hands or feet, by enabling prosthetists to manipulate standardized product templates in several parameters. However, customization remained limited since the construction of the original template incorporated design practices originally associated with mass production, while constricting user-specific inputs to only a few well-defined parameters. If mass production corresponded to representing users in terms of "populations" amenable to the construction of averages, mass customization corresponded to user representations in terms of limited "solution spaces" amenable to configuration within predefined dimensions and fixed boundaries. This was true even of *algorithmic mass customization* as it was used in attempts at automating socket design. Even though advanced software systems translated individual user inscriptions, such as MRI scans, into unique artifacts, the process behind the translation was fixed. Consequently, algorithmic mass customization worked well for users with anatomies amenable to the programmed procedure, while non-standard anatomies could not be so easily inscribed. It can therefore be said that mass customization, even though it is usually associated with the manufacturing of bespoke products on an industrial scale, is based on pervasive standardization, with a limited form of customization added as a secondary process. Where it replaces conventional mass production, its effect will be to allow further differentiation within existing "populations" of users. However, even if each resulting inscription represents a "category of one," the overall user landscape will still be patterned along the *parameters* or *rules* underlying the machine's operation. Where mass customization replaces craft-based custom production, its effect will be to introduce standardization. While this may work to reduce unintended variations in manual processes of user inscription, it will also severely truncate the potential for creatively generating custom products in the interaction between craftsperson and user.

The different varieties of mass customization were, however, not the only possible combinations between custom design and large-scale production. This point was underlined in the discussion of Alpha, an open-source community that evolved around an inscription process I characterized as *scalable custom production*. However, this new pattern of user construction did not, to date, make significant inroads into the industry. This was due to the inadequacies of consumer-grade 3D printing at the time of writing and to the incompatibility of open-source licensing and grass-roots style organizing with the institutional order underpinning the field of prosthetics. For these reasons, scalable custom production was relegated to the margins of the industry, strengthening its connection to people that were excluded from becoming users within the action nets spanned by the conventional industry.

As I will discuss in the following chapter, the effects of this connection were not always as unambiguously inclusive and emancipatory as notions such as the democratization of innovation (Hippel, 2005) or the third industrial revolution (Rifkin, 2011) would lead one to believe.

Notes

1 As Kienitz (2008, pp. 48–57) has shown, for the case of the German prosthetics industry during World War I, such references to historical figures are often an important part of the identity construction of both the designers and users of artificial limbs.

2 Students of the social sciences may be familiar with the cover of Andry's book from a reprint in Foucault's *Discipline and Punish* (1977, p. 169). The image, an engraving of a crooked sapling tied to a straight stake, survives in the prosthetics industry as it has inspired the emblems of many orthopedic associations around the world (see Kohler, 2010).

3 With regard to the term "prosthesis," Jain (1999, p. 32) notes:

> First introduced into English in 1553 as a term of rhetoric meaning 'attached to' or 'setting forth' or, literally, 'adding a syllable to the beginning of a word,' prosthesis did not come to bear the medical sense of the 'replacement of a missing part of the body with an artificial one' until 1704.
>
> (Wills, 1995, p. 215)

Despite early uses of the term, Jain's analysis of the writings of Sigmund Freud and Henry Ford dates the rise of the widespread cultural significance of prosthetics to the beginning of the 20th century.

4 Note that work accidents in industrial factories were themselves a major source of limb loss at that time.

5 ALMA was founded as the US entered WWI in 1917. It was renamed Orthopedic Appliance and Limb Manufacturers Association (OALMA) after WWII. In 1956, it became the American Orthotic and Prosthetic Association (AOPA). AOPA is still active today. I had the good fortune to attend both its centennial celebration marked by a world congress of the profession in 2017 as well as its annual National Meeting in 2018.

6 Dittmer traces the history of the orthopedic profession even further back in time. Elsewhere he mentions the Universal Association which made "surgical instruments, orthopaedic devices and supports" (Dittmer, 2016, p. 5) and was established in Frankfurt as early as 1883. He further dates the establishment of the dual apprenticeship system in what was then Prussia to 1901. Yet, Dittmer, too, concurs that "[d]evelopments in orthopaedic technology and improved production methods became a national challenge during World War I" (ibid.).

7 As Kienitz (2008, pp. 156–170) shows, the bodies of amputees have been subject to the interpretations of professionals from various disciplines including prosthetists, engineers, doctors and psychologists (see also Harrasser, 2009; Harrasser, 2016). Today all these groups are still part of the rehabilitation process and do often work together in teams along with ergo- and physiotherapists. I concentrate on the role of craftspeople and engineers since they were the primary designers and producers of prosthetic devices.

8 The systematic application of engineering principles to prosthetic design seems to have occurred in Germany after WWI (see Borchardt et al., 1919), while in the US craft-based design was still dominant until after the end of WWII (see Contini, 1954).

9 I concentrate here on the case of Germany, but the same dynamic was at play in the US after WWII. There, an influential report on post-war prosthetics noted:

> Perhaps the most striking impression gathered [...] was of the surprisingly close link between artificial-limb development and the development of aircraft and guided missiles. Many of the scientists and gadgeteers who have helped usher in this jet, atomic, electronic and rocket era have also created devices for improving artificial limbs. It requires the same type of thought processes.
>
> (Furman, 1962, p. 3)

10 Herschbach captures how the military's interest in standardization during the US Civil War spilled over into the production of prostheses and other objects that attached to the body:

> Developments in the mechanical measurement and inscription of human locomotion had their origins in a desire to rationalize the movement of troops [...]. The effort to uniform Union troops also made available for the first time sufficient data to set up tables of proportions and produced the first standards for American clothing sizes. As ready-to-wear replaced both homespun and the primitively sized clothes available in antebellum stores, so did factory-made prosthetics absorb the craft-based antebellum producers, supplanting earlier devices made by armourers, cobblers, watchmakers-, harnessmakers and locksmiths. The standardized measuring scales used by limb manufacturers were derived from military data.
>
> (Herschbach, 1997, p. 43)

11 For example, the famous motion studies by Frank and Lillian Gilbreth on human movement took a special interest in the role of workers with amputations (compare Brown, 2002). Similarly, Henry Ford mused about the best way to utilize amputees in industrial production. Quoting a brief excerpt from Ford's autobiography from 1923, Seltzer writes:

> The production of the Model T required 7,882 distinct work operations, but, Ford noted, only 12% of these tasks—only 949 operations—required 'strong, able-bodied, and practically physically perfect men.' Of the remainder—and this is clearly what he sees as the major achievement of his method of production—'we found that 670 could be filled by legless men, 2,637 by onelegged men, two by armless men, 715 by one-armed men and ten by blind men.'
>
> (Seltzer, 1992, p. 157)

12 Note, however, that there are some prostheses which are integrated directly into the user's bone structure using a procedure called "osseointegration." These prostheses do not include sockets at all.

13 Alternatively, the sock can be pulled over a so-called liner, a protective cover made from a soft material such as silicone, if the socket is supposed to be worn with one.

14 Engineers working in the industry frequently question whether the prosthetists' inscriptions indeed correspond to the bodies of amputees. That is, they challenge the sequence of translations established by the prosthetist.

15 To explain the necessity of these alterations, prosthetists occasionally invoked an example I was more familiar with: A well-fitting shoe. Supposedly, a shoe that fits your foot "like a glove" would be terribly uncomfortable when walking. It needs to be tighter in some places and looser in others. Again, engineers were usually skeptical of such metaphors, but often ended up relying on the experiential knowledge of prosthetists, as they lacked evidence of their own to support or refute the prosthetists' claims.

16 Ideally, socket design should account for the different use scenarios for upper and lower limb prostheses. While people stand or walk on their legs, arms hang down from the shoulder. Thus, while lower limb sockets put a premium on strength, often achieved by adding more material, upper limb sockets must be as lightweight as possible. Consequently, if lower limb design principles are applied to the upper extremity, sockets will be too heavy.

17 This does not mean that amputees do not participate in product development. Many people with amputations work in the industry either as prosthetists or technicians or as engineers. Some of the most influential innovations in the field have even been spearheaded by user innovators (see Chapter 6). In claiming that users are rarely present during the development of fit components, I mean that the overwhelming majority of people who are fit with a prosthetic hand or leg have not participated in its development and that, conversely, very few of the amputees who do participate in product development will actually wear the device that they have helped to bring about.

18 To mitigate this structural dependency, large manufacturing firms sometimes hire their own prosthetists or even buy prosthetic clinics. Such strategies are, in turn, resisted by craftspeople and their professional associations.

19 This finding resonates with Wilkie's discussion of different enactments of scale in design-related user representation (Wilkie, 2010, pp. 199–200). Wilkie rightfully points to Foucault's distinction between anatomo-politics and bio-politics as a lens for studying user construction.

20 The examples I give below should not be viewed as excluding other representational techniques. Many firms do, in fact, perform some form of user testing (Chapter 6). However, in the early design stages, many important decisions are based on pre-existing standards or economic constraints, which is my focus here.

21 Lot sizes for different parts differ dramatically, ranging from a few dozens to tens of thousands. For example, over the course of the last 20 years, the four major iterations of the C-Leg, one of the most emblematic prosthetic components currently available, have been fitted to more than 70.000 users according to its manufacturer (Ottobock: https://www.ottobock.de/prothetik/beinprothetik/reclaim-your-life/6.-thema-20-jahre-c-leg/, accessed 2018-09-19). While these numbers are rather small compared to other industries, and many prosthetic fit components are not strictly speaking "mass-produced," the paradigm underlying their design is still qualitatively different from the idea of custom production prevalent in socket design.

22 Stereolithography (SLA), invented in 1984, is another technology that has been used in prototyping and might be used in the manufacturing of certain kinds of components in the future. The Multi Jet Fusion (MJF) method, that has been used in socket manufacturing, is of a more recent vintage and was introduced by HP in 2016.

23 Note that rapid prototyping has been the main application of 3D printers in most industries. As I will show in Chapter 6, the major effects of speeding up product development cycles pertained to the way in which industries were able to react to unexpected use practices.

24 ginger coons has written a very thoughtful book on this kind of mass customization in which she criticizes it for failing to deliver truly custom products (coons, 2022). Interestingly, one of her chapters discusses 3D printing in the design of prosthetic sockets, though her examples are very close to the notion of the "digital plaster cast" analyzed above.

25 Considerations of economies of scale are less important. Similarly, the question of standardizing testing procedures for mass customized products was a contentious issue in the field.

26 The relevance of such tools goes beyond the tension between standardization and customization as discussed in this chapter. Mass customization tools also inspired hopes of involving users as co-creators of their own devices, thereby increasing identification with the product and strengthening compliance with the user roles constructed by the firm.
27 It is noteworthy that at least three of the more successful start-ups producing mass customized fit components were co-founded by amputees themselves, two of whom also had a background in engineering.
28 At the time of the interview, it was still unclear which of the feet's parameters would need to be adjusted to generate the latter effects. Eventually, the firm stopped the development of prosthetic componentry to concentrate on making software tools that were closer to the digital plaster cast model described above.
29 In SLS, powdered material is added layer by layer and melted by a laser to make it stick to the layer below. Eventually, the entire build volume is filled with powder, with the manufactured component buried within. To use the machine efficiently, the build volume is crammed with as many components as possible, which is why SLS providers charge their customers by the volume taken up inside the machine.
30 In practice this did not always happen, due to the incompatibility of file formats, the lack of documentation, and the confusing and fragmented way the community was organized (see Chapter 6).
31 In contrast to the custom design efforts described here, some community members manufactured hundreds of Alpha devices during so-called "makeathons." These devices were usually made for unspecified recipients and were typically circulated in the form of bulk donations (see Chapter 5).
32 Note that 3D printing, and scanning are moving targets. While their basic translational principles (e.g., translating between digital data and physical objects) remain stable, their concrete translational capacities change all the time.

5 Distributing Technology

Mediation between Industry and Users

In this chapter, I address the ways in which user roles are constructed, transformed, or precluded as industrial products are moved from the site of design to the site of production, and on to sometimes unexpected sites of use. Studying the global circulation of artifacts reflects the idea that the construction of user roles does not stop at the doorstep of the R&D department, nor does it first begin when the product meets its prospective user. Instead, an action net perspective draws attention to the intricate processes of *circulation* and *intermediation* that link industrial technology supply and use. Far from the simple distribution of readymade goods, these involve translations that touch upon issues of accessibility and affordability, and include practices of choosing and adapting industrially manufactured products for use within local contexts. In other words, processes of circulation and intermediation regulate which social groups are constituted as an industry's potential users and which remain excluded.

The digitalization of production currently promises to reorganize the ingrained trajectories of industrial products by allowing them to travel as digital files along digital communication infrastructures. Examining these promises, I compare the action nets that evolve and stabilize in conjunction with conventional production devices on the one hand, and both industrial and desktop 3D printers on the other. Attending to both the *infrastructural* and *institutional* conditions of circulation, I show how the distribution of products is shaped by the uneven extension of material networks, constituted by things like roads and warehouses, as well as ingrained professional norms and regulations such as those laid out by national insurance systems. My analysis demonstrates that digital inscription and production devices can be used to construct novel circulation pathways between industries and their users. They may move manufacturing closer to the site of use, remove it from professionally controlled contexts, or give rise to new intermediary actors such as digital platforms. Where they sidestep established infrastructures and institutions, new distribution practices may make prosthetic technology accessible to hitherto excluded or marginalized social groups (Urry & Birtchnell, 2016). However, digitalization does not invariably lead to a decentralization of distribution or a re-localization of manufacturing

DOI: 10.4324/9781003269731-5

(Ferdinand et al., 2016) and could well result in a shift of control to a few powerful actors. Even where manufacturing is moved toward local sites of use, this does neither guarantee the large-scale inclusion of new users, nor the autonomy of local manufacturers (Anderson, 2012). Instead, digital circulation practices may construct new biases between user groups and reproduce well-known power asymmetries.

5.1 The Industrial Order of Circulation

Studying the journey of all the components and materials built into a prosthesis in Europe or North America at the beginning of the 21st century is a tedious task. Until the turn of the 20th century, prostheses were almost exclusively made in independent artisanal workshops. An amputee would have to visit one of these shops and consult with a local craftsperson to have a limb made for them. Within this *decentralized* system of production, the device would then be designed and manufactured *locally*. That is to say, where prostheses were available at all, the social and geographical distances between the sites of designing, manufacturing, and using tended to be rather small. Even though blueprints or models where occasionally shared, artificial limbs did not usually travel very far. When the industrialization of prosthetics took off after the US Civil War, and particularly after World Wars I and II, things began to change (see Chapter 4). In order to deal with the tens of thousands of new amputees, companies like Ohio Willow Wood (US) and Ottobock (Germany) began manufacturing semi-finished componentry that could be ordered by prosthetists. In this new mode of production, fit components, including everything from splints to knee joints, feet, and mechanical hands, were produced in *central factories* and then sent to local workshops for assembly and fitting. Soon, the same was true of the means of socket production, including machines and materials, even though the socket itself was still being produced in local workshops. While this development enabled craftspeople to concentrate on assembling, aligning, and fitting prostheses, it also increasingly removed the design and manufacturing of most parts of the prosthesis from the shop. Thus, while the industrialization of prosthetics helped to scale up fabrication volume, it also led to a system of *remote* production, which dramatically enlarged the distance between the sites of manufacturing and using artificial limbs. This introduced the problem of how to organize the distribution of products across the social and geographical gap between a centralized industry and a range of diversely situated users (see Figure 5.1).

In the first half of the 20th century, the difficulties associated with centralized production were further exacerbated by the same conditions of war and post-war that had given rise to the industry itself. Where infrastructures were destroyed and political borders shifted, the movement of prosthetic components and materials was interrupted, precipitating a state of crisis in user construction. For example, Klaus Dittmer

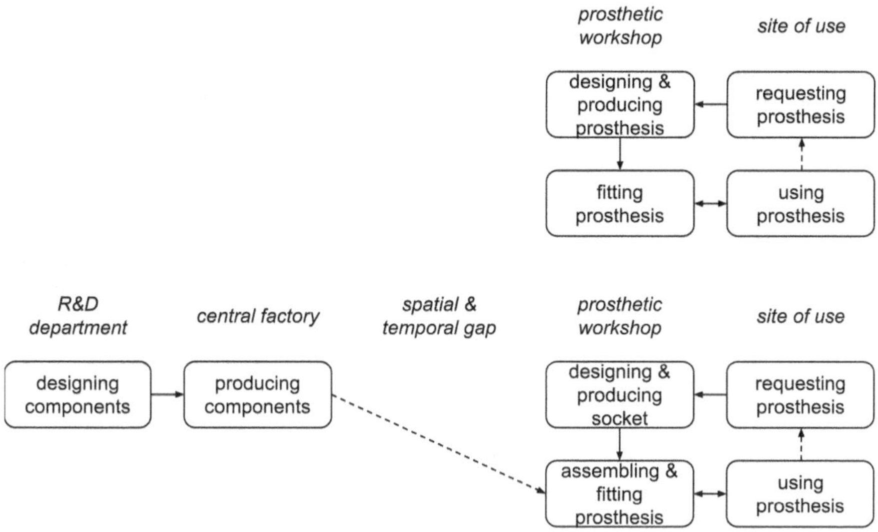

Figure 5.1 During the 19th century prosthetic production was mostly a local affair (above). With the industrialization of prosthetics, the production of fit components was centralized and further removed from the site of use (below). Own figure.

recounts his father's description of working as a prosthetist in isolated West Berlin after WWII.

> Our greatest concern was the sourcing of materials. The pitiful stocks of every single colleague were soon used up, new materials were not coming in, but work and deliver one should. Still to this day, bandages sometimes fall into our hands as symbols of that crisis, made from materials brought in by customers, such as tablecloths or underskirts; flatfoot insoles were made from airplane metal and cartridge sheeting. It was possible to bridge a moment of crisis with these, but for large orthopedic aids it was still necessary to obtain usable materials.
>
> (Bruno Dittmer, 1956, quoted in Dittmer, 2018, pp. 3–4; own translation)

As accounts like this one demonstrate, organizing the distribution of prosthetic supplies and components from manufacturers to local workshops was a major challenge for the young industry, and a failure to address it constantly threatened to undo the entire action net of industrial user construction. The patterns of action that emerged in response to this situation would eventually settle into the industrial order of circulation dominant today, often extending far beyond their place of origin and introducing dramatic consequences for the construction of user roles and identities worldwide.

5.1.1 Setting up Global Distribution Infrastructures

On the infrastructural side, the industry's development was marked by an ever-increasing *centralization of production*, complemented by a *large-scale extension of industrial distribution networks*. With the consolidation of basic distribution infrastructures after WWII, many local workshops turned to ordering semi-finished components from industrial manufacturers. Most of the larger production devices such as milling machines, forges, or galvanizing facilities fell into disuse and eventually disappeared from the shops, as local firms gradually ceased in-house production, or continued it only for professional training purposes. As early as 1955, a member of the American Board of Certification (ABC) for prosthetists and orthotists reported the following:

> Based on a sample survey of representative firms in the industry, it can safely be said that a very large majority of artificial limb companies use pre-fabricated parts to some extent. Probably one-half of the firms use pre-fabricated parts, rather than a hand-made corresponding part, for one-half of their construction requirements or better.
>
> (Hanger, Jr., 1956, p. 73)

Today, this trend toward centralization has been taken even further. The overwhelming majority of components such as pylons, adapters, hands, feet, and joints are produced in a small number of factories, controlled by a handful of large companies.[1] For example, market leader Ottobock, the global market leader in prosthetics, primarily relies on two fabrication plants, with mechatronic components being produced in Austria and mechanical components being manufactured in Germany. Meanwhile, its largest competitor produces all its prosthetic components in Reykjavik, Iceland. Given such a degree of centralization, the gap between producing and using has grown vast.

At the same time, industrial companies have begun setting up large networks of national and international distribution centers to aid the movement of their products around the globe. To be sure, the internationalization of the US and German prosthetics industries had already begun during WWI with American devices such as the Carnes Arm being licensed by German manufacturers (Kienitz, 2008, pp. 165–168), and German prosthetists setting up shop in St. Petersburg (Dittmer, 2018). However, it was only with the relative stabilization of the international system after 1945 that the export of prostheses gained full momentum. For instance, from its first international branch office in Minneapolis, established in 1958, the German company Ottobock went on to build similar distribution centers in more than 55 different countries, while Iceland-based Össur is now active in 18 countries. As a result of these developments, most prosthetic fit components travel vast distances and knot together very differently situated practices of designing, producing, and using. In today's system of centralized industrial mass production, the successful construction of users thus depends on the existence of an intricate logistic infrastructure involving, among other things, transportation networks, warehouses, and distribution companies.

Despite the massive trend toward the centralization of manufacturing, local prosthetic clinics and workshops have not at all disappeared. Rather, they remained indispensable passage points in the industrial distribution network since it was at these facilities that the mediation between the centralized manufacturing activities of the new industry and the local activities of its prospective users took place. To this day, local prosthetists and technicians perform this translation in at least two ways. First, they *produce* the prosthetic socket, which is the material interface between standardized industrial componentry and individual human body (compare Chapter 4). This makes the socket the one major component of contemporary prostheses that is still predominantly manufactured locally.[2] Second, prosthetists *choose*, *assemble*, and *fit* the components that are included in a user's prosthesis. These are critical activities within the industrial system of circulation as it is through them that standardized products are transformed into usable prosthetic devices for individual amputees. Because prosthetic clinics and workshops offer the infrastructural foundation for these crucial translations, the contemporary action net of user construction only extends to places in which such facilities exist.

5.1.2 Co-Evolution of Prosthetics and the Institutional Order of the Post-War Era

Beyond the construction of an infrastructural foundation made up of roads, central factories, decentralized distribution facilities, and local prosthetic clinics, organizing the distribution of industrial fit components also required a set of rules and norms regulating what product should be moved where under which circumstances. In the years after 1945, this institutional aspect of the prosthetics industry closely co-evolved with the overarching institutional order of the post-war era. Of the large number of developments in this period, I will focus on the rise of *professionalism* and the elaboration of the various *national insurance systems*. Both factors continue to be deeply relevant for regulating which prosthetic components are made available to amputees and which user roles and identities they are enabled to perform.

As detailed in Chapter 4, both the importance of prosthetics in nationalist war efforts and emerging competition by other groups led to the formation of professional associations of prosthetists and orthotists in both Germany and the US. As those associations began to stabilize in the post-war years, they also began to implement rules for the conduct of their members. For example, the American Orthopedic Appliance and Limb Manufacturers Association[3] had been around since WWI (1917), but it was only after WWII that it really began to construe and enforce professional standards.[4] One of the former presidents of the organization, McCarthy Hanger writes:

> Although the leaders in the industry starting at the time of World War I recognized the need for improvement in competence and in ethics, progress in this direction was slow and gradual up to 1948. Then the industry set up a voluntary board to establish standards of competence, equipment and ethics, the American Board for Certification of the Prosthetic and Orthopedic Appliance Industry. This Board conducts examinations to determine the qualifications of fitters of artificial limbs and braces and gives qualified candidates the title of Certified Prosthetist or Certified Orthotist.
>
> (Hanger, Jr., 1956, p. 71)

The relevant point here is that, with the growing importance of certification—and according to Hanger, almost 90% of all US prosthetic facilities had undergone certification at the time of his writing—the circulation of prostheses became strictly regulated. In contrast to the idiosyncratic system of the 19th century, the rise of professionalism, placed restrictions on who could legitimately fit limbs to prospective users. From that point onward, this task was reserved exclusively for certified prosthetists.

The second major development critical for shaping the order of circulation in prosthetics was the implementation of national insurance systems in both Germany (*Bundesversorgungsgesetz*, 1950) and the US (Medicare, 1965). The introduction of widespread insurance coverage gave thousands of amputees access to prosthetic devices, which were growing in sophistication as well as price. At the same time, pricing and coverage policies became major points of contention between insurers, prosthetists, and industrial companies. Over the years, their negotiations led to the establishment of a complex set of coding schemes, such as the L-code system in the US, which have become important tools in translating between the actions of the various parties involved in providing artificial limbs. Even though coding schemes are somewhat fragmented and differ widely across countries, they regulate how much an insurer will pay for the provision of a prosthetic device of a certain type and range of functionality.[5] Given the elevated cost of modern prosthetic componentry, a device will only become available to amputees, if it is covered by these coding schemes. If it is deemed too expensive or cannot be translated into one of the existing codes, it will not be ordered by prosthetists and will not find its way to any prospective users.

With the stabilization of both material infrastructures and a set of institutional rules and norms, the problem of organizing the circulation of prosthetic componentry in a centralized production system had at last been resolved in a way that supported the manufacturing operations of the nascent prosthetics industry. With the establishment of centralized factories and decentralized distribution infrastructures, as well as the implementation of

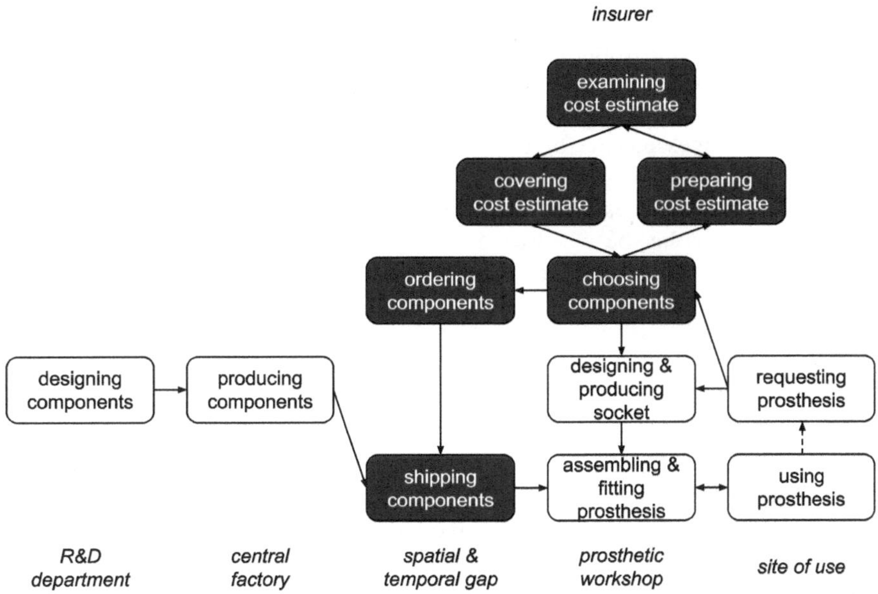

Figure 5.2 The dominant pattern of circulation that bridged the gap between producing and using in the Western prosthetics industry of the 20th century. Own figure.

professional standards and the elaboration of national insurance systems, the major elements of a new *dominant order of circulation* had emerged as one of the central pillars of user construction in prosthetics (compare Figure 5.2). As I will show in the following sections, this system of factory-centered production and global distribution lies at the very heart of contemporary patterns of inclusion and exclusion both at its places of origin and beyond. It shapes who can become a user of what kind of prosthetic device—and who cannot.

5.1.3 Inequalities Within the Dominant Order

Today, both the infrastructural and institutional elements of the dominant order of circulation are deeply taken for granted in Germany, Canada, and the US, the three countries in which I did most of my fieldwork.[6] Material infrastructures and distribution systems—including roads, warehouses, and local clinics—are in place, enabling the swift journey of prosthetic components from the sites of production to the sites of use. Similarly, health insurance as well as professional education and certification systems operate routinely, constituting the institutional backdrop that facilitates and regulates the circulation of prosthetic products. Indeed, these elements operate so smoothly that they are taken for granted under most circumstances.

Yet, even in Germany and the US, which may be called the cradles of the Western prosthetics industry, the conditions of circulation are far from being equally met for all people with limb differences. Rather, even where it functions normally, the dominant order of circulation makes access to prosthetic devices easier for some and harder for others. At times, such inequalities are successfully called out and contested by users, leading to the reorganization of established practices. The situation is thus marked by a constant interplay between taken-for-granted routines, the construction of biases in the user landscape, and the renegotiation of the dominant pattern of action.

5.1.3.1 Biases through Distribution Networks

In Germany, Canada, and the US, the ability to move things quickly and reliably from one place to another is a basic fact of everyday life and prosthetic components are no exception to this rule. When I asked my interviewees to describe the activities involved in moving a prosthetic hand or foot from a central factory to a prosthetic clinic, the question often startled them. "What do you mean?" replied a confused sales manager working for a large industrial manufacturer, "Apart from the obvious answer that we ship it." On the receiving end, prosthetists, too, would take the infrastructural dimension of providing somebody with an artificial limb to be unproblematic. When asked to explain the steps involved in their work, they would frequently leave out logistical aspects, either skipping the processes involved in ordering components or emphasizing the institutional and economic challenges it poses. In short, as infrastructures were firmly in place, the practical miracle of moving components around the globe had become part of the daily routine of ordering and shipping and was hardly ever addressed.

Despite this overall invisibility, material infrastructures did create inequalities between user groups, mostly through their uneven geographical extension. Prosthetic clinics in particular were very unevenly distributed across regions, with much higher concentrations in urban centers as compared to rural areas. This was true even of Germany, were almost 2,000 such facilities exist. From the point of view of amputees living in the rural areas of much larger countries such as the US or Canada, the very description of prosthetic clinics as *local* would have been a stretch, as many of them had to travel quite far to reach the next facility. The problem of accessing qualified professional services was particularly pertinent for people with relatively uncommon limb differences because, despite the standardization of education and equipment, local prosthetists often lacked experience with such cases, and more specialized facilities were few and far between. For example, the rarity of upper limb amputations versus those of the lower limb meant that people in need of an artificial hand would either need to travel farther or settle for a less than ideal solution.

As one of my interviewees, a young man with an upper limb difference, stated:

> Lower limb prosthetists are a dime a thousand. You can drown yourself in people building leg prostheses. But try finding someone who builds an arm prosthesis, I mean a proper one. Well, in all of Germany there are maybe two-three specialists who do upper limb prosthetics. Other than that, you don't get anything, all that's built is crap.
>
> (interview, upper limb amputee, 2016-11-04)

Hence, even in a country in which the prosthetics industry was particularly strong, and at times during which it operated normally, the dominant order of circulation still generated tangible differences between user groups. In this system, the circulation of products depended on the ability of people to access an unevenly distributed infrastructure, rendering the difference between being an urban or a rural, standard or non-standard user highly significant.

Even though such asymmetries were not usually a matter of outright exclusion, many prosthetists feared that the situation might deteriorate in the future, as the industry's distributed infrastructure was difficult to maintain and had become the object of strategic renegotiations. There was a perceived lack of new clinically oriented colleagues coming out of the various national education systems,[7] raising the question as to how the large number of local facilities might be adequately staffed in the future. At the same time, there was a growing tendency among powerful companies—both industrial manufacturers and corporations focused on patient care—to buy smaller shops and reorganize them into larger centers.[8] These firms often legitimized their strategy with the argument that larger facilities would enable more comprehensive services for amputees. However, local prosthetists strongly resisted centralization, arguing that it was beneficial only to industrial manufacturers, while increasing travel times for amputees and undermining their close relationships to local technicians, thus threatening the quality of patient care. As an enraged German prosthetist claimed:

> We know that it [the trend toward centralization, DS] is not right, that it will fail sooner or later. I mean, we have such a great health system in Germany, especially with regard to O&P firms. [...] We have 1900 of them! And this is why there is always a relationship to a specific locality [Ortsbezug in the German original, DS]. When there is an issue with your prosthesis, you don't need to drive far. You can go there quickly, you get an appointment quickly. With your technician! [...] It is a bond of trust that is established there, too! [...] Businesswise there is no question: Centralize everything and then, bam, rake in money. But...the patient! He is what matters!
>
> (interview, German prosthetist, 2016–05–05, own translation)

This conflict between central manufacturers and local prosthetists demonstrates that, even though the overall structure of centralized fabrication and decentralized fitting was not questioned, the specific configuration of this system was subject to ongoing strategic negotiations. In these struggles, centrality and efficient distribution were commonly weighed against locality and the relationship between the industry and its users. Industrial manufacturers rhetorically associated centralization—a tendency that consolidated their distribution network—with the idea of more inclusive services for amputees. Conversely, prosthetists linked a decentralized system that would guarantee the independence of their profession with the availability of locally meaningful services and the formation of trust between technicians and amputees. In short, controversies over the organization of the industrial distribution system were closely related to re-negotiating the mechanisms of inclusion and exclusion in the existing user landscape.

5.1.3.2 Biases in the Institutional Order

A comparable situation pertained with regard to the institutional aspect of organizing the circulation of prosthetic components in Germany, Canada, and the US. Fundamental norms and regulations were rarely questioned in principle. Yet, ingrained action nets still faced users with differential levels of access to prosthetic care. At times, these patterns of inclusion and exclusion were reflected on in practice and served as arguments in renegotiating specific aspects of both professional routines and the insurance system. When this was the case, matters of user construction became intertwined with strategic struggles over industrial reorganization.

Biases through Professional Habits

Prosthetist's routines for choosing the components for the prosthetic limb of a given customer offer an illuminating example of the construction and ongoing contestation of biases in the user landscape. Befitting the importance of such choices for regulating device circulation, there were clear professional norms for how to perform this task. Most importantly, there was the expectation that any *good* prosthetist would begin the process by inquiring about the amputee's goals for using a device and would then go about selecting the right components in an open-ended and dialogical manner. However, in practice, this expectation was not always met. People wearing prosthetic devices frequently complained that their own knowledge and experience was discounted by prosthetists who insisted on deep-seated habits. One of my interviewees reported the following:

> I personally hate it when a technician [...] wants to tell me something like 'yeah, it's best this way and we've been doing it like this for 20 years and it's totally awesome and super, super great'. [...] He is welcome to tell

me that, but he ought not insist on his opinion. I have had technicians, where we yelled at each other. [...] I have lived with this for 28 years! I have worn a prosthesis for almost 28 years! I have seen everything! [...] Some people think they know it better, but they are not themselves affected, so how should they know?"

(interview, upper limb amputee, 2016–11–04, own translation)

Accounts like this one draw attention to the fact that even though professional routines were essential for supporting and regulating the circulation of industrial products, they also lead to the entrenchment of certain user roles at the expense of other possibilities. From the point of view of industrial manufacturers, attempting to shape these routines presented one way of guaranteeing the circulation of their products, and they tried to do so by deploying strategies ranging from advertisement and sales visits to company involvement in professional education programs. From the point of view of amputees, renegotiating their technician's habits could be a matter of great personal importance. Yet, as shown in the above example, doing so risked serious conflicts and could lead to the local break-down of the action net. Where amputees went with the professional's choice, they sometimes ended up with devices that were ill-suited for their purposes and severely limited the kinds of identities they were able to enact. Then again, when amputees decided to challenge their technician's routines, they jeopardized the relationship with their care provider.

Biases through the Insurance System

As with the other elements of the circulation order, the operation of the health insurance system was a taken-for-granted aspect of user construction in the prosthetics industry. For instance, component manufacturers routinely designed their products according to prevailing coding schemes and prosthetists were asked to minutely document their actions to legitimize reimbursement.[9] Supported by these deeply institutionalized practices, the vast majority of amputees in Germany, Canada, and the US could expect the cost of their prostheses to be covered by their insurer. Yet even though coverage of *some form of* prosthetic aid was the norm, many insurance contracts extended to basic products and services only. The insurance system thus played an ambivalent role in device circulation. While it made the mass provision of assistive devices possible, it simultaneously constructed inequalities between users and regularly precluded desirable ways of acting and being in the world. Under these conditions, struggles between amputees, their prosthetists, and their insurers were commonplace and often entailed months-long waiting times, and frustration on all sides.

To avoid such scenarios, amputees, prosthetists, and manufacturers sometimes formed coalitions to convince insurers to extend the coverage for specific components or specific groups of amputees. When successful, such contestations had the potential to change the concrete rules and norms underpinning the circulation of prosthetic devices. A particularly significant example of such a controversy emerged around the so-called C-Leg, the first fully microprocessor-controlled knee joint in the history of the field. Due to its innovative technology, the C-Leg promised enhanced functionality and security, enabling its users to perform a range of activities otherwise precluded to them. However, the use of microprocessors also made the C-Leg about five times as expensive as a conventional knee joint, placing it well beyond the amount covered under the existing reimbursement schemes. In Germany, this situation led to several lawsuits revolving around the question of whether the C-Leg's benefits compelled insurers to pay for the device under German law. Based on multiple clinical studies conducted by its manufacturer, the Federal Social Court eventually found that, under specific conditions, coverage was indeed obligatory (Bundessozialgericht, 2002, 2004). Following that decision, the C-Leg was fitted at prosthetic clinics across the country, enhancing the mobility of thousands of amputees and allowing them to enact new user roles and identities. In this instance, the legal struggle involving amputees, prosthetists, device manufacturers, and insurers led to a reconfiguration of the insurance system and successfully challenged the prevailing order of circulation. However, despite the importance of such changes, the overall regulatory function of the insurance system remained unquestioned, with the circulation of new devices still depending on insurers' reimbursement policies.

In summary, the preceding examples demonstrate that even in places in which the production of prosthetic componentry is highly industrialized and supported by both infrastructures and institutions, the accessibility of prostheses is not equally guaranteed for all users. In fact, specific biases are constructed by the same infrastructures and institutions that enable the translation between the centralized activities of producing and the diversely located actions of using contemporary prostheses. In this situation, concrete inequalities can be contested, although the overall order of circulation remains firmly in place, as do its general mechanisms of inclusion and exclusion.

5.1.4 Global Inequalities in Prosthetic User Construction

It should be clear by now that the Western prosthetics industry has developed in conjunction with a particular order of circulation—one that it helped to construct and that has, over time, come to be a necessary precondition of its daily operation. In Germany, Canada, and the US, this pattern of action and its respective mechanisms of user construction are safely supported by institutions and infrastructures. Serious problems in the circulation of assistive devices are the exception, even though some people are structurally more vulnerable to such hardships than others. Yet, in many other regions of the world, the dominant order of circulation is *chronically* in crisis. According to a widely quoted report by the World Health Organization (WHO), about 30 million people in need of prosthetic or orthotic products live in what the report defines as "developing countries" (WHO, 2011, p. 102), with only 5–15%[10] of them having access to any kind of assistive device. Even those who do have access will usually receive products that would be considered substandard in Germany or the US. In short, from a global perspective, the inaccessibility of appropriate prosthetic products and services is the norm for a majority of amputees. These dramatic inequalities in the global user landscape can be traced to the infrastructural and institutional conditions on which the circulation of Western prostheses has historically been premised. Far from being taken for granted, these conditions are not met in most times and places, positioning the large majority of amputees outside of the Western system of industrial user construction (Harkins et al., 2012).

To begin with, the action net of prosthetic user construction as sketched out so far presupposes the existence of *material infrastructures* connecting remote factories and local sites of use. As I have shown, prosthetic clinics are obligatory passage points in this system, as it is there that standardized industrial products are adjusted to their concrete users. This means that user construction depends on the accessibility of prosthetic clinics and their connection to the industrial distribution system. However, in many regions of the world, prosthetic clinics and workshops do not exist or exist only in urban centers. Moreover, clinics can be difficult to reach where transportation infrastructures are insufficient, or where the mobility of people with limb loss is reduced due to economic deprivation or social stigma (Marino et al., 2015, p. 46). For instance, in Port-au-Prince, Haiti, the clinic in which I did my fieldwork was situated on top of a hill, facing individuals with lower limb loss with a strenuous walk. Yet many of them still arrived there on foot because the taxi fare was unaffordable and local bus drivers refused to take them on board for fears founded in the local Voodoo belief system. Getting to the facility from the Haitian countryside posed even greater challenges, and sometimes took days or a significant amount of money. Hence, in spite of the clinic's existence, prospective users faced serious difficulties reaching it, let alone being on time for their appointment. Consequently, many scheduled amputees never came or did not return for the inevitable repairs and maintenance of their new limbs.

Even where prosthetic clinics are accessible, their connection to the industrial distribution system is not a given. On the one hand, this involves logistic troubles, with shipments taking months, getting lost, or accumulating high costs in duties and taxes. On the other, it is a matter of amputees' ability to pay for prosthetic care (WHO, 2011, pp. 106–107). As alluded to above, Western manufacturers focus on the development and production of advanced and expensive componentry for the European and North American markets. In the absence of private or public *health insurance*, many amputees residing in the countries of the Global South can simply not afford these devices and are thus barred from becoming users. In view of this, large industrial firms deemphasize delivery to parts of the world in which their products cannot be paid for, or only offer a limited range of products to start with. As one high-ranking manager at a large industrial manufacturer explained:

> In Germany you have the best reimbursement worldwide. You are entitled to a maximum compensation for disability and this is why this is obviously a very interesting market for us. In the US, for example, a lot of high-tech is bought by the military for soldiers who were wounded in action. Then there are developing countries, emerging markets, where nothing is paid for, where you can only bring in basic technologies.
>
> (interview, manager at industrial manufacturer, 2016–05–04, own translation)

Given the lack of financial resources and an institutionalized system for covering the cost of medical devices, entire regions of the world are not considered to be "attractive markets" for more sophisticated prosthetic technology. Accordingly, industrial companies do not usually develop devices for people living in these places, nor do they take steps to set up costly distribution networks to secure the circulation of their existing products.

Finally, even where clinics are accessible and funding for appropriate materials can be secured, there is often a lack of *certified professionals* able to assemble, and fit prosthetic devices. As I hinted at above, even in Germany and the US, the shortage of skilled personnel was an issue. Yet, in most other places, the situation was far worse. According to the WHO:

> The International Society for Prosthetics and Orthotics and the World Health Organization have estimated that people needing prostheses or orthotics and related services represent 0.5% of the population in developing countries; and 30 million people in Africa, Asia, and Latin America require an estimated 180,000 rehabilitation professionals. In 2005 there were 24 prosthetic and orthotic schools in developing countries, graduating 400 trainees annually. Worldwide existing training facilities for prosthetic and orthotic professionals and other providers of essential rehabilitation services are deeply inadequate in relation to the need.
>
> (WHO, 2011, p. 102)[11]

Given this lack of trained prosthetists and technicians, the provision of assistive devices became a serious bottleneck for the circulation of prostheses and the construction of corresponding user roles and identities. Even where components and materials were available, choosing, assembling, and fitting them could take months and many amputees had to bide their time.

5.1.5 Strategies for Constructing Users in Troubled Times and Places

In the face of these global inequalities, alternative strategies for making prostheses available in places beyond the Western distribution network are nearly as old as the industry itself. Many of them continue to rely on centralized production and aim at *extending*, *repairing*, *tapping into*, or *copying* the Western action net. In doing so, they often construct precarious user landscapes, which depend on the perilous translation between remote industrial centers and local clinics. By contrast, there have been some successful attempts at setting up action nets around local production. These strategies for constructing users outside of North America and Europe do offer interesting opportunities for studying both the power asymmetries that emerge around centralized industrial production systems and the effects that alternative production technologies may have on configuring a different range of users.

5.1.5.1 Extending the Western Action Net: Between Techno-Imperialism and Healing Hands

Since the rise of large-scale production, Western prosthesis manufacturers have been aiming to *extend* the distribution of their products to ever new places either with the goal of opening up new markets or to lend aid to "developing countries," and quite often both. As Klaus Dittmer shows in his brochure "Orthopedic Technology from Germany: An export model with a 120-year tradition" (Dittmer, 2016), the "export" of Western products and concepts has been part of the prosthetics industry from its inception. Like the industry itself, these ventures were often deeply entangled with histories of war and, in many cases, with histories of colonialism. German prosthetists and technicians traveled to Russia (ca. 1923), Indonesia (1954), Burma (today Myanmar, 1957), the Philippines (1957), Tunisia (1966), Togo (1974), Guinea-Bissau (1974), Vietnam (1978), and Tanzania (1981). They set up prosthetic clinics, brought in tools, materials, and manufacturing techniques and, at times, trained local craftspeople. By running local clinics on Western machines and techniques, these prosthetists effectively set up outposts of the Western prosthetics industry and paved the way for the circulation of its products. As Dittmer writes:

> These returning development aid workers brought experience and know-how back to Germany that benefited the technical developments in orthopaedics, especially in the orthopaedic technology sector, which smoothed the way for 'market access.'
>
> (Dittmer, 2016, p. 9)

As a result of this strategy of extending the action net of prosthetic user construction beyond its places of origin, newly founded prosthetic clinics tended to depend on Western manufacturers for access to machines, materials, and personnel. However, in many cases, circulation remained precarious and action nets were often severed by political upheaval or simply by the fact that funding ran out, causing Western prosthetists to leave the country without having established locally sustainable operations.

These structural dependencies on industrial centers of mass production are very much in place today and are sustained by a system of development aid. As Marino and colleagues (2015) point out in their review of distribution pathways of prosthetic devices in "low-resource settings,"[12] it is often international NGOs and "faith-based organizations," which mediate between local clinics and remote manufacturers. In many cases, these organizations become important mediators that enable and regulate the circulation of prosthetic componentry manufactured by the Western industry. The Haitian clinic I visited provided an illustrative example of this pattern. The clinic's operations were largely based on production technologies manufactured by German firms and donated to the center by a German faith-based organization. Materials and components mostly arrived from North America and were paid for with the help of funding from NGOs and other "healing hands."[13] The clinic had even set up a system of social workers who were responsible for negotiating the coverage of prosthetic care with every amputee. In effect, NGOs *repaired* the Western pattern of action by picking up key tasks that would have been carried out by health insurers in countries of the Global North. By paying for componentry and by regulating the flow of prostheses to prospective users, they allowed the clinic to act much like a comparable facility in Germany, Canada, or the US. The main effect of this was to make local activities compatible with global distribution networks and to enable the circulation of prostheses from central factories located in Europe and North America to prospective users in Haiti.

While this strategy succeeded in connecting the Haitian clinic to the industrial distribution system, this newly constructed link remained highly precarious, placing the entire action net and the users it constructed in constant jeopardy. Relying on international NGOs meant that any change in the volatile economic and political situation might leave the clinic without supplies. For instance, when I joined two representatives of US and Canadian organizations traveling to Haiti, gaining access to the country was difficult, as the travel advisories for US, Canadian, and German citizens had been raised to the maximum warning level due to violent anti-government protests in Port-au-Prince. The International Monetary Fund had threatened to withdraw support for Haiti if the government refused to raise the prices for fuel, diesel, and kerosene. When the government complied with these demands, protests broke out, only to subside when the country's prime minister stepped down. While this change in political leadership made it possible for us to come into the country, and to bring in some materials as well as funding, it severed some of the ties that the clinic's personnel had been able to establish with the previous government. Under these conditions, sustaining the flow of prosthetic components to the clinic was very difficult and user construction remained highly precarious.

5.1.5.2 The Donation Model: Tapping Into Institutionalized Circulation Pathways

Whereas today most of the materials and components at the Haitian clinic are sourced through the conventional practices of choosing, negotiating coverage, and ordering, there was another pattern through which Western prostheses arrived at clinics in the Global South. In this pattern, which reportedly dominated in Haiti after the 2010 earthquake, local facilities do not receive monetary donations to choose and buy their own supplies. Rather, prostheses arrive there as in-kind donations. As described by Marino and colleagues (2015), these devices can be new, but more often they are used. For example, one common practice in Western prosthetics is to return a used prosthesis to the clinic after the recipient has passed away or received a new device. These "second hand" prostheses are collected and given to charities that distribute them to clinics which would otherwise be cut off from the distribution network. In other instances, donations are made by industrial manufacturers themselves, often as a form of disaster relief. In these cases, the institutionalized action net is bypassed as prostheses are not chosen, ordered, or even bought and sold. Instead, they are given away for free or at a very low price.

One central consequence of such donations is that products will circulate to people they were never designed for. This, of course, increases the likelihood of major incongruities between the actions of designing and using prosthetic devices. Many donated devices are unsuited for local use practices and environments, such as work in agriculture. Also, the complexity of Western prostheses presupposes regular maintenance and repair, which often proves difficult in the absence of skilled technicians and a reliable supply of affordable spare parts (Harkins et al., 2012, p. 359). Issues like these represent more general concerns with devices designed in the Global North and used in the Global South. Yet, translation problems are aggravated in the case of bulk donations as they further limit a prosthetist's ability to choose appropriate components for the use of local amputees. Consider, for instance, the following description of a mass-fitting situation in Guatemala, which was based on such donations.

> They [Western prosthetists, DS] went to Guatemala, they collect this bin [filled with donated prostheses], they ship it down. It costs a fortune, it takes months to get there, and they get the clients ready. And here's the standard of care [...]: A client walks in there [...]. They've been waiting six months, they've been waiting a year, they wait outside in the

> streets. One by one they come in. The prosthetist looks at the guy, looks at his limb, starts digging through this bin. Did you have Lego? Looking for that part? Same thing. You dig through the bin. Here? No. Maybe this one? But if I cut off this piece of this one? But maybe that's good for somebody else later? Massive amounts of decision-making. And they basically make these systems on the fly with whatever materials they have: Tape, glue. [...] And they just fit people. As many as they can.
>
> (interview, engineer at non-profit, 2017-09-19)

The unregulated mode of circulation implied by bulk donations clearly invites translation errors of all kinds between the situated activities of Western industry and the differently situated activities of using its products. Donated components, having been designed for an entirely different use context, may offer the wrong kind of functionality, or may not be considered aesthetically pleasing. People may abandon them, or they may break when used in ways unforeseen by their designers. Yet, when repairs, changes, or maintenance become necessary, this ad hoc mode of circulation means that there will rarely be spare parts available. The donation model is therefore prone to construct highly precarious user identities, that may quickly be undone.

5.1.5.3 Alternative Modes of Production, Alternative Modes of Circulation

As the foregoing examples make clear, the dependency on the Western prosthetics industry has created all sorts of problems in places that do not meet the institutional and infrastructural conditions guaranteeing the circulation of its products. In view of this, several projects and organizations have emerged around attempts at decentralizing production and moving it closer to the sites of use. These approaches emphasize independence from the Western prosthetics industry, and they involve ways of designing, producing, and circulating prostheses that center on groups of prospective users that have not been served well by the latter. In effect, they demonstrate that, while Western practices of industrial user construction dominate, they are not without alternatives.

The action net that evolved around the Jaipur foot (Arya & Klenerman, 2008; Srinivasan, 2002) offers a useful example of an alternative order of circulation based on local manufacturing.[14] Developed in the early 1970s by Ram Chander Sharma and Pramod Karan Sethi, the Jaipur foot was first intended to address the needs of amputees in rural India. The inventors had found that the SACH (solid-ankle-cushion-heel) foot, designed and produced by Western manufacturers, was not suitable to local practices, particularly to cross-legged sitting and walking on uneven, wet, or muddy terrain. By replacing the SACH foot's solid ankle with a mix of laminated wood and rubber, Sharma and Sethi designed the Jaipur foot to better suit local conditions. More importantly, they decided to make the device from locally available materials to allow for wide affordability and decentralized fabrication. As a result, not only could the Jaipur foot be made from materials that cost only about 250 Indian Rupees (approximately 3 Euros), thus reducing the need for insurance, but it could also be manufactured by local artisans, thereby sidestepping the reliance on remote industrial manufacturers and even certified professionals (Arya & Klenerman, 2008).

Owing to its local mode of manufacturing, as well as to the fact that Sethi resisted pressures to patent the design, the Jaipur foot has been picked up and further adapted by many local practitioners in places that had hitherto been excluded from the distribution network of the Western prosthetics industry. By far the largest manufacturer of Jaipur feet is an Indian NGO called Bhagwan Mahaveer Viklang Sahayata Samiti (BMVSS). According to its website, the organization has provided prostheses to more than 648,000 recipients in the country since 1975. Despite its large scale, which came with the standardization of manufacturing processes, production is still performed manually and is strongly distributed. Prostheses are produced in 24 permanent centers across India. In addition, BMVSS also offers what they call "on-the-spot fitting camps" in other locations domestically and abroad. For these camps, which are supported by local organizers, BMVSS sends teams of doctors and technicians as well as materials and equipment to temporary workshops, where limbs are made for local recipients in one to three days. In this manner, Jaipur devices have been fitted to 35,900 people across 35 countries, with several temporary "camps" resulting in the establishment of more permanent facilities.

These practices provide a strong contrast to the order of circulation in Western countries. Rather than being manufactured in a central factory using industrial production technology, the Jaipur foot is made by craftspeople in regional centers or even mobile and temporary workshops. In both cases, attempts are made to move the fabrication of both fit components and sockets closer to the sites of use, thus alleviating some of the conditions set on the circulation of conventional devices. This flexible approach has made the Jaipur foot available in places cut off from the distribution networks of Western manufacturers. However, it also raises difficult questions about the consistency and sustainability of products and services (Arya & Klenerman, 2008). It is interesting to observe that the same principles that underpin the circulation of the device in the Global South have limited its success in places in which the institutional order of Western prosthetics prevails (Figure 5.3). Due to its craft-based, local production, the Jaipur foot has not been standardized let alone subjected to the rigorous testing procedures associated with the practices of industrial mass production. As a consequence, the device has not been widely available in Western countries.

This example demonstrates that, while the Western order of circulation is dominant, alternative approaches do exist. Indeed, the institutional and

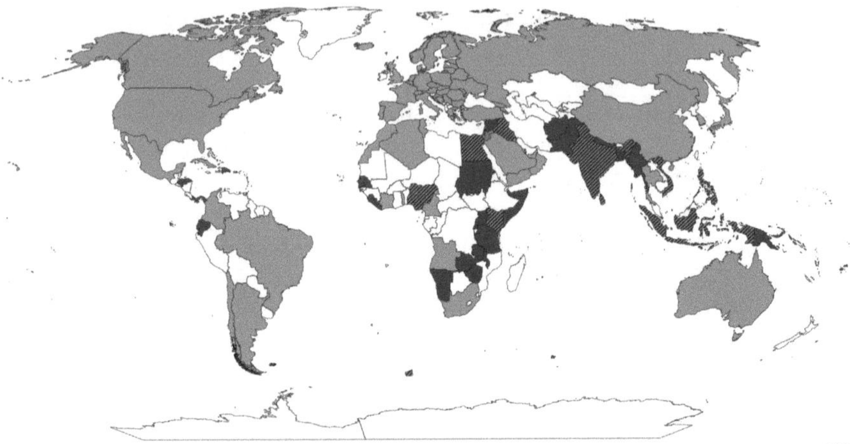

Figure 5.3 The map illustrates the global circulation of Western prostheses and the Jaipur Foot. Blue: Countries with offices or distribution partners of market leader Ottobock; Red: Countries in which BMVSS fitting camps have been held. Green: Overlap. Own figure, using data by Ottobock, and BMVSS.[15]

infrastructural system that has evolved in conjunction with the curious division of labor between centralized mass production and decentralized custom production should be seen as a specific historical configuration of the action nets constituting the supply of prosthetic devices. Even though this pattern may appear rigid and unchangeable, examples such as the Jaipur foot show that changes in the mode of production may well enable different patterns of circulation, with different principles of inclusion and exclusion. As I will show in the next section, this is precisely what is happening with the introduction of digital fabrication.

5.2 Digital Distribution Networks

In this section, I deal with the challenges that the creative application of digital fabrication technologies posed to the dominant order of circulation. My overall argument is that because the prevailing order has evolved in conjunction with the industrialization and centralization of prosthetic production, it may be called into question with the implementation of a new set of production technologies, particularly if they allow for changes in the locus of manufacturing. Digital production technologies, such as 3D scanners and 3D printers, appear to be a case in point, as they are thought to afford a radical decentralization and re-localization of manufacturing (Ferdinand et al., 2016; Schrape, 2019). This promise is based on the technology's capacity to translate between tangible objects and *digital data*—a novel kind of translation that allows industrial products to travel rapidly between sites in the form of digital files rather than material objects. Accordingly, digital distribution networks may now be plotted along an infrastructure spanned by the internet and digital inscription and production devices, rather than along conventional logistic channels made up of roads, warehouses, and delivery centers. In other words, digital fabrication offers new opportunities for organizing the journey of products between industries and their users. Insofar as these changes amount to a reorganization of the dominant order of circulation, they are bound to construct new patterns of accessibility and inaccessibility, and thus new groups of users and non-users.

To examine these claims, I analyze three newly emerging patterns of circulation in the digitalized prosthetics industry: The *outsourcing model*, the *local fabrication model*, and the *open-source model*. I show that digital production devices do allow for changes in the locus of manufacturing, although these may involve centralization as well as decentralization. Moreover, new user roles only emerge where the novel translational capacities of these devices are used to sidestep the existing institutional and infrastructural conditions of circulation. The *outsourcing model*, for instance, resulted in both a centralization of socket production and a decentralization of fit component production, but it did not directly affect end users, because the patterns of circulation changed only within the industry itself. By contrast, in the *local fabrication model* 3D printers were interpreted as part of a digital distribution infrastructure rather than a means of production per se, which helped to sidestep existing infrastructural bottlenecks between industry and users. Inclusive effects remained limited, however, as the model continued to rely on certified professionals and high degrees of centralized control over the flow of both digital data and physical materials. Finally, in the *open-source model*, circulation was based on the free sharing of digital files and the use of privately-owned 3D printers. This allowed volunteer makers to sidestep the institutional and infrastructural conditions set by conventional industry. It did, however, result in the unregulated circulation of devices and the construction of a highly volatile user landscape, in which recipients were often faced with sub-standard products and somewhat unreliable services.

5.2.1 The Outsourcing Model: Reorganization Without New Users

In the prosthetics industry, digital technologies have been associated with the outsourcing of manufacturing since their introduction in the late 1970s and 1980s. In contrast to commonly held beliefs about digital fabrication, this first and foremost referred to the *centralization* of socket production, while the *decentralization* of component production only recently began to gather momentum. Large manufacturers had long sought to expand their factory-centered approach from fit components to all parts of the prosthesis. However, with analogue production technology, removing socket production from local workshops proved to be a troublesome undertaking. In early

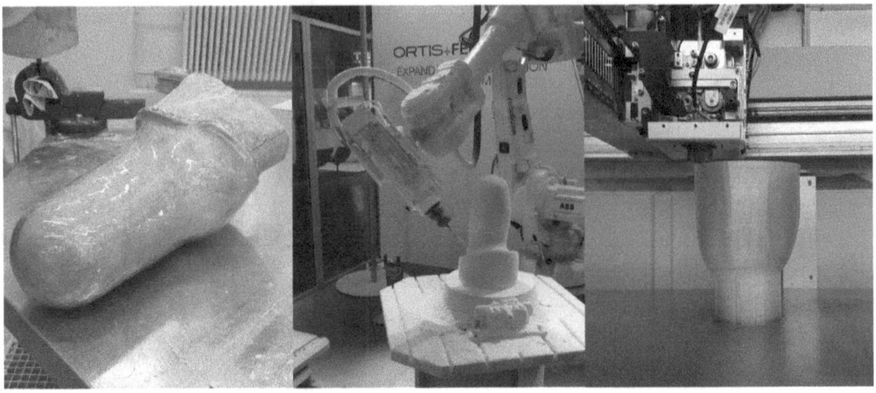

Figure 5.4 Socket "pulled" over plaster model (left), CNC carving a foam model (middle), 3D printing a socket (right), source: own photographs. Own photographs.

incarnations of central manufacturing, a local prosthetist would take and model a plaster cast of the prospective user's limb, just like in the traditional craft-based workflow. However, instead of manufacturing the socket herself, s/he would then pack the cast—a rather large and heavy object (Figure 5.4 left)—and send it off to an external service provider along with a list of specifications for the final product (dotted in Figure 5.5). The concrete manufacturing tasks such as pulling the socket and adding the desired adapters would then be performed by skilled technicians working at a central factory or large workshop. Following production, the socket would be shipped back to the clinic for final adjustments, assembly, and fitting. This method reduced the costs for technicians and lab space born by local clinics. However, it also increased turnaround times for sockets, accumulated shipping charges, and relinquished the prosthetists' control over the quality of the socket. As a consequence, most prosthetists still opted for in-house production.

With the increasing availability of affordable 3D scanners and fast internet connection, the central fabrication of sockets has become more attractive. Using digital inscription devices, it is now possible to translate the limb into a "digital plaster cast" (compare Section 4.2.2), which is modeled in a software tool and can be sent to a central fabricator packaged in the attachment of an e-mail rather than a cardboard box. At the central factory, CNC machine tools are used to translate the digital file back into a tangible object by carving it out of a block of soft foam (Figure 5.4 middle). This foam model is then either shipped back to the clinic to allow for local fabrication or is used as a basis for further manufacturing tasks at the factory. In effect, the new type of intermediary, digital data instead of a heavy block of plaster, made circulation from the local clinic to the central fabricator faster and cheaper,

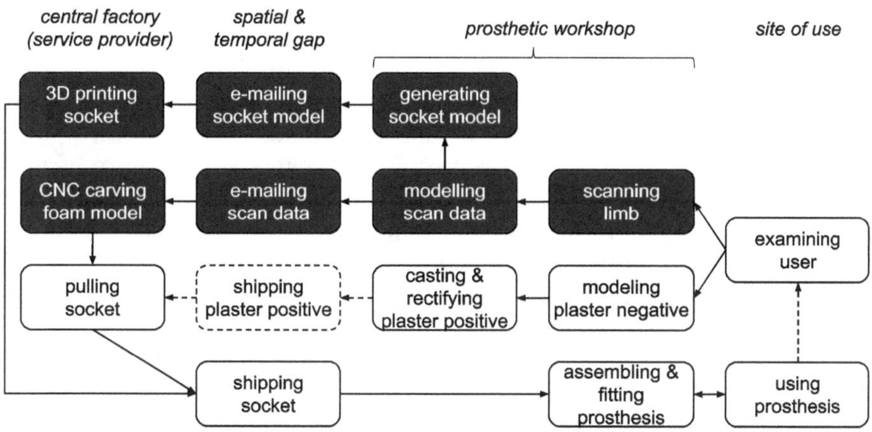

Figure 5.5 The introduction of digital fabrication made the outsourcing of socket production feasible for many smaller companies. Own figure.

contributing to the increasing importance of "c-fab." Whereas in-house production used to be virtually the only option for most prosthetists, by June 2015, 90% of O&P clinics in the US outsourced some portion of their manufacturing.[16]

As central fabrication facilities are adding *industrial-grade 3D printers*[17] to their portfolio of production devices, the trend toward the centralization of socket production appears to be strengthened even further. In contrast to CNC carving, which translates a digital model of the residual limb into a physical foam model that still requires manual production of the socket, 3D printing enables the direct fabrication of the final product based on its digital representation. Socket design can therefore be done in a software program, with any form of bulky intermediary, be it plaster or foam, rendered superfluous. After some assembling and post-production, the socket is then ready for shipping to the clinic.

In addition to strengthening the trend toward the *centralization* of socket production, the introduction of industrial-grade 3D printing has also made the relative *decentralization* of fit component production a more realistic option. Indeed, while some established manufacturers have started buying providers of digital fabrication services, virtually none of the 3D printing-based start-ups have opted for an in-house production approach. Rather than purchasing and maintaining their own equipment, they leverage the already existing infrastructures offered by certified 3D printing service providers. When a prosthetist orders a product from one of these firms, often via an online platform, the company forwards the file to one of their manufacturing partners where it is printed and delivered to the clinic. Again, the outsourcing of production is greatly facilitated by a digital communication infrastructure and the ability to translate between digital files and tangible products.

As this quick overview shows, the advent of digital fabrication has enabled new patterns in the circulation of prosthetic sockets as well as fit components. Both patterns rely on the outsourcing of fabrication to third-party service providers, even though this involves the *centralization* of production in the case of sockets and a *decentralization* of production in the case of fit components. In light of the argument so far, it may be expected that such a reversal would have a drastic effect on the conditions of circulation under which artificial limbs become available to amputees. However, no such shift appears to be forthcoming. Despite the transformation in the spatial organization of production, the outsourcing model has not made prosthetic devices accessible to new groups.

The surprising persistence of the established user landscape can be explained by considering the *infrastructural and institutional conditions* under which products travel from the site of production to the site of use. From this perspective, it becomes clear that the outsourcing model did not sidestep existing conditions, but instead added new ones. From an *infrastructural* point of view, the outsourcing of production presupposes digital distribution pathways *as well as* non-digital ones (Figure 5.5). It depends on the operation of both prosthetic clinics[18] *and* decentralized service providers; it requires that these facilities be connected by an online system to convey digital inputs *in addition* to conventional distribution networks to distribute material outputs. In short: A socket or a foot can be sent to a third-party manufacturer in a digital format, but as long as production is removed from the site of use, the product will still have to be delivered there in its materialized form. With a view to the *institutional* dimension of circulation, the relevant conditions also remain largely the same. While the wording of some insurance schemes may need to be updated to reflect changes in the production process, 3D-printed products are required to conform to the same reimbursement system as their conventional counterparts. Similarly, even though manufacturing itself is outsourced, limbs are still assembled, fitted, and aligned by certified prosthetists at local prosthetic clinics.

In summary, even though start-ups, prosthetists, and service providers are going to great lengths to enable the digital circulation of devices between their respective facilities, these efforts may at best enhance services for a subset of pre-existing user groups. The outsourcing model mainly affects the circulation of intermediaries within industry. It does not alleviate any of the conditions under which products traverse the social and geographical gap between the industry and its users, while in some cases removing production even further from the site of use. The outsourcing of production may thus give companies an advantage over their competitors, but it will not result in the construction of new user roles or identities.

5.2.2 The Local Fabrication Model: Bypassing Conventional Infrastructures

Within the outsourcing model, production was run on industrial-grade 3D printers—large, expensive machines that could only be utilized efficiently only in the context of large fabrication centers. The introduction of *consumer-grade 3D printers*, however, made a difference by making available much smaller and cheaper production devices. In contrast to industrial machines, these could be moved to the desktops of prosthetic clinics, makerspaces, or even private homes with relative ease.

Based on this novel kind of printer, a number of North American NGOs and nonprofits set out to provide prosthetic devices to amputees who had previously been excluded from sufficient prosthetic care due to the infrastructural challenges connected to centralized fabrication. In contrast to classical industrial manufacturers, which would produce all their devices in a *central* factory, these organizations developed low-cost setups consisting of consumer-grade 3D printers as well as scanners and software, which they installed in prosthetic clinics facing financial or logistic hardship. Using this polycentric fabrication infrastructure, prosthetic clinics in places like Nepal and Haiti are now able to produce components *locally*, and partially alleviate their dependence on centers of industrial mass production located in countries of the Global North. Instead of ordering readymade products from *remote* manufacturers—a process that takes months and costs clinics large sums of money in courier charges—they may now use a digital infrastructure to access a range of product files that can be printed and assembled in a matter of hours. As one of the co-founders of an NGO working in Haiti put it:

> From spending a lot of time in Haiti talking with prosthetists, patients and clinic administrators we saw that one of the really big challenges was really just the supply chain logistics and distribution challenges. [...] Getting things into the country and then moving things around within the country. This is something we've kind of seen reports of in many lower-income countries [...] where you don't have Amazon Prime, like we can't just FedEx things. So, one of the things that's valuable about 3D printers in this context is, they basically serve as very slow teleporters. It's just a way of getting something from point A to point B [...]. We really see it as a way to establish a kind of alternative digital supply chain.
>
> (interview, co-founder of an NGO, 2017-09-13)

Consumer-grade 3D printers, thus gave NGOs an alternative way of knotting together the action nets of user construction across vast distances (Figure 5.6). Viewing digital fabrication as a means of *transportation* rather than as a means of *production* per se enabled a faster and cheaper method for

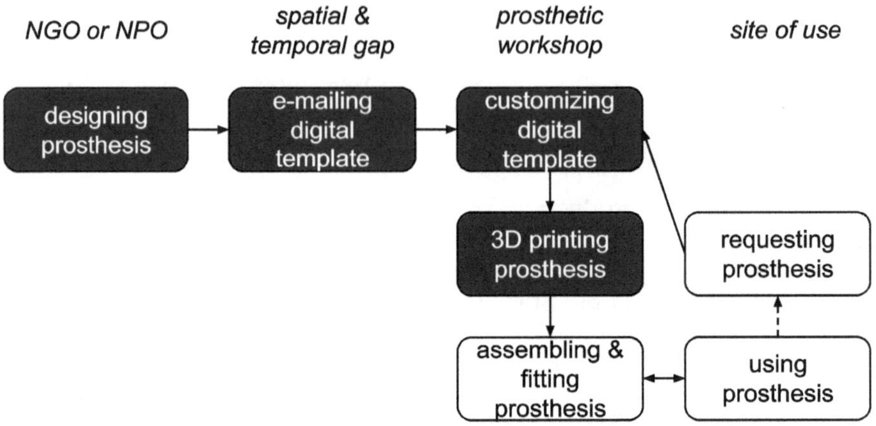

Figure 5.6 NGOs and non-profit organizations (NPOs) use digital fabrication to move production closer to the site of use. Own figure.

making prostheses available at the site of use. This creative use of 3D printers constituted as potential users many of those amputees who were marginalized by the dominant order of circulation that had crystalized around centralized industrial fabrication. In theory, all that had to be done was to set up more digital fabrication facilities in the clinics that asked for them.

5.2.2.1 The Limits of the Local Fabrication Model

In the cases I studied, the installation of local digital fabrication facilities did, indeed, result in the construction of new users by giving prosthetists fast access to prosthetic componentry and by increasing the range of products from which they could choose. Using a digital distribution infrastructure, prostheses could now be distributed more quickly and cheaply from North America to places marginalized by conventional logistic networks. However, despite the common usage of sci-fi metaphors depicting desktop 3D printers as universal replicators or *teleporters*, the new mode of circulation did by no means make prosthetic devices available to everyone who wanted them. In practice, the new technology could only be used to construct a very limited set of user roles and identities. On the one hand, these new biases were due to the material limitations of desktop 3D printers, which narrowed the range of products that could be fabricated with them. On the other, limitations stemmed from the fact that local production remained tethered to remote centers, as NGOs enforced high degrees of technical and organizational standardization to guarantee smooth operations across diverse contexts.

One of the clearest examples of these dynamics of partial inclusion can be found in the case of the Canadian non-profit *Beta* (a pseudonym). Based at the engineering department of a Canadian university, Beta was built around the development and provision of the Beta Hand, a 3D printable upper limb prosthetic system including a mechanical hand, wrist, socket, and harness. Even though the team was rather small, with only one full-time employee and a group of some twenty part-time volunteers, Beta had set up 3D printing facilities in prosthetic clinics in seven countries outside of Canada, including Guatemala, Ecuador, Haiti, Egypt, Uganda, Cambodia, and Nepal.[19] These centers included computers, 3D scanners, desktop 3D printers, and specifically trained local prosthetists. They gave the clinics the ability to produce the Beta Hand without relying on shipments from remote manufacturers. According to the founder of Beta, local digital fabrication played a pivotal role in constructing and sustaining new users in regions marginalized by existing logistic networks:

> We print in the country. Why? Because they [the amputees, DS] don't have to wait for six months. [...] If [a part of the prosthesis] breaks, they go back and they print it for 50 cents. [...] Not 200 Dollars for, you know, a part made in Germany [...]. And then could you imagine the DHL courier charge? [...] Forget about it! If you're a farmer in Guatemala and you've been given a prosthesis, you're not gonna be spending 300 American Dollars to get a little funny piece changed. [Beta] was about if it breaks, somebody in Guatemala makes it for you for 50 cents. That was the magic of 3D printing, that's why you want to 3D print [...] Because it makes it accessible!
>
> (interview, founder of Beta, 2017-09-19)

As this example underlines, using desktop 3D printing as part of a *digital distribution infrastructure* afforded a novel way of translating between prosthesis production, fitting, and use. Moving production closer to the site of use helped to establish viable action nets of user construction in regions of the world that had been excluded from circulation under conditions of centralized mass production.

However, even though the digital system of circulation helped to constitute new user groups, it did not produce anything approaching full inclusion. The efficacy of the digital distribution infrastructure was circumscribed by the translational capacities of the very same consumer-grade 3D printers that had made the extension of the action net possible to begin with. For instance, even though Beta volunteers worked hard to design new products, their portfolio remained limited to upper limb prostheses, as the 3D printers installed in local facilities were technically incapable of producing parts large or robust enough for walking or standing on them.[20] Due to such limitations, Beta's digital infrastructure supported only a *partial extension* of the action net of user construction. While it allowed for the local fabrication of arms and hands, it did not do the same for legs and feet, despite lower limb differences being a far more common problem. As a result, only a

Figure 5.7 Beta's 3D printing facility in a Haitian clinic. Own photograph.

small fraction of amputees visiting the partnering clinics were constituted as potential users of 3D-printed limbs, while the large majority continued to depend on conventional distribution channels. For example, in the Haitian clinic I did my fieldwork in, only about 25 people had been fitted with the Beta Hand in the first four years of the center's operation, while in most other countries, the reported numbers were even lower. The vast majority of amputees at the respective clinics had limb differences that could not be addressed with 3D-printable devices and in some places, local prosthetists were beginning to "run out of people to fit." The user landscape that could be constructed using the digital distribution infrastructure was thus severely limited by the capacities of a production technology commonly represented as universally applicable.

The user landscape was further limited by Beta's way of *organizing* the relationship between designing, distributing, and producing their prostheses. Most importantly, the decentral mode of fabrication that enabled the construction of new user groups in the first place, also confronted Beta with a growing number of diverse local settings of which the organization had little knowledge or control. In order to guarantee the smooth operation of their infrastructure under these circumstances, Beta aimed to reduce the complexity of production by simplifying products and product ranges, and by strictly standardizing and controlling the manufacturing process itself.[21]

However, these measures sometimes ended up further limiting the diversity of viable user identities, as well as reproducing some of the structural dependencies of local clinics on powerful centers in the Global North.

To stabilize their digital distribution network, Beta limited its design efforts to a small range of products with a high degree of simplification, as this was thought to allow Beta hands to be printed and assembled by local prosthetists with little experience in digital technology. Though they were cognizant of the fact that this strategy inevitably reduced the functional and aesthetic versatility of their products, Beta engineers insisted on standardization even in areas where the multi-purpose character of 3D printing was usually seen as one of the major advantages of the new production technology. For instance, when Beta's director explained the composition of the prosthesis to me, I was surprised to learn that the team had limited the number of available forearm geometries to reduce the complexity facing the local prosthetist. Even though Beta had designed a parametric model, which would have allowed for any number of shapes and sizes, they had chosen to make a small, predefined set that would cover most common cases:

I: The outer shell[22] [of the forearm, DS] is parametric that means there's one of 19. [...]

DS (SURPRISED): But theoretically you could make more of those?

I: Yes, we could, yeah. We could make as many as you want. We can make a hundred.

DS: Because they are parametric and you can just [...] scale up, scale down...

I: But for me, knowing human beings, I feel that when you give people more and more options, they get more and more confused, and their decision-making starts to slow down and they're like: Should I choose this one or this one? So, in a way I think 19 is even too much. But with the differences in the human body...I wish we could just have six or something like that, right? [B]ut, you know, it's not enough, right? [...] Everything [Beta Hand] must be deployable by people on the ground, in the country. [...] We are engineers, we would love to make it infinitely complicated, but then nobody will get fit. They'll get stuck.

(interview, director of Beta, 2017-09-19)

As this example illustrates, Beta deliberately limited their product range to allow for the smooth circulation of their products to the site of use.[23] Following this strategy, it was often decided to forego additional functionality or to restrict aesthetic choice, even though it was clear that this would limit the diversity of potential user roles beyond what would have strictly been necessary given the constraints of desktop 3D printing itself. Thus, rather than a result of the translational capacities of digital production devices, this limitation should be understood as an organizational response to the growing complexity and low degrees of control that come with a decentralized mode of production.

Indeed, the idea that standardization and control were necessary to make digital distribution scalable across contexts extended well beyond product design, into the layout and operation of the distribution infrastructure itself. For instance, Beta tightly controlled the machines, and printer settings used in the local production of their hands. In strong contrast to the open-source communities that will be discussed in the next section, Beta never made available the editable source files of their products. Instead, they distributed them in what is known as a G-code, a programming language that directly controls the movement and setting of 3D printers. This was done to guarantee successful local *production*, but also meant that the product itself became practically inaccessible for local *adaptation*. Any changes to the Beta hand's basic design could only be done by the Canadian engineers themselves.

Similarly, Beta also controlled the *materials* used in production, buying them in bulk and distributing supplies to fabrication facilities around the world. Remarkably, this centralized sourcing practice often introduced into Beta's circulation model some of the same infrastructural problems it was meant to overcome, thus partly reproducing the dependency of user construction in the Global South on remote centers in the Global North. This dependency was linked to the fact that even with the help of a digital distribution infrastructure, the Beta Hand could not be manufactured from thin air, as characterizations of 3D printers as "teleporters" or "universal replicators" might suggest. Instead, it was made up of objects that could not be distributed as digital files. Everything from the aquarium-grade silicone used for fingertips, to the metal nuts and bolts used for assembling the prosthesis, to the filament used in the 3D printing process itself had to be delivered via the same cardboard boxes familiar from the central fabrication model. Indeed, whenever one of the Canadian team members visited a production facility (e.g., in Haiti, Nepal…), which they tried to do biannually, they would take a box of materials with them to replenish the local supplies without which the decentralized digital fabrication network would soon have collapsed.

The analytical point to be raised here is that, while *digital distribution* and *local fabrication* might have helped to construct new user groups in places marginalized within the system of centralized mass production, such practices did not necessarily reduce the dependency on powerful organizations located in North America or Europe. In fact, in the local fabrication model, sustaining the newly constructed user groups required a continuous flow of various intermediaries, including *digital files*, *non-digital materials*, and *people* from NGOs located in the Global North to prosthetic clinics located in the Global South. The continued support for new users did, therefore, remain precarious, as it depended on the continued funding of Western NGOs as well as their ability to provide files and materials.

In summary, the idea of using desktop 3D printers as means of transportation, or even "teleportation," allowed NGOs and non-profit organizations to construct an alternative to the infrastructural foundation on which the conventional order of circulation in prosthetics operates. However, this alternative infrastructure could only be used to construct a limited range of user roles, while the majority of amputees continued to depend on the established system. Moreover, the new system did little to address the power asymmetries written into the dominant order of circulation. On the one hand, it enhanced the ability of local prosthetists to choose between prosthetic devices and ways of sourcing them. On the other, its operation continued to depend on the activities of precariously funded North American and European organizations, without which the digital action nets that supported the newly constructed user groups would have collapsed.

5.2.3 The Open-Source Model: Bypassing the Institutional Order

Much like Beta, the open-source community Alpha, introduced in Chapter 4, used desktop 3D printers for the decentralized fabrication of upper limb prostheses for social groups hitherto marginalized by the industry's dominant order of circulation. However, the community drastically differed from Beta in the way it organized the circulation of its products. Beta mainly used digital fabrication as a means to overcome the *infrastructural* challenges of centralized manufacturing, while adhering to the *institutional* aspects of the circulation order, by working with professional prosthetists and by exercising strict control over the design and production of its products. In sharp contrast, Alpha was described by its founder as "a global network of volunteers making assistive technologies through an infrastructure of internet communications, 3D printing and goodwill" (interview, founder of Alpha, 2017-12-14). The community made use of the increasingly widespread private ownership of desktop 3D printers to enact a grass-roots approach to fabrication and distribution. This allowed volunteers to sidestep not only the infrastructural but also the major institutional aspects of circulation, including regulation through professional norms and national insurance systems. By organizing an action net around privately-owned printers and the unpaid work of non-professional makers, Alpha aimed to make assistive devices available to people who had limited access to them through conventional channels.

With a view to the infrastructural dimension of circulation, Alpha was founded on the idea that, given the free availability of printable files on the internet, and the increasing ubiquity of privately owned and publicly available 3D printers, production could be carried out *almost anywhere*. Following this logic, the Alpha community emerged around the organization of (preferably) local matches between makers and amputees. When I interviewed the researcher now credited with founding Alpha, he described the community's inception as follows:

> One morning I was watching YouTube videos and I saw the now famous video about a South African carpenter who teamed up with a costume

> maker from Washington State to create a crude 3D-printed prosthetic hand [compare chapter 4, DS]. They mentioned that it was available open source, they mentioned that [...] this design could help children born missing fingers—and I had an idea. [...] On a whim I added a comment to the YouTube video stream. I said: 'I've made a Google Maps mashup and if you have a printer and you want to help, put a pin on this map and if you know someone who needs a hand, put a pin on this map.' And that video went viral, pins started to appear on the map. People started calling me saying: Ok now what do we do? And so, I created a Google+ community where we could figure it out together and that community now has ten thousand two hundred and fifty people who have signed up and [Alpha] is in eighty countries. There are chapters all over the world.
>
> (interview, founder of Alpha, 2017-12-14)

The approach described here is significant, because it utilizes a new way of making things, desktop 3D printing, to reverse the basic principles of how prosthetic production is organized and how prostheses are delivered to their prospective users. From an infrastructural perspective, fabrication in the Alpha model is based on internet communication and privately-owned production devices. Production is no longer confined to a centralized factory, a third-party manufacturing facility, or even a prosthetic clinic. Rather, it can happen at any site equipped with internet access and a suitable 3D printer, a development signaling a radical *decentralization*. Moreover, as the above quote makes clear, decentralized, private fabrication is paired with a concern for geographically matching potential producers and users of artificial

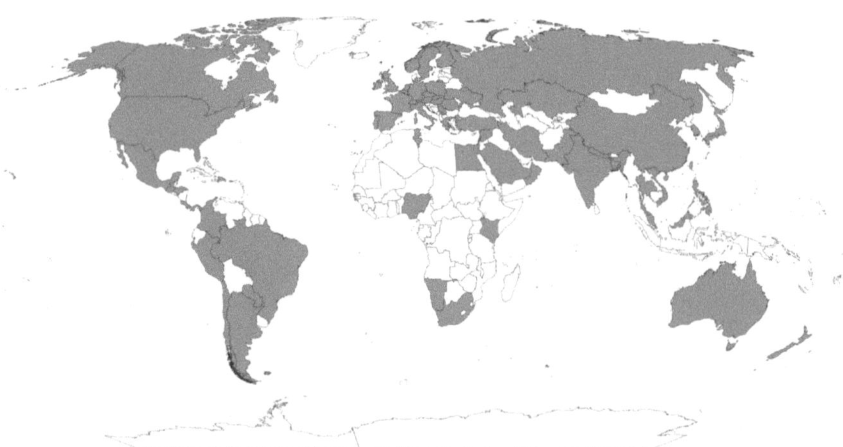

Figure 5.8 Map of countries with Alpha volunteers in 2016, three years after the founding of the community, according to one of the community's websites. Own figure.

limbs. Thus, the Alpha model also promises to ease the translation between producing and using by reducing the spatial distance between them.

From an institutional perspective, too, the ideas of *non-commercial* and *private* fabrication imply a radical break with the dominant order of circulation. The envisioned distance between producing and using is not only *short* in a geographical sense, but also *direct* in the sense that it requires no additional intermediation by professional prosthetists or insurance companies. In the scenario described by its founder, the delivery of devices in the Alpha community is free of charge, organized by the amateur producers themselves, and requires no more regulation than is implied by self-selected matching, internet-based communication, and mutual goodwill:

> Someone who needs a hand gets in touch. In this case, they go to the website, they provide information including measurements and photographs and then people in the community volunteer to work on that case. And then they're put in direct touch with the recipient, and they try to figure out what the recipient wants, and they create a design for the recipient, deliver it and that is sort of the standard case.
>
> (interview, founder of Alpha, 2017-12-14)

What this description implies is that the principle of directly matching prospective users and amateur producers made it possible to sidestep the major institutions governing, and at times constraining, the circulation of assistive devices. Developing, producing, and fitting prostheses *without* the intervention of prosthetists or insurers allowed Alpha to constitute as potential users many of the people who had previously found it difficult to access a satisfactory level of prosthetic care.

The first major group of Alpha hand users were US children with congenital limb differences. In this case, Alpha's ability to sidestep *institutional* constraints on circulation was particularly crucial. Children had

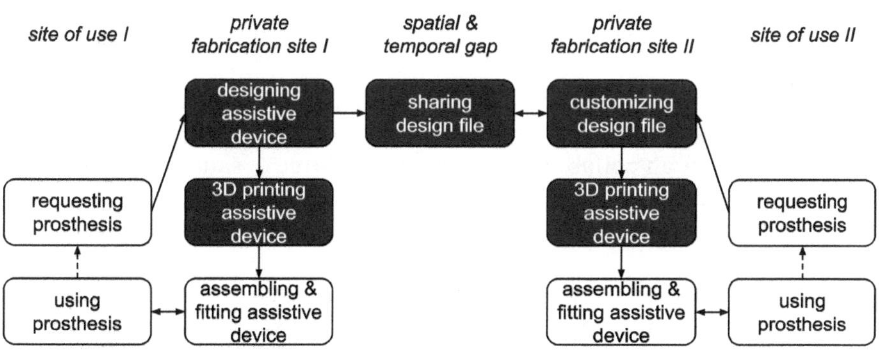

Figure 5.9 Alpha's original model was intended to move production closer to the site of use. Own figure.

been marginalized under the conventional system, partly because standard insurance contracts did not cover the cost of ever new prostheses for their quickly growing bodies. In this situation, Alpha's direct matching system offered parents an alternative way of accessing basic assistive devices for their children, which was free of charge and guaranteed to avoid difficult negotiations with prosthetists and insurers. As may be expected, professionals soon criticized that alternative by questioning the usefulness and safety of homegrown 3D-printed hands.[24] However, Alpha members continuously avoided being subjected to established rules and expectations by further flagging out the differences between their own practices and those of their professional counterparts. For instance, volunteers were adamant that their products were given, not sold, thus emphasizing the charitable nature of their work, and avoiding the complicated certification process required of commercial products. Even more strikingly, many makers even avoided referring to their mechanical hands as "prostheses," to distinguish them from a legally recognized class of medical devices. By labeling their hands as "assistive devices," "wearable tools," or even "toys," volunteers aimed to fend off potential liability issues. However, in doing so, they simultaneously configured the expectations of their potential users and ascribed to them the role of the "recipient" of a free gift, which differed markedly from those of "the customer" or "the patient," so deeply ingrained in the professional belief system of prosthetists and industrial manufacturers.

Inspired by the rapid diffusion of Alpha-style devices among US children, volunteers soon sought to expand operations to other groups. Most importantly, Alpha members identified what they termed "underserved populations" in the Global South as potential recipients. With the expansion of operations beyond the US, the capacity of the open-source model to bypass not only the institutional but the *infrastructural* conditions of circulation came to the fore. As early as 2014, small groups of US-based makers organized the global distribution of 3D-printed hands, while others started local chapters to produce Alpha devices all around the world. Indeed, these operations proliferated rapidly, with the larger community having little control over their activities. By 2019, one of the community's central websites reported that…

> …[T]here are approximately 20,000 [Alpha] volunteers in over 100 countries who have delivered free hands and arms to an estimated 8,000 recipients through collaboration and open-source design to help those in underserved communities who have little to no access to medical care.
> (accessed, 2019-10-17)

Overall, then Alpha's combination of private digital fabrication and a somewhat unregulated voluntarism had led to the emergence of a sizeable action net that operated in parallel to the established practices. By sidestepping the institutional and infrastructural constraints linked to centralized manufacturing and professional fitting, volunteers succeeded in delivering prostheses to people with limb differences, where the conventional industry could not. However, digital fabrication and goodwill alone were not enough to stabilize a global community and the new user roles and identity it had helped to construct.

5.2.3.1 Limitations of the Open-Source Model: User Construction and the Wild West

Alpha's success in constituting previously excluded groups as potential users was at least partly based on its ability to bypass the prosthetics industry's basic institutions, including those related to professionalism and the insurance system. However, at least initially, the community did not develop any shared rules and norms of their own to effectively regulate the rapid expansion of its activities. This low degree of institutionalization meant that, while the new, digitalized action net of user construction continued to proliferate on an "infrastructure of goodwill," it simultaneously remained both fragile and erratic, leading some of my interviewees to liken it to the "Wild West."[25] Where volunteers moved on to other places or interests, the local supply of necessary spare parts collapsed, and new users quickly found themselves without continued support. Conversely, some particularly dedicated enthusiasts sought to adapt the original Alpha model, by extending product distribution *beyond* their local context. They sometimes produced hands for recipients whom they had never met or send devices to communities they believed to be in particular need. These unlikely journeys of 3D-printed hands around the globe are instructive for understanding the relationship of institutions, digital fabrication, and the construction of users and non-users in the open-source model.

5.2.3.2 Remote Fitting: From Germany via France to Morocco

Part of Alpha's original idea had been to re-localize the manufacturing of prostheses by geographically matching potential users with local device manufacturers. However, as the original process was built entirely on self-selection and the altruism of volunteers, there was no guarantee that it would actually result in local matches. On the contrary, the community's internet-based communication infrastructure made it possible for motivated Alpha members to work with amputees living thousands of miles away from them. In many cases, the distance between manufacturers and "recipients" of Alpha hands was far greater than that of traditional prosthetists and their "patients." This growing gap between producers and users was, however, prone to introduce novel translation problems, especially where Alpha hands traversed not only geographical, but also social and cultural distances.

One illustrative example of the complications associated with this "remote fitting model" was described to me by a German group of makers. Having been inspired by stories of the Alpha community and its impact on the lives of American children, they decided to list their 3D printer online and produce Alpha-style hands for whoever needed them. They were contacted by a gentleman from Paris, France, who asked for a device for his nephew, who lived in Casablanca, Morocco, and was born with a partial hand. The makers agreed and eventually delivered a 3D-printed arm based on an Alpha design they had found online. Much to their delight, they soon received several videos showing the recipient using the arm as intended and surpassing the makers' original expectations. However, when I asked about the boy's feedback, they conceded that he had abandoned the new arm for social rather than functional reasons:

> There was actually an incident at the boy's school, where other children talked badly about him. It was literally: 'Don't pick a fight with him, or he will punch you with his robohand', or something like that. It was stupid patter among boys and that upset him so much that he actually does not want to wear the arm anymore—not because he can't use it!
> (interview, Alpha volunteer, 2017-07-11, own translation)

This incident came as a big surprise to the German makers who, having been inspired by the social dimension of providing American children with superhero-themed hands, expected adoration rather than ridicule as a reaction to their product. In spite of the makers' astonishment, such unpleasant surprises were not uncommon in the remote fitting model, as it re-opened the social and geographical gap between the sites of designing, producing, and using. In that model, digital fabrication, internet communication, and the goodwill of volunteers made it possible to deliver prostheses to people who otherwise had no access to them. Yet, in the absence of shared routines for translating between remote production and local use, the danger of translation errors loomed large. This is particularly true, where, as in the above example, digital communication infrastructures weaved together action nets across settings oriented by different cultural norms and expectations.

5.2.3.3 The Digital Donation Model: From the US to India, Syria, Guatemala...[26]

Whereas the remote fitting scenario entailed some, albeit rudimentary, form of mediation between producing and using, Alpha had no way of guarding against even more extreme deviations from its original idea of co-locating production and use. In the absence of shared rules or certification, the free availability of Alpha's designs and the enthusiasm of thousands of hobbyists meant that pretty much *anyone* could now make and distribute Alpha prostheses. In this context, several enthusiasts started initiatives to print *as many hands as possible* for donation to "underserved populations," usually outside of the US. There were virtually no limitations on who could make hands for whom, or how and where they should be produced. Following Alpha's social media channels, it was not uncommon to find unlikely makers introducing themselves with lines like this: "We are a group of 6th grade students challenging anyone and everyone with a 3D Printer [sic!] to print and assemble a prosthetic hand for children!"[27] Nor was it uncommon that such initiatives succeeded in collecting hundreds of hands and shipping them to clinics located, among other places, in India, Syria, and Guatemala without regard for professional quality standards and without any form of routinized translation between the activities of makers and intended recipients.

Interestingly, despite the massive scale on which hands were produced and distributed by such programs, there is virtually no evidence that they were ever put to sustained use. Indeed, contrary to the makers' expectation that their donations would be welcomed in "underserved" regions of the world, local prosthetists would usually turn the hands down for being either disappointing functionally or wildly inappropriate aesthetically. For instance, when I interviewed a prosthetist from India about such donations, he described the following encounter with an Alpha volunteer:

> When we talked about doing something similar in India, he offered me to provide 300 3D-hands that can be distributed in India. And I was very fascinated by the number and the offer, but I had to, unfortunately, respectfully, deny it [...]. I can distribute in mass, it will look pretty nice on Facebook in the news channel, but out of 300 3D-printed devices, I was very, very doubtful that [even one] is going to last more than a week and it is not going to be continued for the long-term use. So that is not our goal, to be in the media, but actually to help an individual that needs it.
>
> (interview, prosthetist, 2017-10-17)

Given such reactions, the commonly held belief within Alpha that having an amateur-made hand is "better than nothing" (interview, 2017-12-14) appears to have been unfounded, at least in scenarios in which prostheses traversed vast geographical, economical, and cultural distances without serious efforts to translate between the actions of designing and using. In the words of one of the few Alpha members with a background in biomedical engineering, Alpha's version of the donation model "was at best a waste of time and a recycling nightmare [...] and at worst damaging psychologically the patients who wanted a hand and got a cheap plastic toy." (interview, engineer & Alpha volunteer, 2017-12-01)

In the face of these difficulties, a significant part of the Alpha community has moved in the direction of stricter regulation, albeit in two different ways. One group of leading Alpha volunteers has split off from the community and aligned themselves more closely with the established prosthetics industry. These groups have decided to stop openly sharing their designs with the larger community and only deliver devices through certified prosthetists.

In fact, many of them have founded formal organizations, including NGOs as well as start-ups, to tighten control over the design, production, and delivery of their products. In doing so they often adopted the local fabrication model described in the previous Section (5.2.2). Another group of volunteers has remained closer to open-source practices. They have begun putting in place a "distributed infrastructure for quality assurance" (interview, 2017-12-14) to complement the "infrastructure of goodwill" alluded to above. Interestingly, the new system mimics some institutional features of the conventional industry without formally interacting with it. For instance, in something like a hobbyist version of the certification process, makers are required to build a test device and have it assessed by the community before being matched with potential recipients. Further, mirroring the division of labor between prosthetists and engineers, makers working at a distance from prospective users are asked to partner with a local liaison who helps to inscribe the recipient's preferences and bodily characteristics as well as to collect feedback. Overall, some years after its inception, Alpha's open-source model has moved away from a "Wild West" state. Some of the volunteers' practices of production and circulation have stabilized around shared rules and norms, signaling the emergence of an institutional order of user construction within the community.

5.3 Digital Circulation: The Limits of Inclusion

In this chapter, I have pursued the question of how the introduction of digital production technologies changes the conditions under which products circulate between the sites of production and use, and how these changes contribute to the constitution of new users and user roles. I have shown how the major infrastructural and institutional elements of the industry's dominant order of circulation have evolved and how they are currently challenged by the rise of digital distribution infrastructures. In this concluding section, I summarize my main findings and relate them to some major arguments within the current scholarly debate around digital fabrication. I argue that 3D printing may be flexibly used in centralized as well as decentralized production systems and that decentralization does not necessarily equal local manufacturing. Even where new patterns of circulation are based on local fabrication, they may tend toward partial realignment with conventional practices as part of their growth and stabilization. The inclusive effects on the existing user landscape may, therefore, remain limited to specific niches for the time being.

Organizing the distribution of goods from the sites of production to the sites of use is a general problem in modern industries because the centralization of manufacturing separates the activities of producing and using in time and space (Hyysalo et al., 2016; compare Toffler's idea of the "second wave," Toffler, 1980). In prosthetics, too, the industrialization of component production has co-evolved with both material distribution infrastructures and institutionalized rules and norms. Today, the circulation of readymade prosthetic components depends on logistic networks linking central factories, regional distribution centers, and local prosthetic workshops. It is regulated by national insurance systems as well as the rules and routines of the prosthetists' profession. Therefore, industrially made prostheses are only available in times and places in which these infrastructural and institutional arrangements are in place. Indeed, the rise of centralized industrial production has historically led to the construction of a highly uneven user landscape. The dominant order of circulation underpins differential access to prosthetic technology in countries of the Global North and further marginalizes people with limb differences living in countries of the Global South.

Against this backdrop, the introduction of digital inscription and production devices affords an opportunity to renegotiate ingrained patterns of circulation and the structural inequalities they entail. The relevant characteristic of these devices is that they enable the translation between digital data and physical objects using multi-purpose technologies. By contrast to the dominant order, this allows the construction of action nets in which industrial products circulate as digital files along digital communication infrastructures rather than as physical artifacts along pathways consisting of roads and distribution centers. In the scholarly debate, these new translational capacities are often linked to the idea of a radical decentralization of manufacturing and a return of production to the site of use (compare Toffler's notion of the "third wave"). The advance of 3D printing is expected to grant people faster, and easier access to all sorts of goods (Ihl & Piller, 2016; Urry & Birtchnell, 2016), or simply allow them to produce whatever they need for themselves (Gershenfeld, 2005; Kostakis et al., 2015; compare Schrape, 2019). Indeed, I have presented two cases, the nonprofit Beta and the open-source community Alpha, in which this ideal was partly realized. Both Beta and Alpha used consumer-grade 3D printers to move production closer to the site of use. Both sidestepped some of the major institutional and infrastructural conditions of circulation, and both succeeded in constituting hitherto marginalized social groups as new users. My findings thus grant some empirical validity to central tenets of the current debate: By using digital production technology as part of a digital distribution infrastructure, the relevant conditions of circulation can be changed, and new user groups can be constructed as a result.

The current study also showed, however, that digitalized patterns of circulation do not always have inclusive effects. One important insight was that digital fabrication does not necessarily move production closer to the site of use. On the contrary, the very fact that digital production devices can be linked to digital communication infrastructures means that they may well be used in the opposite way. As I have demonstrated in my analysis of the *outsourcing model*, in the prosthetics industry digital fabrication was first associated with the *centralization* of socket production. In that model, rather than challenging the order of circulation that had evolved in conjunction with the central fabrication of fit components, new technologies were used to extend a factory-centered pattern to all parts of the product. Even in the community-based *open-source model*, which emerged in explicit opposition to the dominant order, 3D printing did not necessarily involve the co-location of prosthesis production and use. Even though the ideal was for hands to be manufactured locally, in practice makers often lived far away from potential users, and geographical distances could be just as large as they were in the conventional industry. These examples point out that digital production devices may be used in centralized as well as decentralized production systems, and there is no reason to assume that manufacturing will be located in proximity to prospective users. With a view to the structure of the respective action nets, what is reorganized in the outsourcing and remote fitting models is the relationship between designing and producing rather than between producing and using. In these cases, the introduction of 3D printing may lead to a reorganization of industrial activities but is unlikely to involve the construction of new user roles. Indeed, insofar as such novel patterns of action presuppose the circulation of digital as well as physical intermediaries, they may add further conditions to successful user construction and may, therefore, affect only a part of the existing user landscape.

Another finding worth highlighting was that, even where digital fabrication takes place in proximity to the sites of use, the range of new user roles may, at first, be constrained by the infrastructural and organizational challenges of distributed fabrication. As the cases of Beta and Alpha illustrate, the translational capacities of available production devices were one factor limiting the user landscape that emerged around the *local fabrication model* (compare Section 4.3). Contrary to their representation in both popular and scholarly discourse, desktop 3D printers cannot be used to "make almost anything" (Gershenfeld, 2012), nor are 3D printed products necessarily on par with conventionally manufactured ones. For example, desktop 3D printers eased access to mechanical prosthetic hands but left people with lower limb loss dependent on conventional distribution networks. Moreover, infrastructural constraints were complemented by a set of organizational challenges linked to the decentralization of manufacturing. Engineers at Beta found it hard to set up and maintain 3D printing facilities in half a dozen countries, as differences between contexts made it difficult to guarantee smooth operations and a consistent quality of products. These challenges were multiplied in the *open-source model* pioneered by the Alpha community. Here designing and manufacturing were both globally distributed and, at least originally, there were no shared rules or norms for who could manufacture a product or for how volunteer producers should interact with prospective users. Local autonomy and tinkering were encouraged and even technology designers could not control the circulation of Alpha hands.

As I have shown in my description of Alphas "Wild West" phase, the "democratization of production" was prone to encourage patterns of circulation in which products of questionable quality ended up with people who never asked for them or who were disappointed with the properties of homegrown devices. Overall, these examples demonstrate that the inclusive potential of new patterns of circulation can be severely hampered both by the limited capacities of digital production devices to serve as part of larger distribution infrastructures, and by the absence of institutionalized rules and norms to support the organization of decentralized manufacturing. The analysis presented here suggests that, at least initially, digitalized modes of circulation will remain fragile and are as likely to cause mutual frustration as they are to constitute new users.

In light of these challenges, a final insight of the present chapter is that, as new patterns of circulation begin to evolve and stabilize, they have a tendency of becoming re-aligned or entangled with established action nets of user construction. For instance, engineers at Beta chose to stabilize the circulation of their devices by setting up 3D printers at established prosthetic clinics, thus combining the novel element of local fabrication with the conventional element of professional fitting. Similarly, they attempted to maintain control over local operations by centralizing design activities, and regulating production processes and the sourcing of materials, thereby reproducing well-known practices of industrial manufacturers. Even the Alpha community eventually started to cooperate with professional prosthetists and to develop shared practices that resembled key elements of the dominant order of circulation, for instance by requiring the certification of device manufacturers. I argue that these combinations between novel and conventional elements can be interpreted as attempts to stabilize novel action nets of user construction. By partially aligning their activities with established infrastructures and institutionalized practices, novel groups of producers managed to scale up their distribution networks and generate legitimacy within the larger field of prosthetics. However, these alignments also had the unintended effect of limiting the inclusive potential of their original patterns of action. In the Alpha community, some of the most advanced descendants of the Robohand are no longer shared as open-source files, limiting their range of circulation. In the local fabrication model, deeply ingrained power asymmetries are reproduced, as new users in the Global South remain dependent on the activities of remote organizations in the Global North.

Overall, then, their ability to translate back and forth between tangible objects and digital data means that the introduction of digital fabrication technologies offers the potential of sidestepping the infrastructural and institutional conditions under which industrial products travel to the site of use. As I have shown, digital production devices can mediate novel circulation pathways that give rise to new user groups, particularly where they close the gap between central production and local use. However, in contrast to commonly held beliefs about 3D printing, the inclusive effects of these digitalized action nets are likely to be partial and unfold slowly, initially benefitting only a fraction of all possible users. New action nets based on decentralized fabrication in diverse contexts are bound to face difficult infrastructural and organizational challenges. To stabilize their operations, newly formed organizations may choose to partially re-align their activities with the dominant order of circulation. While such re-combinations may reproduce some of the biases of contemporary industrial production, they may also help to scale up emerging patterns of action and pave the way for their eventual normalization and uptake in the industry at large.

Notes

1 Only some purpose-specific prostheses, such as specialized adapters for upper limb devices or high-performance sports prostheses are manufactured as one-off tailormade products at local clinics or specialized workshops.
2 The centralization of socket production proved difficult because it required information about the ever-changing idiosyncrasies of individual bodies as well as several cycles of iteration based on use-feedback. The body of the user could be translated into plaster and forms (see Chapter 4), but since large blocks of plaster tended to be a particularly impractical intermediary to move between sites, socket production remained a local affair until the increasing availability of CAD/CAM systems in the 1990s (see Section 5.2.1).
3 OALMA is still active today, although it changed its name to American Orthotics and Prosthetics Association (AOPA) in 1960. Taking out the *manufacturing* portion of its name reflected the general trend to move production from local shops, staffed with professional prosthetists, to centralized factories.
4 Similarly, a professional association had existed in Germany before the war but had to be newly set up within the radically changed political system after 1945. In West Germany, this was the *Bundesinnungsverband*, which began its work shortly after the end of the war and was officially approved by the government in 1954 (Dittmer, 2018, p. 8).
5 One central difference between countries is the emphasis on either *provision* or *device*. While the German insurance system typically accounts for a prosthetist's work in assembling and fitting a device, in the US it is the cost of the fitted components that matters—a state of affairs US prosthetists frequently lament.
6 There are, of course, important differences between the institutional systems of those countries. However, overall, their patterns of user construction are quite similar, especially when compared to many countries of the Global South, which I will have more to say about in the second part of this chapter.
7 In the US and Canada, training was mostly university-based, and one problem was striking the right balance between clinical and device-oriented education, with most courses being taught by engineers rather than clinicians. In Germany, training was apprenticeship-based, with only a few university programs having been implemented. Even though the quality of that education was deemed high, the concern was that fewer and fewer people showed an interest in a persistently craft-oriented profession.
8 The number of such takeovers varied between countries. In Germany, prosthetists tended to resist takeovers by industrial companies, although some local firms had banded together in larger groups. In the US the situation was different, with many local clinics being bought by a small number of companies, the largest of which controlled approximately 800 clinics across the US.

9 Indeed, securing coverage was such an important aspect of user construction that my interlocutors sometimes mused over whether insurers were not in fact the real users with whom they needed to align their actions.

10 World Health Organization, https://www.who.int/disabilities/technology/en/, accessed 2019-12-20

11 Note that the numbers quoted here represent a very rough estimate only. They may be taken as an illustration of a general problem, yet they do not address the situation in concrete countries and do not allow for differentiated arguments about the kinds of products and services required. As stated in the report itself, this is a more general problem:

> Global data on the need for rehabilitation services, the type and quality of measures provided, and estimates of unmet need do not exist. Data on rehabilitation services are often incomplete and fragmented. When data are available, comparability is hampered by differences in definitions, classifications of measures and personnel, populations under study, measurement methods, indicators, and data sources.
>
> (WHO, 2011, p. 102)

12 A very unfortunate choice of terms, considering how Western organizations continue to extract large quantities of resources from these countries.

13 The phrase "healing hands" was a recurrent one at the clinic and was central to its identity. I had at first assumed that the phrase referred to prostheses and the "healing" of the hands of their users, or possibly to the prosthetists' "magic" or "helping hands." However, after arriving in Port-au-Prince I learned that "healing hands" referred in very important ways to the clinic's sponsors. Each major funder was honored, as a colorful hand-shaped plate with their name was attached to a wall in the central atrium of the building. This wall was immediately visible to everyone who entered and was the final destination of tours given to potential benefactors.

14 Another notable example is the International Committee of the Red Cross (ICRC), which designs devices for non-western settings and strengthens local production capabilities by making instructions freely available online. However, while ICRC devices were originally made from locally available materials, they have since been standardized to exploit economies of scale for greater affordability. ICRC components are now exclusively produced by a Swiss industrial partner.

15 BMVSS: https://www.jaipurfoot.org/img/Brochure%20(July%202021).pdf, accessed 2022-02-24; Ottobock: https://www.ottobock.com/en/company/locations/, accessed 2022-02-24

16 According to a report quoted in O&P Almanac, June 2015 (Issuu Inc., https://issuu.com/americanandp/docs/ june_2015_almanac, accessed 2019-05-31).

17 It should be noted that there are *industrial-grade* variants of various 3D printing technologies, including Selective Laser Sintering (SLS), Fused Deposition Modeling (FDM), Multi Jet Fusion (MJF), and others. In the central fabrication model, components such as feet or covers were more commonly produced using SLS or MJF, while FDM (see Figure 5.4) had been tried for prosthetic sockets. However, in the context of this book, whenever I talk about *consumer-grade* or *desktop* 3D printing, I generally refer only to FDM.

18 In other product classes, such as insoles, the combination of central fabrication and mass customization has allowed the implementation of "direct-to-consumer models." Such products did not have to be fitted at a dedicated clinic but fit well enough "by design." In these cases, the conditions of circulation changed substantially.

19 At the time of writing, Beta had just received a grant to extend their operations to rural areas in North America.

20 The same was true of all other similar organizations included in my data. The notable exception was a Canadian organization running a 3D printing center in a Ugandan clinic. This clinic printed lower limb sockets for children (see coons, 2022). Remarkably, Beta had begun partnering with that organization at the time of writing, which promised to make a larger portfolio of products available to all partnering clinics and thus construct a more diverse user landscape.

21 Despite Beta's best efforts, technological standardization and simplification did not reduce all differences in the usage of the digital fabrication facilities, causing the engineers a good bit of trouble, and at times, prompting rather sociological observations such as this one: "Sometimes I wake up in the morning and think: Why did we do six countries?! Because they are all so unique. Yes, the technology is the same. But what is different is the cultural context!" (Fieldnote, 2018–2008).

22 For all readers with a firm knowledge of prosthetic design, I note that the inner socket was fully customized.

23 This was done even at the price of occasionally having to manually design "one-off sockets" and mailing the files to the respective clinic.

24 The criticism of established actors was ignited when several news articles framed low-cost Alpha hands as functionally equivalent to professionally made prostheses, thus undermining the position of engineers and prosthetists vis-à-vis insurance companies.

25 I chose to retain this politically charged metaphor because I find that, in the context discussed here, it takes on a telling double meaning. My interviewees were referring to the fact that, in the early days of Alpha, there were no common rules. Anyone could make and ship prosthetic hands anywhere without being held accountable for the (sometimes) detrimental effects of their actions. It is important, however, to point to the historical irony that white US Americans at the beginning of the 21st century refer back to an era of settler colonialism to describe the unregulated circulation of prosthetic technology to people for whom they were not intended and who had never asked for them. The "Wild West" thus becomes a way of talking about a new form of "techno-imperialism" (another term borrowed from one of my interviewees), in which people living in "the West" send the devices they make in their spare time out to people they view as underserved, expecting to receive praise for their actions despite the fact that the recipients of their well-intentioned, but often flagrantly unthoughtful gifts may find them entirely disappointing or even outright offensive.

26 Haiti, Pakistan, and Jordan—the list is likely much longer, but these are the countries that my interviewees referred to when discussing this model.

27 Prosthetic Kids Hand Challenge, http://www.handchallenge.com/, accessed 2019-10-22

6 Using Technology

Between Re-Interpretation and Re-Inscription

In this final empirical chapter, I address the carving out of user roles in situated use practices and the ways in which the latter feed back into new design iterations. It is well understood that the roles inscribed in industrially made objects are transformed as the latter become implicated in their users' practical lives. Countless studies have shown that the symbolic and material properties of artifacts remain *interpretatively flexible* (Pinch & Bijker, 1987) and can therefore be transformed or elaborated in use (Lie & Sørensen, 1996). Technical artifacts may suggest, allow, or preclude certain interpretations, but in the last consequence, how a thing is used cannot be fully controlled by its designers. Conversely, unexpected use practices may become *re-inscribed* into new artifacts, as they are picked up by industry (Hyysalo et al., 2016) or as user innovators (Hippel, 2005) design, test, and redesign new generations of products based on their own experience. Analytically speaking, *using* therefore functions as both a constant irritation to industry and as a central source of inspiration for further cycles of *designing* and *producing* new technology (Section 6.1).

In light of these findings, I investigate how the introduction of new production technologies may transform the relationship between *situated use practices* and the emergence of recognizable *user roles*. I begin by analyzing the position of using in the established action net of user construction in prosthetics, paying particular attention to the historical role of users in the industrialization of the field and the institutions that evolved to take their actions into account (6.2 and 6.3). I then contrast this dominant configuration with the action nets that are currently forming around 3D printing (6.4). On the one hand, I compare the ways in which the user roles inscribed into industrial objects are *re-interpreted* as people with limb differences creatively adapt, misuse, or abandon the products that end up with them. On the other, I examine how unexpected interpretations are *re-inscribed* into subsequent design iterations. In the final Section (6.5), I offer some conclusions about the changing relationship between technology use and re-design in times of digitalization. I argue that the introduction of digital fabrication technologies may lead to the rapid emergence of radically new user roles and corresponding design trajectories. Yet, in contrast to the

DOI: 10.4324/9781003269731-6

dominant discourse around 3D printing, I do not ascribe this tendency to a surge in user innovation (Hippel, 2005). Instead, my explanation focuses on the transfer of rapid prototyping techniques to the realm of production, a change allowing technology designers to react more quickly and flexibly to unexpected use practices which are bound to occur once products are released "into the wild."

6.1 The Contingency of Prosthesis Use

The variety of uses to which artificial arms and legs are put is incredibly large, as is the range of meanings attributed to them. It is precisely because prostheses are meant to replace human limbs that they become involved in an almost endless plethora of use practices. People with low degrees of mobility may use their prosthetic legs for walking indoors or within the neatly infrastructured urban environments of the US or Germany. However, more active users may wear them for hiking, running, or swimming. Some particularly athletic users may choose to compete in a large range of sports (Göbel, 2017), each with its own specific requirements and movements. Some people walk barefoot or in flip-flops, others wear sneakers, high heels, drive a car or ride a bike. Some sit at tables, others cross-legged on the floor (Srinivasan, 2002), yet others kneel down to pray. Arguably, the human hand is involved in an even larger array of activities. We use our hands to explore the world we live in, to *get in touch* with things. But also, quite literally, we use them to *manipulate* the things around us from small objects like keys or coins, to larger things like bags, boxes, and stirring wheels. We use our hands to eat or write, but also to paint or play music. Most of us depend on our hands for work, whether it is considered *manual* or not. Not least of all, we use our hands for all kinds of gesticulation, signaling, and other sorts of communication.

All of these ways of *using* human limbs require different properties and movements of the prostheses that are supposed to replace them. Not surprisingly, some of these requirements may be in conflict with one another. A prosthetic foot for a person with low mobility should offer stability and shock absorption, yet a foot for sprinting would need to store and return as much energy as possible to propel its wearer forward, never mind standing still. A prosthetic hand used for heavy labor should be strong and durable. Yet, after work is over, a hand that is light and comfortable may be preferable. In some contexts, the device's most important function may be to simply look like a hand, to allow its wearer to avoid social stigma.

While individual ways of using prostheses are astonishingly diverse, they are also contingent on larger historical configurations. The formation of dominant use practices does depend on the prevalent cultural meaning systems and social institutions as much as it depends on the reasons for limb loss existing in a specific place and time. Here again, the ways in which societies shape and destroy the human body are as diverse as the ways in which these bodies are subsequently interpreted. For instance, the oldest prostheses we know of were found attached to ancient Egyptian mummies. While some of these artificial body parts, such as a wooden toe prosthesis, appear to have been used during the wearer's lifetime (Nerlich et al., 2000), others were only ever manufactured after the person's death to restore an appearance of bodily wholeness in the preparation of the deceased for the afterlife (Gray, 1966). To members of the emerging US urban middle class of the late 19th century, the foremost function of a limb was to "be presentable in polite society" (Mihm, 2002). Their prostheses were made with a focus on concealment rather than mobility, featuring both elegant anthropomorphic movement and outward appearance. Yet, in a sharp demonstration of the social stratification of prosthesis use, limbs for workers and other "persons of limited means" (ibid.: 292) lacked such features. Being used predominantly for manual labor, these latter prostheses focused on durability, ease of maintenance, and cost. In an even starker example, from post–WWI Germany, the perceived need to re-integrate veterans into industrial production was approached within a frame of Tayloristic work organization. In this context, designs emerged that almost entirely sacrificed anthropomorphic form and function to directly couple the user's body to the machine in the name of restoring productivity (Harrasser, 2009).

That the use of prostheses is not purely an individual matter, but a socially structured practice is all the more relevant insofar as the reasons for amputations, too, vary greatly across time and place, and usually affect some social groups more than others. Hence, whose use practices and whose body norms will become relevant in the construction of prevalent user roles depends, to some degree, on which social group is at risk of losing a limb in the first place. Here the construction of meaning and matter, of social expectations and bodily characteristics, interlink most clearly. Society, in other words, does not only structure how specific groups use their prostheses, it also influences which groups will qualify as potential users to begin with. For example, war has historically been the main reason for amputation. Because of that, limb loss first and foremost affected the people involved in the fighting, which more often than not happened to be young men. It is, thus, rather unsurprising that the dominant user roles and role expectations connected to prostheses were gendered male. In fact, David Serlin (2002) has described how the co-evolution of users and prosthetic design in the US after WWII was heavily shaped by male users and the expectations held for them. Yet, war-related limb loss does not solely affect men (landmines, for instance, remain a major source of limb loss in some areas), nor is it the only way in which social differentiation is linked to the risk of bodily injury. In the late 1950s and early 1960s, thousands of children were born with deformed limbs as a result of their mother's thalidomide use during early pregnancy, causing governments to invest significant sums in the development of prostheses for young users. In contrast, today the main reason for amputation in both Germany and the US is cardiovascular diseases of the lower limb, which are more common in elderly persons, thereby moving their use practices into the center of the industry's attention. At other times, the material and symbolic dimensions of human limb loss are woven together even more explicitly. In the Sierra Leone of the late 1990s, the so-called Revolutionary United Front is said to have forcibly amputated the arms and hands of thousands of people to keep them from voting for the eventual winner of the election, Ahmad Tejan Kabbah, who had run his campaign on the slogan "The Future Is in Your Hands."[1] In a different example, among Japanese *yakuza*, the ritual self-amputation of part of a digit, referred to as *yubitsume*, is seen as an apology for violating the code of this mafia-like organization. According to Kaplan and Dubro (2003, p. 14), a 1993 survey by Japan's National Research Institute of Police Science found that 45% of the estimated 80,000 yakuza members had performed yubitsume and 15% of them had done so more than once.

As all of these examples demonstrate, the ways in which purposefully designed prosthetic devices are actually used in practice are shaped by their relationship to complex action nets beyond industrial design and production. To a certain degree prosthesis use reflects the diversity of the individual activities involving human limbs, while also being influenced by the larger societal context in which it is performed. From an action net perspective, this *contingency of using* introduces an iterative dynamic to user construction. On the one hand, it means that the user roles inscribed into prostheses during design and production will inevitably be *re-interpreted* as they become involved in the practical lives of actual people. On the other hand, if such practical re-interpretations are to usher in new user roles, they will eventually need to be *re-inscribed* into industrially made products. Viewed through this lens, the construction of users involves ongoing translations between industrial inscription and re-inscription and the manifold re-interpretations that necessarily occur as artificial limbs are made part of the practical lives of their wearers. In the remainder of this chapter, I will explore how this process is mediated by the system of production prevalent at a given historical juncture.

6.1.1 The Contingency of Use as a Challenge for Industry

As the overview above demonstrates, the introduction of prostheses to the practical lives of their wearers has always entailed a form of re-interpretation and is likely to yield some surprises from the point of view of manufacturers. Yet, for as long as the designing and producing of assistive devices were not professionalized, there were hardly any institutionalized practices for how to react to unexpected forms of *using*. The blacksmiths, cobblers, and dentists of the 19th century had no shared way of collecting feedback from prosthesis use, let alone further configuring use practices within a structured rehabilitation process. Even in cases where they did work with amputees to improve upon existing designs, such developments remained local as there was little exchange between limb makers. Among users, too, there was little systematic coordination or collective articulation of interests vis-à-vis prosthesis manufacturers. On the one hand, until the second half of the 19th century, surviving a major amputation was rare and living with limb loss was mostly viewed as a personal tragedy rather than a systematic problem affecting any recognizable social group. On the other hand, in most places, there were hardly any specialized limb makers that individual or collective demands could have been addressed to. Hence, if amputees wanted to adapt their limbs to their specific pursuits, they were often left with no other option than to make these adaptations themselves.

When the number of amputees grew dramatically as a result of industrial accidents and industrialized warfare on the one side and advances in anesthesia and surgical techniques on the other, the relationship between using and producing prostheses took on a new quality. Clearly, both the professionalization and industrialization of the field were themselves reactions to the fact that limb loss had become a mass phenomenon (compare Chapters 4 and 5). Yet, it soon turned out that scaling up prosthesis design, production, and distribution was not in itself a sufficient solution to the "amputee problem." On the contrary, having constituted thousands of amputees as potential users within a newly emerging mass market, manufacturers were now liable to react more systematically to the ways in which their products were actually used in practice. The potential translations implied in situated acts of using therefore became newly problematic from the point of view of an emerging industry.

This was all the more true since, in the wake of war, veteran amputees almost immediately came to constitute a highly significant social group. Following two World Wars, not only did the sheer number of amputees exceed that of any previous time in history, but wounded veterans had also become symbolically central to the nationalist sentiments of the day. As has been shown time and again, reconstructing the bodies of soldiers wounded in battle was an essential part of post-war nation building in both Germany after World War I (Cohen, 2001; Kienitz, 2008; Perry, 2002) and the US after the Civil War (Herschbach, 1997), and World War II (Serlin, 2002). Even though the conditions were obviously quite different, in all these cases, the use and non-use of prostheses became a matter of national concern, giving amputees new leverage to articulate their own interpretations of the limbs fitted to them, sometimes putting significant pressure on both industry and state to adapt their practices. In World War I Germany, for instance, a group of highly regarded engineers and surgeons reacted to the problem of device-abandonment and general dissatisfaction of prosthesis users by founding the *Prüfstelle für Ersatzglieder*, an institute for testing the artificial limbs put out by the emerging industry (compare Kienitz, 2008, p. 161). Their work was at least partly motivated by the fact that, even though the sudden increase in the number of amputees had caused a surge in prosthetic design and manufacturing activities, amputees found many of these new devices unusable in practice. One of the organization's early reports shows how usability was identified as an issue to be considered more thoroughly in prosthetic design and fabrication.

> [The technically challenging task of designing new upper limb prostheses] as well as the large demand for replacement limbs sparked a fierce invention- and construction activity, which did generate a number of new forms, but created the problem that many less- or non-usable designs, the worth of which was for the most part greatly overestimated by their inventors and manufacturers, were given to the war-disabled.
>
> (Hartmann, 1919, p. 19; own translation)

An even more drastic example of the new relationship between the industry and its users is given by Bess Furman, the journalist tasked by the US government to chronicle the progress of prosthetics following WWII. Underlining the newfound political power of war amputees, she argues that novel ways of organizing prosthetic research were triggered by the publicly articulated dissatisfaction of veterans.

> As an aftermath of World War II, surgeon, engineer, and prosthetist were brought together in a new team type of pioneering in prosthetics. This [...] was mostly the result of a coast-to-coast outcry of amputees that artificial limbs, especially arms, had made scant progress since the Civil War. Some World War II battle victims threw useless hands on the desks of members of Congress. Others told newspaper reporters that their legs had let them down. Overwhelmed by the amputee problem right after Pearl Harbor, the Navy set up the first prosthetics research center in the United States Naval Hospital on Mare Island in 1943.
>
> (Furman, 1962, p. 10)

These examples demonstrate the changing relationship between using and the industrial activities of designing and manufacturing. In both the German and the US cases, the newly emerging industry that had constituted veterans as prostheses users in the first place, was soon forced to answer to that group's publicly voiced dissatisfaction with the products given to them. Indeed, despite the clear differences between the two settings, there were striking parallels in how this challenge was approached.

6.1.1.1 The Birth of Scientific User Testing

The most important parallel was that, in both Germany and the US, the scientific method was called on to establish what users needed, and to re-inscribe these representations into a new generation of products. To do this, systematic user testing under controlled conditions was viewed as indispensable, and so amputees were recruited as test subjects to be examined in university laboratories, hospitals, or state-sponsored R&D departments. In Germany, the *Prüfstelle für Ersatzglieder* was among the first organizations to conduct such science-based testing and re-inscription activities. The organization's goal was to single out and/or develop devices that would be both suitable for mass production and usable within the practical activities of amputees—the latter being imagined first and foremost as working in industry or agriculture. In a first step toward that goal, a large collection of existing prostheses was made, with new inventions being handed in for testing on a regular basis. Having collected this output of the early prosthetics industry, each device was submitted to a series of "scientific" as well as "practical" tests, the results of which were reported to the device's developer as a basis for further adaptations.[2] Systematic user testing was at the heart of this program and mainly occurred within dedicated workshops and test environments which the *Prüfstelle* had set up to approximate the intended sites of use. As described in the following excerpt, amputees were employed by the organization as test users and asked to perform a series of pre-specified tasks under constant supervision.

> For testing, skilled workers [with amputations, DS] are used, who are employed by the *Prüfstelle* for an appropriate wage. The testing operations do include the use of tools, working equipment, and machines and occur, for each replacement arm, in the normal daily working time of several hours, for some weeks. [...] The constant supervision of the worker is done by the shop master and the foreman, the surveillance and determination of the results by the engineers. [...] The assessment of the usefulness of artificial legs involves [...] testing the mechanical limb [*Kunstbein*] during walking on various grounds, during sitting and getting up, climbing stairs and ladders. To make the respective assessments, the *Prüfstelle* has [...] established a walking school in which the walking on even, bumpy, ascending, and descending ground, on hard and soft terrain, over obstacles of various kinds and heights is trained.
>
> (Hartmann, 1919, p. 22; own translation)

As this example makes clear, the *Prüfstelle* had gone to some length to establish one of the first user testing programs in the history of prosthetics. In the model advanced here, using was no longer understood as a private affair separate from designing and developing. Rather, using now played a central role in industrial activities and proving the usefulness of their products became an important requirement for manufacturers, which was certifiable by organizations like the *Prüfstelle*. Ironically, however, the scientific rigor with which using was now approached entailed moving it out of its sociomaterial context and into strictly controlled test environments. Hence, even though using was now directly linked to designing and re-designing, making this connection meant to strip use of much of the contingency that had made it problematic for industry in the first place. While the *Prüfstelle* did, in many cases, continue to observe the conduct of users outside of its own facilities (mostly as part of vocational training), the data collected this way did first and foremost function as a verification of its scientific work (Hartmann, 1919, pp. 33–34). The re-interpretations of certified prostheses that were likely to occur "in the wild" were factored out of the organization's main testing and developing program.

In the US the situation after World War II was similar. Almost 30 years after the founding of the *Prüfstelle*, a nationwide research program mirroring many of the elements of the German case was initiated under the auspices of the National Academy of Sciences.[3] First, a large collection of prostheses was assembled, including the products of military organizations as well as private manufacturers from both the US and Europe, including Germany (Committee on Artificial Limbs, 1947, pp. 9–11). Even though it was originally thought that engineers and surgeons would be able to generate the design criteria for a new generation of prostheses based on this collection alone, it soon turned out that not enough was known about the basic mechanisms of human motion both with and without artificial limbs. Research and development activities were therefore accompanied by fundamental studies of human biomechanics, which in the early 1950s gradually gave way to clinical user testing (Eberhart, 1954; Taylor, 1954). Even more than in the German program, using the scientific method meant bringing users into the laboratory and conducting tests on them within highly controlled environments. To study prosthesis use in action, the partnering organizations invented all kinds of inscription devices to bring out quantifiable and standardizable patterns in their subjects' motions, many of which became the foundation for contemporary laboratory testing and certification. For example, at the University of California, the walking patterns of prosthesis users as well as "normal subjects" were analyzed on a glass walkway to permit photographing from below, while "a special frame was attached to the subject in order to obtain measurements of tilt, twist, lateral and vertical displacement of the pelvis" (Committee on Artificial Limbs, 1947, pp. 42–43). The results of this study were then used as "part of the criteria for functional evaluation of various artificial legs" (ibid.).

Just like the German case, the example of the state-sponsored US research program demonstrates the new importance accorded to using within research and development activities. It further shows that the initial reaction of the prosthetics industry to their users' growing dissatisfaction was characterized by the systematic application of science to re-inscribe a more accurate representation of use into a new generation of products. However, as the below photograph (Figure 6.1) dramatically illustrates, this way of studying use, once again, depended on extracting it from its sociomaterial context and translating it into an activity amenable to the scientific method. Within laboratory-based user testing, the contingency of situated use practices was viewed as a source of error to be avoided, if one were to obtain legitimate scientific results. Systematic clinical studies, which would

Figure 6.1 A prosthesis user taking part in the research and development program at the University of California at Berkeley, ca. 1947. Photograph reproduced from Committee on Artificial Limbs (1947, p. 43).

see the partial release of the new prostheses "into the wild," were not conducted until the early 1950s and did not occur until designs had more or less stabilized (Bechtol, 1957; Eberhart, 1954; Taylor, 1954). As a result, even though surveys were issued after products had been released for general application, including that feedback into subsequent adaptations of those devices was difficult. Rather, the release of a new generation of products was seen as the provisional endpoint of a large-scale national effort by science, state, and industry to fit war amputees with more agreeable devices.

Taken together, the two examples of post-WWI Germany and post-WWII USA make visible a double change in the relationship of the activities of the emerging prosthetics industry and its newly constructed users. On the one side, the re-interpretation of prostheses in use gained a new relevance for manufacturers with users "in the wild" being increasingly able to put pressure on them. Having been constituted as a group of national interest, the dissatisfaction of prosthesis users with existing technology became widely visible and was collectively articulated on a hitherto unknown scale. On the other side, industrial organizations, in tandem with state actors and

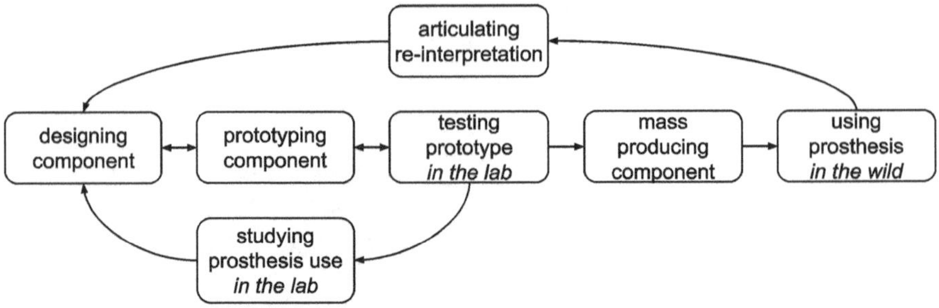

Figure 6.2 As the prosthetic industry struggled to react to the feedback of its users following WWI and II, studying use in the lab became part of the action net of prosthetic user construction. Own figure.

research institutions, aimed to re-inscribe use practices into a new generation of products and doing so by scientific means gradually became the norm. However, studying using in this way meant severing it from the manifold activities making up the practical lives of amputees. Hence, what was taken into account by industry was not the same "using in the wild" that was the source of the contingency facing industrial manufacturers, but a purified form of "using in the lab," which configured amputees as docile test subjects the movements of which could be meticulously measured and translated into new design criteria. Through users' large-scale articulation of discontent and manufacturers' attempts at re-inscription, the integration of use-feedback into industrial activities gradually became the new norm. Whereas situated practices of using artificial limbs had always been an important aspect of identity construction for amputees, it now became an integral component in the action net of industrial user construction.

6.1.2 Mechanisms of Re-Inscription in Contemporary Prosthetics

Today, paying close attention to the use of their products has become a central norm for industrial companies in the field of prosthetics. Large manufacturers take care to present themselves as user-centered and stress that "user-friendly functionality is the key criterion that [their] products have to live up to."[4] Company websites and advertisements are full of quotes and pictures of satisfied users and the idea of doing innovation that "creates value for customers" is emphasized whenever the chance arises. On a more practical level, such normative claims about the centrality of using find their expression in an institutional order that revolves around *using in the lab*. For instance, before including a new product into their reimbursement schemes, thereby making it available for general use, insurers require scientific evidence of that product's usefulness in the form of clinical or field studies. Similarly, large companies have developed internal guidelines and routines for conducting usability testing and entertain large networks of partners to facilitate clinical studies. In short: in contemporary prosthetics, no component enters mass production without having been thoroughly tested for safety and usability within laboratory and clinical settings.

Despite the normative importance accorded to using, use practices situated *in the wild* do not have the same relevance within the prevalent action net of prosthetic user construction. In practice, the re-inscription of user feedback does only rarely occur after a product is first released. Indeed, in the prosthetics industry, the basic features of many products have stayed the same for a long time, and it is not unusual for the same product to remain unchanged for decades. For example, even the C-Leg, the flagship product of the largest manufacturer in the field, has only received three major updates since its release in 1997, while the Utah Arm, one of the most commonly fit myo-electric arm prostheses, has been available in its version "3+" since 2008, after first becoming commercially available in 1974. The relevant point here is that, as product designs do not change for long stretches of time, there are few opportunities for reacting to the contingency that is characteristic of situated use practices. As a result, industrially made prosthetic components may stay incompatible with some or all aspects of their intended users' practical lives, even if their shortcomings are obvious to all involved. One example of such a situation was recounted to me by a prosthetist specializing in fitting upper limb prostheses for children. During a session with one of her younger patients, she complained about the inadequacy of child prostheses, which she described as entirely outdated.

> [Company A's] children's hands have not been refined for 30 years. [...] They have an opening width [...] you can't grip a glass with that, you can't grip anything with that. [...] And also, they really only have this one movement [opening and closing, DS], the heavy motor inside...
>
> (interview, prosthetist, 2016-11-08, own translation)

As this example demonstrates, despite the prevalent norm of user-centeredness, in practice the co-evolution of users and technology is rather sluggish in the area of prosthetic fit components. As designs remain unchanged for surprisingly long periods, the unexpected feedback that is generated in situated use practices can only rarely be re-inscribed into new generations of devices. Consequently, new user roles will be slow to emerge or, as is the case with children using upper limb prostheses, may remain underdeveloped for decades.

The reason for the difficulty of integrating feedback from *using in the wild* into new design iterations can be found in the technological and institutional conditions under which the industrial construction of users operates with regard to fit components. On the technological side, large manufacturers make use of production devices built to thrive on economies of scale, such as injection molding or die casting (compare Chapter 4). These technologies require setting up a dedicated production line for each product, such as a hand or knee, as well as making a new cast or mold for each of its individual components. Given the large initial investments necessary to begin production, making even slight changes to the product's design is likely to be prohibitively expensive once the fabrication infrastructure is in place. Hence, even if it did eventually turn out that the product was being used in an unexpected fashion by one or another group of users, such feedback is unlikely to be re-inscribed into the device, after its original release.

On the institutional side, the symbolic importance as well as the practicality of integrating unexpected feedback from "the wild" is further depleted by the way in which the relationship between using, designing, and producing is organized. More specifically, in a spirit of guaranteeing safety and usability, the prevalent institutional order emphasizes the importance of elaborated user testing procedures *prior* to the large-scale production and commercial distribution of a product. Yet, from the point of view of industrial companies, conducting scientific studies to prove the efficacy of a product, without any guarantee of ever being able to sell it, is a risky, expensive, and time-consuming process. Consider, for example, the following interview excerpt in which a research engineer describes the challenges of putting together a clinical trial to demonstrate the usefulness of new products.

I: The reason it takes some time is, you have to get patients on [the device] and you have to prove [...] that it provides value. And so, there's a kind of a science process behind that. So, if you make something that looks cool but it doesn't provide any patient value, [an insurer] shouldn't be coding for that [...].

DS: So the science process involved in patient testing, what does that look like?

I: It's definitely field testing. You've got to have field testing. You won't get coded for a device until you've got things out there. So, a lot of the time companies will find ways of incentivizing patients, or a prosthetist, to buy their devices for that first couple of years. You know, find some way of providing discounts or rebates or loaners just to get them on patients so they can get the number out there that they need.

(interview, engineer, 2017-12-01)[5]

Given that, within the prevalent institutional order, such large and time-consuming efforts are required *before* a product can actually be marketed to its intended recipients, it becomes clear why manufacturers find it difficult to adapt a product's design during the study, let alone after insurers have decided to bill for it.

Ironically, then, the relationship between using, designing, and producing is organized in such a way that the emphasis on studying using under controlled conditions to some degree reduces the industry's ability to dynamically react to the contingency connected to use practices "in the wild." Hence, despite the efforts of user testing, unexpected ways of using prosthetics do abound and, especially in upper limb prosthetics, many people do not use their prostheses at all. Yet, within the prevailing action net, shaped as it is by technologies of mass production and the institutionalized emphasis on guaranteeing safety and usability, it is difficult for industrial companies to effectively adapt their activities to any unexpected interpretations of their devices that may occur as they are released beyond the lab.

6.1.2.1 Innovation in the Wild

It is particularly in situations in which industrially made prostheses do not easily accommodate the activities central to their wearers' identities that the latter begin tinkering with their artificial limbs, altering them in ways that allow them to go on with their lives. Many of those re-inscriptions do remain rather private affairs and are mostly invisible from the point of view of industry. When people paint their standard-colored foot shells to match the complexion of their feet, when they adjust their legs to change their height, when they refurbish their flats to allow for the one-handed use of appliances, all of these activities are likely to escape the attention of an industry focused on *using in the lab.* In some cases, however, small-scale material and symbolic adaptations are followed up by more thorough design activities conducted by amputees and their peers. At times, inventions originally developed by amputees for their own use do lead to the industrial-scale commercialization of new kinds of devices and their availability to a larger number of potential users (Shah, 2000). In these cases, *using in the wild* feeds back into new industrial design activities, contributing to the emergence and stabilization of new user roles beyond individual re-interpretations.

In the prosthetics industry, innovations by people with limb differences have been a common phenomenon since its very inception. Historically, many noteworthy products, such as the "Hanger limb" (1861), the "Sterling Stump Sock" (1921), the infamous "Flex Foot" (1984), or the "BiOM Ankle System" (2010) were first pioneered by users themselves (Table 6.1). Conversely, they made possible new ways of using prosthetic technology, for instance by affording a more natural-looking gait, by increasing wearing comfort, or by enabling people with limb loss to run, hike, or compete in sports. Following the biographies of these devices (Hyysalo et al., 2019) reveals a pattern of knotting together the actions of designing, producing, and using that diverges in several respects from the conventional action net of industrial user construction in prosthetics. As I will show, the major difference is that, while conventional industrial companies rely on information from *using in the lab,* amputees developing prostheses for themselves are able to draw on an ongoing stream of feedback from *using in the wild.*[6]

First of all, where the conventional sequence in industry begins from designing a novel product and only ever testing it for usability toward the end of that process, people with limb differences start with using an existing product under real-life conditions and realizing it is *not* very useful. Even in 1861, James Edward Hanger, the founder of what is now one of the largest prosthetic service providers in the world, was first fitted with a standard "peg leg." Prolific inventor Bob Radocy reports having "experimented with all types of prosthetic devices" before developing the modular GRIP Prehensile, which today allows hundreds of people to attach dozens of different terminal devices to their body powered arm prosthesis.[7] Hugh Herr, inventor of the BiOM Ankle and professor at MIT, articulates his dissatisfaction with existing devices more forcefully when he publicly argues that it is not amputees but "technology that's broken."[8] In the same vein, Van Phillips, inventor of the Flex Foot, provides a particularly vivid example of the kind of experience that provided the starting point for his own innovative activities. Having lost his foot in a water-skiing accident in 1976, Phillips was fitted with a standard SACH foot,[9] which did not allow him to run or do sports and which he described as follows:

> It's basically inanimate. It's dead. It's heavy. And yet, it's the standard of the world. You basically have to pick it up and put it down. If you forget, it's lagging behind you with every step. Also, as an amputee, you no longer have the ability to plantar flex or point your foot down to the ground. You step off a curb you didn't see, remember landing flat foot and that shutter goes up your spine? That's what it feels like to an amputee with every step, especially trying to run.
>
> (CuspConference, Youtube, https://www.youtube. com/ watch?v=4d7O8UxFJt4, accessed 2020-07-13)

As this example demonstrates, it is the embodied experience of using an industrially made prosthetic aid in their everyday lives that informs and motivates the design activities of amputees. This means that people designing prostheses for their own needs are able to draw on feedback from *using in the wild* from the earliest possible point, whereas designers and engineers working for industrial manufacturers only ever get this kind of feedback toward the very end of their development process.

Information on the device's performance under real-life conditions continues to be an important resource for innovating users throughout the process. This is possible because innovation in the wild is not bound by the same technological and institutional conditions applying to university labs or corporate R&D departments.[10] With regards to production technology, people producing prostheses for their own use are not concerned with the same economic considerations facing engineers designing for mass production. For their initial purposes, it is enough to produce a single device with whatever tools available, tinkering with its design whenever necessary. Similarly, from a point of view of prevailing institutions, privately conducted activities are neither subject to company internal testing procedures and ethics decisions, nor industry-wide regulations concerning safety standards or the generation of scientific evidence. Under these conditions, amputees designing prostheses for their own use can test new versions of their inventions at much earlier stages than is possible for established companies operating in the field of medical devices. Even more importantly, testing will happen under real-life conditions rather than in the controlled environment of clinics or laboratories, thus establishing an ongoing feedback loop between designing and *using in the wild.* For instance, after creating the first functional "Flex Foot" with the help of aircraft-engineer Dale Abildskov, the previously mentioned Van Phillips reportedly designed and built between 200 and 300 similar feet, testing them all himself, and breaking most of them.[11] In an even more drastic example, Hugh Herr, who had lost both his legs during a rock-climbing accident, quickly returned to his passion using various prostheses of his own making and constantly adapting them to new challenges. For example, he added spikes to his feet to enable him to climb walls of ice and built feet slim enough to fit into small cracks. Clearly, while testing a product under real-life conditions may generate invaluable insights for translating between using and re-designing, there are good reasons why none of the testing activities described above would have been permitted by a university's ethics board or a company's R&D guidelines. It is, then, their situatedness outside of the existing industry that allows "user innovators" (von Hippel, 2005) to continuously draw on their personal experience of *using in the wild* throughout the development process.

Advantageous as the position outside conventional industry may be for individual experimentation, it also comes with decisive drawbacks when considering the institutionalization of the new user roles emerging from the work of user innovators. Indeed, from the perspective of the *industrial* construction of user roles, the ways in which users symbolically and materially re-interpret industrial products are always in danger of remaining mere oddities, irrelevant to the lives of others. For new user roles to become more widely relevant, they depend on their re-inscription into industrial products that are manufactured and distributed at large scale.

Remarkably, in all cases discussed here, the prostheses were first commercialized through companies founded by amputees themselves (Table 6.1). It was as these organizations scaled up their production and distribution capabilities, or as they were bought by larger companies, that new prostheses and with them new ways of using became available to a wider range of potential users. In the cases of Hanger (J.E. Hanger Company), and Arbogast (Ohio Willow Wood), their companies did grow into two of the largest firms active in the prosthetics industry today, while Dorrance's company scaled up by merging with A. J. Hosmer Corporation, another organization founded by an amputee. At other times, however, existing companies license in products originally developed by user innovators, not least of all because at that point

Table 6.1 Some noteworthy user innovations and the companies by which they were subsequently manufactured and marketed on a large scale

User Innovator	*Prosthetic Component*	*Year*	*Company Founded by Inventor*	*Company Subsequently Marketing Product*
James E. Hanger	Hanger Limb	1861	J. E. Hanger Company (between 1861 and 1871)	Hanger Inc.
D. W. Dorrance	Split-Hook	1912	D. W. Dorrance Company (1912)	Hosmer-Dorrance Corp. (1941–1996); Fillauer (since 1996)
William E. Arbogast	Sterling Stump Sock	1921	Ohio Willow Wood (1907)	Willow Wood
Bob Radocy	GRIP Prehensile Hand	1980	TRS Inc. (1979)	TRS Inc.
Van Phillips	Flex Foot	1984	Flex-Foot Inc. (1984)	Össur (since 2000)
Hugh Herr	BiOM Ankle	2010	iWalk (2007)	Ottobock (since 2017)

the initial proof of usefulness, so critical for prosthetics manufacturers, has already been provided. This is exactly what happened to the inventions of Hugh Herr and Van Phillips. Phillips founded his own company, Flex Foot Inc. in 1984, which made his running blades available to other amputees. Further underlining the usefulness of the invention, it was put to use by professional athletes such as Dennis Oehler, who, wearing the Flex Foot, won gold medals in the 100-, 200-, and 400-meter sprinting competitions at the 1988 Paralympics, setting new world records in each of them. In the year 2000, Phillips eventually sold Flex Foot Inc. to Össur, one of the largest manufacturers in the field. Since then, Össur has iterated on the basic idea, making energy-storing feed available to thousands of people, partly by marketing the original design through its global distribution network, partly by adapting it for greater versatility.[12] As Össur reports on its website:

> Today more than 90% of amputee athletes worldwide wear some model of the basic Flex-Foot introduced back then, and its widespread availability has given amputees of all activity levels the opportunity to walk, run, hike, even climb mountains, and generally improve their quality of life.
>
> (Össur, https://www.ossur.com.au/ossur-difference/the-history-of-flex-foot, accessed 2019-12-19)

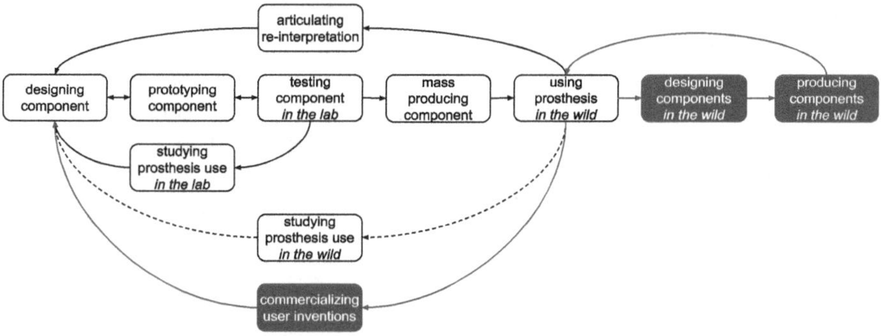

Figure 6.3 The relationship between the re-inscription process within industry and beyond industry. Own figure.

As this example shows, it is when products originally developed by users for their own use feed back into large-scale industrial processes that new design trajectories emerge and enable new user identities to be enacted beyond individual re-interpretation (see Figure 6.3).

In summary, whether re-inscription is done by professional engineers in corporate R&D departments or by prospective users in their private homes, it requires that some form of translation is achieved between industrial *production*, *distribution*, and the practices of *using* situated outside the immediate control of industrial companies. From an action net perspective, the contingent character of *using in the wild*, presents an ongoing challenge for a lasting alignment of those actions, as it involves the constant elaboration and *re-interpretation* of inscribed user roles. Conversely, the industrial scale *re-inscription*[13] of unexpected forms of use into new generations of products provides a measure of stabilization, necessary for the gradual institutionalization of new user roles beyond individual re-interpretations. The industrial construction of users involves the continuous back and forth between both processes throughout a technology's biography.

6.2 3D Printing and the Re-Inscription of Using in the Wild

The increasing availability of digital fabrication technologies promises to reconfigure the relationship between *re-interpretation* in use and *re-inscription* in new design and production efforts. The most common hypothesis links digital technologies to a potential democratization of the means of production, emphasizing the mechanism of user innovation over that of re-inscription by industrial manufacturers. In this view, new user roles do emerge, because digital design and production technologies enable prospective users to design and fabricate almost anything they want, and to freely share their innovations on a large scale using the internet—all *without* the need for conventional manufacturers. In this "age of the consumer-innovator" (von Hippel et al., 2011) or the "digital prosumer" (Ritzer & Jurgenson, 2010), the misalignment between *designing, producing, and distributing on the one side, and using in the wild* on the other, would be bridged, as users take over formerly industrial activities. Traditional companies remain in the picture, but are expected to adapt to these changes by opening up their innovation processes (Chesbrough, 2003), or by supporting and leveraging the productive activities of users (von Hippel 2017: 89–100).

In the following sections, I offer a different analysis. I do concur that new user roles are constructed as the translational capacities of digital production devices become involved in reorganizing the relationship between *producing* and *using*. However, in contrast to proponents of the democratization thesis, I argue that this reorganization revolves around the transfer of rapid prototyping techniques to the realm of manufacturing, and the concurrent move of user testing from *the lab* into *the wild*. Hence, rather than rooting my explanation in users' enhanced ability to design and produce for themselves, I emphasize the mechanism of industrial re-inscription, focusing on the industry's newfound ability to dynamically react to the contingency of situated use practices. In this line of argument, we are not witnessing a democratization of innovation[14] but rather a tighter coupling between using and the activities of industry.

6.2.1 From CAD/CAM to Rapid Prototyping

To understand the effect of digitalization on the link between using and producing, it is instructive to recall the relationship of 3D printing to the development of Computer Aided Design and Computer Aided Manufacturing (CAD/CAM).[15] As Gary Lee Downey (1992a, 1992b) shows in his ethnographic account of the development of CAD/CAM, those technologies first rose to prominence in the 1980s as a possible solution to the US industry's self-diagnosed problem of falling behind Japan with regard to productivity and, especially, the ability to quickly adapt to rapidly changing user preferences. Downey argues the following:

> According to the nationalist script, CAD/CAM technologies promised to streamline product innovation in American industry by merging together the distinct engineering activities of 'design' and 'manufacturing', thus enabling American companies to increase their 'productivity' by responding more quickly and effectively to changing consumer demands.
>
> (Downey, 1992b, pp. 2–3)

As Downey points out, the original thrust of the technology was precisely to establish a more responsive relationship between the industrial activities of designing, and manufacturing on the one side and the ever-changing activities of the industry's users on the other. By enabling the direct translation between easily adaptable digital product models and the numerical control codes steering a new generation of production devices, CAD/CAM was meant to make ingrained systems of mass production more flexible, thus paving the way to faster re-inscription of increasingly unpredictable "consumer demands."

However, as Downey (1992a, p. 154) goes on to show, back in the 1980s this "nationalist script" was not entirely successful, as subsequent developments emphasized "the CAD side of the CAD/CAM division." Technologies such as wireframe modeling or surface modeling did enable *design* engineers to do analysis on computer models, but did not allow for the direct *manufacturing* of these models. Computer-aided design therefore allowed for rapid cycles of designing, analyzing, and redesigning, but did not offer the ability to translate that advantage into the fabrication of end-products that could be materially tested, let alone used. In other words, while computer-aided design models did speed up design, their incompatibility with the requirements of manufacturing kept them separated from the activities of prototyping, lab-based physical testing, or user trials in the wild.

My own argument starts from the observation that the widespread implementation of computer-controlled *production* technologies such as CNC milling machines and 3D printing has changed the situation described by Downey. Arguably, these new technologies are designed precisely to extend the advantages of CAD to the realm of manufacturing, by enabling the rapid translation between digital renderings and tangible objects. It is partly because it embodies the reinvigoration of the original impetus of CAD/CAM that 3D printing is viewed as a technological solution to the industry's problem of flexibly adapting to feedback from ongoing use-practices.

6.2.1.1 Rapid Prototyping in Prosthetics

Historically, the first application of 3D printing in prosthetics was in prototyping. In fact, in products intended for mass production, this way of using the technology has been so dominant that, until recently, the application-oriented term "rapid prototyping" and the technology-oriented term "3D printing" were often used interchangeably. The advantage that digital production offers in this area is that it allows for the semi-automated translation of digital renderings into tangible models which can be used as tools for testing out ideas as well as demonstrating and discussing them with others. With regard to the development of prosthetic fit components, this is precisely how large manufacturers make use of 3D printing today. For example, when asked about the advantages of the technology, an engineer working for such a firm told me:

> With standard products the added value of 3D printing simply is in rapid prototyping. So, when new things are developed here, one can really

> manufacture prototypes very quickly and cost-efficiently, in order to have a tangible model and be able to talk about that.
>
> (interview, engineer, 2016-08-12, own translation)

In contrast to manual prototyping techniques, which require the attention of a dedicated engineer, the ability to produce material objects based on the often already available CAD models made the process both cheaper and faster. Making use of digital fabrication technologies, trying out multiple versions of a prototype or integrating feedback from discussions with colleagues requires nothing more than making a few changes in the digital model, and printing out a new object, rather than starting over and building a new prototype from scratch. As should be expected, this ability was greatly appreciated by industrial companies aiming to reduce the large development costs associated with mass production by rooting out conceptual errors as early as possible in the design process.

Yet, significant as the introduction of rapid prototyping may have been for the process of *designing*, from the point of view of industrial user construction its effects remained limited, as it did not fundamentally alter the industry's relationship to *using*. Despite the ability to translate digital models into tangible prototypes, these objects could hardly be fitted to people with limb differences. For the first decades of their application in prosthetics, the material properties of 3D-printed prototypes were such that they ruled out the idea of actually putting them on prospective users, even in controlled settings. The limited strength and durability of the printed objects meant that they could not bear much weight, while the coarseness of their surfaces impeded most mechanical applications beyond demonstration purposes. Hence, just like CAD models, 3D-printed prototypes mostly remained artifacts of design rather than production. Moreover, as they were unsuited for lab-based testing, let alone field testing, they did not help to elicit feedback

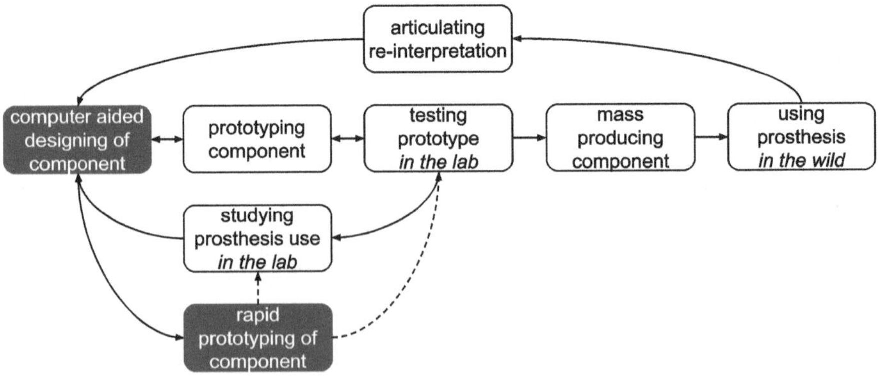

Figure 6.4 Rapid prototyping offered an additional source of feedback informing design, but did not translate into the production of usable objects.

from actual use practices and did, thus, not alter the basic structure of the action net. Prototypes for lab-based functional testing still had to be manufactured manually, and prostheses meant for use under real-life conditions were still made using technologies of mass production.

6.2.2 From Rapid Prototyping to Rapid Production

Over the last decade, the growing sophistication of 3D printers and materials has led to a qualitative change in their application, with 3D printing increasingly being used to manufacture directly usable products instead of prototypes. Following this development, the continuous iteration that digital technologies afforded to the process of design can now, at long last, be extended to the realm of production. Rapid prototyping, in other words, is now complemented by "rapid production" (compare Bak, 2003).[16] This change dramatically transforms the action net of user construction. As the ability to rapidly iterate on existing designs is extended from prototypes to finished products, the integration of feedback from *using in the wild* now becomes feasible. This means that manufacturers can now more readily react to the contingency of situated use practices, paving the way for a faster co-evolution of technology and user roles. Moreover, where designers systematically integrate *using in the wild* as a source of input for product development, the distinction between *testing* and *using* grows increasingly porous, opening the way for new roles, such as the "beta tester." In what follows, I will explore how three different types of organizations, a university-based non-profit, an industrial start-up, and an open-source community, made use of rapid production in practice and how that shaped the action nets of user construction vis-á-vis the established institutional order of the prosthetics industry.

6.2.2.1 Rapid Iteration and the Construction of Scientific Facts

The non-profit Beta[17] was among the first organizations using 3D printing to manufacture end products rather than prototypes. It thus offers a good example of the dynamics triggered by rapid production in terms of the construction of new user roles. Indeed, Beta's ability to draw on feedback from using in the wild speeds up the co-evolution between technology and user roles, with using being increasingly viewed as a form of continuous testing. However, being based at the engineering department of a Canadian university, the Beta case also serves to highlight the ways in which the iterative dynamic between rapid production, and using in the wild is slowed, and in fact halted, by ingrained norms and rules linking medical device development to the construction of scientific facts.

During my stay at Beta, it became readily apparent to me that the team had long since woven the idea of rapid iteration into their design and production practices. In stark contrast to conventional manufacturers that only

Figure 6.5 The "wall of shame" in the Beta lab, displaying some earlier versions of the Beta hand. Own photograph.

release new versions of their products every few years and after thorough testing, when entering the Beta lab, I was faced by the so-called "wall of shame" (see Figure 6.5), displaying a substantial selection of earlier Beta Hands that had been released and subsequently altered or abandoned. The wall, hence, reminded team members and visitors alike of the rapid evolution the device had undergone since it was first fitted to a recipient in 2014. When asked about any of those hands, some senior Beta members were happy to recount the artifacts' history, explaining why some changes were made, kept, or abandoned and thereby offering invaluable insight into the two main sources of feedback orienting Beta's re-inscription practices.

Based on my interlocutors' explanations, as well as my own experience at Beta, a first important type of feedback originates from inside the lab itself and may be based on physical testing as well as the engineers' feedback on assembling and handling the device. While some of the resulting adaptations, such as changes in printing material, are readily visible on the "wall of shame," most are rather incremental in character and difficult to appreciate for an outsider presented with the final product. For an example, consider the situation described in the following fieldnote:

> Margaret [a pseudonym] broke a part while assembling the hand and I mentioned that the same thing had happened to me a day earlier. This incident led to a discussion between a few Beta engineers about how to avoid that problem in the future. After some deliberation, Charley [a pseudonym] says: 'I must go to Solidworks [a CAD program, DS] to show you.' He brings up the CAD model of the hand, navigates to the part that broke earlier and, changing some parameters, adjusts its length by 4mm so that the screw can no longer push through the plastic. [...] As the change is made in the digital file, the edited part can now go on the 3D printer and is indeed finished the next morning. 'Imagine, if I had to go to the machine shop,' Charley says, turning to me, 'that would take forever.'
>
> (Fieldnote, 2018–20-08)

The kind of change described here can be attributed to a form of rapid prototyping, similar to the one practiced at conventional industrial manufacturers. 3D printing gives Beta's engineers the ability to quickly translate between feedback from lab-based activities, the digital CAD model and a new material object. In fact, as pointed out in the above excerpt, the rapid evolutionary dynamic documented on the "wall of shame" would not have been equally supported by conventional prototyping techniques and it was the use of 3D printing that helped Beta to sustain it as part of its routine activities.

Yet, in sharp contrast to most large manufacturers, at Beta, the rapid integration of feedback is not limited to laboratory-based activities. It is precisely because there is no clear material distinction between prototypes and finished products that even early versions of the Beta Hand could be fitted to actual recipients whose situated use practices served as a *second* source of feedback orienting re-inscription activities. For example, when discussing the various changes in wrist design documented on the "Wall of Shame," a senior engineer at Beta told me the following story.

> [W]e've got a young man [...]. We told them, you know: It's only for light duty. Don't do anything difficult! [...] He went and he rode his motorcycle with the hand, right? So, the wrist broke, and I don't want to say he crashed the bike, you know, he fell off the bike. He was fine, he was lucky. And from that moment we actually changed the wrist design substantially. [...] We keep engineering it to be stronger and stronger because as engineers, no matter what you do to design a product, a user will use it however they like.
>
> (interview, engineer, 2017-09-19)

I argue that, from an action net perspective, this example illustrates a fundamental change in the way in which the activities of designing and manufacturing relate to the contingent practices of using prosthetic devices. Specifically, by making use of a combination of CAD and 3D printing, Beta was able to extend the iterative dynamic we have seen in the realm of *rapid prototyping* and *lab-based feedback* to the realm of *rapid production* and *feedback from using in the wild.* As demonstrated by the above example, being able to iterate on already released products enabled Beta to quickly react to unexpected use practices, thus utilizing a feedback mechanism denied to industrial manufacturers operating on conventional technologies of mass production. In this configuration of the action net, continuously drawing on information generated as part of the recipients' practical lives is absolutely critical in shaping the design of new products such as the Beta Hand, as well as the ways in which they can subsequently be used in practice.

Another important transformation, hinted at in the previous example, is that the ability to continuously iterate on already usable products makes the distinctions between *producing* and *prototyping*, as well as *testing* and *using* somewhat arbitrary. As both prototypes and finished products are manufactured in the same way and both remain open for further changes, there is virtually no way of clearly differentiating them. Similarly, as the testing of these objects has moved out of the lab, it is no longer clear whether the people using them should be considered *testers* or full-fledged *users.* Indeed, from the moment the Beta Hand was first tried out in the wild, the engineers learned that, in contrast to traditional laboratory testing, it was next to impossible to delimit how their products would and would not be used. For instance, even when they asked recipients to return the devices, on the grounds of them not being finished products, they found that, after some design iterations, people were reluctant to give up the limbs that had, at that point, become useful parts of their daily lives. In refusing to return the hands, they had moved from acting as testers to acting as users. Conversely, even after years of development and hundreds of deliveries around the world, using retained a quality of testing in the view of engineers. As an expression of that, the fitting of every Beta Hand, is still accompanied by the signing of a liability waiver, identifying the device as a "working prototype based on a new 3D printing technology." Recipients of this peculiar type of object must accept that "there are risks associated with its use, such as unexpected failure of structure, components, or failure during use" (Beta liability waiver, 2017-10). At Beta, then, rapid production had resulted in blurring the boundary between using and testing so clearly institutionalized in conventional prosthetics. While this afforded the rapid co-evolution of user roles and technology, it also meant that the developing organization no longer assumed full responsibility for its ever-changing products. Instead, part of the risk now lay with the users, whose embodied experience was treated as an important resource for further refinement of a product considered "work in progress."

Rapid Production and the Stabilization of Scientific Facts

Owing to the application of rapid prototyping practices to the realm of production and the concurrent move of user testing into the wild, the

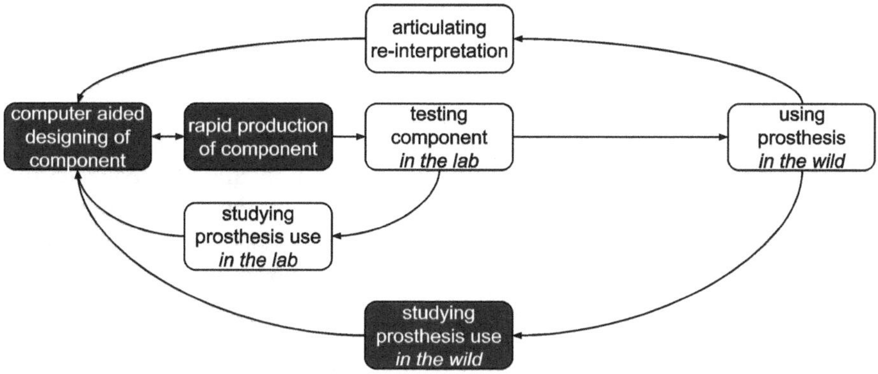

Figure 6.6 The replacement of rapid prototyping with rapid production enables the inclusion of constant feedback from using in the wild. Own figure.

co-evolution of users and technology was much faster at Beta than it was at most conventional manufacturers. However, while the ability to react to unforeseen use practices genuinely pleased the engineers who thought of design as "a never-ending process of feedback and revision" (interview, 2017-09-19), the implementation of rapid iteration also clashed with several of the basic institutions governing the development of medical devices. These incompatibilities at times slowed or stopped the ongoing re-inscription cycle and shaped the way in which user feedback could be taken into account.

One of the most persistent of these incompatibilities facing university-based Beta stemmed from the institutionalized requirement of conducting and *publishing* outcome studies to document the utility of a new prosthetic product. Indeed, the constant evolution of the Beta Hand directly impeded the engineers' ability of establishing scientific facts about its functionality and benefits. In the conventional system of mass production, in which a new prosthetic component enters manufacturing at a rather late point and remains mostly unchanged after that, the norm is to conduct subsequent clinical studies, which are used to convince insurers, prosthetists, and prospective users alike of the product's utility. At Beta, however, products remained malleable even after entering production, and engineers quickly re-inscribed user feedback into ever new versions of the hand. Accordingly, the Beta Hand never stabilized enough for them to put together a study conforming to the scientific standards of engineering or prosthetics journals. This difficulty in publishing was a constant irritation to some Beta members who felt the need to document Beta's success vis-à-vis funding organizations and the scientific community in the field. As becomes clear in the following interview excerpt, this incompatibility between conducting and publishing a credible outcome study and the idea of rapid iteration resulted in a strong motivation to stabilize the Beta Hand's design and stop integrating further feedback:

> We had surveys and we asked people to complete them. We also did some videotaped interviews which were translated and it's great feedback, but it was not publishable. Don't even get me started...fucking publishing. Oh, it just makes my head hurt! You have absolutely ignorant, stupid reviewers who [...] obsess with samples size! Oh, you know: 'You haven't done a survey of 30 people.' My god! [laughs] Like I can't have 30 amputees! [T]he point is, we [...] were changing the design based on feedback. That's why I'm so excited about the 200 Hand [the latest version of the Beta Hand, DS], because it's reached a level of stabilization where I can actually do a survey or a scientific paper. I can actually give it out to 30 people and collect, you know? But before, the hands were evolving. We weren't ready.
>
> (interview, engineer, 2017-09-19)

As this example shows, the question of how to organize the relationship between using and new cycles of designing and producing was shaped by institutionalized patterns of action linking product development to the construction of scientific facts. Beta clearly had the technological means to keep re-inscribing user feedback into new generations of its products, and this ability was deeply appreciated by the engineers. Still, the institutionalized requirement of scientifically proving their products' benefits, acted as a force against the indefinite continuation of the rapid iteration cycle. Under these conditions, Beta eventually decided to "lock down" the design process at least temporarily in order to make the Beta Hand amenable to the construction of stable facts as required by science-based engineering. In result, Beta engineers aligned their practices with the prevalent institutions of the prosthetics industry, foregoing the technologically feasible strategy of continuously adapting their devices to feedback from an ever-growing number of users.

6.2.2.2 Rapid Iteration and Physical Testing

The use of 3D printing at the start-up Omega (compare Section 4.2.2) was similar to that of Beta in that rapid production enabled the organization to routinely draw on feedback from using in the wild to orient its development processes. Just as in the previous case, this increased the speed of co-evolution between users and technology, while blurring the distinction between using and testing, as illustrated by the new role of the "beta tester." However, the necessity of actually selling products within a highly regulated industry meant that Omega was confronted with different aspects of the institutional order, namely the requirement to physically test and certify every new version of its products. Moreover, in contrast to

Beta, Omega did not simply adapt to prevailing institutions, but instead aimed to adapt the latter to better facilitate its own digital development practices.

At Omega, the use of 3D printing was central to the integration of user feedback throughout product development. Using 3D printing for the fabrication of both prototypes and end products alike, even early versions of its prosthetic feet were usable and could be fitted to test users in controlled clinical settings. For example, I participated in a session in which a test-user was fitted with two different 3D-printed feet and was asked to perform a number of different tasks under the oversight of one of Omega's product developers and the technicians of the partnering clinic. After walking around the clinic's corridors, on a treadmill, as well as up and down ramps, the developer asked for his opinion on both feet, which the prosthetist helped him translate back into design changes. The following excerpt demonstrates the way in which feedback was integrated into the design process, by focusing on a discussion that revolved around one specific part of the foot which I will call the "latch."

USER: Like I said, the movement [of the latch] would need to be constrained a bit. Yes. Because that thing slows me down. That's the problem. [...] That latch hits the floor—that's why it's already black.

PROSTHETIST [POINTING TO THE LATCH]: And that here should be softer?

USER: Yes, exactly, or make it softer, because right now it's hard.

DEVELOPER: But should there be more movement in it, too? Is it okay for it to go higher or not?

PROSTHETIST: No, no, no. Otherwise he has no security. The problem is: When he wants to roll over that spot, the latch stops him.

DEVELOPER: Okay. And what if we make the radius steeper at the front? That means adjusting the curve [of the latch] so that, practically, we take off a little of the front?

PROSTHETIST: That will work.

(Recording of feedback session, 2016-03-24)

As a result of feedback sessions like this one, Omega engineers were able to gain some basic insight into the usability of their products much earlier than would have been possible in a system of mass production, where 3D-printed prototypes were used for illustrative purposes only. It was this ability to rapidly iterate on usable prototypes that allowed the start-up to continuously test new product versions and re-inscribe user feedback to evolve their designs.

Omega's collection of feedback did not remain limited to controlled clinical environments either. Instead, the extension of rapid iteration from prototyping to manufacturing was paralleled by an extension of user testing from the lab into the wild. By partnering with prosthetists, who were willing to fit Omega's products to their patients, the start-up was able to recruit

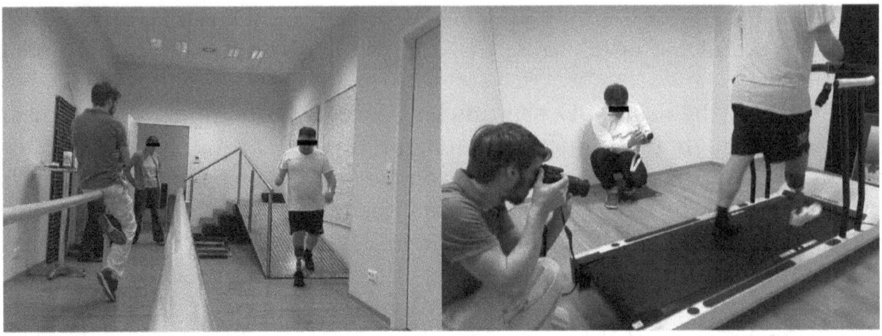

Figure 6.7 User testing of one of Omega's 3D-printed prototypes. Own photograph.

a number of amputees as so-called *beta testers*. The idea of beta testing, a term that Omega borrowed from software development and used in its promotional materials, is to release an unfinished, but usable, version of a product for testing under real-life conditions.[18] The major difference to the field studies done by conventional manufacturers, lies in the recursive relationship that is established between designing and using in the wild. Under conditions of mass production, field testing occurs at a very late stage of the development process, the idea being to prove the usefulness of a device that is supposed to remain virtually unchanged. By contrast, beta testing is done as early as possible in the process, in order to expose the object to the full contingency of human use practices, and to gradually refine the design accordingly. From the point of view of user construction, the major consequence of this is a tightened coupling between re-interpretation in use and re-inscription by industry, leading to the rapid co-evolution of inscribed user roles and situated use practices from an early phase in a product's biography.

Rapid Production and Physical Testing

Omega's idea of "beta testing" aimed at open-ended exploration rather than retrospective legitimation. Because of that, it proved difficult to reconcile with an institutional order that had emerged in tandem with a system of mass production. Particularly, given the industry's emphasis on safety and usability, the idea of releasing an *unfinished* product appeared rather ludicrous. Whereas in software design the mantra is to "release early and often" and to "treat your users as co-developers" (e.g., Raymond, 2001, pp. 27–28), in prosthetics, taking the users' interests into account meant to thoroughly test and certify every product prior to release. As a result, there were several incompatibilities between Omega's philosophy of rapid iteration and the existing set of norms and regulations. For instance, continuous

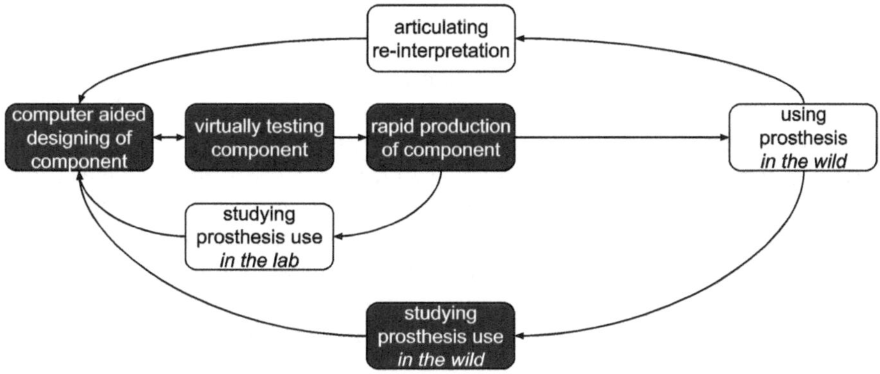

Figure 6.8 By advancing a method for digital testing, Omega aimed to adapt the institutional order to its rapid production model. Own figure.

re-inscription was challenged by the fact that all existing procedures for the certification of new products were based on *physical* testing. Conforming to this institutionalized requirement did, however, introduce a bottleneck to Omega's digital development model. For example, the necessity to test every new version of a prosthetic foot for two million cycles at prespecified laboratories meant that the start-up ended up iterating on the digital versions of their products faster than they could physically test and certify them. Hence, despite the technical feasibility of rapid production, the existing institutional order, tailored to ensure the safety and usability of mass-produced products, was threatening to slow down the speed at which the start-up could re-inscribe the feedback elicited from its beta testers.

Remarkably, however, Omega did not simply change its own practices according to the prevailing order. Rather, at the time of writing, the start-up had begun development of a *digital* testing methodology, which was supposed to adapt existing institutions to a rapid production model. Using finite-element-analysis (FEA) to run virtual tests of its products, the goal was to eventually establish *simulation* as a legitimate alternative to physical testing at external laboratories (Figure 6.8).[19] In contrast to the Beta case, Omega thus aimed to establish compatibility between existing institutions and new practices by adapting the former to the latter rather than the other way around. Essentially, making rapid production work required changing the rules that had been governing the fabrication of prosthetic fit components since WWII.

6.2.2.3 Rapid Iteration and Research in the Wild

Against the backdrop of the two previous cases, the open-source community Alpha offers insight into the dynamics of rapid production *outside* of a conventional R&D context with its institutionalized routines and regulations. Just like Beta and Omega, the Alpha community uses 3D printing to realize an evolutionary development model, releasing new products early and iterating on them fast. However, in contrast to the re-inscription efforts of traditional organizations, Alpha's activities are both *radically decentralized* and largely *unbound by the industry's prevailing institutions* such as those pertaining to physical testing, or outcome studies. As I will show, this mode of organizing allows for a potential multiplication of the kind of direct feedback loops I have traced for other cases of innovation in the wild. Yet, it also raises the challenge of how to properly collect, interpret, and react to that newly available source of information in the absence of shared routines and resources.

At Alpha, the use of freely available CAD tools and affordable desktop 3D printers, combined with the absence of binding norms and regulations, allowed volunteers to engage in the kind of radically iterative development process I have shown in other cases of *rapid production* as well as *innovation in the wild* (compare 7.3.2). Indeed, the community's development model shared properties of both kinds of cases, as the ability to quickly translate between malleable digital files and usable physical prototypes, characteristic of the former, is paired with the continuous unregulated access to feedback, characteristic of the latter. The potential of this combination became apparent even during the development of the two earliest Alpha style devices, the Robofinger and the Robohand.[20] In the video that was to inspire the work of thousands of Alpha volunteers, the two inventors described how they used CAD software and desktop 3D printers to speed up the feedback cycles between re-interpretation in use and re-inscription in design.

CARPENTER: I would do sketches and scan them and [...] e-mail them over, and then he'd script something and send the file back and I'd print it and then I'd say: 'No, hang on, this is not working, and change this and change that.' It was up and down.

PROP MAKER: The impact that utilizing [desktop 3D printing] had upon our design process was incredible. It dramatically increased the speed at which we could prototype and try out ideas.

(MakerBot, Youtube, https://www.youtube.com/watch?v=WT3772yhr0o, accessed 2019-10-14)

As this early example shows, by pairing people with limb loss and people equipped with digital fabrication technology, Alpha linked the ability to quickly iterate on already usable designs, with the availability of direct feedback from ongoing testing and use practices. Yet, while this pattern was effective on the level of individual development projects, it grew even more potent on the level of distributed development in the community at large.

DISTRIBUTED ITERATION

The potential for rapid iteration multiplied, when the two inventors made the printable files of the Robohand publicly available online. This enabled thousands of volunteers to manufacture the device on their own desktop 3D printers, to build on its design in cooperation with recipients, and to share their adaptations with likeminded others. Alpha's way of re-inscribing use-feedback was, thus, closer to the practices of open-source communities (Raymond, 2001; Gläser, 2006, 264–276) than it was to those of the centralized organizations which had hitherto dominated the field of prosthetic componentry. This mode of organizing had two consequences that set Alpha apart from the examples discussed so far. On the one hand, the opportunities for giving and collecting feedback were multiplied, as hundreds of volunteers began working with differently situated recipients all over the world. On the other, volunteers faced the challenge of how to re-inscribe that feedback *lacking* both a centrally organized R&D department and the shared routines and resources necessary to translate the collected information into a form directly usable by other makers (dotted lines in Figure 6.9).[21]

Since many Alpha members directly interacted with prospective users, the community had access to an ongoing stream of user feedback, which shaped its overall development and the kinds of user roles it helped to construct. However, since most volunteers did not systematically collect or document this information, the predominant form in which feedback became

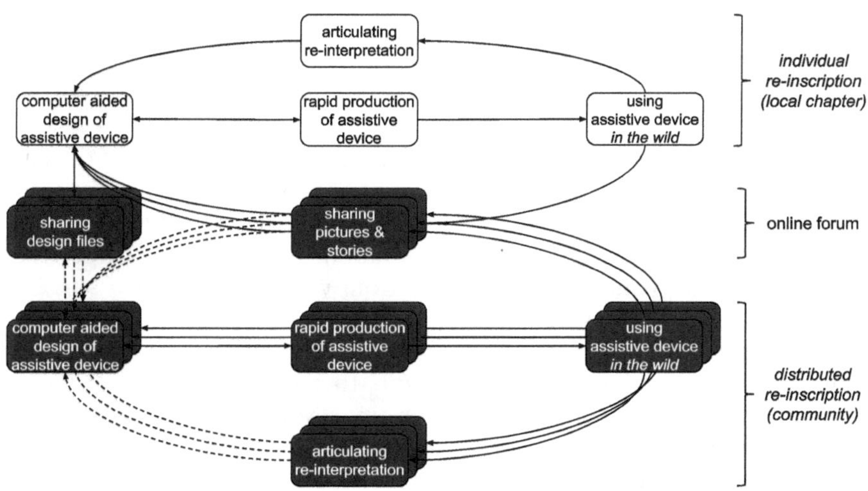

Figure 6.9 Alpha's re-inscription model was highly distributed and relied on the sharing of design files as well as pictures and stories about the use of the assistive devices designed by community members. Own figure.

available to others was that of *anecdotes*. Makers took great delight in sharing pictures and stories of the recipients they worked with and the devices they had made for them. From the start, Alpha's many blogs and forums were full of inspirational content about the lives of people receiving and using 3D-printed hands. This wealth of anecdotal feedback arguably helped Alpha members to gain some general insight into the applicability of hobbyist devices. It also helped them to learn about the most common struggles of their recipients, including things like skin abrasion, social stigma, or trouble with the insurance system. Most importantly, anecdotes shaped new user roles by focusing attention on some of the more surprising usages of Alpha hands, thereby suggesting directions for further development.

In Alpha's early days, this dynamic was triggered by recurring stories about US children who, reportedly, used the unrefined aesthetics of early Robohands to imitate popular superheroes. As Alpha's founder underscored, this surprising re-interpretation guided the subsequent re-inscription efforts by volunteers and contributed to the community's early success.

> So that's one of the reasons why [Alpha] was such a success by the way. It's because we were making devices for children which frankly looked like sort of robotic cyborg hands, because we didn't know how not to do that—and that turned out to be a really big hit with children. You know, prosthetists looked at our devices in the old days and they used to scoff and say those things look like plastic toys. And the kids we were giving them looked at them and they would squeal with delight: 'Those things look like plastic toys and I'm a superhero!' [...] So that was an important lesson and it helped create, I think, the current aesthetic of many 3D-printed prosthetics.
>
> (interview, founder of Alpha, 2017-12-14)

In this example, anecdotes effectively provided Alpha members with some basic insights into the aesthetic preferences of their users and alerted them to a dimension of their devices' utility which professionals refer to as "psychosocial functionality." Indeed, reports about children's favorable reactions, multiplied by massive media attention, were followed by a surge of design activities. Alpha volunteers printed hands in colors resembling figures like Iron Man or Captain America, and developed all sorts of embellishments like Wolverine claws, or Star Wars-themed lightsaber hands. They also designed several new devices which improved on the original Robohand (Figure 6.9). These were openly shared with the larger community and often received telling names like "Cyborg Beast," "Raptor," or "Phoenix," to further stress their perceived symbolic utility.

Remarkably, while the focus on US American children contributed to the community's early growth, it proved problematic when operations expanded to new groups. As Alpha started working with a more diverse cast of users, including adults, and recipients in countries of the Global South, they were faced with rather different interpretations of their products. Volunteers now reported that the padding of early devices was unsuitable for recipients with traumatic rather than congenital limb loss, or that partial hand designs, developed for children with amniotic band syndrome, excluded people with higher degrees of limb loss. Most strikingly, the early focus on extraordinary aesthetics, while popular with US youths, was emphatically rejected by people with other sociocultural backgrounds. Haitian amputees, for instance, took offence at the robotic-looking devices, as they associated them with the figure of the Zombie,[22] rather than with US superheroes. Such stories triggered heated debates about the potentially harmful consequences of open-source hardware design, prompting several leading designers to stop sharing their work with the community (see Section 5.2.3). Yet, they also contributed to another round of re-inscription efforts, which culminated in several new designs. Reacting to the feedback of adult users in Haiti, and other countries of the Global South, these were usually forearm devices that emphasized durability and anthropomorphic appearance, sometimes at the cost of mechanical functionality (Figure 6.10).

As these examples demonstrate, Alpha's community model displayed a strong evolutionary dynamic based on distributed feedback from an increasingly large range of users. Sharing even anecdotal feedback within the community facilitated collective learning and provided general directions for further development. Moreover, each publicly shared design file enriched the portfolio that others could build on. Yet, for all these advantages, truly *collective* development projects remained the rare exception, and most concrete advancements emerged from local rather than community-wide collaboration. For instance, new hand designs were provided by several active father-son-teams, or by dedicated volunteers with an engineering background. Early forearm designs thus came out of local

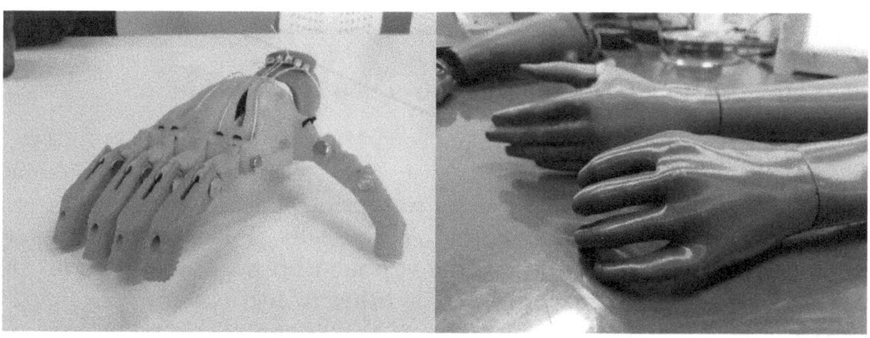

Figure 6.10 Left: A "Cyborg Beast" hand designed for US children, right: Forearm devices designed for Haitian adults, source: own photograph. Own photographs.

groups of Alpha designers working with individual recipients, and further refinements were often made by an emerging network of more strongly coordinated local chapters.

Arguably, more strongly coordinated re-inscription efforts on the community level were hampered by Alpha's loose mode of organizing. The *self-motivated character* of work within the community meant that most volunteers tended toward the tasks considered most rewarding, such as making a hand or giving it to a child. Conversely, they were less interested in the comparably tedious work of documenting design changes, testing products, or conducting outcome studies (dotted in Figure 6.9). The anecdotes they shared usually offered general ideas but provided little concrete information on use practices and contexts, mechanical performance, or long-term durability. Similarly, *self-selection* of members meant that volunteers often lacked the skills and resources necessary to translate the available information into adequate design changes. While most makers had some proficiency in 3D printing, few of them knew very much about computer-aided hardware design, and even fewer had any prior experience in prosthetics. Finally, the community's ability to collectively work on user feedback was impeded by its *low degree of coordination*. Even when insights from local projects were shared, that information was dispersed over various e-mail lists, private websites, forums, social media channels, blogs, and 3D printing repositories, without any clear organizing principle.[23] Hence, despite a wealth of local interaction with a wide range of recipients, little systematic knowledge emerged on the community level and few collaborative design projects were realized. In fact, it was common for Alpha volunteers to miss relevant information, repeat the mistakes of others, and, occasionally, arrive at the same conclusions that had been available all along. While this might be an unavoidable side-effect of an action net emphasizing rapid cycles of trial and error, and globally distributed grass-roots participation, it also meant that Alpha's ability to react to feedback from its users was diminished by various inefficiencies.

6.3 Extending Industrial User Construction into the Wild

From an action net perspective on user construction, the situated practices of *using* play a double role as both a way of integrating industrially made products into the daily pursuits of concrete people and as a central source of input for ever new product designs. Analytically, this twofold character can be captured by stating that using is bound up with other actions on two sides, one pointing to industry, the other to the user's practical life. Using is linked to the complex practices of people who are always more than just users. Industrial products may enable these people to act in ways that were previously precluded to them. Yet, how a product will be interpreted is shaped by the myriad of other activities that make up a person's life, most of which precede the use of the artifact. In this sense, using therefore refers to practices of *re-interpretation*, which make the artifacts of industry compatible with extensive nets of action well beyond the control of designers or manufacturers. At the same time, using has become an integral part of contemporary industrial activity itself. Through mechanisms ranging from the (collective) articulation of dissatisfaction by customers to institutionalized practices such as user testing and outcome studies, the contingency of technology use provides an important source of information for industry. Unexpected ways of using (or not using) influence how new generations of products will be designed, while new user roles are, in turn, stabilized as they are taken up in industrial development and large-scale production. In this second sense, using is therefore a continuous source of feedback, which industrial manufacturers aim to align with their own activities through strategies of *re-inscription* and control.[24]

In this chapter, I have explored how the relationship between using and industrial activity is mediated by the prevalent production devices in order to understand how a change in the latter may contribute to the emergence and stabilization of new user roles.[25] In contrast to existing theories which focus on the ability of users to increasingly engage in hitherto industrial activities, my argument has focused on the ability of producers to increasingly perceive and react to the contingencies of use. To grasp the significance of this transformation, it is helpful to recall the problematic relationship between the action nets constituting systems of industrial mass production and the contingent practices of *using in the wild.*

I found that, *under conditions of mass production*, manufacturers are held accountable for their products by an increasingly large group of customers, to the degree that the latter are able to effectively articulate their demands. However, at the same time, the inflexibility of conventional techniques of mass production, in combination with an institutional order focused on extensive testing and certification, means that industry is hard-pressed to react to any unforeseen feedback once a product has entered production. The widespread practice of bringing "using" into the lab can be understood as a reaction to this predicament, in which manufacturers try to gain feedback from use *before* the product design has been "locked down" for large-scale fabrication. Yet, my study suggests that the success of this strategy remains limited for two reasons. First, pre-production prototypes are, at best, imperfect simulations of the final product. As they are not made using the same production devices, they usually serve as a proof of concept, unlikely to stand up to conditions outside the laboratory. Second, and more importantly, the very act of studying technology use in the lab strips the latter of much of its contingency which is, after all, rooted in its relationship to the myriad other actions of a user's daily life. Hence, even though bringing users into the lab is common in contemporary industries, manufacturers are still bound to be surprised by the ways in which people re-interpret their products, and they will, once more, face the challenge of how to react to that feedback.

Whatever misfits accrue between the user roles inscribed into the products of industrial mass production and the actual pursuits of the people who use them will typically have to be resolved by the latter, be it by rearranging their lives around the product, or by altering the product itself. User-led innovation is a common way in which this adaptation occurs (Hippel, 2005). Owing to the small scale of production and user innovators' lack of institutionalized accountability, feedback loops between designing, producing, using, and re-designing are much tighter and occur much more frequently than is the case with traditional manufacturers. Initially, the rapid co-evolution of technology and user roles is therefore much faster and new user roles emerge more rapidly. However, for any large-scale manufacturing and distribution of their inventions, user innovators do still depend on conventional industry, meaning that the latter retain a key position in the stabilization of new user roles.

Against this backdrop, the decisive question is how the introduction of digital fabrication technologies may alter the relationship between the prevalent system of production and the contingent practices of using. Existing theories of digital fabrication answer this question by postulating the expansion of the second mechanism just mentioned, that of *re-inscription beyond industry*. In contrast, I offer an explanation that is based on the intensification of the first one, which can be characterized as an *extension of industrial re-inscription into the wild.*

6.3.1 The Democratization Hypothesis

Many popular accounts of the digitalization of manufacturing argue that the introduction and increasing ubiquity of digital design tools will lead to a fundamental change in the relationship between users and industry, by giving the former the ability to design and eventually produce *for themselves.* As early as 1980, Alvin Toffler saw signs of a "third wave" in industrial development, which would see the return of what he termed the "prosumer," a role combining the activities of both producing and consuming one's own goods. In a similar vein, Eric von Hippel (2005) proclaimed a democratization of innovation, writing that...

> ...[U]sers' ability to innovate is improving radically and rapidly as a result of the steadily improving quality of computer software and hardware, improved access to easy-to-use tools and components for innovation, and access to a steadily richer innovation commons.
>
> (von Hippel, 2005, p. 13)

Being inspired by the success of open-source software communities (Raymond, 2001), von Hippel argued that part of the potential of user innovation stemmed from the fact that users freely shared both their problems and solutions with others and increasingly formed innovation communities which aided not only the *development*, but also the *distribution* of inventions.

Some years later, Chris Anderson, himself motivated by the recent success of the maker movement, extended this line of argument to include a stronger focus on hardware and *manufacturing*. Showcasing the bold style of a tech journalist, Anderson wrote:

> Because of the expertise, equipment, and costs of producing things on a large scale, manufacturing has been mostly the provenance of big companies and trained professionals. That's about to change. Why? Because making things has gone digital: physical objects now begin as designs on screens, and those designs can be shared online as files. [...] The biggest transformation is not in the way things are done, but in who's doing it. Once things can be done in regular computers, they can be done by anyone. And that's exactly what we're seeing happen now in manufacturing.
>
> (Anderson, 2012, pp. 17–18)

According to the position advanced by all these authors, the introduction and spread of digital production devices will enable users to increasingly perform tasks previously assumed by industry. In this line of argument, user roles are expected to change in two ways. On the one hand, user innovators will represent their own needs differently than industrial manufacturers and thus carve out new roles for themselves, which they inscribe into functionally novel products (Hippel, 2005, p. 8). On the other, the very idea of being a user may take on an entrepreneurial character (Shah & Tripsas, 2007), as an increasing number of people start acting as prosumers, user innovators, or members of maker movements and open-source communities.

Now, without disputing the existence of such phenomena, my own study suggests that a different set of mechanisms is (also) at work, namely those related to the transformation of traditional industrial re-inscription processes. Given that, despite the alleged ubiquity of the means of production, most users neither produce nor innovate,[26] understanding these changes is a critical contribution of a theory of industrial user construction.

6.3.2 The Extension of Industrial User Construction into the Wild

My own account of user construction under conditions of digital fabrication differs from the position just sketched out in terms of both theoretical foundation and practical conclusions. On a theoretical level, the democratization thesis is built with a focus on *actors*. After all, the very idea of "democratization" advanced here is that the group of potential innovators will encompass ever more people, eventually extending to a point where it includes "everyone."[27] In fact, viewed from this vantage point, things are much like Anderson put them: "[t]he biggest transformation is not in the way things are done, but in who's doing it" (2012, p. 18). By contrast, an action net perspective begins from the relationship between *actions*, exploring how changing patterns of activity may give rise to new actorial identities or roles. From that altered vantage point, the main question is not how digital fabrication changes *who* designs, *who* produces, and *who* uses, but how *using* is related to changing practices of *designing, producing, distributing,* and so on.

This difference in theory leads to a different set of observations and practical implications. First and foremost, I found that across various types of actors, digital fabrication technologies are used to tighten the feedback loops between re-interpretation in use and re-inscription in design. As it becomes easier and cheaper to translate between the activities of *using, designing,* and *manufacturing,* the time between the release of new product versions is significantly reduced, meaning that unexpected use practices can be re-inscribed more frequently. Moreover, during the development of each new product iteration, the time frame in which re-inscription is feasible is extended. The incorporation of use-feedback begins earlier than under conditions of mass production (rapid prototyping) and remains feasible even after the product is released "into the wild" (rapid production). Indeed, to the degree that the possibility of re-inscription becomes constant, the process of user construction may be organized in a way that Neff and Stark (2004) call "permanently beta." At this point, the perpetual ability to react to new feedback from using means that there are no longer any discernible differences between prototype and final product, testing and using.

While these tendencies were present in all the cases I studied, their practical consequences depended on the kind of action net that new technologies were introduced to and, especially, the way in which they were related to the institutionalized practices of conventional industry. At Beta and Omega, the two organizations that oriented their activities to the industry's major institutions, the use of digital fabrication allowed an *extension of user testing into the wild.* Whereas under conditions of mass production, manufacturers relied on bringing using into the lab, digital fabrication allowed them to consistently draw on feedback from situated use practices. This new possibility, in turn, was related to two kinds of changes in existing user roles. On the one hand, it allowed a *faster co-evolution* between the user roles inscribed into industrial products and the ways in which these products were actually being used. While most of these changes were incremental, the fact that design was now more directly linked to the full contingency of human use practices meant that more radical changes did occasionally occur.[28] On the other hand, the permanently malleable character of products meant that *using took on the character of perpetual testing.* As an expression of this change, both organizations experimented with new ways of delegating their responsibility to users themselves, for instance by treating them as "beta testers" of products that were by definition unfinished. Yet, these experiments had to be made compatible with the existing institutional order, and their effects largely depended on how this translation was achieved. Beta, for instance, deliberately slowed the speed of iteration to allow for the construction of scientific facts about their products. Conversely, Omega introduced simulation-based "virtual crash tests" to make testing procedures compatible with the speed of their rapid design iterations. In both cases, the effects of digital fabrication therefore depended on how it was related to existing institutions.

By contrast, where digital fabrication technologies were used *beyond* conventional industry, they tied in neatly with the trial-and-error-based tinkering typical of user-led innovation. In scenarios in which the people who used prostheses also directly participated in designing them, 3D printing served as another tool to further speed up rapid cycles of re-interpretation and re-inscription. As theorized by von Hippel (2005), the biggest change lay in the fact that new designs, being available as digital files, could be shared with others who could further iterate on them. Remarkably, however, the community that formed in the case of open-source prosthetics was not a community of users but what could be termed a *charitable innovation community*. It consisted of hobbyists and semi-professional makers who had access to the means of production, be it in the form of privately-owned 3D printers or an infrastructure of shared machine shops, but often lacked the embodied experience of using the devices they produced. The rise of such communities introduces to the realm of "innovation in the wild" two problems that had been typical of conventional industry, namely *how to effectively collect and integrate feedback from ongoing use practices* and *how to establish some form of accountability vis-à-vis the people who use.* While their position outside of conventional industry allows these communities to quickly iterate on products unbound by the requirements of user testing or certification, it also complicates the answer to these questions. After-all, charitable communities lack centralized laboratories as well as shared norms for how to relate to their users. They will, thus, either need to revert to practices well-established in conventional industry or come up with new forms of organizing their distributed innovation efforts.

Given the observations made in this chapter, one of the central questions posed by the digital fabrication of tangible goods is how we want to navigate between the advantages of speeding up the co-evolution of user roles and technology, and the issues of accountability and responsibility linked to releasing unfinished products for use in the wild. As large-scale design and production do become feasible outside of conventional industry, and as manufacturers extend their testing activities beyond the laboratory, we must ask, how we want the contingency of our lives to be taken into account and what kinds of "bugs"[29] we, as users, want to stumble upon in the process.

Notes

1 The Washington Post, https://www.washingtonpost.com/wp-srv/photo/galleries/sierra_leone/part_5.htm?, accessed 2020-01-15
2 The *Prüfstelle* thus pioneered the kind of certification process that has become mandatory for all prosthetic fit components. In fact, its successor organization, Berlin Cert, is still active in the field today.

3 In the US, this program is considered by many as the birth of modern prosthetics. This is at least partly due to its publicly available documentation. The program's early phase is described in the 1947 report by the Committee on Artificial Limbs of the National Research Council, its latter phases are chronicled in the journal *Artificial Limbs: A Review of Current Developments*, which ran from 1954 to 1972.

4 Ottobock, https://www.ottobock.com/en/company/mission/, accessed 2020-03-01

5 It should be noted that even though field studies do involve using the product beyond the clinic, they delimit possible feedback in several ways. For one thing, participants are carefully selected to fit the categories conceived by designers, for another, feedback is usually collected through pre-structured surveys, which further reduce a person's ability to provide rich information on situated use practices. In general, the bulk of (published) research by large companies seemed to aim at legitimation rather than exploration.

6 This is a crucial point in Eric von Hippel's theory of user innovation as well. In his conception, the information needed for solving technical problems is "sticky" and therefore costly to move across sites. Therefore, user innovators and producer innovators, having access to different kinds of information, will likely come up with functionally different kinds of innovation (Hippel, 2005, pp. 66–72). Indeed, an action net perspective, built as it is around the idea of translation, would concur that moving any kind of information across sites is a challenging task, which always involves some form of transformation.

7 Therapeutic Recreational Services Inc., https://www.trsprosthetics.com/, accessed 2020-02-27

8 TED, https://www.ted.com/talks/hugh_herr_the_new_bionics_that_let_us_run_climb_and_dance, accessed 2020-03-23

9 The SACH foot was not designed for the needs of athletes. Coming out of the US national research program described in Chapter 6.2, it was intended as a "generally acceptable and standard manufactured design" (Staros, 1957, p. 23), for basic activities. Its *solid-ankle* and *cushion-heel* provide a measure of stability during walking. Yet, these features also minimize the energy return propelling more active users forward during hiking or running.

10 I found, however, that user innovators often draw on established practices and knowledge, with many of them having a background in engineering or the crafts. Van Phillips, for instance, enrolled as a student at Northwestern University Medical School's Prosthetic-Orthotic Center, where he studied human biomechanics.

11 Smithsonian. National Museum of American History, https://invention.si.edu/innovative-lives-artificial-parts-van-phillips, accessed 2020-03-11

12 Markedly, while Össur continues to manufacture and sell customized versions of the C-shaped Cheetah running prosthesis, a heel has been re-introduced in most versions of the foot that are produced in larger quantities. This allows users to stand and walk more securely instead of just running, which remains a niche use overall.

13 Another relevant mechanism through which the translation between industrial inscriptions and situated use practices is stabilized in prosthetics is *control.* Control, in this context, means the adaptation of situated use practices to a prescribed user role, for instance through therapy, training, or formal contracts, but also through self-discipline. I do not elaborate on that point here, because I find the attempt to control situated use practices through other means than technology design to be a constant factor in all the cases I have studied, regardless of the type of production devices used.

14 I do recognize the importance of "user innovation" and there are several examples in which amputees have used 3D printers to make their own prostheses, or even built their own companies around these inventions. However, as demonstrated in the previous section, this is nothing new in principle and based on my material I find it hard to say whether or not there is a significant increase in such activities.

15 Note that situating 3D printing within the history of CAD/CAM applications stresses its relationship to industrial processes. Conversely, proponents of the democratization thesis like to stress the more recent relationship between the development of *desktop* 3D printing and the maker movement, which occurred once the original patents on key technologies expired, and made the technology available to a larger number of new designers outside industry.

16 A technique that falls somewhat in the middle of the two is "rapid tooling" in which it is the tools and molds used in mass production that are 3D-printed rather than the final product. Rapid tooling is used by several manufacturers in prosthetics, yet it does not feature prominently in my empirical material.

17 Beta is first introduced in Chapter 5. Being based at a Canadian university, the non-profit sets up local 3D printing centers in prosthetic clinics in regions marginalized by the global distribution networks of prosthetic manufacturers. Currently Beta operates in eight countries, including Nepal, Cambodia, Uganda, Kenya, Egypt, Guatemala, Ecuador, and Haiti.

18 To realize this strategy, Omega originally partnered with certified prosthetists and relied on the fact that its mass customized 3D-printed prostheses were considered custom "one-offs" at the time of writing. Hence, the liability for bringing the feet into circulation lay with the prosthetist, rather than the manufacturer.

19 The necessity to develop simulation-based testing stemmed as much from Omega's use of mass customization (Chapter 4) as it was rooted in its use of rapid iteration. In both processes, small changes can be introduced to existing products. However, while mass customization is based on the variation of a standardized template, rapid iteration involves manually introducing changes to that very template. Regardless of this difference, as long as the resulting objects are legally treated as mass-produced medical products rather than custom-made one-offs, it is necessary to test and certify each new variation.

20 As described in Chapter 4, the Robofinger was intended for the carpenter himself, while the Robohand was made for a South African child whose family had contacted the two makers during the development process.

21 Essentially, Alpha lacked both ingredients to construct *facts* about its users in the way sketched out by Latour (1988, 1990): A *laboratory* and the ability to construct *immutable mobiles* which could be accumulated there. At Alpha, re-inscription was "dispersed" (Czarniawska, 2004b) and the important question was, whether translation between the various local activities could be achieved on a community level.

22 According to Murphy (2011), the figure of the Zombie originated in the imagination of enslaved Haitian plantation workers. It remained effective even after the country's independence in 1804 and was still used by the Duvalier regime (1957–1986) to further increase fear of their paramilitary militias, the "Tonton Macoute." The figure became known to a mass audience in the US with the first zombie film, White Zombie (1932).

23 On the technological side the issue of effectively sharing information was made more difficult by the different CAD programs and file formats used. In contrast to open source software, what was shared in Alpha was not necessarily the source files but rather the printable files, which made it even harder to edit them. This appears to be one of the practical roadblocks for translating an open source model to the realm of hardware.

24 I have largely neglected the aspect of industry's direct influence on use activities, which becomes relevant in prosthetics through practices of training and therapy, among others. This was done because these aspects of the action net appeared unaffected by the introduction of new production devices.

25 For the sake of simplicity, the model developed here assumes that the spheres of industrial production and the user's practical lives are *only* mediated by using, which is a vast simplification in at least two ways. First, there appears to be a growing number of cases in which people do care about, and try to influence, the way in which design, circulation, and manufacturing are done. The spread of practices (and labels) such as "open-source development," "ethical production," or "fair trade" do suggest that users may be increasingly concerned with more than the use of industrial products. On the other hand, industrial actors may intentionally or unintentionally shape the lives of people beyond the direct use of their products. For instance, they may employ some of the same people that use their products; they may pollute the environment that users live in, or they may foster brand communities around their own products. To further explore this point, the idea of "concerned groups" reacting to market "overflows" as advanced by Callon and Rabeharisoa (2003; 2007) appears most promising.

26 Even in von Hippel's account, the innovative activities of users are concentrated among so called lead users (Hippel, 1986; Hippel, 2005, pp. 19–31).

27 Note that this argument is politically naive in that, even where the means of production *do* become more widely available, the idea that *everyone* will have the same level of access to them ignores all kinds of power asymmetries and structures of domination that pervade contemporary societies. Put more bluntly, increased access to the means of production for young, well-educated men in the Global North does not equal access for *everyone*, much less any meaningful democratization in the political sense.

28 Arguably, this will be the case more frequently, where the introduction of digital fabrication moves the industry's focus to new user groups, for instance by allowing new forms of *inscription* (Chapter 4) and *distribution* (Chapter 5).

29 This refers, of course, to Eric Raymond's mantra (2001, p. 30), echoed by von Hippel (2005, p. 94), that "more users find more bugs" and "given enough eyeballs, all bugs are shallow." What will happen to this way of thinking, when it is translated from the realm of software to that of hardware?

7 Digitalization and the Future of Use

The central proposition of this book has been that the digitalization of industry has societal effects far beyond the organizations that directly participate in it. I have argued that, in fact, the digitalization of current design, manufacturing, and logistic practices is transforming the user landscape of highly technologized societies. As a consequence, the reorganization of industries concerns the members of these societies not just as workers, makers, and professionals but, perhaps more importantly, as those who use industrially manufactured goods. It is therefore a central task for the social sciences to illuminate *how industries and users relate to one another* and *how user roles will change in the wake of digitalization.*

In this final chapter, I draw together relevant findings in order to attempt a systematic answer to these questions. I present the concept of *modes of user construction* to describe some of the most widespread and longstanding processes that link the intricate action nets constituting industrial organizations to the practical lives of their users. I then show how digital technologies allow for the recombination of established action patterns, thereby paving the way for new and distinctive *digital modes of user construction.* With these contributions, I hope to provide the conceptual tools for comparative studies of the relationship between industrial digitalization and the future of use—well beyond the field of prosthetics.

7.1 Modes of User Construction

In the preceding chapters, I have zoomed in on processes of user construction during specific phases in the biographies of prosthetic technologies. This detailed analysis demonstrated that, even in an industry as specialized as prosthetics, mechanisms such as inscription, circulation, and re-interpretation are realized in a variety of forms. Industrial technology supply and use appear to be linked by highly diversified nets of action that may differ between the products and production technologies involved, the prevalent normative and regulatory regimes, and the kinds of use contexts in which they become entangled. It is precisely this differentiation and even

DOI: 10.4324/9781003269731-7

singularization that is best captured by the notion of *biographies* of artifacts and practices (Hyysalo et al., 2019) or innovations (Lenzen, 2020).

Yet, just like human biographies the biographies of artifacts and practices are never fully individual. When zooming out from singular biographical moments, some recurring patterns can be discerned in terms of the temporal, spatial, and sociomaterial configurations of the relevant action nets. To grasp these, the frog's-eye focus on the diversity of practical action needs to be complemented with a broader bird's-eye-view (Hyysalo, 2021, p. 19). This shift in perspective makes visible widespread regularities in the relationships between technology supply and use and shows how these co-evolve with new generations of production technology over sustained periods of time. In other words, a wider focus brings into view the institutionally and infrastructurally stabilized translations *between* the more intricate mechanisms described previously. The drawback of analysis at this scale is that it necessarily brushes over some of the rich detail we have seen up to this point. The analytical advantage is the ability to identify what may count as *typical* patterns of co-construction between industries and their users.

To denote such longstanding and widespread configurations of action nets that weave together mechanisms of user construction across technology supply and use, I will use the term *modes of user-construction*. The concept builds on several key aspects of the action net analytics outlined in this book and extends them with an emphasis on large-scale patterns of stabilization and transformation.

> *(1) User roles are constructed in patterns of action that span technology design, production, distribution, and use. Modes of user construction give rise to characteristic user landscapes.*

Action net analysis asserts that actorial identities and roles are not given but constructed in action. However, singular actions, and the meanings attributed to them, are enabled and constrained by their relations to other actions in heterogeneous patterns. The analysis of user role construction cannot be limited to either technology design, distribution, or use but must account for their interrelation. Some action nets will of course be unique, exceptional, or ephemeral in character. By contrast, what I call a "mode" marks the other end of the spectrum. It refers to combinations of processes that occur during the biographies *of a large class of technologies*, and that may remain stable for decades. They are made up of recurring "patches of action," such as those I have attended to in previous chapters and which may be understood as typical phases or configurational movements (Hyysalo et al., 2019; compare Williams et al., 2005). Most currently conceivable modes will therefore include some variation of the following basic mechanisms: (a) the *representation* of potential users and the *inscription* of envisioned roles into products, (b) the *circulation* of products between sites and the various forms of *intermediation* that come with it, and (c) the situated *(re-)interpretation* of inscribed user roles and their potential *re-inscription* into technical artifacts. Through the repeated performance of these processes, each mode gives rise to a characteristic set of actorial roles, including a specifically patterned user landscape as well as the corresponding roles of technology designers, manufacturers, distributors, regulators, and so forth.

> *(2) Actions are linked across time, space, and organizational boundaries by processes of translation. Modes emerge as translations are stabilized through institutionalization and materialization.*

In action nets, heterogeneous actions are linked by processes of translation. Translation means that the intermediaries that are acted on—be they digital files, physical products, texts, bodies, or money—are either interchanged or passed on between actions, always involving the potential for transformation. It is in this way that the embodied activities of potential users can be represented in the form of pictures or numbers, which are transformed into sketches and blueprints, and inscribed into physical products. Translation is what enables the interlinking of technology supply and use.

In modes of user construction, these translations have become stabilized. The order and relationship between actions are no longer arbitrary but have become predictable or even taken for granted. The reason for this is that modes of user construction co-evolve with the institutional and infrastructural order of a given industry. Common patterns of action tend to congeal into *institutions*, repeated sequences of action that become supported by formal rules and informal norms. Such institutions, including things like professional routines, insurance systems, or regimes of testing and certification, in turn stabilize modes of user construction by legitimizing certain relations between technology supply and use.

Modes of user construction are further underpinned by the development of material devices and infrastructures. In particular, modes co-evolve with prevalent means of production and distribution, since these facilitate the translations between technology supply and use. *Distribution infrastructures*, including warehouses, roads, and stores help to move intermediaries (e.g., industrial products) from one place to another. *Inscription and production devices* mechanize the translation between intermediaries of different kinds. It is their translational capacities that equate embodied users to the objects of design and further transform the latter into usable products ready for distribution and use.

> *(3) Digital modes of user construction may emerge out of flexible re-combinations of familiar practices that slowly congeal into novel action nets.*

Another insight that I will further develop in this chapter (Section 7.2) is that *digital* modes of user construction may emerge as *institutionalized* patterns of action are re-combined into *novel* action nets. This is due to two conflicting dynamics. On the one hand, new inscription and production devices, as well as novel distribution infrastructures, allow for genuinely new translations between actions. On the other, existing modes of user construction are backed up by a historically grown institutional and infrastructural order that regulates the relationship between technology supply and use. In deeply institutionalized fields like prosthetics, novel modes must be realized against the backdrop of normatively and materially stabilized patterns of action. Under such circumstances, digital modes of user construction are unlikely to occur suddenly or to transform all aspects of an industry's user landscape at the same time. Rather, digital modes may first appear in the form of flexible re-combinations between large patches of action that change at a glacial pace at best.

I demonstrate the analytical potential of the notion of modes of user construction by systematically recasting the major empirical findings of the current study along four different modes observable in the field of prosthetics: The *craft mode*, the *industrial mode*, the *platform mode* and the *community mode*. When spelled out at this level of abstraction, it will become clear that some of the patterns of action observable in prosthetics are also at play in other industries. The modes described here may therefore work as a useful reference point for future studies in other fields. An analysis in terms of modes also yields important insights into the relationship between industrial digitalization and the emergence of new users in its own right. Most importantly, it demonstrates that new modes emerge through partial re-combination of existing practices and that the direction of change is shaped by the interaction of the highly organized activities of technology supply with the diverse lives of the people who use industrially produced goods.

7.1.1 The Craft Mode of User Construction

The craft mode of user construction is one ideal-typical way of weaving together technology design, production, distribution, and use. In prosthetics, we have seen this mode give rise to the actorial roles of prosthetists and orthopedic technicians, as well as a user landscape characterized by high diversification and an emphasis on individual user identities. Beyond prosthetics, craft production has been dominant in most economic sectors of the 19th century and continues to be important in many industries to this day, not only in those involving manual work in the narrow sense (Sennett, 2008).

In terms of *technology design*, the decisive characteristic of the craft mode is that every single product is made for a specific user, be it individual or collective, human, or non-human. Products (e.g., prostheses, shoes, cars) are thus not only unique, but *custom-made* for a specific use scenario. The initial construction of user representations in the craft mode usually involves some form of direct interaction between designers and prospective users, such as taking a person's measurements with a tape measure or interviewing a potential customer. Systematic differences between groups of users may emerge due to the influence of professional rules and routines, yet the goal remains to represent the envisioned user's individual characteristics or preferences and inscribe them into a unique product. In the craft mode, the kind of production device that facilitates the translation of these initial representations into usable products is the tool. That is, while the manufacturing of custom products may involve some degree of automation, the steps necessary to give the product its form and function are controlled manually. This mode of user construction is therefore associated with the mediating role of skilled craftspeople, such as certified prosthetists or orthopedic technicians, which has been variously interpreted as a source of quality or human error.

The craft mode is characterized by a relatively small-scale *distribution* of products rooted in *local production*. Because of the necessity to interact directly with potential users, the sites of production and use are typically close to one another both geographically and in terms of the prevalent institutional order. This means that the circulation of products is relatively free from additional intermediation, be it materially in the form of large-scale infrastructures, or organizationally in the form of distributors, resellers, or regulatory agencies. Rather, products circulate as users pick them up at a local shop, or as a craftsperson visits the user's home or workplace. Under these conditions, even if shared user roles emerge, they will tend to take the form of local practices or styles with a small range of diffusion. Indeed, the circulation of products and user roles is limited by their close entanglement with the practices of a specific social, cultural, and material setting. Even if custom products are moved to a different context, their specificity makes them prone to radical re-interpretations, as we have seen in the case of prosthetics donated from users in the Global North to recipients in the Global South. If the action nets underpinning the craft mode expand, they do so through the addition of local sites of production. These may adapt to new contexts but tend to remain loosely coupled through professional associations and education programs, allowing practices of user representation, production, pricing, feedback collection, and so forth to be shared.

Using custom-made products is commonly associated with the expression of individual identity, since the product's design can be adapted to the user's specific activities and interests. It should be added, however, that in strongly industrialized fields where craft production is not the norm, using custom products may not serve as an expression of individual identity so much as a reflection of social status or affiliation with a specific class or group (Bourdieu, 1984). In either case, a characteristic of technology use in the craft-mode is that situated re-interpretations, both individual and collective, may feed back into new designs relatively quickly. The proximity between using and designing allows for practices of *continuous tinkering* oriented by the principle of trial and error, which results in a continuous back and forth between situated re-interpretation and re-inscription. In this way, feedback from technology use in uncontrolled environments, what I have termed *using in the wild*, can be continuously translated into new design activities. Over time, this close link between using and re-inscribing may lead to the establishment of a stable social relationship between producers and users, which may find its expression in mutual trust or situations of lock-in.

7.1.2 The Industrial Mode of User Construction

The industrial mode of user construction, emblematic of modern societies, represents in many regards the opposite of user construction in a system of craft production. In prosthetics, this mode was associated with the role of engineers, the formation of large industrial organizations, and global distribution networks, as well as a user landscape shaped by the differentiation of relatively large and homogenous populations. Based on technologies of mass production, it has been the emblematic form of user construction in most Western industries throughout the 20th century.

In terms of *technology design*, the central characteristic of the industrial mode is that individual user representations are aggregated into larger categories that inform the development of standardized products capable of being manufactured in large quantities. The social, geographical, and temporal distance between technology supply and use tends to be large and there is rarely any sustained interaction between technology designers and potential users. Instead, technology supply and use are linked by various intermediaries such as marketing departments, resellers, and industry associations (Hyysalo et al., 2016). These mediators use inscription devices and techniques, including surveys and data analysis software, to represent users. They also aggregate representations into larger categories commonly labeled "populations" or "market segments," with these categories occasionally congealing into widely accepted standards or norms (e.g., standard sizes, testing procedures). The effect of this aggregation is to make the heterogeneity of potential users amenable to large-scale production with single-purpose machines in a factory system. This emphasis on efficient production and the disregard for differences between potential users is perhaps best captured in Henry Ford's famous utterance: "Any customer can have a car painted any colour that he wants so long as it is black" (2007[1922], p. 72).

Since the industrial mode is predicated on mass production, the *distribution* of industrially made goods and the user roles inscribed in them proceeds from a central site of manufacturing, both spatially and socially removed from the sites of use. This gap between production and consumption introduces the need to translate between differently situated activities, as products need to circulate across organizational, national, and cultural boundaries. To stabilize these translations, the circulation of products depends on specific regulations (e.g., shared standards, free-trade agreements), and large material infrastructures (e.g., roads, distribution centers). The need to translate between different meaning systems may also give rise to distinct practices of marketing and the emergence of a whole range of market professionals in what Callon and colleagues (2002) have termed the "economy of qualities." It is by the extension of these material and symbolic distribution pathways, rather than through the addition of new sites of production, that genuinely *industrial* action nets of user construction expand to new places and new potential users. These pathways allow industrial products to travel globally yet they also make the industrial mode prone to catastrophic failure in the case of institutional misalignment or infrastructural breakdown following accidents, (trade) wars, natural disasters, or pandemics.

Technology *use* in the industrial mode is faced with the challenge of integrating standardized products into the practical lives of highly diverse users. As already mentioned, industrial actors may attempt to control use and use contexts to guarantee the compliant uptake of their products. This may include everything from advertising to training, from end-user contracts to interface design, and from lobbying to large-scale cultural work. When successful, such strategies construct stable alignments between the spheres of industrial production and consumption that constitute entire populations as users of mass-manufactured goods. Yet, the translation between standardized products and varied practical lives is also taken on by users themselves. In the industrial mode, standardized products are commonly imbued with individual and collective meanings through practices of re-interpretation and domestication. This may be a rather private affair, as suggested in the literature on domestication (Silverstone et al., 1992). However, as we have seen in the case of prosthetics, the very constitution of large homogeneous user groups, typical of the industrial mode, may also give rise to new potentials for collective action. Public articulations in terms of boycotts or demonstrations are possible, as are political lobbying, legal action against manufacturers, or the formation of influential user organizations.

Despite the frequency of re-interpretations, *re-inscription* of the latter remains particularly challenging. From the point of view of industry, the gap between using and producing means that information will not be easily available without renewed efforts at user research. Moreover, the large initial investments associated with mass production and large-scale distribution make it undesirable—or downright impractical—to react to the unexpected use practices that may accrue given the heterogeneity of contexts in which industrial products are taken up. A typical strategy of industrial firms is therefore to examine use practices *prior to* committing to mass production. This may take the form of scientific user testing, "user centered design" (Williams et al., 2005, pp. 68–70) "living labs," or computer simulations to name a few. Nonetheless, all these strategies run the danger of underestimating the contingency of *using in the wild*. As a result of this inability of industrial manufacturers to react to user feedback in a timely and effective manner, *user innovation* is a common feature of highly industrialized societies (Hippel, 2005). While user innovation usually starts out on a small scale and a principle of trial and error resembling the craft mode, it may feed back into industrial action nets through processes of user entrepreneurship (Shah & Tripsas, 2007) or as user innovations are licensed in by conventional manufacturers (Hippel, 2017, compare Chapter 6).

7.2 Digital Modes of User Construction

Modes of user construction are relatively stable, but they are by no means static. In particular, the introduction of a new generation of inscription and production devices, such as 3D scanning and 3D printing, offers new opportunities for organizing the relationship between technology design, distribution, and use. When seized upon, their novel translational capacities may trigger the transformation of established action nets and the user landscapes to which they give rise. Yet, the degree and direction of change are not predetermined. To explain how user roles change in digitalizing industries, one has to grasp the interplay between the *existing institutional and infrastructural order* underpinning current modes of user construction and the *novel translational capacities afforded by digital technology.*

As I have shown throughout the book, new modes of user construction inevitably build on established action nets, which are stabilized by historically grown institutions and material infrastructures. In fact, when new production devices are introduced into strongly institutionalized contexts, such as industrial organizations, they are frequently interpreted in accordance with the status quo, regardless of their novel potentialities. They will be judged against rules and norms shaped by the practices of technology design, manufacturing, and distribution that precede them, and they will be deployed in conjunction with entrenched supply chains and logistic infrastructures. For these reasons, many newly introduced technologies are first used to re-enact well-rehearsed patterns of action. Digital technologies are no exception. In fact, characteristics like modularity, re-programmability, and open-ended malleability arguably make them particularly adaptable to a large range of established routines and context (Orlikowski, 2000). The digitalization of deeply institutionalized industries may therefore not resemble a sudden disruption, as purported by popular accounts, as much as a glacial, partial, and inextricably political process of making new stuff work. We have seen this tendency at work in prosthetics, where digital technologies like design software, 3D scanners, and 3D printers have been symbolically and materially adapted to both the craft and the industrial mode of user construction, resulting in orienting metaphors such as the "digital plaster cast."

The present study has also shown, however, that the wholesale reproduction of established modes of user construction is not necessarily the end of the story. In the long run, the use of digital production technology rarely simply mirrors the social relations between industries and their users. New inscription and production devices by definition *allow for a new set of translations.* They enable genuinely new ways of relating actions to one another, and these will likely be tried out and experimented with, particularly in societies that encourage innovation (Seibt et al., 2023). The question therefore becomes, how the translational capacities of digital production technology can be characterized.

On the most basic level, *digital inscription devices*—from scanners to pressure sensors, and activity trackers—allow for the translation of a growing range of intermediaries (texts, objects, human bodies) into strings of ones and zeroes. These digital data are organized into files, which can be manipulated using software programs and rendered visible on output devices like computer screens. In this way, all kinds of digital objects (Faulkner & Runde, 2019) may be produced. The addition of *digital production devices*—from CNC mills, robotic carvers, and 3D printers—allows for the reverse translation. These machines take certain kinds of digital objects as inputs to produce corresponding physical objects out of a given raw material. In combination, digital inscription and production devices therefore make it possible to translate back and forth between various analogue intermediaries and digital data. It is this translation process that 3D scanning and 3D printing now extend further into the realm of physical objects, of *hard*ware.

A workable equivalence between physical and digital objects means that many operations previously performed on the former, may now be performed on the latter and vice versa. Although not as seamless as often believed, these translations make it possible to leverage the unique properties of digital objects to establish new links between (industrial) technology supply and use. How exactly these properties should be conceptualized is still a matter of scholarly debate (Alaimo & Kallinikos, 2022; Faulkner & Runde, 2019; Kallinikos et al., 2013). However, the current study demonstrates that digital objects should be treated as a new kind of intermediary in action nets (compare Latour, 1990 for a more general discussion of intermediaries), the properties of which enable the restructuring of user construction in at least three ways.[1] The *programmability* and *re-programmability* of digital objects (Kallinikos et al., 2013; Yoo et al., 2010) have enabled new practices of technology design both in terms of individualization and automation. The increased *mobility* and *reproducibility* of digital objects (Rifkin) have opened up new opportunities for the spatial organization of manufacturing and logistics. Finally, the continuous *malleability* of digital objects (Kallinikos et al., 2013; Neff & Stark, 2004) has been used to implement new ways of reacting to user feedback, changing the temporal rhythms of re-design cycles, stabilizing evolutionary dynamics in technology development, and blurring the boundary between testing and using.

To sum up, the digital transformation of user construction is marked by two opposing dynamics. On the one hand, new modes of user construction must build on deeply ingrained institutions and infrastructures. On the other, new inscription and production devices allow for genuinely new ways of translating between actions. The emergence of new modes of user construction therefore requires reconciling both dynamics, save for scenarios in which one of the two dominates entirely. In the field of prosthetics, a typical mechanism of navigating this dual requirement has been the *re-combination of institutionalized action patterns into new action nets.* In these new action nets, some activities, such as the manual modeling of a digital plaster cast, may closely resemble existing practices. Yet, insofar as digital objects allow for new translations between activities, the overall pattern of action may still change. For instance, the increased mobility of the *digital* plaster cast may allow for the centralization of production, while its re-programmability enables a faster reaction to changes in use practices or user bodies. Today, many such new combinations are tried out in the prosthetics industry, either existing side by side or competing with one another. It is when such new action patterns are repeated that they may eventually stabilize as genuinely *digital* modes of user construction, thereby constituting part of a new institutional order in the industry.

There are currently two such re-combinations that appear to be particularly likely candidates for constituting digital modes of user construction. I will label these the *platform mode* and the *community mode of user construction* and explain how both show signs of evolving distinctive sets of infrastructures and institutions, both within prosthetics and beyond. In what follows, I briefly sketch out how these new modes recombine processes typical of the industrial and craft modes into novel action nets that construct user landscapes with distinctive topologies.

7.2.1 Platform Mode of User Construction

A first digital mode of user construction, which I will call the *platform mode*, is characterized by action nets in which formal organizations utilize digital inscription and production devices to link themselves to a wide range of external activities, while retaining a high degree of centralized control over the translations involved. In prosthetics, this pattern of action is epitomized by a host of new organizations, including start-ups and NGOs as well as a range of new user roles that are interpreted as constituting "niche markets." Beyond prosthetics, the potential of platform organizations to use digital technologies to centralize the coordination of heterogeneous user activities has been observed in many industries, with relevant activities spanning communication (Helmond, 2015), transaction (Davis, 2015; Kirchner & Beyer, 2016), and technology development (Chesbrough, 2003; Gawer & Cusumano, 2014).

In the platform mode, crucial aspects of technology *design* are carried out by focal firms in ways similar to the industrial mode. However, due to the re-programmability of digital designs, peripheral aspects of the process may be left to others. In prosthetics, this was most obvious in the case of mass customization platforms and their accompanying software apps. In *mass customization*, technology development begins from the construction of a strictly standardized *digital product template*. As in the industrial mode, the underlying user representations are highly aggregated and the translation between using and designing involves additional mediation. Indeed, user representation may draw on sources also used in conventional industrial design processes, such as anthropometric tables or predefined testing procedures. However, in contrast to analogue designs, the re-programmability of digital templates allows for their adaptation beyond the R&D department (e.g., in a prosthetic workshop), thereby enabling the inscription of individual user specifications. This may be done by adjusting predefined parameters (parametric mass customization) or by applying a set of predefined rules (algorithmic mass customization). In both cases, the semi-automated adaptation of digital objects links a conventional industrial design process that is controlled by a focal firm and based on the accumulation of user data, with a process of partial customization that is oriented toward individual use practices. For this reason, mass customization has long been hailed as a virtuous combination of the efficiency and scale of mass production and the individuality of custom production (Pine, II., 1993). Today, web-based platforms and configurator tools apply such processes to products ranging from computer software to clothes, cars, and furniture. When compared to the industrial mode, this allows for the further differentiation of large, homogenous user categories, increasing the diversity of the user landscape. Yet, the case of prosthetics demonstrates that the variety of user roles remains limited when compared to the craft mode. This is due to the fact that, even though mass customization enables the adaptation of products to user preferences, the latter can only be articulated within a "solution space" predefined by a focal firm.

In the platform mode, the *distribution* of products proceeds from a single center, just as in the industrial mode. However, circulation is not based on material objects, but on digital files. That is, products follow trajectories plotted along digital infrastructures rather than roads, ports, and warehouses. Manufacturing—in the sense of the creation of usable physical artifacts—is delegated to a *global production network* and may occur at any place equipped with suitable digital production devices. The platform mode thus combines centralized design, a characteristic of the industrial mode, with polycentric, or even local production, as associated with the craft mode. In this it resembles processes of outsourcing, licensing, or franchising. Yet, the ubiquity of networked data infrastructures further enhances the speed and reach of distribution, while simultaneously retaining the flexibility of production. These developments may increase inclusivity in the user landscape by making high-quality products available to excluded or marginalized user groups, or by serving specialized user requirements more quickly. However, in the platform mode, the flipside of inclusion is an increased dependence on focal organizations and their digital infrastructures. Just like in the industrial mode, the continued maintenance of action nets depends on circumstances well beyond the control of users and their local communities. Digital production may exacerbate this tendency where it extends the reach of industrial distribution networks, or where local designers and artisans outsource production to third-party fabricators, making their sustenance dependent on production by remote firms.

A final consequence of the platform mode is the potential to combine large-scale production, as associated with the industrial mode, with the ability to continuously re-inscribe feedback from using in the wild, as characteristic of the craft mode. This ability stems from the capacity for *rapid production*, which allows a direct translation between continuously malleable digital objects and the production of immediately usable physical products. Industrial manufacturers thus have the capacity to react to unexpected use practices more easily, which may engender faster feedback loops between re-interpretation and re-inscription and hasten the emergence of new user roles on a large scale. Clearly, this promises greater user participation and influence over product development and the shortening of innovation cycles. However, the case of prosthetics also highlights some of the risks involved. For instance, rapid production enables organizational forms that enroll users as *beta testers* of unfinished products, as industrial firms try to extend their testing procedures beyond the laboratory (Marres & Stark, 2020). Not only does this raise questions about unpaid work (Rieder & Voß, 2010), it may also lead industrial manufacturers to circumvent regulations by permanently labeling their products as prototypes or custom one-offs. While fostering constant product updates and improvements, the platform mode also poses new dependencies and uncertainties for the users it helps to construct.

7.2.2 Community Mode of User Construction

In a second digital mode of user construction, which I will call the *community mode*, digital inscription and production devices link design, production, distribution, and use in a decentralized fashion, thereby reducing the control of industrial organizations. In prosthetics, this mode is mainly associated with the processes pioneered by the Alpha community, although similar approaches have been reported in other industries. Insofar as these collectives have common roots in the maker- and open-source movements (Anderson, 2012; Raymond, 2001) and are based on a growing peer production infrastructure (Benkler, 2006) consisting of shared machine shops (Braybrooke & Smith, 2018), online forums and repositories (Hippel, 2005; Hyysalo, 2021), the community mode can be said to emerge from action nets that cut across classical industry boundaries.

Technology *design* in the community mode involves representational practices based on direct feedback from technology use. Just as in the craft mode, the process begins with the creation of products for individual users. However, in contrast to craft production, the low-cost reproducibility of digital objects means that custom designs can be easily shared with others who can refine and manufacture them without the need for a skilled craftsperson. The community mode therefore links the design of custom products with large-scale distributed manufacturing, allowing for what I have called *scalable custom production*. In this pattern, user identities emerging from local interactions and the design of custom products become the starting point for more widely shared user roles. Similar processes have existed in the context of user innovation, particularly where users started firms based on their own inventions or licensed them to industrial manufacturers (Hippel, 2017; Shah & Tripsas, 2007). Yet, in the community mode, the role of both industrial firms and individual user innovators is deemphasized, due to the low-cost reproducibility of digital objects and the growing availability of the digital means of communication, distribution, and production. The activities of representation and inscription are increasingly distributed in heterogeneous communities, as technology design is based on shared digital infrastructures and repositories like GitHub or Thingiverse, newly emerging rules and norms, exemplified by open-source licenses, and novel practices such as remixing, open documentation, or collective design.

In the community mode, the *distribution* of products relies on the open sharing of digital files and their local fabrication. The major difference with respect to the platform mode is that neither of these processes are centrally controlled by industrial organizations. Instead, they rely on infrastructures and production devices operated by private citizens or loosely organized *peer production networks* and communities. *Private fabrication* (e.g., using desktop 3D printers) is common, but by far not the only option. For more expensive or sophisticated equipment, shared machine shops may be set up, and community members may access industrial-grade production devices by outsourcing production to professional service providers. As a result, large-scale production and distribution is now possible without the involvement of industrial manufacturers. The community mode bypasses not only conventional distribution infrastructures but also evades the strict regulation typical of the craft mode's professions or the industrial mode's regulatory agencies. As we have seen in the case of the Alpha community, this enables the circulation of products to an even wider range of places and potential users than is the case in the platform mode. But insofar as products are manufactured and distributed outside of conventional regulation, the community mode runs the risk of the large-scale diffusion of sub-standard products, or products originally intended for entirely different contexts and use practices. The challenge for communities then is to realize the potential for including a large range of users, while establishing effective rules and norms to tackle issues such as product quality, safety, and reliability of services. As hinted at in the latter stages of Alpha, communities may eventually give rise to formal organizations and platform-like infrastructures to mediate between technology supply and use.

In terms of technology use, one consequence of bypassing prevalent institutions is that the products provided are sometimes sub-par in terms of quality, comfort, or associated services, to industrially produced ones. At the same time, products will tend to be tailored to the user's preferences in a process of trial and error, making them likely to support the construction of pronounced, and unique user identities. Re-interpretations may be particularly radical or surprising when the community mode makes products available to marginalized groups, such as we have seen in the case of Alpha providing 3D-printed prostheses to US children or Haitian adults. In addition, these radical re-interpretations may give rise to widely shared user roles more quickly than in the craft or industrial modes. Globally dispersed communities may evolve a surprising capacity to react to the contingency of using in the wild, owing to the direct feedback loops between technology design and use, and the accumulation of feedback within the wider community. Notably, users do not need to become outright user innovators, as in the industrial mode, but they may participate in the community through small-scale contributions, giving feedback, suggesting small tweaks, or simply raising awareness about the community's products (compare Hyysalo, 2021). *Re-inscription* may thus begin with the kind of individual tinkering typical of the craft mode, but accumulate feedback in ways reminiscent of large-scale user research carried out in research labs and industrial R&D departments. This may be called citizen science (Dickel & Franzen, 2016), *research in the wild* (Callon & Rabeharisoa, 2003), or knowledge management in communities. The decisive point is that re-inscription efforts are increasingly based on a shared wealth of digital data about ongoing use practices in uncontrolled environments. The growing accessibility of digital inscription devices (e.g., sensors, scanners, design software) may further underpin such efforts. The more salient challenge becomes, how to ascertain the rigorous documentation and evaluation of feedback and guard against the construction of new biases in the user landscape that may arise from the ebb and flow of attention in the community and the self-selection of volunteers.

7.3 The Sociomaterial Small Print of the Digital Transformation

Thinking in terms of the emergence of new modes of user construction makes it possible to grasp the overall changes in the relationship between technology supply and use in the age of digitalization. The typology of modes presented here (Table 7.1) may thus serve as a useful heuristic for future analysts and help them to carve out overarching trends from messy fields of action. The highly abstracted form of these modes also makes intelligible similarities and differences between industries, allowing for comparison between studies and promising an avenue toward cumulative theory building. In terms of policy recommendations, the drawing of clear distinctions between modes brings into relief the issues of user diversity, inclusion, and participation at stake in negotiations about industrial digitalization and the future of use.

Table 7.1 Ideal-typical modes of user construction

	Representing—Inscribing	*Intermediating—Circulating*	*Re-interpreting—Re-inscribing*
Industrial Mode	Aggregated user representations inscribed into standardized products (mass production)	Mediated circulation from a single center of production via distribution infrastructures (global distribution network)	Aggregated re-interpretations during "using in the lab" re-inscribed before release (lab-based user research)
Craft Mode	Individual user representations inscribed into custom products (custom production)	Direct circulation from multiple sites of production close to local sites of use (local production)	Re-interpretations from "using in the wild" continuously re-inscribed after release (tinkering)
Platform Mode	Aggregated user representations inscribed into product templates, subsequently customized in predefined "solution space" (mass customization)	Mediated circulation from a single center of design via digital distribution infrastructures to polycentric sites of production (global production network)	Aggregated re-interpretations from using in the wild re-inscribed before release (beta testing)
Community Mode	Individual user representation inscribed into custom designs, subsequently reproduced in other contexts (scalable custom production)	Direct circulation from multiple sites of design via digital distribution infrastructures to sites of local production (private fabrication and peer production network)	Aggregated re-interpretations from "using in the wild" re-inscribed after release (research in the wild)

However, for all their advantages, modes of user construction only present the provisionally stabilized results of much messier processes. The point is not that they fail to capture the richness of action in all its detail. The point is rather that they run the danger of obscuring the contingent processes of their own construction. Yet, if the differences between modes have consequences for the future of use we should be able to say something about *how* one or the other mode comes to prevail in a given field.

I already argued earlier that new modes of user construction start out as *flexible re-combinations* of established patterns of action. In this process, the *range* of possible and conceivable combinations is shaped by the prevalent institutional and infrastructural order of a given industry, as well as the novel translational capacities of inscription and production devices. Yet, the *realization* of a given combinatorial opportunity depends on the stabilization of feedback loops between technology supply and use. In order to explain why a particular mode of user construction emerges and why it affects a particular part of the overall user landscape, it is not enough to focus on the politics involved in the transformation of industry. Nor does it suffice to focus on the material properties of the new technologies involved. Rather, to gauge the pace and direction of change, one also has to consider the *concrete practices of technology use*, their interrelation with the myriad other activities that make up the practical lives of newly constituted users, and the ways in which they feed back into new cycles of technology design.

New modes emerge once the relationship between the activities of industry, the translational capacities of production technologies, and the practical lives of users stabilizes. But it is precisely because of the complex feedback loops between these processes that the decision between multiple possible modes may come down to small events, minor technicalities, or specific user feedback during the early stages of their emergence. With this in mind, a final insight of the present study is that, despite contrary promises, digital modes of user construction do not work equally well for everyone. Instead, they often introduce novel biases in the user landscape. In the case of prosthetics, it was these very biases that linked a digitalizing industry to the concrete lives of highly specific groups of people in ways that proved consequential for both sides. In this book, we have seen practices of mass customization stabilize in conjunction with young adult users in Europe and North America, who popularized the notion that 3D-printed prostheses could be fashionable. We have followed an NGO setting up a multinational network of 3D printing centers which, at first, served only a small number of upper limb amputees whose feedback nevertheless formed the basis for new design iterations. Finally, there was the case of the Alpha community, whose identity and products were so strongly shaped by the feedback of US children that it proved challenging to extend operations to other groups.

These empirical cases have demonstrated that the pace and direction of the digital transformation in user construction is *not* solely a matter of prevalent industrial institutions and novel production technologies. New modes are equally shaped by the users they construct. As new action patterns work only partially and center on a few select groups, the latter's feedback will leave its mark, even as the action net is later extended to other groups. Yet, which groups are constituted as lead users or early adopters is not a straightforward matter. As new production technology is tried out in action, the stabilization or obstruction of feedback loops between technology supply and use may be influenced by seemingly inconsequential events and technicalities.

To complicate things further, the partiality of novel modes of user construction makes it unlikely that any one mode will upend an industry's entire user landscape all at once. As the case of prosthetics demonstrates, several patterns of action may exist in parallel and be associated with different product classes and sub-classes, or even with different components of the same product.

So, what will the digital future of use look like? The model put forth here suggests that digital inscription and production devices systematically enable new kinds of translations between industrial technology supply and use, leading to the re-combination of existing action nets and the formation of novel user landscapes. In principle, new user roles will be shaped by the existing forms of organization in industries and the concrete translational capacities of digital inscription and production devices. Yet, the trouble with predicting the future of use is that, once constructed, users quite literally play a role. In the process of user construction, craftspeople, industrial organizations, platforms, and communities inevitably become tied to the practical endeavors of people that they never fully control. People's lives, quite simply, cannot be reduced to the use of technology. In the end, industries may construct their users, but the latter will ever remain a source of trouble, innovation, and serendipity.

Note

1 This is not an exhaustive list and new ways of knotting together action nets based on digital data are found all the time, not least of all owing to an ever-increasing range of software programs.

Bibliography

Akrich, M. (1992). The De-Scription of Technical Objects. In W. E. Bijker, & J. Law (Eds.), *Shaping Technology/Building Society. Studies in Sociotechnical Change* (pp. 205–224). Cambridge, MA: MIT Press.

Akrich, M. (1995). User Representations. Practices, Methods and Sociology. In A. Rip, T. J. Misa, & J. Schot (Eds.), *Managing Technology in Society. The Approach of Constructive Technology Assessment* (pp. 167–184). London: Pinter Publishers.

Alaimo, C., & Kallinikos, J. (2022). Organizations Decentered: Data Objects, Technology and Knowledge. *Organization Science, 33*(1), 19–37. DOI: 10.1287/orsc.2021.1552.

Ametowobla, D. (2022). *Zur Soziologie der Software. Die Rolle Digitaler Technik bei der Kontrolle von Unsicherheiten*. Wiesbaden: Springer VS.

Anderson, C. (2012). *Makers. The New Industrial Revolution*. New York: Crown Business.

Andersen, H. With. (1988). Technological Trajectories, Cultural Values and the Labour Process. The Development of NC Machinery in the Norwegian Shipbuilding Industry. *Social Studies of Science, 18*(3), 465–482.

Andry, N. (1742). *Orthopædia. Or, the Art of Correcting and Preventing Deformities in Children by Such Means, As May Easily Be Put in Practice by Parents Themselves, and All Such as Are Employed in Educating Children*. London: A. Millar.

Appadurai, A. (1986a). Introduction. Commodities and the Politics of Value. In A. Appadurai (Ed.), *The Social Life of Things. Commodities in Cultural Perspective* (pp. 3–64). Cambridge: Cambridge University Press.

Appadurai, A. (Ed.) (1986b). *The Social Life of Things. Commodities in Cultural Perspective*. Cambridge: Cambridge University Press.

Aronowitz, S. (1978). Marx, Braverman, and the Logic of Capital. *Insurgent Sociologist, 8*(2–3), 26–146. DOI: 10.1177/089692057800800214.

Arya, A. P., & Klenerman, L. (2008). The Jaipur Foot. *The Journal of Bone and Joint Surgery. BritishVolume, 90*(11), 1414–1416. DOI: 10.1302/0301–620X.90B11.21131.

Barley, S. R. (1986). Technology as an Occasion for Structuring. Evidence from Observations of CT Scanners and the Social Order of Radiology Departments. *Administrative Science Quarterly 31*(1), 78–108.

Baudrillard, J. (1998). *The Consumer Society. Myths and Structures*. London: Sage.

Bauer, R. M., & Gegenhuber, T. (2015). Crowdsourcing. Global Search and the Twisted Roles of Consumers and Producers. *Organization, 22*(5), 661–681. DOI: 10.1177/1350508415585030.

Baumgartner, R., & Botta, P. (2008). *Amputation und Prothesenversorgung. Indikationsstellung, operative Technik, Nachbehandlung, Funktionstraining, Rehabilitation*. 3rd edition. Stuttgart: Georg Thieme Verlag.

Bechtol, C. O. (1957). Getting Down to Cases. *Artificial Limbs, 4*(1), 1–3.

Benkler, Y. (2006). *The Wealth of Networks. How Social Production Transforms Markets and Freedom*. New Haven, CT: Yale University Press.

Berker, T., Hartmann, M., Punie, Y., & Ward, K. (Eds.) (2006). *Domestication of Media and Technology*. New York: Open University Press.

Bijker, W. E. (1987). The Social Construction of Bakelite. Toward a Theory of Invention. In W. E. Bijker, T. P. Hughes, & T. Pinch (Eds.), *The Social Construction of Technological Systems. New Directions in the Sociology and History of Technology* (pp. 155–182). Cambridge, MA: MIT Press.

Bijker, W. E. (1992). The Social Construction of Fluorescent Lighting, or How an Artifact Was Invented in Its Diffusion Stage. In W. E. Bijker, & J. Law (Eds.), *Shaping Technology/Building Society. Studies in Sociotechnical Change* (pp. 75–102). Cambridge, MA: MIT Press.

Bijker, W. E. (1995). *Of Bicycles, Bakelites, and Bulbs. Toward a Theory of Sociotechnical Change*. Cambridge, MA: MIT Press.

Blau, P. M., Falbe, C. M., McKinley, W., & Tracy, P. K. (1976). Technology and Organization in Manufacturing. *Administrative Science Quarterly, 21*(1), 20–40. DOI: 10.2307/2391876.

Blauner, R. (1964). *Alienation and Freedom. The Factory Worker and His Industry*. Oxford: Chicago University Press.

Borchardt, M., Hartmann, K., Leymann, Richard, R., Schlesinger, G., & Schwiening, H. (Eds.) (1919). *Ersatzglieder und Arbeitshilfen*. Berlin: Springer.

Bourdieu, P. (1984). *Distinction. A Social Critique of the Judgement of Taste*. Cambridge, MA: Harvard University Press.

Bowker, G. C., & Star, S. L. (1999). *Sorting Things Out. Classification and its Consequences*. Cambridge, MA: MIT Press (Inside technology).

Braverman, H. (1974). *Labor and Monopoly Capitalism. The Degradation of Work in the Twentieth Century*. New York: Monthly Review.

Braybrooke, K., & Smith, A. (2018). Liberatory Technologies for Whom? Exploring a New Generation of Makerspaces Defined by Institutional Encounters. *Journal of Peer Production*, (12), 1–13.

Brown, E. (2002a). The Prosthetics of Management. Motion Study, Photography, and the Industrialized Body in World War I America. In K. Ott, D. Serlin, & S. Mihm (Eds.), *Artificial Parts, Practical Lives. Modern Histories of Prosthetics* (pp. 249–281). New York: New York University Press.

Brown, N., Rappert, B., & Webster, A. (Eds.) (2000). *Contested Futures. A Sociology of Prospective Techno-science*. Aldershot: Ashgate.

Brown, S. D. (2002b). Michel Serres. Science, Translation and the Logic of the Parasite. *Theory, Culture & Society 19*(3), 1–27. DOI: 10.1177/0263276402019003001.

Bruni, A., & Esposito, F. (2019). Digital Platforms: Producing Users in the Age of AirBnB. In U. Meyer, S. Schaupp, & D. Seibt (Eds.), *Digitalization in Industry. Between Domination and Emancipation* (pp. 207–232). Cham: Palgrave Macmillan.

Brynjolfsson, E., & McAfee, A. (2014). *The Second Machine Age*. New York: W.W. Norton & Company.

Burawoy, M. (1979). *Manufacturing Consent. Changes in the Labor Process under Monopoly Capitalism*. Chicago: University of Chicago Press.

Burawoy, M. (1985). *The Politics of Production. Factory Regimes under Capitalism and Socialism.* London: Verso.

Callon, M. (1984). Some Elements of a Sociology of Translation. Domestication of the Scallops and the Fishermen of St Brieuc Bay. *The Sociological Review, 32*(1), 196–233. DOI: 10.1111/j.1467–954X.1984.tb00113.x.

Callon, M. (1991). Techno-economic Networks and Irreversibility. In J. Law (Ed.), *A Sociology of Monsters. Essays on Power, Technology, and Domination* (pp. 132–164). London: Routledge.

Callon, M. (2007). An Essay on the Growing Contribution of Economic Markets to the Proliferation of the Social. *Theory, Culture & Society, 24*(7–8), 139–163. DOI: 10.1177/0263276407084701.

Callon, M., & Latour, B. (1981). Unscrewing the Big Leviathan. How Actors Macro-structure Reality and How Sociologists Help Them to Do So. In K. Knorr-Cetina, & A. V. Cicourel (Eds.), *Advances in Social Theory and Methodology. Toward an Integration of Micro- and Macro-Sociologies* (pp. 277–303). Boston, MA: Routledge.

Callon, M., Méadel, C., & Rabeharisoa, V. (2002). The Economy of Qualities. *Economy and Society, 31*(2), 194–217. DOI: 10.1080/03085140220123126.

Callon, M., & Rabeharisoa, V. (2003). Research "in the Wild" and the Shaping of New Social Identities. *Technology in Society, 25*, 193–204.

Callon, M., & Rabeharisoa, V. (2007). The Growing Engagement of Emergent Concerned Groups in Political and Economic Life. Lessons from the French Association of Neuromuscular Disease Patients. *Science, Technology, & Human Values, 33*(2), 230–261. DOI: 10.1177/0162243907311264.

Callon, M., Rip, A., & Law, J. (Eds.) (1986). *Mapping the Dynamics of Science and Technology. Sociology of Science in the Real World.* London: Palgrave Macmillan Limited.

Castells, M. (2010). *The Rise of the Network Society.* 2nd edition. Chichester, West Sussex: Wiley-Blackwell.

Chesbrough, H. W. (2003). *Open Innovation. The New Imperative for Creating and Profiting from Technology.* Boston, MA: Harvard Business School Press.

Child, J. (1972). Organizational Structure, Environment and Performance. The Role of Strategic Choice. *Sociology, 6*(1), 1–22. DOI: 10.1177/003803857200600101.

Christensen, C. M. (1997). *The Innovator's Dilemma. When New Technologies Cause Great Firms to Fail.* Boston, MA: Harvard Business School Press.

Clarke, A. E. (1998). *Disciplining Reproduction. Modernity, American Life Sciences and "the Problems of Sex".* Berkeley: University of California Press.

Clifford, J., & Marcus, G. E. (Eds.) (1986). *Writing Culture. The Poetics and Politics of Ethnography.* Berkeley: University of California Press.

Cohen, D. (2001). *The War Come Home. Disabled Veterans in Britain and Germany, 1914–1939.* Berkeley: University of California Press.

Committee on Artificial Limbs (1947). *Terminal Research Reports on Artificial Limbs.* Edited by National Research Council. Washington, DC. https://collections.nlm.nih.gov/catalog/nlm:nlmuid-36210050R-bk

Contini, R. (1954). Prosthetics Research and the Engineering Profession. *Artificial Limbs, 1*(3), 47–76. http://www.oandplibrary.org/al/pdf/1954_03_047.pdf.

Cooley, M. (1980). Computerization - Taylor's Latest Disguise. *Economic and Industrial Democracy, 1*, 523–539.

coons, g. (2022). *The Digital Bespoke. Promises and Pitfalls of Mass Customization.* London: Routledge.

Cowan, R. S. (1983). *More Work for Mother. The Ironies of Household Technology from the Open Hearth to the Microwave*. New York: Basic Books.

Cowan, R. S. (1987). The Consumption Junction. A Proposal for Research Strategies in the Sociology of Technology. In W. E. Bijker, T. P. Hughes, & T. Pinch (Eds.), *The Social Construction of Technological Systems. New Directions in the Sociology and History of Technology* (pp. 253–272). Cambridge, MA: MIT Press.

Czarniawska, B. (1997). *Narrating the Organization. Dramas of Institutional Identity*. Chicago: University of Chicago Press.

Czarniawska, B. (1998). *A Narrative Approach to Organization Studies*. Thousand Oaks, CA: Sage.

Czarniawska, B. (2004a). *Narratives in Social Science Research*. Los Angeles, CA: Sage.

Czarniawska, B. (2004b). On Time, Space, and Action Nets. *Organization, 11*(6), 773–791. DOI: 10.1177/1350508404047251.

Czarniawska, B. (2014). *A Theory of Organizing*. 2nd edition. Cheltenham: Edward Elgar.

Czarniawska, B., & Sevón, G. (2005). *Global Ideas. How Ideas, Objects and Practices Travel in the Global Economy*. Malmö: Liber.

D'Adderio, L. (2010). Artifacts at the Centre of Routines. Performing the Material Turn in Routines Theory. *Journal of Institutional Economics*, 7(02), 197–230. DOI: 10.1017/S174413741000024X.

Dahlander, L., & Magnusson, M. G. (2005). Relationships between Open Source Software Companies and Communities: Observations from Nordic Firms. *Research Policy, 34*(4), 481–493. DOI: 10.1016/j.respol.2005.02.003.

Dahlander, L., & Magnusson, M. G. (2008). How do Firms Make Use of Open Source Communities? *Long Range Planning, 41*(6), 629–649. DOI: 10.1016/j.lrp.2008.09.003.

Davis, G. F. (2015). What Might Replace the Modern Corporation? Uberization and the Web Page Enterprise. *Seattle University Law Review, 39*, 501–515.

Davis, S. M. (1987). *Future Perfect*. Reading, MA: Addison-Wesley Pub.

Deleuze, G., & Guattari, F. (1987). *A Thousand Plateaus. Capitalism and Schizophrenia*. Minneapolis: University of Minnesota Press.

DeSanctis, G., & Poole, M. S. (1994). Capturing the Complexity in Advanced Technology Use. Adaptive Structuration Theory. *Organization Science, 5*(2), 121–147.

Dickel, S., & Franzen, M. (2016). The "Problem of Extension" Revisited. New Modes of Digital Participation in Science. *Journal of Science Communication, 15*(Special Issue: Citizen Science Part I), 1–15.

Dickel, S., & Schrape, J.-F. (2017). The Logic of Digital Utopianism. *Nanoethics, 11*(1), 47–58. DOI: 10.1007/s11569-017-0285-6.

DiMaggio, P. J., & Powell, W. W. (1983). The Iron Cage Revisited. Institutional Isomorphism and Collective Rationality in Organizational Fields. *American Sociological Review, 48*(2), 147–160.

Dittmer, K. (2016). Orthopaedic Technology from Germany. An Export Model with a 120-Year Tradition. *Orthopädie Technik* (special print), 1–10.

Dittmer, K. (2018). Orthopädietechnik in Deutschland Nach 1945. Ein Rückblick Auf 60 Jahre Handwerks- und Verbandsgeschichte. *Orthopädie Technik* (Sonderausgabe OT World), 1–19.

Dosi, G. (1982). Technological Paradigms and Technological Trajectories. A Suggested Interpretation of the Determinants and Directions of Technical Change. *Research Policy, 11*, 147–162.

Douglas, M., & Isherwood, B. (1979). *The World of Goods. Towards an Anthropology of Consumption*. New York: Basic Books.

Downey, G. L. (1992a). CAD/CAM saves the nation?: Toward an Anthropology of Technology. *Knowledge and Society, 9*(9), 143–168.

Downey, G. L. (1992b). Human Agency in CAD/CAM Technology. *Anthropology Today, 8*(5), 2–6.

Drewlani, T., & Seibt, D. (2018). Configuring the Independent Developer. *Journal of Peer Production*, (12), 96–114. http://peerproduction.net/issues/issue-12-makerspaces-and-institutions/peer-reviewed-papers/configuring-the-independent-developer/.

Eberhart, H. D. (1954). The Objectives of the Lower-Extremity Prosthetics Program. *Artificial Limbs, 1*(2), 4–7.

Epstein, S. (2003). Inclusion, Diversity, and Biomedical Knowledge Making. The Multiple Politics of Representation. In N. Oudshoorn, & T. Pinch (Eds.), *How Users Matter. The Co-Construction of Users and Technologies* (pp. 173–190). Cambridge, MA: MIT Press.

Estalella, A., & Sánchez Criado, T. (2019). *Experimental Collaborations. Ethnography Through Fieldwork Devices*. New York: Berghahn Books.

Faulkner, P., & Runde, J. (2019). Theorizing the Digital Object. *MIS Quarterly, 43*(4), 1279–1302.

Feldman, M. S., & Orlikowski, W. J. (2011). Theorizing Practice and Practicing Theory. *Organization Science, 22*(5), 1240–1253. DOI: 10.1287/orsc.1100.0612.

Ferdinand, J.-P. (2018). *Entrepreneurship in Innovation Communities. Insights from 3D Printing Startups and the Dilemma of Open Source Hardware*. Cham: Springer.

Ferdinand, J.-P., & Meyer, U. (2017). The Social Dynamics of Heterogeneous Innovation Ecosystems. *International Journal of Engineering Business Management, 9*, 1–16. DOI: 10.1177/1847979017721617.

Ferdinand, J.-P., Petschow, U., & Dickel, S. (Eds.) (2016). *Decentralized and Networked Future of Value Creation*. Cham: Springer.

Fleck, J. (1988). *Innofusion or Diffusation? The Nature of Technological Development in Robotics* (Edinburgh PICT Working Paper 4).

Flichy, P. (2007a). *The Internet Imaginaire*. Cambridge, MA: MIT Press.

Flichy, P. (2007b). *Understanding Technological Innovation. A Socio-Technical Approach*. Cheltenham: Edward Elgar.

Fogliatto, F. S., da Silveira, G. J. C., & Borenstein, D. (2012). The Mass Customization Decade. An Updated Review of the Literature. *International Journal of Production Economics, 138*(1), 14–25. DOI: 10.1016/j.ijpe.2012.03.002.

Ford, H. (2007[1922]). *My Life and Work*. New York: Cosimo Classics.

Foucault, M. (1977). *Discipline and Punish. The Birth of the Prison*. New York: Vintage Books.

Frey, C. B., & Osborne, M. (2013). *The Future of Employment. How Susceptible Are Jobs to Computerization*? (Oxford Martin School Working Paper), from https://www.oxfordmartin.ox.ac.uk/downloads/academic/future-of-employment.pdf.

Furman, B. (1962). *Progress in Prosthetics. A Summary Under Sponsorship of the Prosthetics Research Board of the National Academy of Sciences*. Washington, DC: U.S. Department of Health, Education, and Welfare.

Gawer, A., & Cusumano, M. A. (2014). Industry Platforms and Ecosystem Innovation. *Journal of Product Innovation Management, 31*(3), 417–433. DOI: 10.1111/jpim.12105.

Gershenfeld, N. (2005). *FAB. The Coming Revolution on Your Desktop - From Personal Computers to Personal Fabrication.* New York: Basic Books.

Gershenfeld, N. (2012). How to Make Almost Anything. The Digital Fabrication Revolution. *Foreign Affairs, 91*(6), 43–57.

Gherardi, S., & Nicolini, D. (2005). Actor-Networks. Ecology and Entrepreneurs. In B. Czarniawska, & T. Hernes (Eds.), *Actor-Network Theory and Organizing* (pp. 285–306). Malmö: Liber.

Giddens, A. (1984). *The Constitution of Society. Outline of the Theory of Structuration.* Cambridge, MA: Polity Press.

Glaser, B. G., & Strauss, A. L. (1967). *The Discovery of Grounded Theory. Strategies for Qualitative Research.* Chicago, IL: Aldine.

Glaser, V. L., Pollock, N., & D'Adderio, L. (2021). The Biography of an Algorithm: Performing Algorithmic Technologies in Organizations. *Organization Theory, 2*(2), 263178772110046. DOI: 10.1177/26317877211004609.

Gläser, J. (2006). *Wissenschaftliche Produktionsgemeinschaften. Die soziale Ordnung der Forschung.* Frankfurt am Main, New York: Campus.

Gläser, J., & Laudel, G. (2009). *Experteninterviews und Qualitative Inhaltsanalyse. Als Instrumente Rekonstruierender Untersuchungen.* 3rd edition. Wiesbaden: VS Verlag für Sozialwissenschaften.

Gläser, J., & Laudel, G. (2013). Life With and Without Coding. Two Methods for Early-Stage Data Analysis in Qualitative Research Aiming at Causal Explanations. *Forum: Qualitative Social Research, 14*(2). https://www.qualitative-research.net/index.php/fqs/article/view/1886

Gläser, J., & Laudel, G. (2019). The Discovery of Causal Mechanisms. Extractive Qualitative Content Analysis as a Tool for Process Tracing. *Forum: Qualitative Social Research, 20*(3), Article 29. DOI: 10.17169/fqs-20.3.3386.

Göbel, H. K. (2017). Passungen Herstellen. Zur Affizierungspraxis von Körpern und Prothesen in der Leichtathletik. In G. Klein, & H. K. Göbel (Eds.), *Performance und Praxis. Praxeologische Erkundungen in Tanz, Theater, Sport und Alltag* (pp. 167–190). Bielefeld: Transcript.

Grabher, G., & Ibert, O. (2014). Distance as Asset? Knowledge Collaboration in Hybrid Virtual Communities. *Journal of Economic Geography, 14*(1), 97–123. DOI: 10.1093/jeg/lbt014.

Granovetter, M. (1973). The Strength of Weak Ties. *American Journal of Sociology, 78*(6), 1360–1380.

Gray, P. H. K. (1966). Embalmers' "Restorations." *The Journal of Egyptian Archaeology, 52*(1), 138–140. DOI: 10.1177/030751336605200116.

Greimas, A. J., & Courtés, J. (1982). *Semiotics and Language. An Analytical Dictionary.* Bloomington: Indiana University Press.

Hanger, M., Jr. (1956). Economic Aspects of the Artificial Limb Industry. *Orthotics and Prosthetics, 10*(2), 65–79.

Haraway, D. J. (1988). Situated Knowledges. The Science Question in Feminism and the Privilege of Partial Perspective. *Feminist Studies, 14*(3), 575. DOI: 10.2307/3178066.

Haraway, D. J. (1991). A Cyborg Manifesto. Science, Technology, and Socialist-Feminism in the Late Twentieth Century. In D. J. Haraway (Ed.), *Simians, Cyborgs, and Women. The Reinvention of Nature* (pp. 149–181). New York: Routledge.

Haraway, D. J. (1994). A Game of Cat's Cradle. Science Studies, Feminist Theory, Cultural Studies. *Configurations, 2*(1), 59–71. DOI: 10.1353/con.1994.0009.

Harkins, C. S., McGarry, A., & Buis, A. (2012). Provision of Prosthetic and Orthotic Services in Low-Income Countries: A Review of the Literature. *Prosthetics and Orthotics International, 37*(5), 353–361. DOI: 10.1177/0309364612470963.

Harrasser, K. (2009). Passung Durch Rückkopplung. Konzepte der Selbstregulierung in der Prothetik des Ersten Weltkriegs. In S. Fischer, E. Maehle, & R. Reischuk (Eds.), *Informatik. Im Focus das Leben* (pp. 788–801). Bonn: Gesellschaft für Informatik e.

Harrasser, K. (2013a). *Körper 2.0. Über die Technische Erweiterbarkeit des Menschen.* Bielefeld: Transcript.

Harrasser, K. (2013b). Sensible Prothesen. Medien der Wiederherstellung von Produktivität. *Body Politics, 1*(1), 99–117.

Harrasser, K. (2016). *Prothesen. Figuren Einer Lädierten Moderne.* Berlin: Vorwerk 8.

Hartmann, K. (1919). Die Prüfstelle für Ersatzglieder. In M. Borchardt, K. Hartmann, Leymann, R. Radike, G. Schlesinger, & H. Schwiening (Eds.), *Ersatzglieder und Arbeitshilfen* (pp. 18–57). Berlin: Springer.

Helmond, A. (2015). The Platformization of the Web. Making Web Data Platform Ready. *Social Media + Society, 1*(2), 1–11. DOI: 10.1177/2056305115603080.

Henderson, K. (1991). Flexible Sketches and Inflexible Data Bases. Visual Communication, Conscription Devices, and Boundary Objects in Design Engineering. *Science, Technology, & Human Values, 16*(4), 448–473.

Hernigou, P. (2013). Ambroise Paré IV. The Early History of Artificial Limbs (from Robotic to Prostheses). *International Orthopaedics, 37*(6), 1195–1197. DOI: 10.1007/s00264-013-1884-7.

Herschbach, L. (1997). Prosthetic Reconstructions. Making the Industry, Re-Making the Body, Modelling the Nation. *History Workshop Journal, 44*, 23–57.

Hickson, D. J., Pugh, D. S., & Pheysey, D. C. (1969). Operations Technology and Organization Structure. An Empirical Reappraisal. *Administrative Science Quarterly, 14*(3), 378. DOI: 10.2307/2391134.

Hine, C. (2007). Multi-sited Ethnography as a Middle Range Methodology for Contemporary STS. *Science, Technology, & Human Values, 32*(6), 652–671. DOI: 10.1177/0162243907303598.

Hippel, E. von (1986). Lead Users. A Source of Novel Product Concepts. *Management Science, 32*(7), 791–805.

Hippel, E. von. (1988). *The Sources of Innovation.* New York: Oxford University Press.

Hippel, E. von. (2005). *Democratizing Innovation.* Cambridge, MA: MIT Press.

Hippel, E. von, Ogawa, S., & De Jong, Jeroen P. J. (2011). The Age of the Consumer-Innovator. *MIT Sloan Management Review, 53*(1), 27–35.

Hippel, E. von. (2017). *Free Innovation.* Cambridge, MA: MIT Press.

Hippel, E. von, & Katz, R. (2002). Shifting Innovation to Users via Toolkits. *Management Science, 48*(7), 821–833. DOI: 10.1287/mnsc.48.7.821.2817.

Hughes, T. P. (1983). *Networks of Power. Electrification in Western Society, 1880–1930.* Baltimore, MD: Johns Hopkins University Press.

Hyysalo, S. (2006). Representations of Use and Practice-Bound Imaginaries in Automating the Safety of the Elderly. *Social Studies of Science, 36*(4), 599–626.

Hyysalo, S. (2009). Figuring Technologies, Users, and Designers. Steps Towards an Adequate Vocabulary for Design-Use Relations. In F. Prenkert, E. Baraldi, H. Håkansson, & A. Waluszewski (Eds.), *Use of Science and Technology in Business.*

Exploring the Impact of Using Activity for Systems, Organizations, and People (pp. 291–314). Bingley: Emerald.

Hyysalo, S. (2010). *Health Technology Development and Use. From Practice-Bound Imagination to Evolving Impacts.* London: Routledge.

Hyysalo, S. (2021). *Citizen Activities in Energy Transition. User Innovation, New Communities, and the Shaping of a Sustainable Future.* New York: Routledge.

Hyysalo, S., Jensen, T. E., & Oudshoorn, N. (2016a). Introduction to the New Production of Users. In S. Hyysalo, T. E. Jensen, & N. Oudshoorn (Eds.), *The New Production of Users. Changing Innovation Collectives and Involvement Strategies* (pp. 1–42). New York: Routledge.

Hyysalo, S., Jensen, T. E., & Oudshoorn, N. (Eds.) (2016b). *The New Production of Users. Changing Innovation Collectives and Involvement Strategies.* New York: Routledge.

Hyysalo, S., & Johnson, M. (2016). User Representation. A Journey towards Conceptual Maturation. In S. Hyysalo, T. E. Jensen, & N. Oudshoorn (Eds.), *The New Production of Users. Changing Innovation Collectives and Involvement Strategies* (pp. 75–100). New York: Routledge.

Hyysalo, S., Pollock, N., & Williams, R. A. (2019). Method Matters in the Social Study of Technology: Investigating the Biographies of Artifacts and Practices. *Science & Technology Studies, 32*(3), 2–25. DOI: 10.23987/sts.65532.

Hyysalo, S., & Usenyuk, S. (2015). The User Dominated Technology Era. Dynamics of Dispersed Peer-Innovation. *Research Policy, 44*(3), 560–576. DOI: 10.1016/j.respol.2015.01.002.

Ihl, C., & Piller, F. (2016). 3D Printing as Driver of Localized Manufacturing. Expected Benefits from Producer and Consumer Perspectives. In J.-P. Ferdinand, U. Petschow, & S. Dickel (Eds.), *Decentralized and Networked Future of Value Creation* (pp. 179–204). Cham: Springer.

Jain, S. S. (1999). The Prosthetic Imagination. Enabling and Disabling the Prosthesis Trope. Science, *Technology, & Human Values, 24*(1), 31–54.

Joerges, B., & Czarniawska, B. (1998). The Question of Technology, or How Organizations Inscribe the World. *Organization Studies, 19*(3), 363–385. DOI: 10.1177/017084069801900301.

Johnson, M. (2007). Unscrambling the "Average User" of Habbo Hotel. *Human Technology, 3*(2), 127–153.

Johnson, M., Mozaffar, H., Campagnolo, G. M., Hyysalo, S., Pollock, N., & Williams, R. (2014). The Managed Prosumer. Evolving Knowledge Strategies in the Design of Information Infrastructures. *Information, Communication & Society, 17*(7), 795–813. DOI: 10.1080/1369118X.2013.830635.

Kallinikos, J., Aaltonen, A., & Marton, A. (2013). The Ambivalent Ontology of Digital Artifacts. *MIS Quarterly, 37*(2), 357–370.

Kaplan, D. E., & Dubro, A. (2003). *Yakuza. Japan's Criminal Underworld.* Expanded edition. Berkeley: University of California Press.

Kienitz, S. (2008). *Beschädigte Helden. Kriegsinvalidität und Körperbilder 1914–1923.* Paderborn: Ferdinand Schöningh.

Kirchner, S., & Beyer, J. (2016). Die Plattformlogik als Digitale Marktordnung. *Zeitschrift für Soziologie, 45*(5), 324–339. DOI: 10.1515/zfsoz-2015-1019.

Kivimaa, P., Boon, W., Hyysalo, S., & Klerkx, L. (2019). Towards a Typology of Intermediaries in Sustainability Transitions: A Systematic Review and a Research Agenda. *Research Policy, 48*(4), 1062–1075. DOI: 10.1016/j.respol.2018.10.006.

Kline, R., & Pinch, T. (1996). Users as Agents of Technological Change. The Social Construction of the Automobile in the Rural United States. *Technology and Culture, 37*(4), 763. DOI: 10.2307/3107097.

Knoblauch, H. (2005). Focused Ethnography. *Forum: Qualitative Social Research, 6*(3). http://www.qualitative-research.net/index.php/fqs/article/view/20/44.

Knorr-Cetina, K. (1981). *The Manufacture of Knowledge. An Essay on the Constructivist and Contextual Nature of Science.* Oxford: Pergamon Press.

Kohler, R. (2010). Nicolas Andry de Bois-Regard (Lyon 1658-Paris 1742). The Inventor of the Word "Orthopaedics" and the Father of Parasitology. *Journal of Children's Orthopaedics, 4*(4), 349–355. DOI: 10.1007/s11832-010-0255–9.

Kohtala, C., Hyysalo, S., & Whalen, J. (2020). A Taxonomy of Users' Active Design Engagement in the 21st Century. *Design Studies, 67*(4), 27–54. DOI: 10.1016/j.destud.2019.11.008.

Kopytoff, I. (1986). The Cultural Biography of Things. Commoditization as Process. In A. Appadurai (Ed.), *The Social Life of Things. Commodities in Cultural Perspective* (pp. 64–91). Cambridge: Cambridge University Press.

Kostakis, V., Niaros, V., Dafermos, G., & Bauwens, M. (2015). Design Global, Manufacture Local: Exploring the Contours of an Emerging Productive Model. *Futures, 73*(2–3), 126–135. DOI: 10.1016/j.futures.2015.09.001.

Laet, M. de, & Annemarie, M. (2000). The Zimbabwe Bush Pump. Mechanics of a Fluid Technology. *Social Studies of Science, 30*(2), 225–263.

Latour, B. (1983). Give me a Laboratory and I will Raise the World. In K. D. Knorr-Cetina, & M. Mulkay (Eds.), *Science Observed. Perspectives on the Social Study of Science* (pp. 141–170). London: Sage.

Latour, B. (1986). The Power of Associations. In J. Law (Ed.), *Power, Action, and Belief. A New Sociology of Knowledge?* (pp. 264–280). London: Routledge.

Latour, B. (1987). *Science in Action.* Cambridge, MA: Harvard University Press.

Latour, B. (1990). Drawing Things Together. In M. Lynch, & S. Woolgar (Eds.), *Representation in Scientific Practice* (pp. 19–68). London: MIT Press.

Latour, B. (1991). Technology Is Society Made Durable. In J. Law (Ed.), *A Sociology of Monsters. Essays on Power, Technology, and Domination* (pp. 103–131). London: Routledge.

Latour, B. (1992). Where Are the Missing Masses? The Sociology of a Few Mundane Artifacts. In W. E. Bijker, & J. Law (Eds.), *Shaping Technology/Building Society. Studies in Sociotechnical Change* (pp. 225–258). Cambridge, MA: MIT Press.

Latour, B. (1999). *Pandora's Hope. Essays on the Reality of Science Studies.* Cambridge, MA: Harvard University Press.

Latour, B., & Akrich, M. (1992). A Summary of a Convenient Vocabulary for the Semiotics of Human and Nonhuman Assemblies. In W. E. Bijker, & J. Law (Eds.), *Shaping Technology/Building Society. Studies in Sociotechnical Change* (pp. 259–264). Cambridge, MA: MIT Press.

Latour, B., & Woolgar, S. (1986). *Laboratory Life. The Construction of Scientific Facts.* Princeton: Princeton University Press.

Law, J. (1987). Technology and Heterogeneous Engineering. The Case of Portuguese Expansion. In W. E. Bijker, T. P. Hughes, & T. Pinch (Eds.), *The Social Construction of Technological Systems. New Directions in the Sociology and History of Technology* (pp. 105–128). Cambridge, MA: MIT Press.

Law, J. (1991). Introduction. Monsters, machines, and sociotechnical relations. In J. Law (Ed.), *A Sociology of monsters. Essays on power, technology, and domination* (pp. 1–25). London: Routledge.

Law, J. (1999). After Ant. Complexity, Naming and Topology. *The Sociological Review, 47*(1), 1–14. DOI: 10.1111/j.1467-954X.1999.tb03479.x.

Law, J. (2003). *Traduction/Trahison. Notes on ANT.* Edited by Department of Sociology, Lancaster University, from https://www.lancaster.ac.uk/fass/resources/sociology-online-papers/papers/law-traduction-trahison.pdf.

Law, J, & Bijker, W. E. (1992). Postscript. Technology, Stability, and Social Theory. In W. E. Bijker, & J. Law (Eds.), *Shaping Technology/Building Society. Studies in Sociotechnical Change* (pp. 290–308). Cambridge, MA: MIT Press.

Law, J., & Ruppert, E. (2013). The Social Life of Methods. Devices. *Journal of Cultural Economy, 6*(3), 229–240. DOI: 10.1080/17530350.2013.812042.

Lee, N., & Brown, S. (1994). Otherness and the Actor Network. The Undiscovered Continent. *American Behavioral Scientist, 37*(6), 772–790. DOI: 10.1177/0002764294037006005.

Lenzen, K. (2020). *Die Multiple Identität der Technik. Eine Innovationsbiographie der Augmented Reality-Technologie.* Bielefeld: Transcript.

Leonardi, P. M. (2013). Theoretical Foundations for the Study of Sociomateriality. *Information and Organization, 23*(2), 59–76. DOI: 10.1016/j.infoandorg.2013.02.002.

Leonardi, P. M., & Barley, S. R. (2008). Materiality and Change. Challenges to Building Better Theory About Technology and Organizing. *Information and Organization, 18*(3), 159–176. DOI: 10.1016/j.infoandorg.2008.03.001.

Leonardi, P. M., Nardi, B. A., & Kallinikos, J. (Eds.) (2012). *Materiality and Organizing. Social Interaction in a Technological World.* Oxford: Oxford University Press.

Lie, M., & Sørensen, K. H. (1996). *Making Technology Our Own? Domesticating Technology into Everyday Life.* Oslo: Scandinavian University Press.

Lindberg, K., & Czarniawska, B. (2006). Knotting the Action Net, or Organizing Between Organizations. *Scandinavian Journal of Management, 22*(4), 292–306. DOI: 10.1016/j.scaman.2006.09.001.

Lundvall, B.-Å. (1988). Innovation as an Interactive Process. From User-Producer Interaction to the National System of Innovation. In G. Dosi, C. Freeman, R. R. Nelson, G. Silverberg, & L. Soete (Eds.), *Technical Change and Economic Theory* (pp. 349–369). London: Pinter Publishers.

Mackay, H., Carne, C., Beynon-Davies, P., & Tudhope, D. (2000). Reconfiguring the User. Using Rapid Application Development. *Social Studies of Science, 30*(5), 737–757.

Mackay, H., & Gillespie, G. (1992). Extending the Social Shaping of Technology Approach. Ideology and Appropriation. *Social Studies of Science, 22*, 685–716.

MacKenzie, D. (1984). Marx and the Machine. *Technology and Culture, 25*(3), 473. DOI: 10.2307/3104202.

MacKenzie, D. A., & Wajcman, J. (Eds.) (1985). *The Social Shaping of Technology. How the Refrigerator Got its Hum.* Milton Keynes: Open University Press.

Marcus, G. E. (1986). Contemporary Problems of Ethnography in the Modern World System. In J. Clifford, & G. E. Marcus (Eds.), *Writing Culture. The Poetics and Politics of Ethnography* (pp. 165–193). Berkeley: University of California Press.

Marcus, G. E. (1995). Ethnography in/of the World System. The Emergence of Multi-Sited Ethnography. *Annual Review of Anthropology, 24*, 95–117.

Marino, M., Pattni, S., Greenberg, M., Miller, A., Hocker, E., Ritter, S., & Mehta, K. (2015). Access to Prosthetic Devices in Developing Countries. Pathways and Challenges. *IEEE 2015 Global Humanitarian Technology*, 45–51.

Marres, N., & Stark, D. (2020). Put to the Test: For a New Sociology of Testing. *The British Journal of Sociology, 71*(3), 423–443. DOI: 10.1111/1468–4446.12746.

Marx, K. (1976). *Capital. A Critique of Political Economy.* Volume 1. London: Penguin Books.

Mason, P. (2015). *Postcapitalism. A Guide to Our Future.* London: Penguin Books.

Mauss, M. (1990). *The Gift. Forms and Functions of Exchange in Archaic Societies.* London: Routledge.

McAfee, A., & Brynjolfsson, E. (2017). *Machine, Platform, Crowd. Harnessing the Digital Revolution.* New York: W.W. Norton and Company.

Meyer, J. W., & Jepperson, R. L. (2000). The “Actors” of Modern Society. The Cultural Construction of Social Agency. *Sociological Theory, 18*(1), 100–120.

Meyer, U. (2019). The Emergence of an Envisioned Future. Sensemaking in the Case of “Industrie 4.0” in Germany. *Futures, 109*, 130–141. DOI: 10.1016/j.futures.2019.03.001. https://www.sciencedirect.com/science/article/abs/pii/S0016328718300077

Meyer, U, Schaupp, S., & Seibt, D. (Eds.) (2019). *Digitalization in Industry. Between Domination and Emancipation.* Cham: Palgrave Macmillan.

Michael, M. (2012). What Are We Busy Doing? *Science, Technology, & Human Values, 37*(5), 528–554. DOI: 10.1177/0162243911428624.

Mihm, S. (2002). “A Limb Which Shall Be Presentable in Polite Society.” Prosthetic Technologies in the Nineteenth Century. In K. Ott, D. Serlin, & S. Mihm (Eds.), *Artificial Parts, Practical Lives. Modern Histories of Prosthetics* (pp. 282–299). New York: New York University Press.

Miller, D. (1987). *Material Culture and Mass Consumption.* Oxford: Blackwell.

Mol, A. (2002). *The Body Multiple. Ontology in Medical Practice.* Durham, NC: Duke University Press.

Moser, I. (2006). Disability and the Promises of Technology. Technology, Subjectivity and Embodiment Within an Order of the Normal. *Information, Communication & Society, 9*(3), 373–395. DOI: 10.1080/13691180600751348.

Mosley, N. (2000 [1990]). *Hopeful Monsters.* London: Dalkey Archive Press.

Mozaffar, H. (2016). User Communities as Multi-Functional Spaces. Innovation, Collective Voice, Demand Articulation, Peer Informing and Professional Identity (and More). In S. Hyysalo, T. E. Jensen, & N. Oudshoorn (Eds.), *The New Production of Users. Changing Innovation Collectives and Involvement Strategies* (pp. 219–246). New York: Routledge.

Murphy, K. M. (2011). White Zombie. *Contemporary French and Francophone Studies, 15*(1), 47–55. DOI: 10.1080/17409292.2011.535263.

Neff, G., & Stark, D. (2004). Permanently Beta. Responsive Organization in the Internet Era. In P. N. Howard, & S. Jones (Eds.), *Society Online. The Internet in Context* (pp. 173–188). Thousand Oaks, CA: Sage Publications.

Nelson, R. R., & Winter, S. G. (1982). *An Evolutionary Theory of Economic Change.* Cambridge, MA: The Belknap Press of Harvard University Press.

Nerlich, A. G., Zink, A., Szeimies, U., & Hagedorn, H. G. (2000). Ancient Egyptian Prosthesis of the Big Toe. *The Lancet, 356*(9248), 2176–2179. DOI: 10.1016/S0140–6736(00)03507-8.

Neves da Rocha, F., & Pollock, N. (2019). *Innovating in Digital Platforms: An Integrative Approach.* In Proceedings of the 21st International Conference on Enterprise Information Systems, pp. 505–515.

Nicolai, A. (1919). Der Schmuckarm. In M. Borchardt, K. Hartmann, Leymann, R. Radike, G. Schlesinger, & H. Schwiening (Eds.), *Ersatzglieder und Arbeitshilfen* (pp. 683–708). Berlin: Springer.

Noble, D. F. (1978). Social Choice in Machine Design. The Case of Automatically Controlled Machine Tools, and a Challenge for Labor. *Politics & Society 8*(3–4), 313–347. DOI: 10.1177/003232927800800302.

Noble, D. F. (1979). Social Choice in Machine Design. The Case of Automatically Controlled Machine Tools. In A. S. Zimbalist (Ed.), *Case Studies on the Labor Process* (pp. 18–50). New York: Monthly Review Press.

Noble, D. F. (1984). *Forces of Production. A Social History of Industrial Automation.* New Brunswick: Transaction Publishers.

Noble, D. F. (1985). Social Choice in Machine Design: The Case of Automatically Controlled Machine Tools. In D. A. MacKenzie, & J. Wajcman (Eds.), *The Social Shaping of Technology. How the Refrigerator Got its Hum* (pp. 109–124). Milton Keynes: Open University Press.

Orlikowski, W. J. (1992). The Duality of Technology. Rethinking the Concept of Technology in Organizations. *Organization Science, 3*(3), 398–427.

Orlikowski, W. J. (2000). Using Technology and Constituting Structures. A Practice Lens for Studying Technology in Organizations. *Organization Science, 11*(4), 404–428.

Orlikowski, W. J. (2007). Sociomaterial Practices. Exploring Technology at Work. *Organization Studies, 28*(9), 1435–1448. DOI: 10.1177/0170840607081138.

Orlikowski, W. J., & Barley, S. R. (2001). Technology and Institutions. What Can Research on Information Technology and Research on Organizations Learn from Each Other? *MIS Quarterly, 25*(2), 145. DOI: 10.2307/3250927.

Orlikowski, W. J., & Scott, S. V. (2008). Sociomateriality. Challenging the Separation of Technology, Work and Organization. *The Academy of Management Annals, 2*(1), 433–474. DOI: 10.1080/19416520802211644.

Oudshoorn, N. (2003). *The Male Pill. A Biography of a Technology in the Making.* Durham, NC: Duke University Press.

Oudshoorn, N. (2011). *Telecare Technologies and the Transformation of Healthcare.* New York: Palgrave Macmillan.

Oudshoorn, N. (2016). The Vulnerability of Cyborgs. The Case of ICD Shocks. *Science, Technology, & Human Values, 41*(5), 767–792. DOI: 10.1177/0162243916633755.

Oudshoorn, N. (2019). Placing Users and Nonusers at the Heart of Technology. In T. L. Pittinsky (Ed.), *Science, Technology, and Society. New Perspectives and Directions* (pp. 163–175). Cambridge: Cambridge University Press.

Oudshoorn, N. (2020). *Resilient Cyborgs. Living and Dying with Pacemakers and Defibrillators.* Singapore: Palgrave Macmillan.

Oudshoorn, N., & Pinch, T. (Eds.) (2003). *How Users Matter. The Co-Construction of Users and Technologies.* Cambridge, MA: MIT Press.

Oudshoorn, N., & Pinch, T. (2008). User-Technology Relationships. Some Recent Developments. In E. J. Hackett, O. Amsterdamska, M. Lynch, & J. Wajcman (Eds.), *The Handbook of Science and Technology Studies* (3rd edition, pp. 541–566). Cambridge, MA: MIT Press.

Oudshoorn, N, Rommes, E., & Stienstra, M. (2004). Configuring the User as Everybody. Gender and Design Cultures in Information and Communication Technologies. *Science, Technology, & Human Values, 29*(1), 30–63. DOI: 10.1177/0162243903259190.

Pentland, B. T. (1999). Organizations as Networks of Action. In Joel A. C. Baum, & B. McKelvey (Eds.), *Variations in Organization Science: In Honor of Donald T. Campbell* (pp. 237–253). Thousand Oaks, CA: Sage.

Pentland, B. T., & Feldman, M. S. (2007). Narrative Networks. Patterns of Technology and Organization. *Organization Science, 18*(5), 781–795. DOI: 10.1287/orsc.1070.0283.

Pentland, B. T., & Feldman, M. S. (2008). Designing Routines. On the Folly of Designing Artifacts, While Hoping for Patterns of Action. *Information and Organization, 18*(4), 235–250. DOI: 10.1016/j.infoandorg.2008.08.001.

Perrow, C. (1967). A Framework for the Comparative Analysis of Organizations. *American Sociological Review, 32*(2), 194. DOI: 10.2307/2091811.

Perry, H. (2002). Re-Arming the Disabled Veteran. Artificially Rebuilding State and Society in World War One Germany. In K. Ott, D. Serlin, & S. Mihm (Eds.), *Artificial Parts, Practical Lives. Modern Histories of Prosthetics* (pp. 75–101). New York: New York University Press.

Pfaffenberger, B. (1992). Technological Dramas. *Science, Technology, & Human Values, 17*(3), 282–312. DOI: 10.1177/016224399201700302.

Pfeiffer, S. (2017). The Vision of "Industrie 4.0" in the Making-a Case of Future Told, Tamed, and Traded. *Nanoethics, 11*(1), 107–121. DOI: 10.1007/s11569-016-0280–3.

Pfeiffer, S. (2022). *Digital Capitalism and Distributive Forces.* Bielefeld: Transcript Verlag.

Pickering, A. (1993). The Mangle of Practice. Agency and Emergence in the Sociology of Science. *American Journal of Sociology, 99*(3), 559–589.

Pinch, T., & Bijker, W. E. (1987). The Social Construction of Facts and Artifact. Or How the Sociology of Science and the Sociology of Technology Might Benefit Each Other. In W. E. Bijker, T. P. Hughes, & T. Pinch (Eds.), *The Social Construction of Technological Systems. New Directions in the Sociology and History of Technology* (pp. 11–44). Cambridge, MA: MIT Press.

Pine, B. Joseph, II. (1993). *Mass Customization. The New Frontier in Business Competition.* Boston, MA: Harvard Business School Press.

Pollock, N., & Hyysalo, S. (2014). The Business of Being a User. The Role of the Reference Actor in Shaping Packaged Enterprise System Acquisition and Development. *MIS Quarterly, 38*(2), 473–496.

Pollock, N., & Williams, R. (2009). *Software and Organisations. The Biography of the Enterprise-Wide System or How SAP Conquered the World.* London: Routledge.

Pollock, N., Williams, R., & Procter, R. (2003). Fitting Standard Software Packages to Non-Standard Organizations: The "Biography" of an Enterprise-Wide System. *Technology Analysis & Strategic Management, 15*(3), 317–332. DOI: 10.1080/0953732031000160l504.

Powell, W. W., & DiMaggio, P. J. (Eds.) (1991). *The New Institutionalism in Organizational Analysis.* Chicago: The University of Chicago Press.

Powell, W. W., & Grodal, S. (2005). Networks of Innovators. In J. Fagerberg, D. C. Mowery, & R. R. Nelson (Eds.), *The Oxford Handbook of Innovation* (pp. 56–85). Oxford: Oxford University Press.

Pugh, D. S., Hickson, D. J., Hinings, C. R., Macdonald, K. M., Turner, C., & Lupton, T. (1963). A Conceptual Scheme for Organizational Analysis. *Administrative Science Quarterly, 8*(3), 289. DOI: 10.2307/2390971.

Raymond, E. S. (2001). *The Cathedral and the Bazaar. Musings on Linux and Open Source by an Accidental Revolutionary.* Revised edition. Beijing: O'Reilly.

Reeves, T. K., Turner, B. A., & Woodward, J. (1970). Technology and Organizational Behaviour. In J. Woodward (Ed.), *Industrial Organization. Behaviour and Control* (pp. 3–18). London: Oxford University Press.

Rieder, K., & Voß, G. G. (2010). The Working Customer – an Emerging New Type of Consumer. *Psychology of Everyday Activity, 3*(2), 2–10.

Rifkin, J. (2011). *The Third Industrial Revolution. How Lateral Power is Inspiring a Generation and Transforming the World.* Basingstoke: Palgrave Macmillan.

Rifkin, J. (2014). *The Zero Marginal Cost Society. The Internet of Things, the Collaborative Commons, and the Eclipse of Capitalism.* New York: Palgrave Macmillan.

Ritzer, G., & Jurgenson, N. (2010). Production, Consumption, Prosumption. The Nature of Capitalism in the Age of the Digital "Prosumer." *Journal of Consumer Culture, 10*(1), 13–36.

Rogers, E. M. (1983). *Diffusion of Innovations.* 3rd edition. New York: Free Press.

Rohracher, H. (Ed.) (2005). *User involvement in Innovation Processes. Strategies and Limitations from a Socio-Technical Perspective.* München: Profil.

Rosen, P. (2002). *Framing Production. Technology, Culture, and Change in the British Bicycle Industry.* Cambridge, MA: MIT Press (Inside technology).

Russell, S., & Williams, R. (2002). Social Shaping of Technology. Frameworks, Findings and Implications for Policy. with Glossary of Social Shaping. In K. H. Sørensen, & R. Williams (Eds.), *Shaping Technology, Guiding Policy. Concepts, Spaces and Tools* (pp. 35–112). Cheltenham: Edward Elgar.

Schlesinger, G. (1919). Der Mechanische Aufbau Der künstlichen Glieder. In M. Borchardt, K. Hartmann, Leymann, R. Radike, G. Schlesinger, & H. Schwiening (Eds.), *Ersatzglieder und Arbeitshilfen* (pp. 321–661). Berlin: Springer.

Schneider, C. (2018). *Opening Digital Fabrication. Transforming TechKnowledgies.* Karlsruhe: KIT Scientific Publishing.

Schot, J., Kanger, L., & Verbong, G. (2016). The Roles of Users in Shaping Transitions to New Energy Systems. *Nat Energy, 1*(5), 71. DOI: 10.1038/nenergy.2016.54.

Schrape, J.-F. (2019). *Technology and the Promise of Decentralization. Origins, Development, Patterns of Arguments.* (SOI Discussion Paper, 2019-01).

Schreier, M. (2012). *Qualitative Content Analysis in Practice.* Los Angeles, CA: Sage.

Schulz-Schaeffer, I. (2016). *The Position Fields of Technology. A Role-Theoretical Approach to Socio-Technical Networks.* Technical University Berlin. Berlin (TUTS Working Papers, 2–2016).

Seibt, D., Schaupp, S., & Meyer, U. (2019). Towards an Analytical Understanding of Domination and Emancipation in Digitalizing Industries. In U. Meyer, S. Schaupp, & D. Seibt (Eds.), *Digitalization in Industry. Between Domination and Emancipation* (pp. 1–25). Cham: Palgrave Macmillan.

Seibt, D., Windeler, A., & Schulz-Schaeffer, I. (2023). Einleitung. Das Programm Der Innovationsgesellschaft Heute und Seine Perspektiven. In I. Schulz-Schaeffer, A. Windeler, & D. Seibt (Eds.), *Innovationsgesellschaft. Befunde und Ausblicke.* Wiesbaden: Springer VS.

Seltzer, M. (1992). *Bodies and Machines.* New York: Routledge.

Selznick, P. (1949). *TVA and the Grass Roots. A Study in the Sociology of Formal Organizations.* Berkeley: University of California Press.

Sennett, R. (2008). *The Craftsman.* New Haven, CT: Yale University Press.

Serlin, D. (2002). Engineering Masculinity. Veterans and Prosthetics After World War Two. In K. Ott, D. Serlin, & S. Mihm (Eds.), *Artificial Parts, Practical Lives. Modern Histories of Prosthetics* (pp. 45–74). New York: New York University Press.

Shah, S. K. (2000). *Sources and Patterns of Innovation in a Consumer Products Field.* Innovations in Sporting Equipment (Sloan Working Paper, #4105).

Shah, S. K., & Tripsas, M. (2007). The Accidental Entrepreneur. The Emergent and Collective Process of User Entrepreneurship. *Strategic Entrepreneurship Journal, 1*(1–2), 123–140. DOI: 10.1002/sej.15.

Shaiken, H. (1985). *Work Transformed. Automation and Labor in the Computer Age.* New York: Holt, Rinehart and Winston.

Silvast, A., & Virtanen, M. J. (2021). On Theory–Methods Packages in Science and Technology Studies. *Science, Technology, & Human Values, 48*(1), 167–189.

Silverstone, R., & Hirsch, E. (Eds.) (1992). *Consuming Technologies. Media and Information in Domestic Spaces.* London: Routledge.

Silverstone, R., Hirsch, E., & Morley, D. (1992). Information and Communication Technologies and the Moral Economy of the Household. In R. Silverstone, & E. Hirsch (Eds.), *Consuming Technologies. Media and Information in Domestic Spaces* (pp. 9–28). London: Routledge.

Söderberg, J. (2013a). Automating Amateurs in the 3D Printing Community. Connecting the Dots Between "Deskilling" and "User-Friendliness." *Work Organisation, Labour & Globalisation, 7*(1), 124–139.

Söderberg, J. (2013b). Legal Highs - Legal Definitions Versus "Open Innovation." In R. Leenes, & E. Kosta (Eds.), *Bridging Distances in Technology and Regulation* (pp. 71–82). Oisterwijk: Wolf Legal Publishers.

Söderberg, J. (2016). The Cloud Factory. Making Things and Making a Living with Desktop 3D Printing. *Culture and Organization, 25*(1), 65–81. DOI: 10.1080/14759551.2016.1203313.

Söderberg, J., & Maxigas. (Eds.) (2014). *Book of Peer Production. Journal of Peer Production.* Gothenburg: NSU Press.

Solav, D., Moerman, K. M., Jaeger, A. M., & Herr, H. M. (2019). A Framework for Measuring the Time-Varying Shape and Full-Field Deformation of Residual Limbs Using 3-D Digital Image Correlation. *IEEE Transactions on Bio-Medical Engineering, 66*(10), 2740–2752. DOI: 10.1109/TBME.2019.2895283.

Sørensen, K. H. (1996). *Learning Technology, Constructing Culture. Socio-Technical Change as Social Learning.* Norwegian University of Science and Technology (STS Working Paper, 18/96).

Sørensen, K. H., & Williams, R. (Eds.) (2002). *Shaping Technology, Guiding Policy. Concepts, Spaces and Tools.* Cheltenham: Edward Elgar.

Srinivasan, R. (2002). Technology Sits Cross-Legged. Developing the Jaipur Foot Prosthesis. In K. Ott, D. Serlin, & S. Mihm (Eds.), *Artificial Parts, Practical Lives. Modern Histories of Prosthetics* (pp. 327–348). New York: New York University Press.

Srnicek, N., & Williams, A. (2015). *Inventing the Future. Post Capitalism and a World Without Work.* London: Verso.

Star, S. L. (1991). Power, Technologies, and the Phenomenology of Conventions. On Being Allergic to Onions. In J. Law (Ed.), *A Sociology of Monsters. Essays on Power, Technology, and Domination* (pp. 26–57). London: Routledge.

Star, S. L. (1999). The Ethnography of Infrastructure. *American Behavioral Scientist, 43*(3), 377–391. DOI: 10.1177/00027649921955326.

Starbuck, W. H. (1965). Organizational Growth and Development. In J. G. March (Ed.), *Handbook of Organizations* (pp. 451–533). Chicago: Rand McNally & Company.

Staros, A. (1957). The SACH (Solid-Ankle Cushion-Heel) Foot. *Orthopedic & Prosthetic Appliance Journal, 11*(2), 23–31.

Stewart, J. (2007). Local Experts in the Domestication of Information and Communication Technologies. *Information, Communication & Society, 10*(4), 547–569. DOI: 10.1080/13691180701560093.

Stewart, J., & Hyysalo, S. (2008). Intermediaries, Users and Social Learning in Technological Innovation. *International Journal of Innovation Management, 12*(3), 295–325.

Stewart, J., & Williams, R. (2005). The Wrong Trousers? Beyond the Design Falacy. Social Learning and the User. In D. Howcroft, & E. Moore Trauth (Eds.), *Handbook of Information Systems Research. Critical Perspectives on Information Systems Design, Development and Implementation* (pp. 195–221). Cheltenham: Edward Elgar.

Strong, F. S. [Jr.] (1954). Artificial Limbs. Today and Tomorrow. *Artificial Limbs, 1*(1), 1–3.

Suchman, L. (1987). *Plans and Situated Actions. The Problem of Human-Machine Communication*. New York: Cambridge University Press.

Suchman, L. (2007). *Human-Machine Reconfigurations. Plans and Situated Actions*. 2nd edition. Cambridge: Cambridge University Press.

Suchman, L. (2012). Configuration. In C. Lury, & N. Wakeford (Eds.), *Inventive Methods. The Happening of the Social* (pp. 48–60). London: Routledge.

Taylor, C. L. (1954). The Objectives of the Upper-Extremity Prosthetics Program. *Artificial Limbs, 1*(1), 4–8.

Taylor, F. W. (1919). *The Principles of Scientific Management*. New York: Harper & Brothers Publishers.

Thompson, J. D. (1967). *Organizations in Action*. New York: McGraw.

Toffler, A. (1980). *The Third Wave*. New York: Morrow.

Trist, E. L., Higgin, G. W., Murray H., & Pollock, A. B. (1963). *Organizational Choice. Capabilities of Groups at the Coal Face under Changing Technologies. The Loss, Re-discovery & Transformation of a Work Tradition*. London: Tavistock Publications.

Troxler, P. (2013). Making the Third Industrial Revolution. The Struggle for Polycentric Structures and a New Peer-Production Commons in the FabLab Community. In J. Walter-Herrmann, & C. Büching (Eds.), *FabLab. Of Machines, Makers and Inventors* (pp. 181–198). Bielefeld: Transcript.

Tseng, M. M., Wang, Y., & Jiao, R. J. (2017). Mass Customization. In The International Academy for Production Engineering, S. Chatti, & T. Tolio (Eds.), *CIRP Encyclopedia of Production Engineering* (pp. 1–8). Berlin: Springer. https://link.springer.com/referenceworkentry/10.1007/978-3-642-35950-7_16701-3#citeas.

Turner, R. H. (2001). Role Theory. In J. H. Turner (Ed.), *Handbook of Sociological Theory* (Vol. 15, pp. 233–254). New York: Springer.

Urry, J. (2016). *What Is the Future*? Cambridge, UK: Polity.

Urry, J., & Birtchnell, T. (2016). *A New Industrial Future? 3D Printing and the Reconfiguring of Production, Distribution, and Consumption*. New York: Routledge.

van den B, H., & Rip, A. (1987). The Nelson-Winter-Dosi Model and Synthetic Dye Chemistry. In W. E. Bijker, T. P. Hughes, & T. Pinch (Eds.), *The Social Construction of Technological Systems. New directions in the Sociology and History of Technology* (pp. 129–154). Cambridge, MA: MIT Press.

van den Scott, L.-Jo K., Sanders, C., & Puddephatt, A. J. (2017). Reconceptualizing Users through Enriching Ethnography. In U. Felt, F. Rayvon, C. A. Miller,

& L. Smith-Doerr (Eds.), *The Handbook of Science and Technology Studies* (4th edition, pp. 501–527). Cambridge, MA: MIT Press.

van Kammen, J. (2003). Who Represents the Users? Critical Encounters Between Women's Health Advocates and Scientists in Contraceptive R&D. In N. Oudshoorn, & T. Pinch (Eds.), *How Users Matter. The Co-Construction of Users and Technologies* (pp. 151–172). Cambridge, MA: MIT Press.

Wajcman, J. (2017). Automation. Is It Really Different This Time? *The British Journal of Sociology, 68*(1), 119–127. DOI: 10.1111/1468–4446.12239.

Weick, K. E. (1995). *Sensemaking in Organizations.* Thousand Oaks, CA: Sage.

Wellerson, T. L. (1957). Historical Development of Upper Extremity Prosthetics. *Orthotics and Prosthetics, 11*(3), 73–77.

Wenten, K.-A. (2019). Controlling Labor in Makeathons. On the Recuperation of Emancipation in Industrial Labor Processes. In U. Meyer, S. Schaupp, & D. Seibt (Eds.), *Digitalization in Industry. Between Domination and Emancipation* (pp. 153–178). Cham: Palgrave Macmillan.

WHO (2011). *World Report on Disability.* Geneva: WHO Press. http://whqlibdoc.who.int/publications/2011/9789240685215_eng.pdf.

Wilkie, A. (2010). *User Assemblages in Design. An Ethnographic Study.* Dissertation. Goldsmiths, University of London, London.

Williams, R., & Edge, D. (1996). The Social Shaping of Technology. *Research Policy, 25*(6), 865–899. DOI: 10.1016/0048–7333(96)00885-2.

Williams, R., Stewart, J., & Slack, R. (2005). *Social Learning in Technological Innovation. Experimenting with ICTs.* Aldershot: Edward Elgar.

Wilson, A. B., Jr. (1992). History of Amputation Surgery and Prosthetics. In J. H. Bowker, J. W. Michael (Eds.), *Atlas of Limb Prosthetics. Surgical, Prosthetic, and Rehabilitation Principles* (pp. 3–16). 2nd edition. Rosemont: American Academy of Orthopaedic Surgeons. http://www.oandplibrary.org/alp/chap01-01.asp?searchquery=history.

Woodward, J. (1958). *Management and Technology.* London: Her Majesty's Stationery Office.

Woodward, J. (1965). *Industrial Organization. Theory and Practice.* 2nd edition. Oxford: Oxford University Press.

Woolgar, S. (1991). Configuring the User. The Case of Usability Trials. In J. Law (Ed.), *A Sociology of Monsters. Essays on Power, Technology, and Domination* (pp. 57–103). London: Routledge.

Wyatt, S. (2003). Non-Users Also Matter. The Construction of Users and Non-Users of the Internet. In N. Oudshoorn, & T. Pinch (Eds.), *How Users Matter. The Co-Construction of Users and Technologies* (pp. 67–80). Cambridge, MA: MIT Press.

Yoo, Y., Henfridsson, O., & Lyytinen, K. (2010). Research Commentary — The New Organizing Logic of Digital Innovation. An Agenda for Information Systems Research. *Information Systems Research, 21*(4), 724–735. DOI: 10.1287/isre.1100.0322.

Zuboff, S. (1985). Automate/Informate. The Two Faces of Intelligent Technology. *Organizational Dynamics, 14*(2), 5–18.

Zuboff, S. (1988). *In the Age of the Smart Machine. The Future of Work and Power.* New York: Basic Books.

Index

Note: Page numbers followed by "n" denote endnotes.

MIX
Papier | Fördert gute Waldnutzung
FSC® C083411

Kolibri 360 GmbH
Ferdinand-Jühlke-Straße 7
99095 Erfurt, Deutschland
produktsicherheit@kolibri360.de